Health and Wellness Tourism

Health and Wellness Tourism

Melanie Smith
László Puczkó

AMSTERDAM • BOSTON • HEIDELBERG • LONDON • OXFORD • NEW YORK
PARIS • SAN DIEGO • SAN FRANCISCO • SINGAPORE • SYDNEY • TOKYO
Butterworth-Heinemann is an imprint of Elsevier

Butterworth-Heinemann is an imprint of Elsevier
Linacre House, Jordan Hill, Oxford OX2 8DP, UK
30 Corporate Drive, Suite 400, Burlington, MA 01803, USA

British Library Cataloguing-in-Publication Data
A catalogue record for this book is available from the British Library

Library of Congress Cataloging-in-Publication Data
A catalog record for this book is available from the Library of Congress

ISBN: 978-0-7506-8343-2

For information on all Butterworth-Heinemann publications
visit our web site at www.elsevierdirect.com

Typeset by Charon Tec Ltd., A Macmillan Company.
(www.macmillansolutions.com)

Printed and bound in Hungary

09 10 11 12 13   10 9 8 7 6 5 4 3 2 1

*To our dear little son Levente, who has given a whole
new meaning to the term wellness…*

Contents

List of Contributors

Ilja Castermans-Godfried
Centre of Research for Cultural Tourism
Zuyd University
Sittard, The Netherlands

Jennifer Kim Lian Chan
School of Business and Economics
Universiti Malaysia Sabah
Kota Kinabalu, Sabah
Malaysia

Rob Davidson
Department of Property and Construction
University of Westminster
London, United Kingdom

Sonia Ferrari
Dipartimento di Scienze Aziendali
Università della Calabria
Arcavacata di Rende (CS)
Italy

Alon Gelbman
Department of Tourism and Hospitality Studies
Kinneret College on the Sea of Galilee
Kfar-Tavor, Israel

Babu P. George
School of Management
Pondicherry University
Pondicherry, India

Roos Gerritsma
Leisure and Tourism Department
School of Economics
INholland University
Amsterdam/Diemen, The Netherlands

Nuno Gustavo
Escola Superior de Hotelaria e Turismo do Estoril
Estoril, Portugal

Kevin Hannam
School of Arts, Design, Media and Culture
University of Sunderland
Sunderland, United Kingdom

Henna Kangas
Centre for Tourism Studies, University of Joensuu
Savonlinna
Finland

Jennifer Laing
Tourism Research Unit
Monash University
Berwick Campus, Berwick, Melbourne, Australia

Chantal Laws
Department of Leisure, Tourism and Hospitality
University of Gloucestershire
Park Campus, Cheltenham, United Kingdom

Veronique Nelly Paul Marie Joukes
CETRAD, The University of Trás-os-Montes and Alto Douro
Vila Real, Portugal

Inna Petroune
International Relations
Sochi State University of Tourism and Recreation
Sochi, Russia

László Puczkó
Xellum Ltd
Budapest, Hungary

Tamara Rátz
Department of Tourism
Kodolányi János College
Székesfehérvár
Hungary

Sonja Sibila Lebe
Faculty of Economics and Business
University of Maribor
Maribor, Slovenia

Melanie Smith
Institute for Environmental Sciences
Faculty of Business
Corvinus University
Budapest, Hungary

Anja Tuohino
Centre for Tourism Studies, University of Joensuu
Savonlinna, Finland

Elena Yachina
Institute of Rehabilitilogy under Sochi
State University for Tourism and Recreation
Sochi Research
Institute of Balneology
Sochi, Russia

Preface

Travelling … is either an escape or a discovery
(Rosie Thomas, b. 1947)

The decision to write this book came after many years of a growing interest in health and wellness. It started around 10 years ago when I first discovered yoga during a visit to India and subsequently bought several books and taught myself the basics. This was followed by the enrolment in classes, regular practice at home, and culminated in a British Wheel of Yoga Teachers' Training Foundation course. This journey included the discovery of meditation and other spiritual activities, attendance at Yoga and Body-Mind-Spirit fairs and trade shows in London, and yoga and holistic weekend workshops in the United Kingdom. Whilst at the University of Greenwich in London, an interesting collaboration began with Dr Catherine Kelly*, who had similar research and personal interests. Over a period of 3 years, we became involved in researching holistic tourism. This included creating a database of over 500 holistic retreat centres around the world, surveying retreat centre operators about their motivations and practices, participant observation during different holistic retreats and workshops, and a research trip to Goa, which included face-to-face interviews with holistic practitioners. In 2006 we edited a special edition of the journal *Tourism Recreation Research* on Wellness Tourism, which was very kindly supported by Tej Vir Singh. The research period then culminated for me in a 5 week trip to Thailand, where I learnt the principles of Thai

---

*Catherine Kelly is still an academic at the University of Greenwich, but she has also set up her own successful holistic holiday company in 2007 called *Core Journeys* (http://www.corejourneys.com), which runs retreats in a range of locations. Thank you to Catherine for this very inspiring and interesting period of our lives and research.

Massage at the International Training Massage School (ITM) in Chiang Mai. This was, it has to be said, a wonderful experience!

A very different understanding of health and wellness emerged for me during the next 3 years when I moved to Budapest in Hungary. The concept of holistic tourism was almost unknown there, except for a few yoga classes and the rare offer of Thai massage or Ayurveda in one or two spas. It was there that I first started offering whole courses on Health and Wellness Tourism to BA Tourism students. These varied considerably from the courses being taught in Hungarian, which focused almost exclusively on historic spa management. Many of the ideas for this book emerged from the writing of materials and case studies for these courses, as well as discussing concepts with students. Some of them went on to write Dissertations in this subject, which allowed for more in-depth study of the different aspects of wellness. In parallel, my co-author (and husband) and I spent a great deal of time travelling around the region visiting spas and wellness facilities in Hungary, Austria, Czech Republic, Slovakia, and Slovenia. This gave us considerable insight into some of the most innovative developments in health and wellness tourism, but also some of the most uninspiring! A great deal can be learnt from those destinations and sites which need improvement, and much of our current and future work is based on trying to enhance the quality and creativeness of the sector.

Finally, in 2006, László Puczkó and I established the Spa and Wellness Tourism Special Interest Group (SIG) within ATLAS, which is the Association for Tourism and Leisure Education (http://www.atlas-euro.org). This was inspired by a tribute lecture which I gave to to the late Marin Bachvarov, who was Professor in the Dept of Geography and Tourism at the University of Łódź in Poland. Marin sadly died in 2006, but he had carried out some interesting work on the development of health and wellness tourism in Central and Eastern Europe, which formed the foundation for some of the work in this book. We had the first official Expert Meeting of the ATLAS SIG in Budapest in June 2007, and the members were invited to contribute case studies to this book. In Part Three, you can therefore read about the interesting and diverse research of some of the group members. We are discussing educational and curriculum development, definitional frameworks, policy and management issues. In addition, we are carrying out visitor profile and motivation surveys in a range of health and wellness facilities, which is expected to have global coverage in the coming few years.

We have tried to use our experiences and knowledge in this book to make it as interesting, informative and useful as possible. We hope you enjoy this journey into health and wellness as much as we have.

Melanie Smith
Corvinus University, Budapest

My own journey started long before I left, and was over before I returned.

(John Steinbeck, b. 1902)

I like bathing in warm waters. I always have. This may be genetic, or it may be locational, since Hungary has some of the best assets of thermal waters in the world. The circumstances were ideal to become a spa-fan. I grew up in a small, historic spa town (Gyula) and during my childhood, I could visit almost all the major baths around Hungary. Ever since, anywhere I travel I tend to visit spas and if possible I try spa hotels and day spas, too. I have been lucky and I could visit various facilities in different continents, but my favourites are in Europe.

I started more than just enjoying spas around 10 years ago, when I got involved in some curriculum development (e.g. for a European Union funded Socrates programme), and then later in consultancy projects. I worked together with Dr Tamara Rátz (one of the case study authors in this book) on the first global analyses of health tourism. In the last 8–10 years I consulted on many developments and was involved in numerous research and strategy formulation projects. I always found it almost painful when I saw that the developers or destination managers could not really take in the complex nature of health and wellness tourism. This was one of the main reasons, apart from being a fan, to start this book.

I believe that among the myriad things and activities one can do, participating in a health and wellness trip is maybe the best choice, especially, if the traveller can pay attention to all three elements, that is body, mind, and spirit. A trip like that *can* actually do a traveller the world of good, and giving something that is physically, biologically, emotionally, or psychologically beneficial to a guest is almost priceless. I also like experiences. By that I mean places and facilities that put a great deal of thought into what they offer.

In my head the ideal plan is to develop and run an eco-fit, hol-life retreat spa ☺!

László Puczkó
Xellum Ltd, Budapest

PART 1

History, definitions, and scope

CHAPTER 1

Introduction

> *What we anticipate in our destinations is not holiness or divine visions, but something even more miraculous – the opportunity to feel different from the way we feel at home. It is as if the act of travelling to a certain place in the world entitles us to feel happier and more alive.*
>
> (Chaline, 2002:67)

In the Introduction of a new title, authors tend to summarize the rationale and the content of their book. This already presents some challenges, as the definitions and labels used for this form of tourism are almost endless. This leaves us with the difficulty of clearly defining contents and meanings. As you will see later in the book, different countries and different organizations use labels such as health, wellness, medical, and spa almost interchangeably. Back in 1990, Bywater stated that:

> *Despite the growing interest in health and fitness, spas and thermal health resorts in the European Community are enjoying mixed fortunes. Opinion is divided on whether this sector represents medicine or tourism, and whether and to what extent the two can meet …*
>
> (Bywater, 1990:52)

The term 'health tourism' has not been well defined. The IUTO in 1973 stated that health tourism is '… the provision of health facilities utilizing the natural resources of the country, in particular mineral water and climate' (p. 7). Goodrich and Goodrich (1987:217) defined it as:

> *… an attempt on the part of a tourist facility (e.g. hotel) or destination (e.g. Baden, Switzerland) to attract tourists by deliberately promoting its health-care services and facilities, in addition to its regular amenities. These health-care services may include medical examinations by qualified doctors and nurses at the resort or hotel, special diets, acupuncture, transvital injections, vitamin-complex intakes, special medical treatments for various diseases such as arthritis, and herbal remedies.*

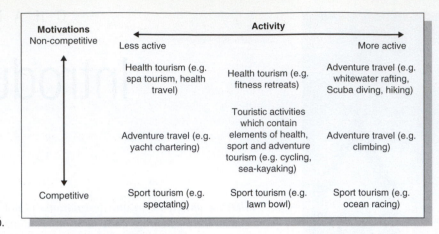

| **Motivations** | | **Activity** | |
Non-competitive	Less active		More active
	Health tourism (e.g. spa tourism, health travel)	Health tourism (e.g. fitness retreats)	Adventure travel (e.g. whitewater rafting, Scuba diving, hiking)
	Adventure travel (e.g. yacht chartering)	Touristic activities which contain elements of health, sport and adventure tourism (e.g. cycling, sea-kayaking)	Adventure travel (e.g. climbing)
Competitive	Sport tourism (e.g. spectating)	Sport tourism (e.g. lawn bowl)	Sport tourism (e.g. ocean racing)

Figure 1.1
Health Tourism Activity and Motivation Spectrum.
Source: Smith and Puczkó.

Hall (1992:151) refers to Van Spielen who defined health tourism as '… staying away from home, health as the most important motive, and done in a leisure setting'. Van Spielen also formulated five components, each identifying a more specific market segment, that is:

- Sun and fun activities
- Engaging in healthy activities, but health is not the central motive (adventure and sports tourism activities such as hiking, cycling, or golf)
- Principle motive for travel is health (e.g. sea cruise or travel to a different climate)
- Travel for sauna, massage, and other health activities (spa resort)
- Medical treatment.

Hall (1992) provided an analysis of health tourism within the context of adventure and sport tourism. Health tourism was compared to the other two forms of tourism based on its activity levels and motivation spectrum (Figure 1.1).

Hall's analysis did not consider the body–mind–spirit approach in his comparison, which is important when defining wellness tourism as we will see.

There is a wealth of literature about health and wellness tourism in the German language which is not always referred to in this publication, as we instead aim to fill gaps in the English language market. However, it can be seen that German, Austrian and Swiss academics and practitioners have made some useful distinctions between health and wellness. For example, Müller and Kaufmann (2000) regard wellness tourism as being a subset of health tourism, and distinguish between 'cure' (in German 'kur') tourists and those who seek more general wellness. According to Dunn (1959) who was one of the first doctors to talk about the philosophy of 'wellness', this is a state of health which comprises an overall sense of wellbeing and sees a person as consisting of body, mind, and spirit. Lifestyle and self-responsibility for health are paramount in the quest for a better quality of life. Müller and Kaufmann (2000) define wellness tourism as:

> *The sum of all the relationships and phenomena resulting from a journey and residence by people whose main motive is to preserve or promote their health. They stay in a specialised hotel which provides the appropriate professional know-how and individual care. They require a comprehensive service package comprising physical fitness/ beauty care, healthy nutrition/diet, relaxation/meditation and mental activity/education.*

They go on to discuss how wellness is pursued by 'healthy' people with the prime aim of prevention, whereas 'cure' tourists want to be healed, recover or recuperate from illness. The most common resources for this have traditionally been mineral waters and climate, but increasingly, health tourism includes not only physical but also mental and psychological problems. This is when the definitions of health and wellness start to become more complex and convergent.

In Germany, there is considerable emphasis on the term 'medical wellness', which somehow aims to combine the idea of health (cure) and wellness. This is defined by the Deutscher Wellness Verband (2008) as a form of 'behavioural medicine' where clients are guided by qualified practitioners to make specific changes to their lifestyle which can help lead to optimum wellness. This concept aims to democratize health and wellness in the sense that it is not only available to the few privileged, rich individuals who can afford to visit luxury spas, hotels, and clinics.

However, the growth of the medical wellness concept in Germany is not fully embraced by all academics and practitioners, who see it as somehow too narrow. The work of Wolfgang Nahrstedt over the past decade or more has analysed changing definitions of health and wellness. He suggests that the term 'wellness' came from a combination of the World Health Organization's (WHO, 1948) notion of 'well-being' and the later (1950s) concept of 'fit-ness'. In recent years, the term 'medical wellness' has been at the centre of German health and wellness developments, but he argues that this does not meet the goal of complete wellbeing, whereas the concept of 'cultural wellness' combined with 'wellness education' takes us to a form of 'high level wellness'. This is a more holistic approach which goes back to Dunn's (1959) idea of balancing body, mind, spirit with the social environment, culture, and spirituality (Nahrstedt, 2008).

There are clearly different historic, cultural, and linguistic understandings of health and wellness. In some languages (e.g. Hebrew) there is no word for 'wellness', and it is merely translated as 'health'. However, it seems to be increasingly common that the term 'wellness' is used internationally, even in those countries where the language is very different from English (e.g. Hungary) or in countries which are protectionist about language (e.g. France). Translating the term for the purposes of marketing or carrying out research can create a few problems. For example, in Finnish, there is not an easy direct translation of the word 'wellness' and the

Finnish version corresponds more closely to 'wellbeing'. In Slovenian, the translation is more like 'well-feeling'. In German-speaking countries, not only is the term wellness (in English) fully embraced, but it has even been taken a stage further with the concepts of 'selfness' and 'mindness' being developed. These concepts are discussed in Chapter Eleven. Interestingly, as noted by the BMWA (2002), some anglicisms like the term 'wellness' (and even less, 'selfness' and 'mindness') are not so well understood in the UK, neither is the term 'health tourism', mainly because of the lack of a 'kur' or medical wellness tradition.

Irrespective of terminology, health and wellness as a concept clearly means different things in different countries and cultures. Chan's (2007) research in Malaysia showed that local people associated health and wellness mainly with personal wellbeing and lifestyle, stress release for working people in urban areas and a new form of leisure/tourism activities for foreign tourists. This includes spa and body treatments for personal wellbeing (stress release) and beauty/cosmetic surgery. In Central and Eastern Europe, the term health is closely related to physical and medical healing. The existence of medical waters and spas means that the main association for people in the region is with these forms of activity. Many Western Europeans are familiar with the concept of historic, thermal spa tourism as well as thalassotherapy (cures based on sea elements), especially on the Atlantic coast. In Southern Europe, there is an emphasis on seaside wellness, where sunshine, sea air and thalassotherapies are used to enhance wellbeing. In addition, the pace of life is relaxed and siestas are common, and the Mediterranean diet is considered to be one of the healthiest in the world. Turkish baths are used in Turkey and similar facilities exist in some parts of Spain (e.g. Andalucia) where the legacy of the Moors is dominant. In Scandinavia, there is a large emphasis on outdoor recreation such as Nordic walking, cross-country skiing, and lake swimming, even in winter. In Finland especially, almost all people have a sauna in their house or in the close vicinity as this is seen as an integral part of everyday wellness. In Germany, Austria, and Switzerland, physical fitness is also seen as being extremely important, but this is combined with other principles of optimum wellness, including healthy eating, rest and relaxation, and some forms of spiritual activity such as yoga and meditation. There is an increasing shift towards self-responsibility and a balanced approach to life. 'Selfness' and 'mindness' imply that people are taking responsibility for their own lifestyle and making relevant physical, emotional, psychological, and social changes.

In Asian countries, many spiritual activities such as yoga, meditation, and massage are more integrated into everyday life than they are in most Western countries. The use of energy flows is a more accepted form of healing (e.g. Reiki, Shiatsu) and balance creation for living space (e.g. Feng Shui, Vasati). In Middle Eastern and North African countries where religion is a much more central focus of life, spirituality is not seen as an 'optional extra'. Enhanced physical wellness may come from physical healing (e.g. using spas) or medical intervention (e.g. medical trips to India). In the UK, US, Canada, and Australasia, the use of day spas or health and beauty farms is fairly widespread. Emphasis is more on cosmetic treatments, relaxation and pampering than it is about medical treatments. However, there are also clear growth trends in occupational wellness (e.g. work-life balance, stress management) as well as the need for enhanced spirituality as organized religion declines.

The concept of wellness clearly means different things in different contexts and countries. The age old tradition of sitting in spa waters in Europe is far removed from the spiritual traditions of Asia, and different again from more modern forms of wellness, such as occupational psychology workshops or cosmetic surgery holidays. What is clear, however, is that there is an increasing globalization and hybridization of wellness products, whereby eastern philosophies and traditions infiltrate western contexts; traditional spas expand to include emotional and spiritual activities as well as physical ones; and pop psychology blends with more esoteric practices to enhance mental wellness. Figure 1.2 demonstrates the wide

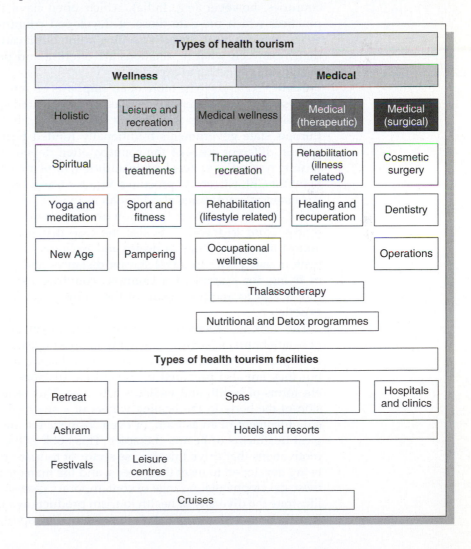

Figure 1.2
Spectrum of Health Tourism. *Source*: Smith and Puczkó.

range of health and wellness products and facilities which have emerged in recent years.

Visitors still find it difficult to anticipate what kind of services they are likely to experience at a health or wellness destination or site, so labelling and marketing are extremely important. We will highlight regional and product-related differences, as well as giving a global overview of the recent situation and the likely trends in the future. To make reading and understanding easier, we will mainly use the term health tourism, with the understanding that wellness tourism is a subset, and that it is a holistic concept. One differentiation would be that medical activities play an important role in health tourism however, most forms of wellness tourism do not include a medical or cure dimension.

Because of its focus on tourism, this book tends to be biased towards those nations which generate international tourists (i.e. developed countries). The destinations visited by tourists may be located in developing countries, however (e.g. India), which often have traditional, spiritual practices which pre-date those of developed countries by thousands of years. This can be an attractive selling point, but it can also result in a mismatch between what destinations are offering and promoting, and what visitors are expecting to experience.

There also tends to be more of an emphasis on international rather than domestic tourism. Often it is implied and not stated specifically that tourists enjoy the facilities within their own country. In Central and Eastern Europe, state governments traditionally funded health trips to baths or spas in different areas of the country, often depending on what kind of healing properties waters had. In addition, until after 1989, it was very difficult for CEE citizens to procure a Visa for travel outside their own country. Financial constraints also limit an individual's ability to travel abroad, and it is only the élite in transition or developing countries who can currently afford to travel. It is also the case that some countries can offer almost the whole range of health and wellness products domestically, so visitors may prefer to travel shorter distances and avoid long-haul travel or flying, for example. For example, countries like India are vast therefore a visit to another region of the country can afford a very different experience.

The book will focus on the development, management and marketing of health tourism. Not only are many people increasingly concerned about their physical, social, and psychological wellbeing in their everyday lives, but they are also prepared to travel long distances to experience different forms of health and wellness activities. This ranges from the immersion of the body in the healing waters of a spa to the quest for spiritual enlightenment in an ashram, or even cosmetic enhancement through surgical treatments or beauty therapies. This book will examine the range of motivations that drive this diverse sector of tourists, the products that are being developed to meet their needs, and the management implications of these developments. A range of contemporary case studies will be used to illustrate the diversity of health tourism products available internationally. It will also examine new trends in fashion, diet, sport, fitness, leisure and recreation, and their relationship to tourism. Tourism can contribute to many dimensions of health, though obviously it is debatable as to how far a transitory phenomenon can make a significant difference to long-term health. The links between lifestyle changes and tourism therefore need to be explored.

Tourism has always been seen as a process of self-regeneration as well as relaxation, education or indulgence (Ryan, 1997). Hallab (2006:71) describes how 'In the fields of travel and tourism, health has been approached from the angle of tourism experiences' effects on an individual's well-being'. The concept of wellbeing implies our everyday levels of satisfaction and contentment. These are enhanced by regular breaks from routine, periods of rest and relaxation, fantasy and escapism, even the mere pleasure of planning and anticipating a trip. The psychological as well as the physical benefits of tourism appear to have gained increasing importance. As stated by Seaton and Bennett (1996:69) 'In modern days the emphasis is more likely to be put on mental rather than physical improvement'. There are debates within the book as to whether wellness tourism concerns escapism *from* the self (and the world) to environments that offer pure relaxation, or, whether it is about *confrontation* of the self and re-negotiation of one's place in the world and relationships to others.

Wellness tourists (perhaps ironically) need to be in good enough physical health to embark on a journey, as well as being materially affluent. As with all forms of tourism, the flows of tourists are predominantly from more developed to less developed countries. The pursuit of wellness is time consuming and expensive (e.g. Smith & Kelly's, 2006, research shows that the average cost of a week's holistic holiday is 520 pounds sterling (about 800 EUROs) and the average cost of a massage or life-coaching session is prohibitive for the majority of people – anything from 50 to 150 EUROs). Indulgence in wellness activities is therefore largely the premise of the middle classes, except in countries where governments subsidize medical activities (e.g. spas in Central and Eastern Europe during the socialist era) or where yoga and/or meditation are integrated into everyday life (e.g. India, Thailand). The recent trend seems to be for Western tourists to seek solace in Eastern philosophies and therapies (e.g. Chinese medicine, Buddhist meditation, Indian Ayurveda, Thai massage). Such alternatives already pervade many Western societies, but tourists are often just as keen to visit the origin of the practice.

If wellness tourism was merely about relaxation, then one might argue that the traditional beach holiday with its emphasis on sunbathing is the ultimate form of meditation! Similarly, spa tourism sometimes offers little more than a soak in warm thermal or medicinal waters. In order to qualify as a contemporary wellness tourism experience, we would contend that some deliberate contribution has to be made to psychological, spiritual or emotional wellbeing in addition to physical. This takes wellness tourism from the realm of being merely a passive form of tourism with a focus on escapism to one where tourists are purposefully driven by the desire to actively seek enhanced wellness. The majority of wellness tourists are already active at home in some form of wellness-enhancing activity (e.g. fitness, yoga, meditation, massage, healthy eating). Those that are not often aim to engage further in the wellness activities they have experienced on holiday, thus demonstrating that even a short trip can have a long-lasting effect on one's everyday life.

The destination in wellness tourism is often an alternative space in which one can engage in self-analysis without the stresses and distractions of home. Tourists frequently seek locations and activities that are transcendent. For example, De Botton (2002) describes how travellers are attracted to 'sublime' landscapes that benefit their soul by making them feel small, yet part of an infinite and universal cycle. It is no coincidence then that many wellness centres are located beside the ocean or on a mountain top. For example, Pechlaner and Fischer (2006) note the importance of location in the context of Alpine Wellness, a product developed in the Alpine region of Europe.

However, for some wellness tourists, the traditional preoccupation with rest, relaxation and escapism reigns supreme. But arguably all wellness tourists are self-aware, active seekers of enhanced wellbeing, health, and happiness. Of course, wellness is not a static concept and is subjective and relative, thus always in flux. The needs of wellness tourists will clearly vary enormously at different times and stages of their lives. The current diversification of this sector is therefore a welcome development and one which is worthy of close observation and dedicated research.

SUMMARY OF PART ONE: HISTORY, DEFINITIONS, AND SCOPE

Chapter Two – Historical overview

This chapter provides an overview of the international development of health over the past centuries dating back as far as 5000 BC when Ayurveda was being practised in India, the first known use of Chinese medicine in 1000 BC, and numerous indigenous traditions in Australasia, Africa, and the Americas. It covers Ancient Egyptian customs of bathing and the use of cosmetics; Greek and Roman building of thermal and medical baths, fitness regimes, and the consultation of 'oracles' in the hope of curing sickness; the development of Arabian and Ottoman hamams or steam baths; the visiting of Japanese onsens; European traditions of spa and seaside bathing and oxygen therapy, including those resorts built in the colonies. The chapter outlines the main practices of health in the principle regions of the world, and the extent to which travel played a role in the development of resorts and destinations. Although the spread of health tourism was very limited until the 20th century, there is some evidence of travelling for medical purposes in Roman times and even earlier.

Chapter Three – Contemporary definitions

This chapter discusses some of the terminology that is currently used in health tourism, especially the problems of differentiating between terms which are closely related. The definition of 'health' is becoming broader and much closer to that of 'wellness', thus the terms are sometimes used interchangeably. The same is true of 'wellbeing', 'happiness', and 'quality of life', therefore recent theories from sociology or psychology are used to make some distinctions. More esoteric notions of wellness have traditionally been known as 'New Age', a term that is often used in a derogatory way, therefore 'holism' is becoming more common. Spirituality is viewed as an important dimension of wellness, but this tends to be more and more secular and disconnected from religion. Wellness overall implies a balance of different areas of one's life (e.g. physical, social, spiritual, intellectual, occupational, and emotional). Health has closer links to illness and medical treatments, but it follows the same philosophy of achieving balance of both physical and mental dimensions in life.

Chapter Four – Leisure, lifestyle, and tourism

This chapter explores the relationship between the practices of everyday life and leisure and the way these relate to tourism. The chapter starts with an overview of some of the tools that are used to boost health or enhance wellness, such as medicine (conventional and complementary), therapy, psychology, nutrition, rehabilitation, and cosmetics. Many of these trends are led by the media and peoples' personal faith in new products. The second part of the chapter focuses on the political, environmental, and social factors that encourage people to seek enhanced wellness, such as the breakdown of communities, obsession with the self and celebrities, the desire to downsize, the decline of traditional religion, new media and technology, work-related stress, etc. Although this chapter is somewhat biased in the sense that it focuses mainly on developed, capitalist countries, it is argued that these are the main generating countries for tourism, and secondly, many 'emergent' or 'transition' countries (e.g. CEE, China, India) seem to be heading the same way in terms of economic and social pressures and trends.

Chapter Five – Typologies of health and wellness tourism

This chapter examines the whole spectrum of health tourism, including those facilities which focus mainly on physical and medical treatment, through to those which emphasize rather the spiritual or self-development aspects of the self. The chapter is divided into a number of sub-sectors in order to facilitate the discussion as the products, facilities and services can differ greatly according to which dimensions of health are catered for. Even within the sub-sectors, a further breakdown is required, for example, there is a big difference between a spa which focuses on medical treatments and another which emphasizes beauty. Holistic tourism can be about self-development in retreat centres, but some visitors may just want to enjoy yoga or meditation for relaxation purposes or stress relief. Medical tourism now takes place outside spas as well as within them, and may not involve any other treatments except an operation and the required recovery period. Occupational wellness can take place in large hotels or in small retreat centres. A number of case studies and examples are used to illustrate the complexity and diversity of the various typologies of health tourism.

Chapter Six – An international and regional analysis

This chapter takes a geographical approach and considers the way in which health and wellness tourism have developed in different regions of the world. Whereas the history chapter (Chapter Two) focuses on past developments in health in a number of regions, this chapter analyses in more detail contemporary developments and their relationship to tourism. The chapter starts by discussing briefly the linguistic and cultural differences which influence the way in which wellness is defined before going on to an analysis of the regions. The regions chosen include Western, Central and Eastern, Southern and Northern Europe; the Middle East and North Africa, which are seen as being geographically and culturally similar; Eastern, Western, and Southern Africa; Asia; Australasia and the South Pacific; the Americas and the Caribbean. There is also some discussion of indigenous traditions in many developing countries, which pre-date those of the colonizing society by thousands of years, and which are now becoming fashionable again in contemporary spas and wellness centres.

SUMMARY OF PART TWO: MANAGING AND MARKETING HEALTH AND WELLNESS TOURISM

Chapter Seven – Demand, motivations, and profiles

This chapter discusses the profiles and motivations of typical health tourists, making a distinction between different typologies of health tourism (e.g. traditional spas, hotel spas, medical spas, holistic and spiritual retreats, medical centres, etc.). There is a discussion of current trends with some explanations of why the health market is still mainly dominated by women and people who are over 40 years of age. Some distinctions are made between nationalities (e.g. the health patterns of the Japanese can differ somewhat from those of North Americans). For each of the typologies of health tourism, examples of research are given to highlight the trends in consumer behaviour. Different methods of segmentation are given as examples of some of the most recent research being undertaken in this field, and there is an analysis of the importance of lifestyle practices and their influence on tourist behaviour.

Chapter Eight – Planning and development

This chapter discusses some of the issues that are important when planning health and wellness tourism destinations, including the likely impacts of tourism development, location and design of facilities, development concepts and philosophies, and the main challenges for profitability and longevity. Although it is recognized that a certain degree of organic and spontaneous development can be attractive, especially for holistic tourism destinations, this does not guarantee a high quality of experience for visitors, nor does it protect their health and safety. In order to maximize the positive impacts of tourism for destinations and to minimize the negative impacts, a certain amount of planning is necessary. This can take place at a number of levels – national, regional, local, and site level. Priorities differ depending on the level of planning, but the harmonization of development can help to ensure sustainability (e.g. national strategies can inform regional decisions or local regulations).

Chapter Nine – Managing destinations and sites

This chapter describes the way in which health tourism is managed starting with a distinction between the different levels of management, for example, geographical (i.e. national, regional and local levels), and asset or resource-based management. This includes references to the organizational structures involved and the way in which developments are managed. Emphasis is mainly placed on the need to create high quality and memorable experiences in a wellness context, including the design of the facilities, atmosphere creation, staff training and regulation, and service management. The management of visitor expectations is also crucial, including information provision, pre- and after-care, health and safety assurance, and many other issues relating to the provision of treatments. The chapter makes a distinction between different types of wellness facilities and destinations (e.g. resort spas, day spas, medical spas, wellness hotels, and holistic centres) and identifies the key management issues for each.

Chapter Ten – Reaching customers

This chapter focuses on the way in which health and wellness products are marketed and promoted to customers. This includes an analysis of marketing communications and the levels at which this operates (i.e. cognitive, behavioural, and affective). The segmenting and targeting strategies of different countries and organizations are also considered, including their use of slogans and images. Branding is a key focus of the chapter, looking at the way in which global, national, regional, local, and organizational brands are created and communicated. This also includes theming and packaging of products. The use of language is considered to be especially important when creating a unique or distinctive image, yet many destinations or sites seem to revert to standardized or clichéd expressions. This means that customers are not always able to distinguish between companies and products. However, this makes those organizations which do this well really stand out. Several examples of good practice are therefore given. Finally, the chapter looks briefly at tour operations, distribution, and pricing.

Chapter Eleven – Product development

This chapter starts with an overview of the globalization of health tourism analysing the extent to which product development is becoming standardized with the same facilities and services available all over the world. On the one hand, this ensures a diversity of products, but on the other hand, it means that unique experiences are harder to create and find. Health tourism is becoming more and more competitive with some markets already reaching saturation point, therefore innovation is becoming essential. For this reason, many spas and wellness hotels develop signature treatments in the hope of making themselves stand out; some desinations sell their unique natural resources or landscapes; others promote the expertise of their practitioners and use 'big names' to attract visitors (e.g. in holistic and wellness centres). In addition, the chapter examines the trend towards more integrated experiences, that is the search for balance of body–mind–soul or work/life balance. For this, destinations need to offer a diverse range of products and to advise their clients carefully in their choice of workshops or treatments.

Chapter Twelve – Conclusions: The future of health and wellness tourism

This final chapter discusses the likely future of health tourism using industry trends – prediction data. This includes the shift towards wellness as a lifestyle and not just as an exceptional leisure or tourism activity. The growing demands and motivations of consumers are analysed in depth, including the emergence of new markets (e.g. teens) and preferences for more natural and indigenous products and treatments. The delivery of services is changing and making increasing use of online technology (e.g. not just for bookings, but also for pre- and after-care, even online retreats). There is a growing concern about issues relating to sustainability and environmental impacts of health tourism, thus there is a notable 'greening' of the industry. Some operators and businesses are more concerned about the apparent saturation of the wellness market and the need to diversify products or attract new markets. Finally, some recommendations are made for health practitioners as well as for researchers in this field.

SUMMARY OF PART THREE: OPERATIONAL AND MANAGEMENT ISSUES IN HEALTH AND WELLNESS TOURISM

This section provides a number of case studies from around the world which exemplify many of the issues discussed in the first two sections of the book. This includes the historical development of spas and their subsequent decline and regeneration; product development and innovation for existing and new destinations; the diversification of health and wellness tourism markets; organizational and management strategies; and marketing and promotion.

1. Heritage of spa and health tourism in Russia (Inna Petroune and Elena Yachina)

This case study provides an overview of the history of Russian health tourism, and some of the barriers to the development of spa tourism, especially in the transition years following 1989. Many of the problems relate to the previous system of state subsidy and control, and subsequent inadequate political policies and financial investment. As a result, such countries struggle to modernize their facilities, to improve their services and to enhance their image. One of the major challenges is to re-orientate destinations and products from state-subsidized medical tourism to more private funded leisure and recreational tourism. Such problems are not unique to Russia and are common to many other former socialist countries, especially in Central and Eastern Europe. However, future developments are likely to involve far more product innovation, quality enhancement, staff training, and more effective organizational structures and networks.

2. The health spa resort Rogaška Slatina returning to its past glory (Sonja Sibila Lebe)

This case study discusses how the oldest spa resort in Slovenia, like many other spas in Central and Eastern Europe, has suffered from lack of investment during World War II and thereafter to become a somewhat rundown medical facility. However, since 1991, there has been considerable re-investment in health spa resorts and many spas have introduced different kinds of wellness programmes, Rogaška Slatina included. The problems of mixed markets still have to be addressed, to accommodate medical visitors on the one hand, and recreational guests on the other. The subsequent labelling and promotion of the resort to appeal to an international market with different understandings of terms like 'spa' and 'wellness' is another dilemma facing this and many other similar resorts in this region.

3. Regeneration of an historic spa town: A case study of spa in Belgium (Melanie Smith)

Spa in Belgium has a long history going back to Roman times, and the town enjoyed a glamorous heyday in the 18th century. Despite a decline in the early part of the 20th century, Spa went on to benefit from state-supported health tourism in the post World War II years until the 1980s, when support was withdrawn. As a result, there was a shift to leisure rather than health-based tourism. However, this was not enough to save the historic spa facilities from degeneration, and eventually they were no longer used. Instead, a new thermal complex was built on the hill above the town with an emphasis on 'thermoludism' or recreational/fun use of the waters. Despite the popularity of the development, there is some debate about the potential longevity of its success, as well as controversy about the construction of new facilities instead of the renovation of historic ones.

4. Vidago and Pedras Salgadas Spas: The revival of a tourism attraction or a marketing technique for beverages? (Veronique Nelly Paul Marie Joukes)

This case study discusses the redevelopment and linking of two traditional but under-visited spas in the North of Portugal. Although they are geographically isolated, the potential for tourism is arguably significant because of the area's diverse resources. Significant funds are being used to support the project, therefore the redevelopments will be large scale, creating employment, attracting subsequent investment, and enhancing the image of the region and the country as a whole. Overall, this is an ambitious, potentially risky project, which represents the high hopes that goverments and investors are now attaching to 'flagship' wellness developments.

5. The Luigiane thermal baths: A tool for the deseasonalization of the tourist demand in Calabria (Italy) (Sonia Ferrari)

The Luigiane thermal baths in Calabria, Italy represent an ideal opportunity for extending the tourist season. The baths function almost as a thermal town with five hotels and several leisure facilities. The case study discusses research that has been undertaken in the area with main stakeholders and clients, and shows how there is an increasing interest in the concept of wellness and not just therapeutic or curative tourism. The diversification of the market is also likely to be based on other attractions in the region, such as culture, gastronomy, the sea, and sports. This case study exemplifies the need to redevelop traditional health resorts to incorporate broader concepts of wellness and attract new markets.

6. Hotel Herttua: Spa and rehabilitation centre in Eastern Finland (Anja Tuohino and Henna Kangas)

This case study discusses the Hotel Herttua in Finland which is located in a beautiful but relatively unknown landscape. It has traditionally attracted rehabilitation customers on social holidays supported by state funding that is those who want to improve their working ability, as well as war veterans (a market which has a finite lifespan). In the summer, however, tourists come whose motivations are different. The e-GOOD cooperation network is currently carrying out research to find new innovative solutions for the changing demand of visitors and to identify new potential segments for wellness tourism. One of the suggestions is to develop a concept of 'Lake Wellness'.

7. São Pedro do Sul Thermal Centre: Between health and wellness tourism (Nuno Gustavo)

This case study describes a thermal centre in Portugal which dates back to 1884, and its current organizational and management structure. Its buildings tend to attract two markets: health visitors and wellness visitors. Research has shown that these visitors have different needs and therefore future developments should take into consideration the need for differentiation of spaces, infrastructures, models of management, and communication. This case study highlights some of the difficulties for traditional spas wishing to diversify their wellness products and attract new and different markets.

8. Healing hills and wellness in luxury (the Netherlands) (Ilja Castermans-Godfried)

This case study focuses on the South-Limburg region of the Netherlands which is aiming to attract more 'silver tourists' that is those over 50 years or more, who will represent up to 40% of the Dutch population in 20 years. An example of one project called 'Healing Hills' in Heuvelland is given, in which the tourism industry and medical sector are cooperating to provide a recovery centre for those who have undergone operations. 'Wellness in Luxury' is another project which will aim to make Valkenburg a city of wellness with a spa and health resort and a wellness boulevard. The focus of both case studies is innovation and the cooperation of many stakeholders.

9. Peninsula Hot Springs: A new spa tourism experience 'down under' (Jennifer Laing)

This case study describes a relatively new spa development in Australia called Peninsula Hot Springs which was opened to visitors in June 2005. It is one of the 'flagship' projects in the State government's desire to position Victoria as the main health destination in Australia. Although the spa facilities for tourists are new, the natural resources (e.g. geothermal and fresh water aquifers) and indigenous Aboriginal products are thousands of years old. The development is expanding all the time with plans to extend the target markets to include international tourists in addition to the existing urban visitors from nearby Melbourne. This case study shows clearly the challenges of combining ancient traditions with new facilities and services, as well as the need to cater for a diversifying health market.

10. Using wellness elements for branding an exclusive image of tourism sites in the North of Israel (Alon Gelbman)

This case study analyses the branding of wellness facilities in the North of Israel. Although wellness is often only a small part of the actual tourism offer, many businesses consider the image or brand it creates to be highly attractive, symbolizing exclusivity and luxury. Unfortunately, the reality behind the image does not always turn out to be as attractive as the promise, as many small businesses cannot afford to run proper wellness facilities nor employ qualified staff. A content analysis of 39 tourist destinations shows the variations between the image promoted and the levels of actual wellness development. Often the label 'spa' seems to be overused and is often misleading, as it does not refer to a spa in the traditional sense. Although beautiful natural landscapes and healthy, organic food are also promoted, this is perhaps not enough to constitute a wellness tourism destination in terms of what tourists might expect.

11. Ayurvedic health tourism in Kerala, India (Kevin Hannam)

This case study focuses on the way that Ayurveda is being used to market the Indian state of Kerala. Tourism is of crucial importance to Kerala and visitor numbers are increasing each year. One of the main products being promoted is traditional, holistic 'health' tourism in the form of Ayurveda. However, the concept of Ayurveda is becoming oversold, resulting in many unlicensed and ill-equipped health centres being developed and promoted to tourists. Although there is a voluntary certification code of conduct, it is not widely accepted. Many tourists see Ayurveda as an attractive 'extra' rather than a primary motivating factor for visiting the region, but there are still concerns that Kerala's image is being damaged by unplanned and unregulated developments.

12. Hot springs in Japanese domestic and international tourism (Tamara Rátz)

This case study analyses the traditional and contemporary development of Japanese onsens. Historically, the hot springs have been used for health, spiritual, educational, and cultural purposes, and more recently, leisure, recreation, and tourism. The modern onsen experience includes nutrition, sightseeing, exercise, and relaxation in natural surroundings. The medical or health dimension has become less significant as support from insurance declines, however with the ageing population, a resurgence of interest is likely. Whilst many Japanese visitors enjoy the onsen for relaxation purposes, international visitors expect and would like a cultural heritage experience. The modernization of onsen is therefore not always a welcome development, especially as it is hard for visitors to access more remote, traditional, and 'authentic' locations.

13. CHI spa at the Shangri-la, Sabah, Malaysia: Its philosophy and management concept and 'a journey of experiences' (Jennifer Kim Lian Chan)

This case study discusses the development and management of spas in the hotel industry in Malaysia, focusing in particular on the CHI Spa Center in the Shangri-la hotel in Sabah. This is part of a hotel chain in Asia with similar hotels in Penang and Bangkok. The philosophy of design and development are based on Chinese concepts of CHI energy flows, Yin and

Yang, and the five elements. The signature therapies are based on these principles, as well as some healing traditions from the Himalayas. This case study exemplifies the increasing use of ancient and indigenous traditions in regional and global chain hotels, and the desire to give a local or regional flavour to international tourism facilities.

14. The Big Chill Festival, England, UK (Chantal Laws)

This case study discusses the Big Chill Festival in the UK, a 3-day festival which includes not only music and the usual festival facilities, but also a Body and Soul area where holistic health practices are offered. The main market for the festival is older than average with an audience of predominantly thirty-somethings. The festival is similar to counter-culture celebrations in the 1960s and 1970s, which had strong links to New Age ideologies. The emphasis is on creating an alternative space in which an atmosphere of spirituality, transcendence, and community are created. This case study shows how some festivals are moving towards a more integrated form of experience and embracing the holistic notion of body–mind–spirit.

15. The growing yoga community in the Netherlands: How yoga is becoming a lifestyle product including tourism activities (Roos Gerritsma)

This case study shows how yoga is growing in the Netherlands as a lifestyle-enhancing activity, still mostly used by women, but increasingly also by men, stressed-out workers, even children. Many forms of yoga are offered as well as being blended with other activities (e.g. 'body balance'), and although people may turn to yoga for physical health reasons, they sometimes then discover the meditative or spiritual benefits. This can lead to an intensification of practice, such as all-day or weekend workshops, events, as well as holidays. Many new magazines, TV programmes and internet sites are facilitating the practice of yoga and the promotion of products and services. Online yoga 'communities' can even share ideas and reviews of experiences, such as workshops or trips. As yoga tourism has been relatively under-researched, the case study ends with some recommendations for future research.

16. Medical tourism in India: A case study of Apollo Hospitals (Babu P. George)

This case study focuses on the exponential growth of medical tourism in India and the business of the Apollo Hospitals Group, the largest healthcare group in Asia. After the deregulation of the Indian economy in the 1990s, the Apollo chain could expand there with fewer bureaucratic barriers and the easier importing of the latest technology. The benefits of an international cluster mean a guarantee of quality, training, resource management, and technology. Their networks and contacts are extensive and their marketing is well established. Although there are criticisms that Apollo shows little concern for the indigenous populations' health, in terms of medical tourism for international tourists, this represents a major opportunity for India.

17. The use of spas by meetings participants: The case of the US (Rob Davidson)

Business and politics was frequently discussed in spas in ancient times (e.g. Greek and Roman baths). This case study describes how there has been something of a renaissance in the combination of water-based activities and business tourism. Many companies are choosing spa hotels as a location for their meetings and conferences, as it is believed that spas help to motivate and relax people and provide incentives for better performance. Spas can provide the ideal social environment for team building and can be conducive to networking. Participants are usually offered lesiure based rather than medical packages and treatments, but increasingly workshops aiming at easing stress and dealing with other psychological or lifestyle issues are becoming more common. Massages and relaxation treatments might also be offered to participants during a meeting or conference. There is a considerable growth rate in this form of wellness tourism in the US, but the trend is likely to increase everywhere.

CHAPTER 2

Historical overview

Your town is only a perfect town when there is a bath in it.
(Abu Sir in Lee, 2004)

This chapter provides an overview of the history and development of health and wellness, emphasizing the different ways in
which health is understood in various regions and countries of
the world. This helps to pave the way for later chapters which
focus on contemporary understandings of health and some of
the definitions that have emerged in recent years. As health
becomes more globalized as a result of international travel and
increased mobility through immigration and guest working,
there is a chance that products and services will become more
homogenized and ubiquitous (i.e. the same or similar products
will be available all over the world). However, in historical terms,
health and wellness practices have been very much embedded
in regional and local traditions and cultures, with available natural resources also determining the forms of wellness that were
developed. Clearly, the concept of travelling for health reasons
is a relatively late addition to the history of health; therefore the
emphasis on tourism is fairly minimal in this chapter. However,
later chapters (e.g. Chapter Six) show just how these regions have
developed their tourism facilities and resources over the past few
decades using their unique traditions as described here.

A brief international overview of health and wellness

Many visitors to modern day health and wellness centres are
often unaware of the cultural origins of the treatments they enjoy.
They may not realize that Indian Ayurvedic practices go back as
far as 5000 BC, or that Egyptian women in 3000 BC used similar

cosmetics to the ones that are sometimes used today. The earliest known writings about Chinese medicine go back to 1000 BC, yet Chinese medicine in Western societies is viewed as something 'new' and exotic. The earliest reference to magical healing waters according to the Spas Research Fellowship (2008) is about 1700 BC. Hippocrates, the classic philosopher and physician of the Hellenistic age, and a prophet of natural healing methods, said: '… water is still, after all, the best'. The most ancient evidence of bathing culture was found in the valleys beside the river Indus where an ancient culture with water ducts, bathrooms and bath pools existed. Crebbin-Bailey et al. (2005) provide a comprehensive timeline showing how ancient Greek civilizations from 700 BC introduced cold water bathing for warriors, Persians (600–300 BC) already used steam and mud baths, Hebrews introduced ritual purification by water through immersion in the Dead Sea in 200 BC, and Thais (then Siamese) practised massage as far back as 100 BC. The Roman Empire left an incredible legacy of baths, one of the principle ones being in Bath in Britain in 76 AD, as well as the discovery of thermal springs in still-popular destinations like Spa in Belgium before 100 AD and Baden-Baden in Germany in 211 AD. The term 'therme' was used for elegant leisure facilities whereas the term 'balnea' was used for simple and mainly healing oriented bathing establishments.

The Baths of Caracalla near Rome were in use for three centuries before they lost their aqueduct water supply in the siege of Rome 537 AD. The baths could accommodate between 6,000 and 8,000 bathers a day (Spas Research Fellowship, 2008). Lomine (2005) describes how Augustan Society in Rome during the Roman Empire (44 BC to 69 AD) travelled fairly extensively for health reasons to relaxing landscapes, seaside resorts, and hot springs. Medicine was not very developed and the average lifespan was about 40 years, so wealthy citizens would travel in the hope of finding treatment or recovering in a healthier climate. Typical trips would include sea voyages from Italy to Alexandria in Egypt or visits to mineral springs in what are now Vichy, Aix-en-Provence, Bath, and Wiesbaden. Augustans would also travel to consult oracles or 'fortune tellers' for example, in Delphi (Greece), Delos (Aegean Sea) or Claros (Asia Minor). Health and religion were combined in the case of visits to Asclepius' (the Greek god of medicine) sanctuaries, where visitors entered the sanctuary, took a bath to get purified, entered the god's temple, prayed, and laid down to sleep where the god would visit them and magically cure them or give advice about what treatment to take.

The Ottoman Empire built Turkish baths in 800 AD and knights from Britain experienced them during crusades in 1200 AD. Saunas began appearing along the Baltic in Finland as early as 1000 AD. The 14th century saw the development of the first shower in the baths of Bormie in Italy, as well as the discovery of warm springs in Central Europe (e.g. Buda – now Budapest in Hungary and Carlsbad in Germany – now Karlovy Vary in the Czech Republic). Unfortunately, in some parts of Europe (e.g. Britain) by the 15th century there were concerns about public bathing in warm waters because of the spread of diseases like syphilis, leprosy, and plague. Naked, mixed bathing was also deemed immoral by the Bishop of Bath and Wells (which may explain the tendency in Britain today to still bathe in spas partly clothed!).

The Renaissance in Europe (16th century) witnessed a boost to balneo-therapy (water therapy treatments) as a medical practice, especially in Italy where there were famous sulphurous springs in Abano, mud baths in Padua, Lucca, and Caldiero. In 1553, the first European Spa Directory was printed in Venice listing more than 200 spas. Elizabeth I popularized public bathing in 1571 in Britain to discourage the British from travelling to Spa in Belgium. The chemical and mineral properties of spa water were discovered in the mid-17th century (for drinking and douching as well as bathing) and their effects were gradually listed and understood, and the effects of different temperatures were also researched. Many European Kings and Queens supported the visiting of spas. The late 18th century saw the recognition of the benefits of seawater, the beginning of thalassotherapy, which was particularly popular in France. Modern massage techniques began to be developed in the early 19th century, particularly in Sweden. In the US, the spiritual value of indigenous (Native American Indian) landscapes started to be appreciated, and spas were built around springs there. In Germany, the first modern hydrotherapy spa was developed in the early 19th century offering health packages of treatments, such as fresh air, cold water, and diet. This started a trend in both Europe and America. In 1880, Father Sebastian Kneipp started practising hydrotherapy for the poor, and his ideas still continue today. By the turn of the 19th century, travel guides were promoting the health treatments of air and sun cures all over the world, including the resorts of the Caribbean and spas in North Africa as well as Europe or Russia. There was an increased enthusiasm for health and exercise amongst the upper classes, and active tourism became popular (MacKenzie, 2005). By the early 20th century, the benefits of spas for the war wounded were well recognized all over Europe, and visits to the seaside were recommended for industrial workers.

We clearly see a growing awareness of the health-giving properties of water, whether sea, thermal or mineral water. Greeks and Romans focused on both cleanliness and fitness and understood the health benefits of various types of water treatments. However, it should also be remembered that the ancient civilizations of Asia and the Middle East and indigenous peoples all over the world have been aware of the benefits of massage, yoga, meditation, herbal medicines, and other forms of healing and spiritual practice for many more centuries than in Europe. The Japanese also had their own spas known as 'onsens', which are based on natural thermal springs. In 737 AD, Japan's first onsen (hot spring) opened near Izumo, and centuries later the first 'ryoken' (inns) were built, offering fine food, accommodations, Zen gardens, outdoor baths and indoor soaking tubs called cypress ofuro (SpaFinder, 2008). Although the standard of living and quality of life of many people throughout the world is still deemed low by western standards (e.g. in India, Africa, or amongst indigenous tribal groups), those people have found their own ways of preserving health and maintaining wellbeing. Although illness may triumph more quickly over wellness in conditions of deprivation, some of the indigenous traditions and techniques are becoming more and more valued in modern day spas, as we shall see later in the book. Tourists are also becoming keen to visit the 'homes' of certain practices and traditions like Ayurveda and Thai massage.

The following sections provide a more comprehensive overview of the way in which health and wellness tourism has developed in different regions of the world. The kinds of destinations and products which are promoted to tourists in these different regions are discussed in more detail in Chapter Six. This chapter rather provides an historical overview so that it is clear where practices originated when discussed later in the book. Although it is impossible to be fully representative of the whole world, these sections give a good understanding of the available resources, cultures and traditions of several regions of the world, in which the individual countries tend to have much in common with each other. Of course, the geography of the world has changed considerably over the past centuries, with numerous empires being created and dismantled; European colonial powers in Africa, India, and the Americas ruling for several decades but the regions later regaining independence; and towns which were once in one country are now in another or have been completely re-named. Therefore, geography can be as complex as history when explaining the distribution of health and wellness traditions. For the purposes of simplicity, some reference is made to this multi-layering of history (e.g. indigenous traditions versus those of colonial rulers), but much of the analysis is more resource based according to what was available in regions, with some reference made to the influence of cultures. Health and wellness practices in Egypt and North African countries like Tunisia and Morocco tend to have more in common with Middle Eastern traditions than East, West, or South African ones, so the decision has been made here and in Chapter Six to discuss these countries along with the Middle Eastern region rather than Africa.

Europe

The history of health tourism in Europe has tended to be based around spas and seawater treatments, mainly because of the large numbers of thermal and mineral springs and sea coasts. The word Spa is thought maybe to have originated from Latin and phrases such as *'sanitas per aqua'*, or from the Walloon word 'espa' for fountain. The town of Spa in Belgium was one of the first, so it is sometimes thought that the term comes from this name. Hydrotherapy or water-based treatments are the cornerstone of what European spas have traditionally had to offer with a focus on health and physical wellbeing. It is only in recent years that cosmetic or beauty treatments have become more popular, as well as more spiritual or psychological activities. As the need for the treatment of illness declined in Europe with better healthcare regimes and preventative wellness techniques, spas have increasingly shifted from physical and medical to more relaxing and pampering activities. However, historically they were viewed as places to rehabilitate and 'take the waters' or 'take the cure'. Mineral water, thermal water, seawater, muds, climate therapy, oxygen therapy, and sometimes special diets were the main focus.

The Romans built very sophisticated baths all over Europe which were integral to their way of life, and would consist of a series of cool to hot baths and a final cold plunge pool. Roman (Latin) terms like frigidarium (cool), tepidarium (lukewarm), caldarium (warm), laconium (hot), etc. are still used in spas today. Baths or spas as they were later called were places where people met to discuss issues, like politics and philosophy, and they were the centres of social life for soldiers and administrators (Crebbin-Bailey et al., 2005).

The Roman Bath Experience

- Ideally undertake sports or a workout.
- Enter a tepidarium (lukewarm room of 35°C) and treatment begins.
- Receive an oil massage to soften the skin and then relax for a while.
- Enter the laconium (a hot, dry room of 80°C like a sauna) to initiate the detoxifying process.
- Receive a body scrub to remove dead skin in preparation for a vigorous massage.
- Enter the caldarium (a warm, damp room like a steam bath) and relax.
- Plunge into a cold pool to close the pores of the skin and invigorate the body.
- Rest and read in a library or quiet room.

The Romans travelled to different spas for healing purposes, with Spa in Belgium being one of the best known at that time, as well as destinations like Bath in the UK, Baden-Baden in Germany, Budapest in Hungary, and Gerona in Spain. The Roman baths in Gerona were later used by the Arab occupiers in the 12th century. Many of Europe's historic spa towns were built around healing springs between the 14th and 16th centuries, such as Vichy in France. Originally, travel to such destinations was common for royalty or nobility, but this later declined as domestic bathing conditions improved. From the 16th to the 20th centuries, religion flourished and the church became more of a centre for social activities than spas. However, in the late 20th and early 21st centuries, as traditional religion once again declined, spas became one of the most desirable public spaces in which to congregate.

Case Study: Vichy

Since Roman times, for almost 2,000 years now, Vichy waters have been famous for their beneficial virtues: already since the 17th century, for example to stimulate natural defence mechanisms. Under Louis XIV, or Napoleon III the town and thermal spa were renovated and Vichy was not only a resort to take the waters, but also a place of pleasure and elegance (it was called 'the second Paris') and Vichy became 'the queen of Spa towns' (the King was Baden-Baden in Germany). Today, Vichy waters can be taken for different therapeutic reasons, for example rheumatology, gastroenterology, and of course for dermatological or dermocosmetic problems. The town and the thermal waters gave the name to the world-wide known Vichy pharmaceutical company, specialized in skin care (to make the brand even more different from other brands, Vichy products are sold in pharmacies only). The Thermal establishment 'Dômes de Vichy', birthplace of the brand, is where the Laboratoires Vichy have located their Dermocosmetic Centre. During the 1990s, Vichy developed spa therapy using Thermal Spa Waters: going back to health and beauty treatments for the balance of body and mind, like the holistic health-beauty concept of the Vichy Spa Les Célestins (7.500 m^2 of care facilities connected to a four-star hotel). Les Célestins provides more than just skin care, for example:

- Vichy Nutritional Centre and Vichy Slimming (besides on site treatments, offering 6-month post-treatment follow up, as well. Former guests can log on and receive on-line treatment to help their weight loss programme
- 'Hands of the World' (different massages each day during the stay)
- Rituals, for example the Bourbon Ritual
- Escapes and wellbeing (packages for 2 days)
- The *Célestins* Complexion (making skin softer).

There are 15 multiple-use thermal spa sources in Vichy town, which are incorporated in external treatments or taken internally as cures. One of them is bottled and sold commercially: Vichy Célestins.

(Vichy Thermes, 2008)

By the end of the 18th century, spa treatments and sea bathing seemed to develop concomitantly. Hydrotherapy was studied as a scientific way as another form of medicine, and confidence in the curative properties of water, both as bathing and drinking spread throughout Europe in the first half of the 19th century. Numerous mountain climatic resorts were built in the Alps, the Carpathians or around the Mediterranean. By 1889, there were 188 spas in Spain, for example (Larrinaga, 2005). However, gradually the motivation for coming to spas changed from being predominantly about health and cures to a desire for leisure, thus many spas started to develop casinos and dance halls, as well as other entertainment facilities. The first International Balneological Congress was organized in Budapest (the world's only spa capital city) in 1937.

After World War II, spa resorts in Western Europe went into stagnation. For example, Bacon (1998) describes how spas in the UK (unlike in continental Europe) tended to be eclipsed by seaside resorts in the 19th century. However, in communist Central and Eastern Europe and in the Soviet Union the spas or thermal baths entered a new phase of development, with treatment mainly sponsored by the state or the trade unions in their specialized facilities. The democratization of access to the spas was coupled with a narrow specialization in medical treatment. A profound change occurred in the appearance of the spas. A dominating feature of their physical planning became the trade union rest houses, hotels, and sanatoria. Spas became 'healing combinats' for the people, based on mineral waters, climate, and other local natural resources. The accommodation facilities were typically large buildings with mineral water basins and healing devices, with a residential part, dining facilities and meeting halls. Other services were almost absent.

In Finland, one of the compensations offered to wounded Finnish soldiers after the World War II was veteran spa rehabilitation. A system of regular periods (usually 1–3 weeks) of physical rehabilitation was created and the state paid the costs. The Finnish 'golden spa age' had been in the 1800s, and the density of spas was the highest in Europe from the early 1890s, even though there were only a few natural spas (i.e. thermal/mineral waters) in Finland. From the 1960s onwards, war veterans were given good quality professional medical care in these spas, as well as some leisure/wellness activities and facilities. In the future when the war veterans are no longer alive, a new use for such spas will need to be created, which may be based on wellness rather than medical tourism (Aho, 2007).

Lee (2004) suggests that the European health and wellness model has been based around the four elements: water, fire, earth, and air (Indian Ayurveda and Chinese philosophy do this too, but in a slightly different way as discussed later in the chapter). The balance or harmonization of these elements was considered essential to wellness by Greek philosophers. Water therapies help to heal and soothe the body; heat treatments induce sweating and accelerate circulation of the blood; earth offers numerous natural herbs, flowers, plants, muds, and fruit; and fresh air and oxygen are the essence of life. Greeks and other ancient civilizations believed that thermal and mineral springs were a gift from the Gods and built temples for various deities near to them. There is often a connection between spas and spirituality, for example, Lourdes in France is both a healing spring and a pilgrimage destination. Diet, exercise, massage along with water were seen by the Greeks and Romans as being essential for combating disease and preserving good health. Bathing in the sea or rivers was always considered to be health giving, a process akin to baptism or rebirth in which individuals were symbolically purified and cleansed. Cleanliness and hygiene were considered essential, a philosophy which was later forgotten in mediaeval and Renaissance Europe, when public diseases in spas became rife. Thalassotherapy or the use of seawater in health and wellness was practised by ancient Egyptians, but the Greeks added more treatments, such as the use of mud to this tradition (pelotherapy). Later, this expanded to include salt scrubs, seaweed wraps, and salt inhalation, amongst others. Roscoff in France and Varberg in Sweden became popular destinations for seawater cures.

The principle of fire was first developed in the context of health and wellness in Roman baths (where thousands could congregate at once in heated rooms), Turkish hamams or steam baths, Russian 'white' or 'black' banias (a steam room and sauna, respectively), and Finnish saunas. Some farmers in Germany in the 18th century also used dry heated rooms where flax or hemp was stored, and Austrian farmers used hay-storing barns with a stove. Sweat bathing was thought to ease aching muscles after a long day in the fields as it could draw toxins out of the body, such as lactic acid. Finns and Russians used the sauna as an integral part of everyday life and one in which to celebrate special occasions (e.g. birth, weddings, death). Russian banias were traditionally more vigorous than Finnish saunas, and whipping with twigs was not uncommon. The air was generally wetter and special oils were used such as eucalyptus or mint (a common practice in spas today). Although it is recommended that alcohol should not be drunk before, during, or immediately after a sauna, it was not unusual in Russia or Finland to consume vodka or other alcoholic beverages like beer as part of the social experience!

Air is another integral part of health and wellness everywhere, but in Europe this usually meant (and still does) going to the seaside or to mountain regions to escape heavily polluted cities. Pure air therapy is sometimes known as climatotherapy, which harnesses facets of the environment such as air, climate, atmosphere, temperature, humidity, and light. The movement from one climate to another is well known in European wellness tourism, for example, Northern Europeans going to Southern Europe for warmer, drier climates, and more sunshine, or city dwellers going to the mountains or the sea to recharge and relax. Those with tuberculosis or blood problems traditionally convalesced in the mountains, and those with bronchitis or rheumatism went to the seaside. Regular exercise and fitness programmes were also known to assist better respiration. Beckerson and Walton (2005) describe how from the mid-18th century onwards, resort visiting in Britain (and later in Belgium) was based mainly on the healthy qualities of the seaside air, and by the late 19th century, it was even more important than sea bathing. It was much later in the 20th century when sunshine started to become even more popular. Publicists promoted 'ozone' as being fresh, revitalizing, and invigorating. Mountain and countryside air was also thought to have numerous health benefits, especially for workers from industrial cities. Increasingly in European spas, breathing work is being done as part of yoga or meditation, but this is usually derived from Asian traditions. Oxygen therapy is also sometimes used to improve skin damage. Ozone treatment in medical spas was traditionally used with oxygen and injected into the body to inactivate bacteria, oxidize certain poisons, increase blood circulation and strengthen the immune system, but its usage is a bit more controversial these days.

Finally, earth elements in Europe mainly consisted of muds, which were derived from a number of sources (e.g. moors, bogs, volcanoes, seabeds), herbs or plant extracts used in medicines, flower essences use in remedies (e.g. Bach Flower Remedies), essential oils most commonly used in aromatherapy or caves used in climatotherapy. The use of medical mud originated in France as a way of treating war wounds in World War II, and was then used in massage by the mid-1950s. Farmers in Europe sometimes fell asleep in the hay and this was thought to have a therapeutic effect and now forms the basis of some Alpine Wellness techniques. Phytotherapy (the use of plants for healing or therapeutic uses) and Western herbalism is still treated with some scepticism by medical practitioners as it is unscientifically proven for the most part. However, the ancient Egyptians, Greeks, Romans, and Indians all used essential oils as perfumes or for massage. Vinotherapy – the therapeutic use of wine and grapes in beauty and health treatments is believed to date back to Egypt in 3200 BC but became widespread in France in the Bordeaux region only recently when grape seeds were found to have healing properties for the skin. The first vinotherapy spa did not open in Caudalie until 1999, where elements from grapes and wine were combined with warm spring water for baths, massages, masks, scrubs, and wraps. Caves with special climatic conditions are used for medical healing, especially in pulmonology.

In terms of balancing the elements, Kneipp, the 19th century priest prescribed alternating hot and cold baths, compresses, steam baths, showers, wraps, footbaths (Kneipp footbaths can be found in numerous spas around the world today) as well as herbal therapies, nutrition, fresh air, sunshine, and rest. Kneipp's legacy continues in healing traditions today, especially in the German 'kur' (or cure) system, with the national health programme sometimes paying for stays in a Kneipp Kurhaus if prescribed by a doctor. This represents an early form of holistic or integrated wellness, which is preventative as well as curative.

Middle East and North Africa

Arabian medicine was originally influenced by that of Greeks and Romans, however by the Dark Ages in Europe, medical developments in Arabia were far superior and even today, the Middle East is one of the major growth regions for medical tourism. Egyptians were particularly focused on diseases of the eye, and it is thought that kohl eyeliner pencils were originally used to disinfect the eye rather than for cosmetic purposes. However, beauty cosmetics were used in ancient Egypt as far back as 1400 BC, including skin oils, face creams, deodorants, toothpaste, henna and hair dyes, red ochre lip gloss, and perfumes. Sunburn and prickly heat treatments were developed throughout the region as the desert sun was so intense (an even more major issue for tourists today). Egyptians and Babylonians used bathing to heal the spirit and treat the body. Whereas European bathing focused on medical or physical health-giving properties, Egyptians believed that they should be clean and beautiful to reach a higher spirituality. Cleansing involved exfoliating and massaging the skin in a warm bath using yoghurt and honey. It was said that Queen Cleopatra (69–30 BC) bathed in milk to keep her skin soft, hence the modern day spa's 'Cleopatra Bath' treatment.

Egyptians used thermals baths, whereas Arabian hamams or Turkish steam baths played a fundamental role in Ottoman culture (around 600 AD), and were places of social gathering and ritual. There were separate quarters for men and women, and like Roman baths there was a graduating sequence of heat, as well as scrub massages. Since the time of Aristotle (304–322 BC) people also visited the Dead Sea to experience its healing waters and therapeutic climate, as well as mud wraps. The Rasul is a traditional Arabian cleansing ritual that is administered in an elaborately tiled steam chamber that has a domed starlit ceiling. A steam injector infuses a mixture of aromatic dried herbs which cleanse and detoxify. Visitors take a short shower, medicinal muds are applied to the skin to cleanse and exfoliate, the mud is then massaged until it hardens. The mud starts to liquefy as the humidity increases, and after about 20 minutes a tropical rain shower falls from the dome of the Rasul and washes away the mud. Nowadays, more and more luxury spas where the Arabic architecture and traditions blend with Western-style spa resorts are opening along the coastline in Qatar, Saudi Arabia, Oman or Dubai.

Arabian medicine tends to use Hippocrates' idea of the 'four humours' (yellow bile, black bile, phlegm, and blood), their respective qualities (choleric, melancholic, phlegmatic, and sanguineous), and their natures (hot, dry, humid, and cold), and the seasons. It is these elements that needed to be in harmony or balance to attain optimal health. Astrological influence was also considered important, as well as the will of Allah. Diet and bathing were both considered important, as well as herbal and natural medicines, such as cassia (cinnamon), cloves, myrrh, nutmeg, sienna, and sandalwood, as well as drugs like opium, cannabis, and camphor to balance body and mind. The rose and its oils were considered to be the most important flower and it was used for a range of health problems as well as for its scent. Although not only indigenous to Arabia and the Middle East (many of the traditions are Indian), other therapies were used to help balance energies within the body. These include crystal and gem therapy, aura readings, colour therapy, and chakra cleansing. Gold was also commonly used, as it is believed to ease tension, feelings of inferiority and anger as well as encouraging the realization of one's innate potential (Van der Meulen & O'Brien, 2006).

Alexander (2001) describes the holistic system of medicine known as 'Tibb', which was mainly practised in Persia and Turkey in the past, but increasingly in the Middle East, India, Pakistan, Bangladesh, Afghanistan, and Malaysia. It combines elements of ancient Egyptian and Greek medicine, Chinese and Indian traditions, and the healing wisdom of Persia and the Middle East. It recognizes the vital energy known as 'qawa' in Arabic, and shares the concept that medicine needs to be holistic, to look at the whole person, balance the elements, and use herbal remedies to heal the body. Tibb focuses on lifestyle rather than just diet alone (the traditional Chinese starting point), including breathing, emotions (counselling or psychotherapy is deemed valuable), sleeping patterns, eating patterns, a person's working life, their ability to relax, and finally, their spiritual state. This appears to be one of the precursors of holistic wellness as discussed later in the book, for which many people travel to retreats or special workshops to experience.

The Key Principles of Tibb

- Get up early before sunrise and certainly before 7 a.m.
- Eat a good breakfast, a reasonable sized lunch but a small dinner at least 2 hours before bedtime.
- Take regular exercise to keep you healthy in body and mind.
- Make sure you get enough rest, as people in the West tend to be over-stimulated.
- Take a siesta in the afternoon for 30 minutes. Take a day off work if you are tired. Have a warm bath with essential oils.
- Incorporate spirituality into your life, for example prayer, meditation, or simple contemplation of the beauty in the world.
- Don't go to bed too late, 11 p.m. at the latest.
- Cultivate good sleep. Try meditating or gentle massage before bed.

(Alexander, 2001).

Jews also take part in ritual bathing, since traditionally orthodox Jews have to go to the 'mikveh'. The water comes from a barrel in which they collect rainwater. This then has to be purified to become 'kosher', in which women and men can bathe separately.

Of course, one of the main natural resources in this region is the Dead Sea, which has attracted visitors from around the Mediterranean basin for thousands of years. Biblically, it was a place of refuge for King David, and it was one of the world's first health resorts (e.g. for Herod the Great).

Asia-Pacific

Asia's wellness traditions take a holistic approach of treating the body, mind, and spirit as one, trying to identify the root cause of a problem and encouraging the body to heal itself. The natural healing approach in Asia is therefore usually rooted in tradition and spirituality rather than based on natural assets. This is, however, a little different in Japan, where onsens (traditional bathing establishments) are often visited by locals looking for relaxation or meditation and increasingly by tourists. An onsen is a Japanese hot spring. As it is a volcanically active country, Japan has thousands of onsen, and they were traditionally thought to have spiritual beings living in them which gave vision and guidance. The Balneotherapy Institute was founded by Kyushu University in 1931 and by 1955, there were over 90 medical facilities in the mineral spring locations in Japan. Like European spas or Arabic hamams, onsens are social spaces as well as sites of purification and ritual. Therapies like Shiatsu massage or Reiki have also emerged from Japan and are commonly used in western spas nowadays.

India's cultural and historical legacy predates even that of Ancient Egypt, and Ayurveda ('the science of life') is regarded by scholars as the oldest healing system in the world. It is the prime healing tradition in India, Sri Lanka, and Nepal. It is interesting therefore that it has only been in recent years that Ayurveda has started to be used in modern spas. It is a long-term lifestyle choice, but can increasingly be experienced in small doses whilst on holiday in the form of massage or diet. Balance should be achieved in the three universal governing forces or doshas: vata (air), pitta (fire), and kapha (earth). One of these forces tends to dominate in most individuals and the task of Ayurveda is to redress the balance through appropriate diet, oil and massage therapies, herbal remedies, yoga and meditation.

As stated, spirituality is an important and inherent part of most Asian traditions, and this is particularly true in India. There are close connections to religion and pilgrimage in some cases, for example, the world famous 'Kumbha Mela':

Case Study: Mela Festivals in India

Sacred festivals in India are called 'Melas' and they are an important part of the Hindu pilgrimage tradition. The greatest of these is the Kumbha Mela, which is a riverside festival held four times every 12 years in different locations, such as Allahabad at the confluence of the river Ganges and Yamuna. Bathing in these sacred waters is thought to be cleansing for body, mind, and spirit and is said to purge pilgrims of all their sins.

In theory, the Kumbha Mela festivals are supposed to occur every 3 years, rotating between four cities, but this is dependent on astrological factors. Such festivals can attract up to five million pilgrims or more. It is thought that not only is the Kumbha Mela the largest religious gathering in the world, it may also be the oldest. Although historical research on this festival is not conclusive, it is thought that its origins date back to the 9th century, when a philosopher called Sankaracharaya organized the Kumbha Mela in Prayaga (Allahabad) so that yogis, sadhus and sages from all corners of India could meet in a central location. One of the reasons to meet was to create an environment of mutual understanding between different religious sects. Another was to give ordinary householders the chance to interact with normally reclusive holy men.

At the most auspicious hour on the most auspicious day of the festival many thousands of holy men from various sects will bathe in the river. Following the ceremonial bathing of the sadhus, millions of other people rush to enter the river. For a devout Hindu, to bathe at the Kumbha Mela sites at this auspicious time is considered an event of immeasurable spiritual significance. Unfortunately, this great religious fervour has often resulted in hundreds of pilgrims being crushed to death as the masses race towards the river banks. Furthermore, many Hindus consider the Kumbha Mela sites to be the most favoured places to die, and ritual suicide, though discouraged by the government, is still practised.

(Sacred Sites, 2008)

Traditional or Chinese medicine (TCM) forms the basis of many Asian therapies, although therapies vary from one country to another. Originally, medicine was based on ancestral worship, shamanism, and magic, but these principles became more philosophical, scientific, and rational over time.

Chinese practices focus on the individual and provide a unique combination of therapies based on the 'Three Treasures' listed below:

- Energy – or life force, called Qi or Chi
- Jing – the essence which governs vitality and longevity
- Shen – the mind or spirit, responsible for consciousness and mental ability.

There is always an attempt to balance Yin (feminine, cold, static) and Yang (masculine, warm, dynamic), the opposing but complementary forces which govern Chi. The philosophy of Yin and Yang is further refined into the theory of five elements of earth, fire, metal, water, and wood, where each nurtures and supports the others. This balance of energy and elements forms the basis of Feng Shui philosophy. Chinese medicine, like Indian Ayurveda, tends to be a holistic and preventative approach to health including diet, movement, spiritual, and emotional wellbeing. A number of therapies are offered such as herbal medicine, acupuncture, reflexology, Qi Gong or Tai Chi, as well as massages which focus on meridians or energy lines in the body.

Thailand is famous for Thai massage which is exported to wellness centres all over the world. It is given clothed and involves a system of stretching, loosening joints, and easing muscle tension through a sequence of yoga-like movements, as well as manipulating meridian or sen lines. The technique is around 2,500 years old and was developed by an Ayurvedic doctor, Shivago Komarpaj. The massage has a spiritual as well as a physical dimension, and it is common for masseurs to say a short prayer before they begin wishing improved health to their patient. Other countries in Asia have developed their own approaches to health and wellness, like Jamu in Indonesia which is a blend of a selection out of 150 possible ingredients to make health-giving drinks, cosmetics, medicines, and remedies. The development of the modern Asian spa market is relatively young compared to that of Europe. For example, Thailand's first three major spas were not opened until 1993 (Crebbin-Bailey et al., 2005). By the 21st century, Thailand, Singapore, and India have become a major destination for medical, especially surgical tourism.

The indigenous peoples in the Asia-Pacific region (including Australian Aborigines and New Zealand Maori) have always used traditional herbal remedies, massages, and deep spiritual beliefs in holistic ways to preserve good health and enhance wellbeing. Many of the products found in modern day spas in Australia, for example, have been used for more than 40,000 years by Aboriginal Australians (e.g. the Li'Tya range). Rotorua in New Zealand has numerous hot springs in its vicinity because of its volcanic landscape. Maori people were originally attracted to the springs and built whole villages in the area. The British found the modern town of Rotorua in the 1830s and soon discovered the curative effects of the hot springs. The Maori Te Arawa people were instrumental in bringing the tourism industry into the town and they formed a guild of hospitable tour guides who showed Europeans around the place. Word got around and curious tourists from Europe and America visited Rotorua. Since the early 20th century, the town has developed a tourism industry that revolves around the hot springs and millions of people have been drawn to the place because of the curative power of its mineral-enriched water. The Rotorua Baths complex was built in mock Tudor style during the 1920s.

Africa

Africa has a wide range of indigenous herbs and plants which have been used for centuries for health and healing. Different tribes in Africa have traditionally drawn on the natural world for all kinds of remedies, using sand from the deserts, mud or clay from the soil, salt from the oceans, and plant and herbs from the jungles. Masai tribes people in Kenya and Tanzania administered massage to each other to ease backs and shoulders after carrying heavy loads or hunting all day. Zulu warriors had different ways of preparing for the fight ahead, using physical, psychological, and spiritual techniques to do so. Ancient Bushmen in countries like Botswana used a combination of drumming and trance dance to heal sickness.

MacKenzie (2005) describes some of the guidebooks which promoted Africa in late 19th and early 20th centuries, especially in southern Africa where railway lines had spread to support the gold rush. Cruises were seen as being a health-giving experience because of the healthy air on the sea and the warm climate. Sulphur and hot springs were also discovered around the Cape and putative health resorts with hotels and sanatoria in the mountains and drier areas of the region were promoted. Lung diseases were particularly thought to benefit from a stay in Africa.

However, the main evidence of health and wellness tourism in Africa is in the development of European colonial hill stations, spas, and seaside resorts, and other enclaves that catered to the health and welfare of the expatriate community. Jennings (2007) describes a 1924 advertisement for one of France's spas: 'Beware! Against the poison that is Africa, there is but one antidote: Vichy'. His book describes how throughout the French empire, water cures and high-altitude resorts were widely believed to serve important therapeutic and even prophylactic functions against tropical disease and the tropics themselves. Although colonizers sometimes frequented spas back home as the advertisement suggested, it was more common to build spa retreats in the colonies. The Ministry of the Colonies published bulletins accrediting a number of spas thought to treat tropical diseases ranging from malaria to yellow fever and specialist guidebooks gave advice on the best spas for colonial ills. Treatments were based on acclimatization theory and the development of a science of hydrotherapy. Many spas and hill stations served as a refuge from disease, heat, insects, and wildlife, and other perceived 'dangers', including contact with indigenous peoples! Crossette (1998) notes that the age of the hill station mirrored the period when seaside resorts, spas, and great mountains lodges were being built in Europe and the US, and how in some cases, the style and atmosphere of these European or American mountain retreats were copied in the colonies. Hill stations usually had to be around 5,000 to 8,000 feet above sea level beyond the reach of mosquitoes, and had to be more than just resorts. They were also a medical centre of sorts used for recovery and recuperation, as well as a retreat from reality for home-sick Europeans. Although more common in Asia, they were also built in Kenya, Uganda, and elsewhere in Africa where Europeans had colonized. South Africa was particularly rich in thermal spring resorts.

The Americas

Clearly, when we talk about the Americas we have to make a distinction between the modern spas of the past 100 years or so in the USA and Canada, Central, and South America, and the traditions of indigenous peoples throughout the region which predate those spas by thousands of years. South America has thousands of hot springs, volcanic thermal waterfalls (e.g. Costa Rica, Ecuador or the Caribbean), some of which were traditionally used by indigenous peoples such as the Incas. Influences of ancient civilizations are pervasive throughout the region. For example, in Maroma Spa (Mexico) the orientation of the rooms follow the Ancient Maya traditions. This will apparently allow the positive energy from planets and stars to come to the rooms. According to Mayan spirituality this has a good impact both on the soul and body of those who stay in the rooms. Guests at the Ikal del Mar on the Mexican Riviera can enjoy facials and massages influenced by Mayan traditions such as the Mayan Bath, the Mayan massage, the Hammock Massage where the colour hammock is chosen according to the guest's desired energy and the Temazcal Spiritual Mayan Sauna. The word Temazcal, in the Nahuatl language, is a combination of the words Temaz, meaning bath, and Calli, meaning home. The ceremony was practised by the Mayans and other indigenous groups as a therapeutic and purifying ritual. In Mexico the Temazcal is a ritual ceremony that has been practised by indigenous people for hundreds of years. It is similar to a Sweat Lodge, and is a thanksgiving to the four elements, and a healing for the body, mind, and spirit. Participants are often asked to fast the day before and the experience (traditionally led by a medicine man) can be intense. Mexico's Mayan Riviera also boasts one of the world's most extensive varieties of native herbs. Therefore, spa treatments tend to offer a combination of natural marine elements with native herbs and aromas. The One and Only resorts offer an 'Aztec Aromatic Ritual', where the spiciness of the wrap was traditionally used as a curative treatment to heal headaches, arthritis and muscular aches. An ancient village recipe of aromatic spices provides a warm and stimulating sensation.

Traditionally, Native Americans viewed mineral and healing springs as inherently spiritual. They also used other rituals for preserving health and wellbeing, such as 'sweat lodges'. There are several styles of Native American Indian (e.g. Navaho) sweat lodges that include a domed or oblong hut similar to a wickiup, a teepee, or even a simple hole dug into the ground and covered with planks or tree trunks. Stones are heated in an exterior fire and then placed in a central pit in the ground. Often the stones are granite and they glow red in the dark lodge. Rituals and traditions vary from region to region and tribe to tribe. They often include prayers, drumming, and offerings to the spirit world. Other typical Native American Indian traditions and tools (which are increasingly being used in retreats and holistic centres) include:

Native American Traditions and Tools

- *Animal totems*: The appearance of birds and animals, either in reality or dreamtime, are considered to be totem messengers offering spiritual guidance.
- *Dreamcatchers*: The earliest dreamcatchers (sacred hoops) were crafted for children to protect them from nightmares.
- *Feather fetishes*: Fetishes are sacred objects used as a tool to facilitate an awakening into your whole self, used in prayer, or utilized for protection and healing.
- *Smudge sticks*: Using a smoking smudge wand for purification is part of many Native American traditions.
- *Curanderismo*: Blending and evolution of Native and Hispanic healing techniques involving herbs, sweats, diet, and magick.
- *Medicine wheels*: Each direction of the medicine wheel offers its own lessons, colour association, and *animal spirit guide*.
- *Talking sticks*: Passing the talking stick from speaker to speaker is a respectful way to communicate and share opinions. This tradition is especially helpful in keeping disagreements from getting out of hand.

(Holistic Healing, 2008)

1806 saw the first coming together of indigenous traditions and modern spa culture when John Arnold of Rhode Island opened the US's first European-style spa in Saratoga (New York), a native American Indian word for the 'place of the medicine waters of the great spirit':

Case Study: Saratoga Springs

Saratoga Springs is one of the oldest spas in America, and was based on natural, carbonated mineral water. Native Americans had been frequenting the mineral springs since the 14th century, and they believed the springs had healing powers, and that they were also sacred. In the late 1700s, Sir William Johnson, a friend of the Native Americans, became ill and he was transported to the springs to drink the water and to bathe. He is believed to be the first white man to visit the springs. By the 1800s, Saratoga was already a very popular tourist attraction, and water was being bottled and shipped around the world. In the 1900s, the carbon dioxide from the waters was used to make Ice Cream soda fountains, but this eventually led to over-drilling of wells and the running dry of the waters by commercial companies. In 1908, the State of New York therefore passed laws limiting the amount of pumping and eventually, Saratoga Spa State Park was created as a means of protection and management.

Amongst others, Simon Baruch, a hydrotherapist (a medical doctor who believed in the healing powers of the mineral waters), advocated the development of the springs in Saratoga into a health spa. When Franklin D. Roosevelt was Governor of New York State, he hired an architect to study the spas in Europe, which served as tourist and health centres, and to design the grandest spa in the world at Saratoga to compete. The US became a centre of spa innovation when Saratoga Springs emerged as a fashionable retreat for luminaries such as Edgar Allan Poe as well as the President. In the summer of 2002, Saratoga Springs was named by the National Trust for Historic Preservation as one of the Dozen Distinctive Destinations in the country.

(Saratoga State Park, 2008)

The American Hydropathic Institute opened in New York in 1851 and was said to be the first medical school based on water cure principles. The concept of 'naturotherapy' also originated in New York. It focuses on the vital curative force within the body (Alexander, 2001). As well as water-based treatments, natural cures are derived from diet and fasting, fresh air and sunlight, relaxation, and psychological counselling. Remedial exercises in water were developed in the early 1920s for those with mobility problems. The Boyes Hot Spring near Calistoga dated from 1895 and was redeveloped and re-named in 1928 as the Sonoma Mission inn and Spa. Towards the end of the 20th century, it started to offer additional services such as massage, beauty treatments and fitness activities.

However, generally spas in America tended to be more social than therapeutic, and demanded little from patients (Crebbin-Bailey et al., 2005). The first day spa, Manhattan's Red Door Salon, was introduced by Elizabeth Arden in 1910, offering manicures, facials and the signature 'Arden Wax' (in addition to serving as a finishing school). A second-generation American, Deborah Szekely, also created the first destination spa, Rancho La Puerta, located just south of the border in Baja California. In 1958, Szekely also opened the pioneering Golden Door spa in California, offering individualized weight loss and fitness programs (and purportedly introducing Jane Fonda to aerobics). The first fitness spa, The Ashram, also debuted in California, in 1974, brandishing a gruelling weight loss/fitness regimen that was toned down and popularized by Tucson's Canyon Ranch in 1979. By 1997, innovative US doctors began to introduce 'medical spas', combining Western and holistic medicine in a luxurious, spa-inspired environment alongside spa services (SpaFinder, 2007). Overall, in the past 40 years or so, numerous so-called 'super spas' have emerged in America which preserve the privacy of individuals and shelter them from the outside world so that they can relax, be pampered and rejuvenate (e.g. vine spas or spa and golf, or ski and spa products).

Conclusion

This chapter has demonstrated the diversity of health and wellness traditions which exist in different regions of world, providing an overview of their origins and their continuity over time. Although the degree of travel within most regions was somewhat limited by transport until the latter part of the 20th century, there was nevertheless some movement to spa or thermal destinations as early as Roman times, if not before. The influence of the most ancient cultures on subsequent cultures is clearly widespread, whether it is the indigenous peoples of the Americas, Africa or Australasia, Indian traditions in Arabic countries, or Chinese medicine in Asian ones. As time goes on, we see an even greater degree of cross-over and hybridization as indigenous and traditional cultures increasingly influence western ones (e.g. Feng Shui sauna or Aquaveda) and vice versa (e.g. spa resorts in Arabia). It seems that the globalization of health and wellness can only be a positive development as the whole world starts to share in practices that often remained within one small region or locality for thousands of years. It seems that the route to optimum wellness is one in which ideas are shared, especially through travel, tourism, and increased mobility of practitioners from one region of the world to another. Although many wellness systems have much in common with one another (i.e. the tendency towards holistic and lifestyle-based approaches), the tools and techniques that are used can vary greatly, therefore an increased choice for consumers and tourists alike is one of the most welcome developments of the 21st century.

Contemporary definitions

Wordsworth had urged us to travel through landscapes to feel emotions that would benefit our souls.

(De Botton, 2002: 159)

This chapter explores some of the terminology that tends to be confused with or used synonymously with the concept of health. The previous chapter demonstrated clearly that there has been a traditional emphasis on healing or resting the physical body, usually by going to spas or to seaside destinations. There has been very little focus on the mental, emotional, or spiritual side of health. Although mediaeval pilgrimage could be thought of as an early form of spiritual tourism, it was based on specific, organized religions and religious destinations. Contemporary societies, on the other hand, are becoming more drawn to those health practices which offer them the chance to experience physical, mental and spiritual balance or integration. As a result, the terminology that is used to define contemporary health and wellness is evolving constantly and needs to be redefined in order to understand fully the needs of modern consumers. This chapter therefore explores some of the concepts that are related to the health and wellness sectors, especially those which are currently being researched or are being used as labels to sell products and services.

Health

As discussed briefly in the Introduction, opinions about what constitutes 'wellness' diverge greatly, and the term is often confused with definitions of health. The widely accepted definition of health is that of the World Health Organization (WHO, 1948), which states that 'health is a state of complete physical, mental, and social wellbeing and not merely the absence of disease or infirmity'. Saracci (1997) questioned this definition, suggesting that this state corresponds much more closely to happiness than to health. He argues that common existential problems relating to emotions, passions, personal values, and questions on the meaning of life do not make one happier, but they are equally not strictly reducible to health problems. However, since 1948, the WHO has broadened its definition further so that there is something of a convergence between issues relating to physical and mental health and broader issues of wellness and lifestyle management. For example, WHO (1984) stated that health is also:

> *The extent to which an individual or a group is able to realize aspirations and satisfy needs, and to change or cope with the environment. Health is a resource for everyday life, not the objective of living; it is a positive concept, emphasizing social and personal resources as well as physical capabilities.*

> (WHO, 1984)

In addition to freedom from the risk of disease and untimely death, the WTO also refers to peoples' abilities to perform family, work, and community roles; their ability to deal with physical, biological, psychological, and social stress; the extent to which they experience feelings of wellbeing; and their state of equilibrium with their environment. It seems to be the case that the concept of health and wellness are increasingly being used inter-changeably, but it should still be emphasized that health tourism includes medical or cure aspects, and that wellness is more preventative than curative.

Wellness is supposed to create harmony in mental, physical, spiritual, or biological health in general and has stronger ties with changing lifestyle or doing something healthy than with curing a specific disease. People consuming wellness services tend to show higher health awareness than others. They are eager to do something for a healthier lifestyle, they are conscious about their nutrition and often do physical exercise. Wellness addresses human health in a holistic or comprehensive sense and assumes that each person will actively participate in protecting their health, in preventing diseases and will not leave all this to medication. Myers et al. (2000) define wellness as being 'a way of life oriented towards optimal health and wellbeing in which the body, mind, and spirit are integrated by the individual to live more fully within the human and natural community'.

Travel can contribute to all aspects of health if we consider the physical and mental benefits of rest and relaxation, the social aspects of mixing with other tourists and local people, and the intellectual stimulation that can come from learning about new places. Some holidays may have a specific health focus (e.g. those that involve visiting medical spas or having specific medical treatments such as operations) whilst others can provide more indirect health benefits even if the wellness label is not used at all.

Illness

It is necessary to refer to illness since it is assumed that we would do anything, including travelling to get our health back or at least improve it. Henderson (2004) differentiates between travel for reasons of wellness (e.g. leisure and beauty spas) and travel for reasons of illness (e.g. medical interventions and health check-ups). Illness or disease is one of the key motivations for those people who travel to medical spas, and they often have a prescription from their doctor confirming that they need a specific treatment for an illness, disease or debilitating condition. Although some sick visitors may just enjoy the chance to relax and recuperate in a spa or by the sea, the motivations are somewhat different from those visitors who are in good health and simply want to enhance wellbeing and live better. It is also rare that mental and psychological problems are given the same consideration as physical illnesses, and treatment is rarely state subsidized. An exception might be where occupational or work-based wellness is encouraged through incentive trips to spas or stress relief workshops. Usually those people with non-diagnosed mental troubles are forced to pay high prices for a wellness-enhancing holiday. However, this situation may change in the future as it becomes even more economically sound for governments to encourage preventative wellness (i.e. preserving good health rather than curing illness) through, for example, physical exercise, healthy nutrition, stress management, spa visits, etc. The visitation of spa or wellness facilities can be motivated by the result of the individual's self-analysis, that is 'I am not feeling 100% right now' or 'I am feeling tired'. This can lead to ad-hoc decisions of visiting a spa. Furthermore, illness as a motivation can refer to surgical trips, when visitors travel to a third country because it is cheaper or faster to have certain operations there. Several countries in Asia or in Central and Eastern Europe opened up their existing or developed new medical facilities to treat foreigners. Since the financial situation of national health insurances is not getting any better, patients face long waiting lists, therefore many consider having the necessary treatment in a third county for less.

Wellbeing

The Stanford Encyclopedia of Philosophy (2007) describes wellbeing as 'what is non-instrumentally or ultimately good *for* a person' and how well a person's life is going for that person. It may be difficult to define what is good for a person, as there are short- and long-term considerations. For example, a hedonist may engage in constant short-term pleasurable experiences but which will damage him/her physically or psychologically in the long term. There is a need to make a distinction between what is good *for* a person and what seems good *to* a person.

The NEF (2004) make a distinction between happiness and wellbeing: 'Wellbeing is more than just happiness. As well as feeling satisfied and happy, wellbeing means developing as a person, being fulfilled, and making a contribution to the community'.

In their Wellness Manifesto, Hamilton et al. (2008) state that:

The evidence shows that a good marriage, the company of friends, rewarding work, sufficient money, a good diet, physical activity, sound sleep, engaging leisure and religious or spiritual belief and practice all enhance our wellbeing, and their absence diminishes it. Optimism, trust, self-respect and autonomy make us happier. Gratitude and kindness lift our spirits; indeed, giving support can be at least as beneficial as receiving it. Having clear goals that we can work towards, a 'sense of place' and belonging, a coherent and positive view of the world, and the belief that we are part of something bigger than ourselves foster wellbeing.

Two leading American wellbeing researchers, Diener and Seligman (2004) say a (partial) formula for high wellbeing is to:

- live in a democratic and stable society that meets material needs;
- have supportive friends and family;
- have rewarding and engaging work and an adequate income;
- be reasonably healthy and able to treat mental health problems;
- have important goals related to one's values;
- have a philosophy or religion that provides guidance, purpose and meaning to one's life.

Travel is generally thought to enhance wellbeing, although it could be argued that holidays correspond more closely to a state of temporary happiness in which we are on a short-lived 'high'. Many people engage in exaggerated behaviour when they are away from home (e.g. drinking more alcohol, eating richer foods, partying more). This is a good example of short-term behaviour creating artificial highs which are not long-lasting and could even be detrimental if they became part of one's everyday routine. Many people experience a crushing sense of disappointment when they have to return from a dream holiday, implying that travel is only really of benefit when we are fully immersed in it. However, the anticipation of a trip and the relived memories can contribute to a sense of wellbeing, especially if travel is a constant or regular feature of one's everyday life.

Quality of Life

More recently, the term 'quality of life' (QoL) seems to be used with increasing frequency. It tries to define the things that make a life good – quality relationships, good housing, leisure, freedom from pain, etc. as well as a happy state of mind. Diener (2005) states that QoL usually refers to the degree to which a person's life is desirable versus undesirable, often with an emphasis on external components, such as environmental factors and income. In contrast to subjective wellbeing, which is based on subjective experience, QoL is often expressed as more 'objective' and describes the circumstances of a person's life rather than his or her reaction to those circumstances. However, some scholars define QoL more broadly, to include not only the QoL circumstances, but also the person's perceptions, thoughts, feelings, and reactions to those circumstances. Indexes that combine objective and subjective measures, such as happy life years and healthy life expectancy, have also been proposed.

The Scottish Executive Committee (2006) describes how QoL is a vague and difficult concept to define, and even though it is widely used, this is with little consistency. Some researchers suggest that QoL cannot be defined exactly and that the definition assigned to the term, and the way in which it is used, are contingent upon research objectives and context. Consequently, there is a lack of consensus about its meaning, and there are potentially over 100 definitions. A uni-dimensional definition would be synonymous with health alone, whereas a multi-dimensional definition would focus on several core dimensions (e.g. physical, material, social, emotional, psychological, personal, and inter-personal). Generally, however, QoL seems to refer to peoples' satisfaction with their lives, their physical, mental, social and emotional health, and the nature of the environment in which they are living. Cynics may suggest that everything can therefore be included in QoL. However, usually it is measured by more qualitative indicators than Standard of Living, which may indicate that someone is financially secure with a high income and a 'good' job. Nevertheless, this does not mean that they are satisfied with their life or happy as a result.

There are clearly objective and subjective indicators which can be used to measure QoL (Table 3.1). A good way of thinking about these is to consider which aspects of life are beyond the control of most individuals (e.g. poverty rate of a neighbourhood, healthcare, or education provision) and

Table 3.1 Objective and Subjective Indicators of Quality of Life.

Objective Indicators	Subjective Indicators
Life expectancy	Happiness
Employment status	Job satisfaction
Marital status	Sense of community
Education	Family relationships
Working hours per week	Social relationships
Housing conditions	Stress levels
Crime rates	Use of leisure time
Poverty level	Degree of spirituality
Healthcare provision	Sense of safety
Legal rights	Holidays taken

which aspects are open to individual choice or perception (e.g. family relationships, social life, leisure activities).

QoL implies a balance of these different domains. Much of the time, it is impossible to change the objective indicators and these may or may not affect peoples' levels of satisfaction and stress. For example, an area could indicate low levels of crime according to official statistics, but some residents may still not feel safe. A neighbourhood could be less poor with better housing than some others, but there will always be somewhere even better that people may dream of living. QoL may be just as perceptual as it is material.

Peoples' ability to afford travel will be dependent on their amount of free time and disposable income. It is generally considered to be desirable to have long periods of paid leave when holidays can be taken, thus long working hours (e.g. UK, Hungary) and short vacation times (e.g. USA, Japan) may be impediments to travel. However, there is not always a correlation. Leisure trends suggest that even those who have little free time manage to travel as extensively but for shorter periods of time (e.g. Tyrell & Mai, 2001). Disposable income may be a bigger barrier, thus those living in poorer countries will be unlikely to include tourism in their QoL analysis unless it represents a lifelong dream.

The pilot research commissioned by the Ministry of Local Government and Regional Government (Hungary) concluded that tourism and travelling does have a positive impact on the QoL. One of the key findings of this research (ÖTM, 2007) was the formulation of the Tourism-specific Quality of Life Index (TQoL). Using this index, decision makers as well as citizens can have a better understanding of the complex impacts of tourism on domains of QoL.

Tourism-specific Quality of Life Index (TQoL)

The Ministry of Local Government and Regional Development in Hungary was assigned a project to develop the Tourism-specific Quality of Life Index (TQoL) (as part of the implementation of the National Tourism Development Strategy, accepted in 2006).

From the many definitions and models the approach of Rahmann (Kovács et al., 2006) was selected as a basis. According to Rahmann's approach, it is anticipated that all the eight domains, directly or indirectly have some kind of relationship to and with tourism (Figure 3.1).

This project was a pilot one, since related research projects did not study the likely relationship between tourism and QoL in its anticipated complexity. Rather, these studies were focusing on the relationship between one or some of the elements of tourism and QoL (e.g. satisfaction with trip elements and QoL).

One of the main challenges of this work was, however, to identify the likely relationships and develop a structure in which the domains relate to and stem from tourism. It is understood that tourism is 'only' one of those factors that can have an impact on QoL, for

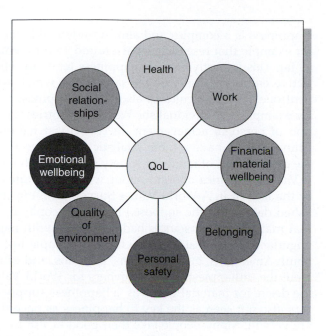

Figure 3.1 Quality of Life Domains. *Source*: Kovács et al., 2006.

example through the economic and social development of a destination or the life and life conditions of those directly or indirectly working in tourism, and those who do not have anything to do with tourism. Also, tourism can influence the level of satisfaction with life and, based on personal experiences as a tourist, the reactions to changes in QoL at home.

Amalgamating the definition by Meeberg (1993) and the findings of the research on definitions and approaches, the definition of TQoL was created.

QoL is a feeling of overall life satisfaction, as determined by the mentally alert individual whose life is being evaluated. In the formulation of the individual's opinion, which is fundamentally based on subjective factors, tourism can play a role (after Meeberg, 1993).

The new model does not only analyse general domains, but it examines the interlinkages between general QoL domains and the elements of tourism. Five TQoL domains were identified combining the so-called objective (Scandinavian) and subjective (American) approaches:

- The Attitudes towards Travelling as an Activity (ATA)
- Motivations of the Visit (or) (MV)
- The Qualities of the Trip (QT)
- The Characteristics of the Destination (CD)
- The Impacts of Tourism (IT).

A model and the tool were tested in three pilot locations and further, international testing was planned from 2008.

Happiness

Happiness is a complex and almost undefinable term. Bond (2003) notes, for example that researchers have found 15 different academic definitions so far. This is partly because happiness tends to reflect a temporary, subjective emotional state, unlike satisfaction which reflects a more permanent one. Different cultures also value happiness in very different ways, for example, in individualistic Western countries it is often seen as a reflection of personal achievement. In collectivist nations such as Japan and China, people have a more fatalistic attitude to happiness, and meeting the expectations of family or society will be much more important.

Various theories abound about what constitutes or causes happiness or the lack of it. A World Values Survey (2003) in the New Scientist published data about the supposed happiest people in the world, concluding that material circumstances had little to do with happiness. For example, Nigerians were considered the happiest people in the world followed by South Americans, but Romanians, Russians, and other Eastern Europeans were the unhappiest. The researchers for World Values Survey described the desire for material goods as 'a happiness suppressant'. Physical health was also not seen as the key to happiness as once thought, unless people are very ill. Many people take their good health for granted and are none the happier for it (Elias, 2002). Connor (2003) describes how Buddhists are often considered to be some of the happiest people in the world, but they are not born with a happiness gene as once thought. Instead, research shows that the practice of meditation and mindfulness can help to alleviate negative emotions and depression and to promote happiness.

Bond (2003) points out that many of the so-called happiest nations paradoxically often have the highest suicide rates, it is thought mainly due to the individualistic culture and lack of social and community support. Shah and Marks (2004) suggest in their research that the happiest people tend to be altruistic, generous, tolerant, and sociable. This perhaps has implications for the wellness industry, as it arguably needs to create more opportunities for social interaction. Tourism can certainly contribute, as it is by nature a sociable and often collective activity.

Characteristics of the Happiest People

Surround themselves with family and friends
Lose themselves in daily activities or 'flow'
Are not focused on materialism
Are not obsessed with image, social status, and fame
Are grateful for and satisfied with what they have
Are altruistic and help others
Trust others and cooperate
Live in 'happy', politically stable nations
Have good genes!

(Adapted from Elias, 2002; Bond, 2003; Ravilious, 2005)

Travel no doubt creates happiness on many levels, but it is largely the premise of wealthy, western nations, therefore international levels of happiness cannot easily be measured in research. We should not forget, however, that there are several tourism forms that somehow contribute to happiness, for example visiting friends and relatives or participating in voluntary activities. In any, not only in western and wealthy country trips to relatives and friends take place and the feeling of belonging and love definitely forms an important part of happiness.

Spirituality

Some authors have argued that spirituality is at the core of wellness (e.g. Devereux & Carnegie, 2006; Pernecky & Johnston, 2006; Steiner & Reisinger, 2006). This represents a shift away from orthodox religion towards a kind of transcendent spirituality, where one aims to develop beyond the self and the ego. Heelas and Woodhead (2005) suggest that a slow but steady spiritual revolution is taking place in which secular spirituality is taking over from traditional religion. Some Western psychologists such as Freud believed that religion was detrimental to the emotional health of the individual. Others like Jung believed that spirituality was the essence of what it meant to be human. Indeed, the word 'spirituality' comes from the Latin 'spiritualitas', an abstract word, related to the Greek word 'pneuma' meaning breath, the essence of life.

Elkins et al. (1988) described spirituality as a multi-dimensional construct with the following nine major dimensions:

1. *Transcendent dimension*: Belief in more than that which is seen, that may or may not be belief in God; and belief that personal power is drawn through harmonious contact with this dimension.
2. *Meaning and purpose in life*: Deep confidence that one's life has purpose, emerging from a quest for meaning.
3. *Mission in life*: Sense of responsibility to life; knowing that in 'losing one's life' one 'finds it'.
4. *Sacredness of life*: Belief that all life is holy.
5. *Material values*: Realization that ultimate satisfaction is from spiritual, not material things.
6. *Altruism*: Belief in social justice, and awareness that 'no man is an island'.
7. *Idealism*: Commitment to the actualization of positive potential in all aspects of one's life.
8. *Awareness of the tragic*: Deep awareness of human pain, suffering, and death, and that life has value.
9. *Fruits of spirituality*: Benefits of spirituality realized in relationships with self, others, nature, and what one perceives as the Ultimate.

Woods Smith (1994) collapsed the nine dimensions of spirituality identified by Elkins et al. (1988) into four as follows:

1. Feeling confident that life is meaningful, which includes having a sense of mission in life.

2. Having a commitment to the actualization of positive potential in all aspects of life, which includes realizing that spiritual values offer more satisfaction than material ones and that spirituality is integral with one's relationship with self and all else.
3. Being aware of the interconnectedness of life, which includes being conscious of the tragic and touched by the pain of others.
4. Believing that contact with a transcendent dimension is beneficial, which includes feeling that all of life is sacred.

Some researchers have developed 'wheels of wellness' (denoting an ideal balance of activities in life) some of which place spirituality at the centre (e.g. Myers et al., 2000). Spirituality is a holistic discipline which is not limited to the 'explorations of the explicitly religious' but considers all aspects of the spiritual experience, namely, 'the psychological, bodily, historical, political, aesthetic, intellectual, and other dimensions of the human subject' (Schneiders, 1989:693). Davie (1994) described spirituality as 'believing without belonging', which arguably suits more individualistic societies. Sociological research has suggested that the development of more individualistic cultures and societies has increased social alienation, rendering a greater need for seeking spiritual solace.

Cohen (1996) describes how the quest for a 'spiritual centre' is an integral part of tourism, especially when people feel socially alienated. Traditional aspects of spiritual retreats have often been in the form of pilgrimages for religious tourists (Carrasco, 1996; Devereux & Carnegie, 2006), but the secular tourist may seek other forms of spiritual enlightenment. Spiritual tourism can include visiting religious sites or buildings, spiritual landscapes, pilgrimage centres, ashrams, retreats, or gurus. The spiritual quest is seen as more abstract than a specifically religious one, focusing on the balance of body, mind, and spirit. Graburn (2002) discusses how the inner and outer journey – that is, the inner world of consciousness and the outer world of experience – can be reconciled through travel. This may be achieved through the contemplation of certain landscapes, which may variously inspire awe, introspection, or wonder, reminding us of our place in the world and our relationship to the universe.

Case Study: Confusing the Religious and the Spiritual? Ananda, Assisi

Ananda was founded in 1968 by Swami Kriyananda, a direct disciple of the Indian yoga guru Paramhansa Yogananda (author of the influential *Autobiography of a Yogi* first published in 1946). Paramhansa Yogananda was the first great Indian master to live most of his life in the Western world. Yogananda emphasized the universality of religion. The inner essence of all religions, he said, is one and the same: the way to union with the Infinite, known as 'Self-realization', which will be the religion of the future.

Ananda is a network of seven spiritual communities, with hundreds of centres and meditation groups in the United States and in Europe. The teaching at Ananda blends Western and Eastern spiritual disciplines with special emphasis being given to both the teachings of Christ and to India's scientific and ancient gift of yoga and meditation.

Ananda Europa was founded in Italy in 1983 and has been flourishing at its present location near Assisi since 1986. There are about 80 residents at Ananda, some living within the community and others, including families and children, in homes nearby. Ananda specializes in community living and in applying spiritual principles to every aspect of life: work, family, relationships, educating children, religion, how to solve problems and overcome crises, healing, creativity, and much more. Open all year round, Ananda offers residential weekend, week-long and intensive programs on a variety of subjects, for example:

- Meditation and Self-realization
- Ananda Yoga
- Ananda Yoga Teacher Training
- Ananda Raja Yoga Teacher Training
- Material Success
- Spiritual Self-Healing
- Vegetarian Cooking
- Kriya Yoga
- Vedic Astrology
- Spirituality in Daily Life
- Pilgrimages in Italy: 'Spirit Walk' and 'In the Footsteps of St. Francis'

They also lead pilgrimages, Himalayan Adventures, and Ayurveda Vacations in India.

For many visitors, the blend of Western religion and Eastern spirituality may work, however, it is a controversial juxtaposition, especially with the religious town of Assisi nearby. As a result, Assisi has been investigated even raided by police on more than one occasion and accused of being a cult and brainwashing weak and vulnerable people, and being involved in criminal activities or sex scandals. There is some debate about the accuracy of the charges, but this perhaps demonstrates the difficulties of trying to blend conventional religion with 'universal' spirituality.

(Ananda Answers (2008); Ananda Retreats, 2008)

Magyar (2008) compiled the most popular spiritual destinations around the world by collecting information from major spiritual travel-oriented websites. We can see that there are some destinations that may not be mentioned top of mind, for example Alaska, which is mainly visited because of its untouched nature and spiritual atmosphere.

- Jerusalem (Israel)
- Mecca (Saudi Arabia)
- The Vatican and Rome (Italy)
- Tibet, Nepal and Mount Everest
- Goa and Benares (India)
- Machu Picchu (Peru)

- Egypt
- Mount Fuji (Japan)
- Navaho Region (USA)
- Rio de Janeiro (Brasil)
- Alaska (USA)

New Age

Many of the more esoteric aspects of wellness are sometimes described as 'New Age', with the term often being used in a derogatory way. However, New Age beliefs are interesting as they are closely connected to non-religious spirituality and their proponents tend to be much more open minded to new experiences than those who deride it. Religious Tolerance (2006), an online forum describes New Age as 'a free-flowing spiritual movement; a network of believers and practitioners who share somewhat similar beliefs and practices, which they add on to whichever formal religion that they follow'.

New Age teachings started in England in the 1960s and became globally popular in the 1970s therefore they are often associated with the Hippy era and 'Baby Boomers'. They were largely a reaction to the failure of organized religion to meet the spiritual needs of all people. Heelas (1996) asserts that the essence of the New Age movement is self-spirituality, that is the notion that the self is sacred and that spirituality lies within the individual person. Miller (1994) discussed the New Age movement and its commercial dimensions. According to her, people want to believe in something, to have some hope and faith, and the selling of spirituality offers divine dividends. New Age products have become very lucrative, with a wild boom in the 1990s when spirituality was the buzzword in the merchandising business (Green & Aldred, 2002).

However, by the 1980s and 1990s the movement came under criticism because healing methods were seen as unscientific (e.g. Crystals, Tarot), many New Age leaders were accused of being charlatans, and some rituals were confused with the Occult or Satanism.

Typical New Age activities include the following:

- *Channelling* (conjuring up spirits of the dead)
- *Crystals* (i.e. their healing energy)
- *Meditating* (blanking the mind and releasing oneself from conscious thinking)
- *New Age music* (melodic, inspirational music used for healing, massage therapy, and relaxation)
- *Holistic health* (healing techniques from traditional medical models which aim to balance body, mind, and spirit. Examples are acupuncture, crystal healing, homoeopathy, iridology, massage, various meditation methods, polarity therapy, psychic healing, therapeutic touch, reflexology, etc.)
- *Human potential movement* (individual and group mental and physical techniques used to advance spirituality. Examples include Gestalt Therapy, Primal Scream Therapy, Transactional Analysis, Transcendental Meditation, and Yoga).

Today, many people may subscribe to New Age beliefs without even giving them a label. For example, Religious Tolerance (2006) states that a recent survey in the United States showed that many Americans hold at least some New Age beliefs:

- 8% believe in astrology as a method of foretelling the future
- 7% believe that crystals are a source of healing or energizing power
- 9% believe that Tarot Cards are a reliable base for life decisions.

About 1 in 4 believe in a non-traditional concept of the nature of God which is often associated with New Age thinking:

- 11% believe that God is *'a state of higher consciousness that a person may reach'*
- 8% define God as *'the total realization of personal, human potential'*
- 3% believe that each person is God.

In terms of tourism, it seems that the number of people who are engaging in New Age activities whilst on holiday are growing. For example, many holistic centres such as Skyros in Greece or Cortijjo Romero in Spain include such activities. In some cases, whole centres are devoted to the practices and visitors come specifically to meet or join like-minded communities. Findhorn is a good example:

Case Study of a New Age Community: Findhorn Foundation, Scotland

The Findhorn Foundation in Inverness Scotland welcomes more than 14,000 visitors every year, from more than 70 countries. The Findhorn Community was established in 1962 by Peter and Eileen Caddy and Dorothy Maclean, who began by cultivating a world-famous garden which attracted more and more people seeking to join a nature-based, self-sufficient community. In the late 1960s the Park Sanctuary for meditation, and a Community Centre, were built by Peter and community members in accordance with Eileen's guidance (she used the guidance from spirits to influence both the cultivation of the garden and the construction of the centre).

In 1970 a young American spiritual teacher named David Spangler arrived in the community and with his partner Myrtle Glines helped to develop the spiritual education programmes of the Findhorn Community. Today the Centre runs almost 200 week-long courses every year. There are also conferences, trainings, worldwide pilgrimages, and an outreach programme of educational workshops which are taken round the world. Those who wish to take a course are asked to attend *Experience Week* first, which introduces the main principles of life in the community, including love in action, meditation, sacred dance, and nature outings. Examples of courses include *Ecovillage Training*, a month long programme which has an ecological focus; or *Essence of the Arts in Community*, a 3 month programme focusing on visual and performing arts. There are also shorter workshops on Healing, Meditation, Dance, Enlightened Leadership, Conflict Resolution, Shamanism, Manifestation, Energy Management, Yoga and many more. Retreat weeks also exist, including vegetarian cookery courses, pilgrimages, even gay, and lesbian retreats.

By the 1990s the Findhorn Foundation became the heart of a diverse community of hundreds of people who spanned dozens of holistic businesses and initiatives. They were all linked by a commitment to non-doctrinal spirituality and a shared positive vision for humanity and the earth. In 1997 the Foundation was recognized as an official United Nations NGO.

(Findhorn, 2007)

New Age tourism destinations have an apparently spiritual dimension. Even some of the world's major monuments and World Heritage Sites such as Stonehenge in the UK, the Pyramids in Egypt and Machu Picchu in Peru are sometimes sold as being 'New Age' destinations. New Agers tend to visit sites and events belonging to different cultures and religions.

New Age Tourism Activities: A Classification

- *Power/sacred places*
  (sacred sites/stones, temples, pilgrimages, holy sites, visiting tribes, rituals, etc.)
- *Wellness and holistic health*
  (Reflexology, Bach Flower Therapy, Aromatherapy, Reiki, Acupuncture, Homoeopathy, etc.)
- *Divination*
  (Visiting places to foretell future; I ching, Runes, Scrying, Tarot Cards, Pendulum movements etc.)
- *Greenery and eco-spirit*
  (Spirituality related visits to Nature, Deep ecology, Mother Earth, Goddess, etc.)
- *Workshops/seminars/festivals*
  (Visualization, Feng-Shui, Karma, Reincarnation, Auras, Sacred Dance/Song, Self-Development, Gurus etc.)
- *Other*
  (Retreat Centres, New Age Accommodation, Spas, UFO, purchase of crystals or other goods etc.)

(After Pernecky and Johnston, 2006)

Holism

For decades, scholars have emphasized the value of the connections between mind and body that can contribute to wellness (Chopra, 1993; Weil, 1995; Pesek et al., 2006), but society is now becoming more interested in the role of spirituality in wellbeing and healing, and in exploring body–mind–spirit philosophies (Gallup & Lindsay, 1999; Ables, 2000; Pesek et al., 2006). There is relative consensus amongst researchers that optimum wellness comes from a balance between wellbeing in the body, the mind, and the spirit (i.e. a holistic approach to life). The American Holistic Health Association (AHHA) (2007) suggests that there are two standard definitions that are used for 'holistic':

1. Holistic as a whole made up of interdependent parts. You are most likely to hear these parts referred to as the mind/body connection; mind/body/spirit, or physical/mental/emotional/spiritual aspects. When this meaning is applied to illness, it is called holistic medicine and includes a number of factors, such as dealing with the root cause of an illness; increasing patient involvement; and considering both conventional (allopathic) and complementary (alternative) therapies.
2. Holistic as a synonym for alternative therapies. By this definition, 'going holistic' means turning away from any conventional medical options and using alternative treatment exclusively. This meaning mainly relates to illness situations, and sometimes is used for controversial therapies.

According to AHHA (2007) holistic health as an approach to creating wellness encourages you to:

- Balance and integrate your physical, mental, emotional, and spiritual aspects.
- Establish respectful, cooperative relationships with others and the environment.
- Make wellness-oriented lifestyle choices.
- Actively participate in your health decisions and healing process.

Holistic approaches can also be interpreted as somewhat 'New Age' or esoteric depending on the treatments that are offered under this label. Many practitioners focus on 'life energy' of the body using massage or other techniques (e.g. reiki) to activate or calm this force. Some practitioners who were participating in the Body, Soul, and Spirit Expo (in Canada) were asked by Chandler (2007) what the word 'holistic' meant to them, and here are some of their responses:

'Holistic means bringing the body, mind, spirit, and emotions to a place of wholeness and balance'.

'Faith healing, unorthodox medicine, folk medicine, holistic medicine, natural medicine, unconventional medicine to name a few however we are always developing our energies to aid others in the quest for knowledge, wisdom, healing, and humanitarian efforts ...'

'To clear space for the individual to remember their strength and wholeness, regardless what outside circumstances look like. To hold the energy so their own inner voice and inner healer can step forward'.

'Holistic to me means every aspect, embracing all consciously – the good and the bad ... I'm passionate about living one's life to the full, relationships between men and women (how to make then fulfilling), opening my heart to love as fully as I can, being completely present in the moment, the beautiful earth'.

Holistic tourism tends to be mainly offered at 'retreat centres' which are usually purpose built (as opposed to temporary venues that can be hired for multiple purposes by multiple users) and owner run. A retreat centre has multiple meanings; it can be a place for quiet reflection and rejuvenation, an opportunity to regain good health, and/or it can mean a time for spiritual reassessment and renewal, either alone, in silence, or in a group (Retreats Online, 2006).

Wellness

As stated in the Introduction, the concept of wellness was developed by Dunn (1959) as 'a special state of health comprising an overall sense of wellbeing which sees 'Man' as consisting of body, spirit, and mind and being dependent on his environment'. Müller and Kaufmann (2000) later made an attempt to combine the understanding of wellness in North-America and in Europe, suggesting that wellness is a state of health featuring the harmony of the body, mind, and spirit, self-responsibility, physical fitness, beauty care, healthy nutrition, relaxation, meditation, mental activity, education, environmental sensitivity, and social contacts as fundamental elements.

The Deutscher Wellness Verband (2008) suggest that the term 'medical wellness' can be used to somehow integrate the concepts of health and wellness, in the sense that there is a medically supervised programme of wellness for clients. This involves making specific changes to lifestyle which can help to achieve optimum wellness. However, it could be argued as stated in the Introduction, that this term is somewhat narrow and does not take into consideration some of the broader aspects of wellness (Nahrstedt, 2008).

Wellness is clearly a complex concept, incorporating elements of lifestyle, physical, mental, and spiritual wellbeing, and one's relationship to oneself, others and the environment. It could be argued based on the above discussions that wellness as a concept incorporates or balances all of the dimensions of life mentioned so far: wellbeing, happiness, QoL, holistic practice, spiritual beliefs. This makes it a wide ranging and complex field with multiple dimensions. If we want to talk about wellness activities or wellness tourism we need to start thinking in terms of subsets or sub-sectors.

Adams (2003) refers to four main principles of wellness:

1. Wellness is multi-dimensional.
2. Wellness research and practice should be oriented towards identifying causes of wellness rather than cause of illness.
3. Wellness is about balance.
4. Wellness is relative, subjective or perceptual.

The final point is an interesting one, implying that wellness is more of a psychological than a physical state. The National Wellness Institute (2007) defines wellness as: 'an active process through which people become aware of, and make choices towards, a more successful existence'. They advocate a positive and optimistic outlook and a holistic and balanced approach to life. Their six-dimensional model focuses on the physical, spiritual, intellectual, emotional, social, and occupational aspects of life:

Social

The social dimension encourages contributing to one's environment and community. It emphasizes the interdependence between others and nature. As you travel a wellness path, you'll become more aware of your importance in society as well as the impact you have on multiple environments. You'll take an active part in improving our world by encouraging healthier living and initiating better communication with those around you. You'll actively seek ways to preserve the beauty and balance of nature along the pathway as you discover the power to make willful choices to enhance personal relationships, important friendships, and build a better living space, and community. Social wellness follows these tenets:

- It is better to contribute to the common welfare of our community than to think only of ourselves.
- It is better to live in harmony with others and our environment than to live in conflict with them.

Occupational

The occupational dimension recognizes personal satisfaction and enrichment in one's life through work. At the centre of occupational wellness is the premise that occupational development is related to one's attitude about one's work. Travelling a path towards your occupational wellness, you'll contribute your unique gifts, skills and talents to work that is both personally meaningful and rewarding. You'll convey your values through your involvement in activities that are gratifying for you. The choice of profession, job satisfaction, career ambitions, and personal performance are all important components of your path's terrain. Occupational wellness follows these tenets:

- It is better to choose a career which is consistent with our personal values interests and beliefs than to select one that is unrewarding to us.
- It is better to develop functional, transferable skills through structured involvement opportunities than to remain inactive and uninvolved.

Spiritual

The spiritual dimension recognizes our search for meaning and purpose in human existence. It includes the development of a deep appreciation for the depth and expanse of life and natural forces that exist in the universe. Your search will be characterized by a peaceful harmony between internal personal feelings and emotions and the rough and rugged stretches of your path. While travelling the path, you may experience many feelings of doubt, despair, fear, disappointment, and dislocation as well as feelings of pleasure, joy, happiness, and discovery – these are all important experiences and components to your search and will be displayed in the value system you will adapt to bring meaning to your existence. You'll know you're becoming spiritually well when your actions become more consistent with your beliefs and values, resulting in a 'world view.' Spiritual wellness follows these tenets:

- It is better to ponder the meaning of life for ourselves and to be tolerant of the beliefs of others than to close our minds and become intolerant.
- It is better to live each day in a way that is consistent with our values and beliefs than to do otherwise and feel untrue to ourselves.

Physical

The physical dimension recognizes the need for regular physical activity. Physical development encourages learning about diet and nutrition while discouraging the use of tobacco, drugs, and excessive alcohol consumption. Optimal wellness is met through the combination of good exercise and eating habits. As you travel the wellness path, you'll strive to spend time building physical strength, flexibility, and endurance while also taking safety precautions so you may travel your path successfully, including medical self-care and appropriate use of a medical system. The physical dimension of wellness entails personal responsibility and care for minor illnesses and also knowing when professional medical attention is needed. By travelling the wellness path, you'll be able to monitor your own vital signs and understand your body's warning signs. You'll understand and appreciate the relationship between sound nutrition and how your body performs. The physical benefits of looking good and feeling terrific most often lead to the psychological benefits of enhanced self-esteem, self-control, determination, and a sense of direction. Physical wellness follows these tenets:

- It is better to consume foods and beverages that enhance good health rather than those which impair it.
- It is better to be physically fit than out of shape.

Intellectual

The intellectual dimension recognizes one's creative, stimulating mental activities. A well person expands their knowledge and skills while discovering the potential for sharing their gifts with others. Using intellectual and cultural activities in the classroom and beyond the classroom combined with the human resources and learning resources available within the university community and the larger community, a well person cherishes intellectual growth and stimulation. Travelling a wellness path, you'll explore issues related to problem solving, creativity, and learning. You'll spend more time pursuing personal interests, reading books, magazines, and newspapers, while keeping abreast of current issues and ideas. As you develop your intellectual curiosity, you'll actively strive to expand and challenge your mind with creative endeavours. Intellectual wellness follows these tenets:

- It is better to stretch and challenge our minds with intellectual and creative pursuits than to become self-satisfied and unproductive.
- It is better to identify potential problems and choose appropriate courses of action based on available information than to wait, worry and contend with major concerns later.

Emotional

The emotional dimension recognizes awareness and acceptance of one's feelings. Emotional wellness includes the degree to which one feels positive and enthusiastic about oneself and life. It includes the capacity to manage one's feelings and related behaviours including the realistic assessment of one's limitations, development of autonomy, and ability to cope effectively with stress. The well person maintains satisfying relationships with others. Awareness of and accepting a wide range of feelings in yourself and others is essential to wellness. On the wellness path, you'll be able to express feelings freely and manage feelings effectively. You'll be able to arrive at personal choices and decisions based upon the synthesis of feelings, thoughts, philosophies, and behaviour. You'll live and work independently while realizing the importance of seeking and appreciating the support and assistance of others. You'll be able to form interdependent relationships with others based upon a foundation of mutual commitment, trust, and respect. You'll take on challenges, take risks, and recognize conflict as being potentially healthy. Managing your life in personally rewarding ways, and taking responsibility for your actions, will help you see life as an exciting, hopeful adventure. Emotional wellness follows these tenets:

- It is better to be aware of and accept our feelings than to deny them.
- It is better to be optimistic in our approach to life than pessimistic.

(National Wellness Institute, 2007)

The notion of balance is a much cited one too, and numerous wheels of wellness' can be found when researching this phenomenon, which are similar to the National Wellness Institute's six-dimensional model. The authors' own model (Figure 3.2) shows in visual form the main dimensions which constitute wellness:

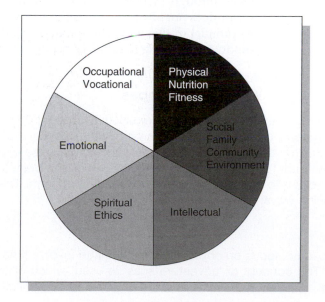

Figure 3.2
Wheel of Wellness. *Source*:
Smith and Puczkó.

It is unlikely that travel can contribute to all of these domains simultaneously, unless the tourist in question wishes to work exceptionally hard on holiday! Although occupational wellness is becoming a growth sector and some tailor-made trips are catering for such needs (e.g. life-coaching or stress management retreats), it is more common that people go on holiday to escape from the pressures of working. Nevertheless, the increasing number of business trips which incorporate a wellness element (e.g. a conference in a spa hotel) means that one's occupation, travel, and wellness are becoming more closely connected.

Not all tourists will want to embark on a spiritual journey either, especially those who crave escapism from existential matters. On holiday, time and space are somehow distorted and the reality of one's real life can seem far away. Equally, people sometimes travel to escape from emotional problems and dilemmas, rather than to confront them. It is only the recently developing wellness sector that offers tourists the chance to deal with their emotional baggage in an environment far away from home. To many, this is not at all appealing.

Even within the wellness market, not all wellness tourists are seeking healing and/or renewal of body, mind, *and* spirit. Indeed, a visitor with strong interests in yoga as a form of exercise, for example would be unlikely to have an interest in a psychotherapeutic style course at a retreat centre. A typical spa visitor would not expect nor want to receive a psychological or spiritual experience. A religious visitor on a sacred retreat would not be interested in crystal healing or reiki. Equally, a visitor learning about neurolinguistic programming or life coaching may have little interest in yoga or Tai Chi. The complexity of visitors' priorities is difficult to understand, and it appears that providers of wellness tourism do not always try 'to cover every base' in terms of their provision either. So whilst it seems that optimum wellness is to be achieved at a personal level, through synergies of body–mind–spirit–environment, the tourism sector does not always have the holistic know-how or the desire to deliver its product in this way. Those that do tend to categorize or separate their products according to different needs as the following case study shows:

Case Study of Wellbeing Escapes

Wellbeing Escapes is an online service based in London, UK which provides a range of so-called wellbeing holidays which focus on health, lifestyle, and individual needs, especially recharging from the stress of modern life. The holidays are expensive with the average trip costing around 1500 pounds (about 2400 EUROs) but many of them are all-inclusive and they also claim to enhance peoples' lives in the long term. The holidays are categorized in the following ways:

Active

These holidays focus on physical challenges and involve fitness activities as well as visits to spas. The concept of 'adventure spas' is used, which claim to boost stamina, provide stress relief and make people feel younger. Most of the spas are located in areas of great natural beauty and some packages even combine for example, spas and safaris in Kenya or spas and golf in Cyprus.

Ayurveda

The Ayurvedic holidays offered are guaranteed to be authentic experiences using only properly qualified practitioners, whether they take place in India (the home of Ayurveda) or in another location (e.g. London). Ayurveda uses treatments such as massage, nutrition, and lifestyle changes to enhance wellbeing. Typical destinations apart from India include Sri Lanka, Mauritius, and Bali.

Destination spa

These luxury spas are exotic destinations in themselves and provide all-inclusive programs complete with fitness activities, lifestyle coaching, healthy cuisine, and a whole range of body and beauty treatments. Emphasis is placed on creating lasting benefits for visitors, such as more energy, a more positive outlook, greater ability to focus, and enhanced creativity. Many of these destination spas are located in Asia or the Caribbean, and some are world famous such as Chiva Som in Thailand.

Detox: weight loss

Detox programmes aim to boost the immune system and to rejuvenate the body. This is done through the removal of toxic substances such as alcohol and refined sugar. A weight-loss diet can also be included in the programme as well as fitness activities or special treatments (e.g. Ayurveda or Thalassotherapy). Participants can learn about healthy eating for life. Destinations include the USA, Malta, Hungary, and Greece.

Holistic

Holistic holidays are seen as being about the whole person – mental, physical, and spiritual and creating balance and harmony within. The focus is more on 'spiritual fitness' than physical fitness. Visitors can take an inner journey using meditation, yoga, ayurveda, tai chi, massage, or reiki. Creative activities are also included in many of the programmes which take place in beautiful settings in Thailand, Malaysia, Sri Lanka, the Maldives, and Mauritius.

Pampering

Pampering escapes offer 'time out' from everyday life in luxury surroundings in Austria, Morocco, Monaco, Cyprus, and Malta amongst others. The focus is mainly on body and beauty treatments, including massage, steam and sauna, and relaxation in pools and baths.

Thalassotherapy

Thalassotherapy takes place in areas which are close to the sea and uses the beneficial aspects of the marine environment, such as the climate, sea water, seaweed, algae, mud, and sand. They are often seen as more therapeutic than pampering. Thalassotherapy is good for weight loss, cellulite reduction, post-natal toning, back problems, water retention, circulation problems, and joint pain. Water-based exercise classes like aqua aerobics are often included. Typical destinations offered are Crete, Cyprus, and Ireland.

Thermal

Thermal holidays are taken in traditional spa resorts in destinations like Austria, Hungary, Slovakia, and Italy. Treatments include soaks in the thermal and mineral waters, mud wraps and massage. They can be used to ease specific medical problems or just to relax and alleviate stress. Medical spas focus on therapeutic and preventative approaches as well as aesthetic or cosmetic ones.

Yoga

Yoga holidays focus on the practice of physical asanas as well as meditation to promote stress relief and calm. These can be combined with nature-based or other activities, as well as healthy living programmes.

(Wellbeing Escapes, 2007)

Conclusion

It is clear that wellness is a multi-dimensional concept which incorporates aspects of both physical and mental health, as well as environmental and social factors. In the past, there was much more emphasis on curing health problems through conventional or traditional medicine prescribed by a doctor, whereas in recent years, it has become more common to try to maintain a healthy lifestyle and prevent illnesses, often using self-prescribed methods. The burgeoning wellness industry offers individuals the chance to try out a whole range of activities which claim to balance body, mind, and soul. Some of these are scientifically tested but the majority rely on peoples' belief in their ability to work. This does not mean that wellness activities are a mere placebo, but they sometimes take a leap of faith on the part of individuals, many of whom are relatively uninformed about impacts and effects. The propensity to travel for reasons of wellness are increasing, not just because there is a need for escapism from stress, but also because people sometimes need to take a step back from their lives to truly know themselves. It is also perhaps true to say that when we travel, we are more inclined to take risks, to try new things and to focus on what is most important to us, whether that is our health, our emotions, our need to express ourselves or the desire to simply have fun!

CHAPTER 4

Leisure, lifestyle, and tourism

In order to walk the path of wellness, one must first have a clear understanding of what it means to be a human being, of how to conceive of one's own self in relation to the rest of the world.
(Wolsko et al., 2006)

There is clearly a need to identify which tools are available to help in the pursuit of wellness, as travel is only one of many. This chapter focuses on the lifestyle habits that are characteristic of contemporary societies, starting with some of the approaches that can be used in our quest for enhancement of health, well-being, and quality of life. Many of these are not new, but they have started to evolve in interesting ways to accommodate changing tastes and preferences. The second half of the chapter analyses some of the factors which are encouraging more and more people to seek wellness services and activities, including travel. The stresses of living in work-obsessed, time-pressured, materialistic and overly-individualistic societies is taking its toll on larger numbers of people, but as this book will demonstrate, help is at hand!

Medicine

Conventional medicine is provided by qualified doctors and their allied staff such as registered nurses and healthcare professionals, physical therapists, and psychologists. The treatments or medicines that are given are scientifically proven to be effective and are carefully monitored and regulated. Many medical spas have waters which have special medical or healing properties, and they are generally used by those with a prescription from their doctor for a specified amount of time. Although other visitors may use the waters for leisure or recreation, the time recommended in medical waters is fairly limited (e.g. 20 minutes at any one time). Medical facilities are also clearly the main focus of medical tourism trips which may involve some form of intervention such as surgery or treatments, including dentistry and cosmetics.

In addition to conventional medicine, there is also a growing market for CAM or Complementary and Alternative Medicine. This can be used as an alternative to conventional medicine or in combination (sometimes called 'integrative medicine'). Often CAM medical systems developed and evolved much earlier than conventional medical systems. Examples in Western cultures include homoeopathic or naturopathic medicine, and in non-Western cultures traditional Chinese medicine or Indian Ayurveda. Mind-Body medicine is also an important part of CAM, although techniques like support-groups or cognitive-behavioural therapy have become mainstream. Others like meditation, prayer, mental healing, and therapies that use creative outlets like art, music, and dance are still being researched. Biologically based practices use substances found in food, herbs, or vitamins. Manipulative or body-based practices use movement or manipulation such as chiropractic or osteopathic techniques, as well as massage. Energy therapies involve the use of energy fields, for example through Therapeutic Touch, Qi Gong, or Reiki (National Center for Alternative and Complementary Medicine, 2007).

Many conventional medical practitioners remain sceptical about the impacts of CAM, arguing that there is no such thing as alternative medicine – just medicine that is untested and unproven to work! However, a survey released in May 2004 by the National Center for Complementary and Alternative Medicine in the United States, found that in 2002, 36% of Americans used some form of alternative therapy in the past 12 months, and in the United Kingdom, a 2000 report ordered by the House of Lords suggested that CAM use in Britain was high and rising. The most common CAM therapies used in the United States in 2002 were prayer (45.2%), herbalism (18.9%), breathing meditation (11.6%), meditation (7.6%), chiropractic medicine (7.5%), yoga (5.1%), body work (5.0%), diet-based therapy (3.5%), progressive relaxation (3.0%), mega-vitamin therapy (2.8%), and visualization (2.1%). However, the sector is largely unregulated therefore people tend to self-medicate and so-called 'experts' may not be properly qualified to advise. A small but increasing number of 'celebrity' practitioners are advocating the use of alternative and complementary medicines, for example, the Barefoot Doctor in the United Kingdom who writes a weekly column in a national broadsheet newspaper and has written several popular books. He also participated in a New Year Retreat with the holistic travel company Core Journeys (http://www.corejourneys.com) in 2008.

Many alternative and complementary medicine practices are used in holistic centres and retreats, whereas conventional medicine is used in medical spas and in destinations which provide specific medical services. Even some leisure and recreational spas offer visitors health checks with a doctor, for example, measuring their fitness levels, weight, body fat, blood pressure, cholesterol, etc. and making recommendations for a healthier life.

Therapy and healing

If something is therapeutic, it has healing powers. These days, almost all wellness activities seem to be described as 'therapeutic', whether they are relaxing massages, yoga classes, water-based treatments, or physical exercise. We can talk about psychological therapy, sex therapy, beauty therapy, diet therapy, de-tox therapy, trauma therapy, stress therapy, etc. Most therapies are administered by a qualified practitioner on a regular basis, for a set time period and with specified outcomes. For example, Therapeutic Recreation organizations (e.g. the American Therapeutic Recreation Association) focus on rehabilitating people with illnesses or disabling conditions. Health, well-being and quality of life are improved through recreational activities such as creativity, cookery, gardening, fitness and sports. Sometimes the word 'therapy' implies that individuals or groups are receiving some form of counselling or engaging in activities which help them to deal with mental and emotional problems. This brings us into the realms of psychology, especially the more popular forms of it which are starting to pervade the field of wellness.

Case Study of Therapeutic Recreation: Experience Therapy

Hole in the Wall Camps are the world's largest family of camps for children with serious illnesses and life-threatening conditions. To date, more than 114,000 children from over 30 countries have attended free of charge, since 1988. The philosophy of the chain of camps can be summarized as follows:

- *Laughter and More Laughter*: More and more it's been shown that for children with serious illnesses, laughter really is the best medicine. In addition to the contagious laughter found at each Camp and Programme, there is 24-hour, high quality medical care provided for each camper. Each facility is staffed by trained medical professionals. The medical presence at Camp is carefully kept in the background so that the children can fully concentrate on the fun activities.
- *Plus Total Care*: Children with cancer, HIV, sickle cell anaemia, and other serious illnesses can feel safe and cared for. Doctors and nurses volunteer their time and talents, and attend to every child's needs. Each medical facility accommodates the full array of treatments for the medical conditions they serve, whether it's a chemotherapy treatment, a dialysis procedure, or daily infusions. Our medical facilities are designed to be as welcoming as possible. They are friendly, brightly-painted places that blend in with the look and feel of other camp structures. And their catchy names reflect the distinct charm and personality of each camp:

The OK Corral, The Patch, Goody's Body Shop, Paul's Body Shop, The Well Shell, The Beehive, The Med Shed and Club Med.

> • *Serious Medicine with a Light Touch*: Collectively, Hole in the Wall Camps served more than 15,000 campers with over 50 medical conditions in 2006. Our camps continue to expand their services to include new medical conditions each year and enhance the level of care they provide to campers during their time at Camp. Last year, Hole in the Wall Camps welcomed new campers and families for a Transverse Myelitis Weekend, a Little People of America summer session and Autism Family Day(s).
>
> (Hole in the Wall Camps, 2008)

Many spas are thought to have therapeutic properties because of the mineral content of the waters, mud or even climate. Patients can benefit from internal therapy such as drinking the waters, inhalation therapy (e.g. inhaling droplets or fumes of water), lavages (oral, nasal, gynachaeological), as well as external therapy which can include baths and showers, hydromassaging, balneotherapy (using thermal and healing waters for bathing, drinking, or inhalation), or fangotherapy (applying mud to those parts of the body that suffer from various disorders). Many visitors choose their spa destination carefully according to which therapies are offered, for example, Thalassotherapy which makes use of sea water, mud, seaweed, etc. One of the most attractive offers in recent years has been Aromatherapy where essential oils are blended to create different effects and are used for massage or inhalation. Many holistic centres and retreats offer a range of healing techniques and therapies, and tend to be more creative and experimental than medically proven. This might include Colour or Sound Therapy, Bach Flower Remedies, Angel or Animal Medicine Therapies, amongst others.

Psychology

Psychological wellness focuses mainly on control of the mind and emotions. This could include tools and techniques such as the development of mindfulness, meditation, building self-esteem, becoming a better communicator, reducing stress, managing anxiety, and overcoming depression.

The reference to 'popular' or 'pop' psychology which is used most frequently in wellness circles (as opposed to medical ones) is often used in a derogatory way, as many of the theories are scientifically unproven. However, there is a large and growing 'self-help' industry based on the books, TV, and radio programmes and workshops of 'famous' gurus such as Deepak Chopra. Individuals can begin to diagnose and solve their own psychological problems using books about relationships, stress, depression, anger, etc. or they can attend a workshop or training programme. Many holistic holidays and retreat centres focus on self-help, usually in the form of group workshops. Some of the more tried and tested methods may include psycho-drama, a form of drama therapy which explores the problems of people in a working group. For example, in psychodrama, participants explore internal conflicts through acting out their emotions and interpersonal interactions on stage. The Hoffman Process is an 8 day intensive residential course in which participants are shown how to let go of the past, release pent-up stress and resentments, and break self-limiting behaviour patterns, especially those based on their childhood experiences. There are many more, but some have a firmer basis in traditional psychology than others.

If work/life balance is the problem, then Life-coaching may provide better advice, and is being increasingly offered as a form of occupational wellness. Life-coaching is not counselling and not therapy instead it is described as 'a practical, forward-looking way to gain clarity on what you don't like and what you can do about it. It's also a powerful support system to keep you moving in the right direction. It provides an external perspective on your life' (UK Life Coaching, 2007). Life-coaches tend to focus on a number of domains within a person's life such as work, home, finances, social life, partner, health, dreams, spiritual, and work/life balance. Techniques like NLP (Neuro-Linguistic-Programming) are used which aims to understand how people think, behave and change. NLP helps to master the mind, improve communication, and re-think how we experience the world.

Cosmetics

The use of make-up by women is an ancient concept, but never before has its usage been so intensive and commercialized. Whole magazines are devoted to the subject of beauty and haircare with the suggestion that total transformation is only a colour palate away! Women who choose NOT to wear make-up in Western societies are the exception rather than the norm. However, the most impressive trick is to imply that no make-up has been used at all and one's look is almost entirely natural and effortless. This places considerable pressure on the majority of women to invest in expensive skin and haircare products in the attempt to look naturally younger and more beautiful. This is the major focus of day spas and many hotel spas too, which offer facials, manicures, pedicures, haircare, etc. Taking this a stage further, the admittance even advocating of plastic surgery by many – especially American – celebrities has led to the increasing demand for such services, with many women choosing to go on holiday for surgery to enjoy a relaxing recuperation or merely cheaper prices. The quest for the body beautiful can lead women in particular to diet endlessly in an attempt to be an elusive size zero after their favourite Hollywood stars. Men on the other hand struggle to pump up or tone their bodies to an artificial and usually unretainable level using steroids, proteins, or other aids which can irreparably harm the body in the long term. Nutritional and exercise programmes exist in spas and fitness centres which can help women or men to obtain the perfect physique, but these are ideally monitored or guided by medical or healthcare professionals.

Nutrition

The subject of healthy nutrition has become something of a public education campaign in recent years, in many countries. It is hard to turn a corner without seeing a book, magazine or a TV programme about diets, healthy eating or de-toxing. United States style 'fat camps' are becoming more common to which overweight and obsese children are sent during their summer holidays for a diet and fitness programme. In the United Kingdom Celebrity chefs like Jamie Oliver are revolutionizing school dinners and home-cooking, and pseudo-doctors like Gillian McKeith are encouraging (even terrorising!) the nation into making healthier diet choices. Diets like the Atkins or Weight Watchers have become world-famous, and now numerous celebrities are promoting the need to 'detox', even though it has been scientifically proven not to be necessary.

Detox, short for detoxification, is the body's natural, ongoing process of neutralizing or eliminating toxins from the body. Although detox used to be primarily thought of as a treatment for alcohol or drug dependence, the term is also used to refer to diets, herbs, and other methods of removing environmental and dietary toxins from the body for optimum health. A de-tox diet aims to minimize the amount of chemicals ingested (e.g. by the use of organic food), it emphasizes foods that provide the vitamins, nutrients, and antioxidants that the body needs for detoxification, and it contains foods, such as high fibre foods and water, that draw out and eliminate toxins by increasing the frequency of bowel movements and urination. A de-tox diet is thought to improve the health problems created by a build up of toxins such as indigestion, bad breath, fatigue, poor skin, and muscle pain, giving the individual more energy, concentration, clarity and an overall feeling of wellness (Wong, 2007).

Unfortunately, the cult of celebrity and obsession with models has also led to a worldwide increase in eating disorders such as anorexia and bulimia. In 2007 the Eating Disorders Coalition took action to curb eating disorders among models and to promote healthy weight in fashion. The British Medical Association had intervened back in 2000 when it was clear that there was a direct link between teenage anorexia and unrealistic role models in fashion. For example, their report stated that models and actresses in the 1990s commonly had body fat levels as low as 10% – the average for a healthy woman is 22%–26% (BBC News, 2000). Numerous reports have been emerging since stating that not only is there a rise in adult eating disorders (e.g. especially in women over 40 and gay males) but even in children as young as 5 (Kinsey, 2005).

Many retreats and holistic centres offer nutrition-based programmes especially for vegetarians, those who want to de-tox, eat raw or organic food, to lose weight, or simply learn to eat more healthily. Some clinics focus specifically on digestive health (e.g. the Mayr Centre in Austria). Spas and wellness hotels are starting to recognize the need to provide healthier food for visitors (those in Central and Eastern Europe traditionally offered high calorie, fatty foods with little consideration of the health consequences). Visitors may be able to choose from certain menus (e.g. vegetarian, gluten and wheat-free, low calorie) or there may be a diverse buffet with clearly labelled dishes. This allows visitors to make their own choices, although even in countries like Germany and Austria with relatively high nutritional awareness, the provision of sweet and high calories foods provides too much temptation for the average visitor!

Rehabilitation

The Spas Research Fellowship (2008) describes how spa treatments are increasingly being perceived as a potential tool in the rehabilitation of people with alcohol and drug problems. Even back in the mid-19th century, hydrotherapy was being used to treat alcoholics who would detoxify by drinking the mineral waters, bathing in hot, warm and cold baths, applying wet packs and taking showers. Immersion and flotation were also deemed important treatments for detoxification. Since 1957, the East West Detox Centre in Thailand has been using a detoxification process based on the combination of a hundred herbs and plant extracts administered as a daily drink. This is complemented by other therapies including herbal steam baths, diet and nutrition as well as counselling and guidance. Ozone therapy can also be used.

Rehabilitation can refer to the process of enabling people with disabilities, serious or long-term illnesses to reach and maintain their optimal physical, sensory, intellectual, psychological and social functional levels. However, the term 'rehab' is these days more commonly associated with recovering alcoholics, drug or sex addicts, especially famous celebrities. An unusual form of tourism maybe, but one which is becoming increasingly familiar to those who have drink and drug problems is to rehabilitate in luxury surroundings. Instead of the kind of tough programmes previously administered, addicts can now enjoy gourmet food and whale watching as part of their treatment. In Southern California, a number of new rehab centres with enticing names such as 'Harmony Place' and 'Renaissance' offer ocean views, massage and horse riding. Celebrities must pay for the privilege of rehabilitating, however, with a month's stay costing as much as 80,000 United States Dollars. It seems that people get better quicker in pleasant surroundings (Reuters, 2006). We Care Holistic Spa even offers pre-Oscar detox for strung-out celebrities in Palm Springs!

Case Study: The Sanctuary in Byron Bay, Australia

'My vision for The Sanctuary was to create one of those places you dream about going to feel healed, nurtured, held, and cared for.'

(The Sanctuary, 2007)

The Sanctuary is a luxury Therapeutic Retreat which specializes in the treatment of addictions, alcoholism, eating disorders and other physical and psychological issues such as depression, anxiety, stress-related disorders, trauma or chronic pain. Like many other contemporary rehabilitation retreats, the style is not one that is similar to a 'bootcamp', but offers a programme that is customized to suit individual needs and life experiences. The Sanctuary offers complementary medical therapies from both east and west. Personal healing is the primary function of the retreat.

Individuals are offered personal interviews to determine their needs and famous clientele are guaranteed anonymity. Each visitor can expect the following staff to assist them:

- personal therapists;
- doctor and registered nursing staff;
- psychiatrist (as required);
- physiotherapist;
- acupuncturist;
- naturopathic consultant incorporating nutrition, iridology and herbal medicine;
- massage therapist integrating shiatsu, qigong and deep tissue;
- yoga and meditation teacher;
- personal fitness instructor;
- 24-hour carers;
- personal chef;
- dietician (where required); and
- chauffeured private vehicle.

In addition to treating specific addictions or problems, the Sanctuary helps visitors to reconnect with their passions and interests in life. Excursions are encouraged into nature, such as bushwalks or whale watching, as well as participation in creative activities such as dance, art, music or martial arts. This approach which also takes into consideration diet, nutrition and exercise as well as spiritual well-being is truly holistic.

Three main programmes are included:

De-toxification: where the visitor recovers from substance misuse (e.g. drugs and alcohol) by removing toxins from the body as well as coping with withdrawal symptoms.
Intensive: which runs from 8 a.m. until 5 or 6 p.m. everyday and involves around 12 daily treatments or therapies. These will be customized or tailored to individual needs.
Transitional: here, the client takes part in a down-scaled programme which consists of more life-enhancing activities and learns self-motivation and self-responsibility. Reconnection with friends and family will be encouraged and they are allowed to visit the client. This stage is the beginning of the return home where after-care support will also be provided.

There are never more than four residents at the same time. The fees can be as much as 28,000 dollars per week, so this retreat is only for the very rich or famous.

At this juncture, the question clearly needs to be asked why all of these tools, treatments and techniques are needed to enhance peoples' life and wellbeing. The commercialization of wellness services in the form of leisure and tourism implies that the need is demand-led, but it could also be argued that the media plays a huge role in peoples' desire to be slimmer, more beautiful, look younger, and live longer. The workplace becomes more exacting, peer pressure mounts, technology speeds up our lives, and overall stress levels are increasing exponentially. The following sections analyse in more detail the factors which appear to be influencing the need for wellness activities both at home and on holiday.

Factors influencing the need for wellness tourism

Dann & Cohen (1996) describe how anomie tends to be prevalent in tourism generating societies, reflecting a general normlessness or meaninglessness, which acts as a major 'push' factor in travel motivation (Dann, 1977). Sharpley (2002) describes how alienation (e.g. from work, community and nature) has become an extrinsic motivating factor in tourism. The growth of the wellness tourism sector as a whole can arguably be attributed to a number of common factors, many of which are discussed below. Most of these are, however, mainly applicable to 'postmodern', capitalist societies with a relatively long history of outbound tourism. It should be recognized that the majority of countries generating wellness tourists are relatively wealthy and usually Western, although there is a large existing domestic and regional market for medical spa tourism in Central and Eastern Europe, where spa visits were traditionally state-subsidised through insurance or holiday vouchers. Not only resort, but even business hotels open their own spas or extend existing fitness rooms with wellness elements. Richards (2006) also notes that large numbers of Chinese tourists are now travelling to other Asian countries for medical tourism. The Japanese have their own onsens which are similar to European historic spas and therefore attract other Asian visitors. Middle Eastern tourists (especially men) are also travelling both within and outside the region to visit spas or have medical treatments. There is likely to be an increasing flow of outbound tourists from India, although domestic tourism already affords a plethora of wellness opportunities from yoga to meditation to Ayurveda. The factors below are nevertheless biased more towards Western, capitalist countries, therefore this bias should be recognized, although similar trends are arguably already emerging in transition countries (e.g. in Central and Eastern Europe and large Asian cities).

The search for community

Communities are becoming increasingly dislocated and fragmented in modern society. Growing international mobility has resulted in many people leaving their home town or even home country and spending long periods of their life far away from family or friends. The number of single people has increased with larger numbers of women choosing to pursue a career before settling down. As a result, the birth rate or number of children per family in many Western countries is decreasing. Divorce rates are also high with up to 50% in many European countries. Unlike Asia where collectivity is valued highly, European societies tend to value individual-ity and independence. The decreasing importance of organized religion has also exacerbated this phenomenon.

The globalization process has led to wider definitions and concepts of community, and more acceptance of the fluidity of changing social struc-tures. In some cases, virtual communities (e.g. those on the Internet) may have replaced actual ones. Bauman (2001) describes how many people now make fleeting attempts to join transient 'aesthetic communities' based on collective appreciation of entertainment or media-based activities. One of the most prevalent current trends in the United Kingdom, for example, is to idolise celebrities or to follow TV docu-dramas like 'Big Brother'. Whole media communities become (virtually) united in their hero(ine) worship or addiction to soap operas. These form the basis of friable and short-lived bonds between citizens in much the same way as sporting or arts events – described by Bauman (2001:72) as 'carnival communities'.

Bauman (2001) also suggests that the 'global elite' (i.e. tourists) may be less concerned with a sense of place and community than their more deprived counterparts, living as they do in a state of 'exterritoriality'. They actively seek out 'community-free zones' and virtually identical 'socio-cultural bubbles' (e.g. global hotel chains and restaurants, conference centres, air-conditioned offices, airports). Nevertheless, the global elite fre-quently succumb to feelings of loneliness and depression, no doubt engen-dered partly by their own (often self-imposed) isolation. Most people have a strong need to belong somewhere, and a certain desire for familiarity, continuity and security in their surroundings. For example, people may start to feel alienated from their locality because of its anonymity (e.g. not knowing their neighbours, no friendly postman or milkman). The stand-ardization or 'placelessness' of the shopping mall or supermarket complex as opposed to the local corner shop might engender a feeling of anonym-ity. Bauman (2001) describes how this engenders nostalgia for an idyll of community as a kind of 'paradise lost'.

The increasing need for 'community' as part of the wellness quest is noted by many authors (e.g. Devereux & Carnegie, 2006; Smith & Kelly, 2006). Bauman's (2001, 2003) seminal works on the fragmentation of trad-itional societies and communities conclude that 'Human community' looks today as remote from current planetary reality as it was at the beginning of the modern adventure (Bauman, 2003:149). This explains the tendency in holistic retreats and ashrams to create communities around collective, 'karmic' activities. For example, Dina Glouberman (2002) describes how her desire to establish the well-known holistic holiday centre *Skyros* was partly based on her own yearning for community. Edmond and Deborah Szekely did alike with their Golden Door in Southern California (1958). Many well-ness tourists are seeking a sense of community, perhaps within a holistic centre, a yoga retreat, at a New Age festival, or on a pilgrimage. Although their primary focus may be on self-development, they wish to enter into a kind of psychological, emotional or spiritual communion with others.

Temporary communities are formed during a medical holiday, where guests, or patients tend to spend at least a week (but three-four weeks are not unknown either). During these weeks the days are spent with very similar activities, guests eat with the same people day-by-day. This gives the opportunity to talk and to socialize. Many ill and especially older people are looking for understanding and sympathy, which they may not have from healthy people, but can expect it from people in a similar situation. In countries, where medical trips are at least partially financed by the state health insurance, an unknown, but supposedly significant percent of the trips are motivated by looking for company.

Obsession with the self and celebrity

As concepts of community become increasingly blurred and diminished, obsession with the self is reaching an all-time high thanks to new media, technology and consumer-orientated services. This is often played out in terms of fixations on body image, clothing, consumerism and a growing fascination with celebrity and its supposed set of ideal existence characteristics. At one end of the spectrum lies an engagement with the outer self – 'the physical body', and at the other, a search for the inner self, or spirit. However, the route to creating individual identities is often based on a superficial obsession with celebrity figures who appear to embody the characteristics that we are aspiring to.

Harrison (2006) describes how around one third of Americans are suffering from 'celebrity-worship syndrome' or CWS. Social psychologists seem to think that people alleviate boredom through celebrity obsession, as well as searching for identity. Fantasy relationships can seem easier than real ones in a world where fragmentation of society and communities is becoming more common. Fame appears to be like a new religion and celebrities are our Gods! Series like Big Brother tranform unknown people into stardom, a dream for many people leading humdrum, ordinary or poverty-stricken lives. Although celebrity worship can be harmless escapism, it can also lead to fanaticism and unhealthy self-image (e.g. inducing anorexia, promoting the need for cosmetic surgery). Identity construction of stars is mesmerizing but also fickle (e.g. Madonna's transformation from Virgin to Vamp to Earth Mother to Yogic Guru to Kabbalah Spiritualist).

The desire to downsize: Voluntary simplicity

Employment stability is a thing of the past these days and it is not uncommon for people to be suddenly made redundant and take time to find a new job. Sometimes, substantial financial compensation means that the individual concerned has the money to re-think what he or she would like to do in the future with regards to a career. In other cases, consequent financial hardship means a radical downsizing in terms of expenditure and lifestyle. However, in some cases, the voluntary desire to downsize comes from a need to escape from the 'rat race' of constant working, long hours, excessive stress and too much focus on material living. It is clear that many inhabitants in Western cultures are not overly happy with the environment that they have been complicit in creating. Ironically, opulent, self-indulgent lifestyles overwhelmed by choice and opportunities are the very thing driving many citizens towards simpler lives. The Trends Research Institute, a think-tank of educators and specialists that predict social trends, estimates that by the end of the decade, 15% of American adults will be living 'the simple life', the main reason being that they want to improve the quality of their life (Humphreys, 2007).

The tendency of the over 30s to simplify their lives has led to the increased use of labels such as 'downsizers', 'downshifters', and 'simple livers'. Such people voluntarily give up stressful, high-paying jobs in favour of other kinds of 'luxuries' – a job that helps others, for example, or free time to enjoy hobbies, family and friends. Some people simply opt for a less stressful, time-consuming job and subsequently spend less, whereas others change location completely and purchase a smaller home in a more natural, calmer environment. In some cases, people may decide to follow their dream of running a small retreat or yoga centre. Many of the holistic practitioners running retreat centres questioned by Kelly & Smith (2008) were motivated by the desire to simplify their lives.

Other ways of simplifying life may be to de-clutter. There are now many Life-coaching and Lifestyle 'gurus' who advocate clearing out any unwanted material possessions. Happiness surveys have consistently shown that the collection of material possessions does not lead to happiness, in fact, quite the reverse. However, there is much emotional baggage around the retention of objects, especially those which represent our past. As older people move to smaller homes, they may face the agony of having to dispose of possessions simply due to lack of space. In some cultures (e.g. Asia) lack of living space may be a constant feature of life therefore a more minimalist approach to possessions is common. In fact, the terms 'feng shui' or 'zen' are frequently used in the context of de-cluttering as it is thought that dealing with physical clutter can help to make way for a better emotional and spiritual life. By de-cluttering your home, you push away bad energy and make space for new energy to enter. Wellness gurus suggest that much unwanted time, energy and emotion is wasted on excessive material goods, especially clothes. Therefore anything we own, possess, or do that does not enhance our lives on a regular basis should go. De-cluttering is now even described as a 'therapy' where help is required to decided which clothes, books, papers, furniture, etc. to throw away. Even in tourism this is an important feature for those trying to travel light, avoid an airline's excess charges or waiting for baggage reclaim! More interestingly, de-clutter workshops are becoming more and more mainstream and are starting to feature in holistic retreat programmes.

Towards a new spirituality

The role of religion in health and wellness is quite significant, as many of the rituals and traditions to do with bathing were a way of purifying the body and washing away sins. Ancient cultures also believed that spirits lived in certain springs and mineral waters and were responsible for healing sickness. Religion can dictate certain aspects of diet and other lifestyle factors, such as the daily routine. Many monks and nuns practise regular meditation (or prayer), fasting, and tend to rise and go to bed early. However, many Western capitalist societies have moved towards increasing secularization, its citizens either disillusioned with, or alienated from the faith that they were brought up with. At the same time, mass immigration has led to the embracing of multi-faith communities and their cultures, highlighting even further the gap between traditional and (post)modern societies. Coupled with this parallel and somewhat contradictory phenomenon, is the notion of religious 'fundamentalism', which has, in recent times, pervaded the lives of Western societies. Mutual misunderstandings abound in the aftermath of global terrorism, with religion often being cited as the root cause of international crises and Western fear. Relationships between religion and spirituality are notoriously difficult to define. The latter, however, appears to have gained strength in recent times (albeit in new and sometimes unconventional formats) at the expense of the former. For example, new explorations of the relationship between Western psychology and Eastern spiritualism are gaining increased interest among researchers and practitioners (e.g. Kowalski 2001). Blurred boundaries between faith, religion, psychology and spirituality continue to be dynamically re-negotiated in contemporary Western society.

Fosarelli (2002:207) describes how 'In addition to taking better care of their bodies, many people are searching for new ways to make themselves healthier by paying more attention to their emotional and spiritual lives'. Many people aspire towards finding their spiritual centre within another society and culture through travel. As stated by Coelho (in Arias, 2001:20) 'More spiritual adventurers exist today than most people think'. Many of these are using tourism as a means of visiting locations which are viewed as more spiritual than home (India and Thailand being good examples). In such locations, spiritual activities such as yoga, massage or meditation may be an integral part of everyday life, and many tourists want to learn how to change their whole philosophy of or approach to life. Brown (1998) explores the various engagements that a so-called 'spiritual tourist' may be involved in (e.g. visiting retreats, ashrams, gurus). Although there has been concern about the exploitative nature of spiritual tourism with its sometimes fake or charlatan gurus, the majority of tourists appear to find what they are looking for, and many find themselves staying longer than they intended to or returning periodically throughout their lives.

Case Study: Ashram Tourism

The Osho Commune International in Pune, India is a well-known ashram. Osho was an inspirational (sometimes controversial) guru who died in 1990 but left the legacy of his ashram as well as many publications. Up to 200,000 visitors from every religion come to visit the ashram every year and take part in the meditation programmes, other courses and everyday life in the Commune. The average age of visitors is 35–45 years old and 34% have University degrees. 40% of these visitors are Indian, but visitors from over 100 countries can be found visiting at any one time, either for a short visit or for many months. The religious backgrounds of Osho's disciples are as follows: 20% are Jewish, 40% are Christian, about 30% Hindu, 5% Shinto/Buddhist, and 5% from other religious beliefs (Indiatravelite, 2007). In accordance with Osho's wishes participants in the Osho Commune International wear maroon most of the time and for evening meditation they wear white. They have to take AIDS tests before entering the commune, which has unsurprisingly created speculation about the nature of activities within the centre!

As well as meditation auditoria, the facilities at the ashram include beautiful landscaped zen gardens, a large swimming lagoon, and a sports facility. The Commune also runs an organic farming project. The ashram attracts many artists and musicians who provide cultural performances. Many meditations take place every day starting at sunrise, and other courses includes western therapy approaches, healing arts, esoteric sciences, creative arts, martial arts, tantra, zen, and sufism. One unique therapy designed by Osho is the Mystic Rose, a 3-week course, in which the participant laughs for 3 hours a day the first week, cries for the same period the next week and sinks into silence the third week.

The Commune has sometimes been referred to as a 'Spiritual Disney Land' with Osho described as 'a guru of hedonism' or 'an impressario of spiritual Mardi Gras'. Osho was frequently criticized for his materialistic practices (saying that material poverty was not a spiritual value) for example, acquiring 93 Rolls-Royces, and was also accused of sex scandals (he attracted thousands of followers in the 1970's and 1980's with talk about sex as a path to super-consciousness). He and his followers set up a commune in Oregon before he was arrested and deported for immigration violations in 1985. Soon after, he returned to India and founded the still-flourishing Pune commune. Despite the controversies his legacy lives on and there are still thousands of people who are subscribing to his philosophy of life, visiting his ashram, and reading his numerous publications with translations published in 55 languages.

(Pune Commune, 2008; Osho, 2008)

New media and technology

The amount of time that the majority of individuals spend watching television, surfing the net or playing computer games has increased exponentially in recent years. Florida (2002) gives a case study of a 26 year old man who re-named himself 'DotComGuy' in January 2000. He moved into a suburban house and lived from goods and services only purchased on the Internet for a whole year! Groceries or fast food were delivered; for entertainment he surfed the net or watched TV; to socialize he went into chat rooms & even dated online. He was seen as so innovative and commercially popular that corporate sponsors paid for all his needs in exchange for publicity through his website. His choice was variously praised or condemned, as he was described as 'A house-bound king of infinite cyberspace' as well as a 'Poster Child for Internet Idiocy'. However, his experiment proved that it is possible to live a virtual life for an indefinite period of time with little more than new technology for company. Although most people do not aspire to a life lived through a modem, many are unable to tear themselves away from their addiction to media, technology and communications. Television watching is one of the few leisure activities that continues to increase. Most people cannot easily be parted from their laptop or mobile phone, even on holiday.

Sociological researchers suggest that many people in postmodern societies are unable to differentiate fact from fiction or reality from fantasy. Heritage sites, museums, arts venues and other tourist attractions have to compete for peoples' leisure time and the increasing demand for interactive, high tech experiences. The development of whole simulated worlds in hotels or theme parks in destinations like Las Vegas or Dubai are becoming more and more popular. Even wellness facilities are starting to be themed (regardless of their location) creating North African or Turkish-style steam baths, Scandinavian saunas, Japanese onsens, or Buddhist meditation zones. As a result, the visitor could technically be anywhere in the world, as long as escapism, entertainment or excitement is guaranteed.

Fitness and sports

Statistics have started to reveal that worldwide obesity is at an all-time high with up to a quarter of the population in countries like the United States and Britain being obese. Excess body weight is pandemic therefore there is a need not only to advocate good diet but also to encourage fitness and sports. In most Western societies life expectancy is increasing, therefore there are growing numbers of older people who want and should be encouraged to remain fit and healthy. However, awareness of the close relationship between exercise and a healthy lifestyle needs to be integrated into the education of young children if it is to succeed in later life.

In their survey of the Top Ten Fitness Trends for 2007, the American College of Sports Medicine (2007) named the following:

Top Ten Fitness Trends for 2007

1. *Children and Obesity*: Programme development to reduce obesity among children was the number-one trend identified in the survey. Health and fitness professionals predict schools are unlikely to increase time devoted to physical education or nutrition education, and providing physical activity for kids may fall in the hands of the health/fitness industry along with fitness professionals.
2. *Special Fitness Programmes for Older Adults*: Fitness clubs and retirement communities stand to benefit from health and fitness programmes that cater to the older adult. The number-two prediction notes the baby boom generation is growing older and living longer, and their physicians are recommending they remain active.

3. *Educated and Experienced Fitness Professionals*: Fully accredited education and certification programmes for health/fitness professionals are on the rise. The importance of obtaining certification through academic accreditation is highly recognized by the fitness industry.

4. *Functional Fitness*: Functional fitness training, using strength training to improve performance for activities of daily living, will become more prominent in 2007. Exercises that mimic actual job tasks or other activities will help improve balance, coordination, strength, and endurance.

5. *Core Training*: A greater emphasis on and understanding of core training will occur, focused on forming the foundation for training the upper and lower extremities, including sport skill development. Core exercises, which strengthen, condition, and stabilize the abdominal and back muscles, often use props such as stability balls, BOSU balance balls, wobble boards, and foam rollers to provide support for the spine.

6. *Strength Training*: The health benefits of incorporating strength training into a fitness regimen will receive continued emphasis. Women and older adults are credited with keeping this long-lasting trend popular.

7. *Personal Training*: Personal trainers will continue to gain recognition and credibility among other health care professionals for higher professional standards and accreditation. Also, now more than ever, the personal trainer is more accessible to potential clients.

8. *Mind/Body Exercise*: Variations of yoga, Pilates, Tai Chi and other mind/body exercises will be introduced and remain popular next year. Research supports that the mind benefits from these programmes as much as the physical improvements in muscular strength, aerobic capacity, flexibility and balance.

9. *Exercise and Weight Loss*: Weight-loss programs will include an exercise component. Most diet programmes already incorporate some exercise/physical activity recommendations, but professionals expect more visibility to be placed on energy balance in the weight-loss equation.

10. *Outcome Measurements*: Defining and tracking outcomes of a fitness programmes will have a higher profile in the future. Professionals expect advances in technology to help determine success in disease management or changes in negative lifestyle behaviours.

It is clear from these trends that there is a growing awareness of the connection between fitness, sports, lifestyle, quality of life and wellness. This includes the mental and emotional balance that can come from more spiritual activities such as yoga and Pilates or the need to follow certain exercise and diet programmes to boost health. However, the survey only targeted fitness and sports practitioners and did not address the issue of participation. Many nations are actually becoming less active rather than more so. Britain is a good example, where it is predicted that half the population do no sport or active recreation at all (BBC News Online, 2006). However, Finland has turned itself around from being one of the world's unhealthiest nations to one of the fittest with an emphasis on outdoor pursuits like Nordic walking, cycling, cross-country skiing (Guardian Unlimited, 2005). Many people in Western countries have decreasing leisure time as a result of long working hours and use their lack of time or energy as an excuse for not exercising. Slumping in front of the TV with a takeaway meal after a long day in the office can seem far more appealing! However, public education campaigns are starting to suggest ways in which fitness can be integrated into everyday life (e.g. walking to work, using stairs instead of lifts, taking a short walk in the lunch break). Fitness and sport programmes are also a very common feature in wellness hotels, resorts and destinations.

Time-poor, cash-rich Élites

More and more people are 'cash-rich' and 'time-poor' in Western societies today. Working hours have increased in many countries to the extent that our leisure time seems greatly diminished. Most statistics reveal that working mothers have the least time for themselves and leisure activities. However, research by the Future Foundation in the United Kingdom (2007) has shown that women participate, on average, in ten different leisure pursuits a year, compared to around six 20 years ago. They therefore suggest that our determination to fit in yoga, paragliding, hiking and wine-tasting classes etc., on top of our jobs, might be stoking our belief that we have less free time nowadays.

Interestingly, although watching television and surfing the net are the main pastimes for many people, the Foundation's research also shows a growing desire for self-improvement: around half of British adults believe that free time should be spent on worthy pastimes, such as visiting art galleries, rather than on frivolous activities. 'Personal fulfilment' was the top priority for 50% of British adults, compared with 25% in 1983.

> *There's this emerging idea of ourselves as projects — we are no longer labelled by our education or gender, or born into a social situation that we then play out for the rest of our lives. We can do new things, pick up new skills, learn a new language. Because we're living longer, we have more time to think about who we really want to be. We are all asking ourselves, 'How can I get more out of my life?'*

This has important implications for the wellness industry and might explain why there are growing numbers of people, who are willing to spend their hard-earned cash on the pursuit of self-development, even on holiday. People may have less time to travel for leisure purposes, but they want to ensure that their trips create a memorable experience which they can savour for a long time. In many cases, there will be more trips but of a shorter duration (e.g. long weekends). In particular, women have more and more spending power. For example, Marks & Spencers (2007) shows how the 'Bridget Jones Generation's' spending power has increased by as much as 50% in the last 20 years with an increase in women working full-time and earning 75% of what men earn. Table 4.1 compares expenditure on leisure, travel and other activities.

Table 4.1   Changes in Womens' Spending Patterns.

Twenty years ago money was spent on...	Today money is spent on...
• One holiday a year to close destinations, for example Europe	• Several holidays a year, including long-haul destinations
• Eating out infrequently, typically in pubs	• Meals out in restaurants (on average once a week)
• Basic food for home cooking	• Luxury ready meals
• Bottles of sweet European wine, for example Liebfraumilch, or spirits and cocktails	• Dry 'new world' wines, beer and alcopops
• Shared use of a 'family' car	• Own car
• Mass-market chocolate once or twice a week	• Chocolate more often, and luxury or premium brands
• Quick-fix slimming food	• Diet products and gym memberships
• Share of partner's financial services	• Own financial products
• Basic clothes and toys for child she has in her late-20s	• Designer clothes and latest toys for child she has in her early to mid 30s
	• 'Me' items such as spa days, beauty treatments, jewellery, and perfume

(Marks & Spencers, 2007)

So-called 'lifestyle' purchases are clearly becoming more common, including fitness and wellness activities such as gyms, spas and beauty salons, and more travel to longer haul destinations. Grainger (2007) describes how many 'time-poor, cash-rich' women are booking themselves on 'therapy holidays' complete with life-coaches, nutritionists, psychologists and fitness instructors. Such holidays involve people getting away for a relatively long period of time (e.g. 3 weeks) and re-assessing their life using professional help. Such trips are expensive – as much as 6,000 pounds! (about 9600 EUROs) Grainger (2007) describes how:

> *A decade ago therapy holidays in five-star settings were rare. Alternative magazines and festivals advertised dozens of retreats offering courses in yoga, meditation, nutrition, art, dancing or self-improvement, but most were set in old, rambling country houses with shared rooms, basic vegetarian food and group tuition.*

Although such holidays still exist, there is a definite shift towards the luxury market. In 2006, according to Mintel, 205,000 British people went on a 'wellness holiday'. The biggest boom seems to have been at the top end of the market, where counsellors are flown around the world to cater for rich clients and provide therapies for the famous.

However, the article also questions the extent to which a holiday can have long-lasting effects on peoples' lives, suggesting they create a 'geographic fallacy' that by changing location people can change what they are unhappy about. There is also a debate about whether holidays should be pleasurable or painful (e.g. retreats which use extreme emotional counselling such as the Hoffmann Process are exhausting, even traumatic). People often need post-holiday counselling when they return just to deal with the impacts of their trip! Some holistic holiday companies such as Skyros advise people not to make any major decisions about their life until at least 2 months after their return, and Cortijo Romero aims to send people away stronger and more in control of their lives, rather than weaker and more vulnerable.

Fashion versus tradition

Visiting spas and using a variety of services can also be influenced by tradition or fashion. Countries, where evidence based medicine has been accepted for many years or the use of natural assets and traditions are deeply rooted in culture and society, may find the hype of wellness in Western countries a little surprising. Certainly, we cannot know all the possible treatments and traditions that were applied during history, therefore relabelling traditional services as 'new' can appeal to a lot of visitors.

In Western societies the term wellness is so often used that marketers may start to look for a new buzzword(s). Toiletries, shampoos, magazines even carwashes label themselves as wellness products and services. In TV or Internet draws, a wellness holiday, that is in a seaside spa resort seems to be an ultimate prize. Not only can those who have already come across the real term and its meaning but almost everybody can now develop some kind of association with the term wellness.

This media attention makes people curious and may choose a 'spa' or 'wellness' trip next, or stay in a spahotel instead of a 'normal' hotel. Less adventurous guests may book a treatment, participate in aquagym session 'for fun'. One can hope that these guests may taste the flavour of a healthier lifestyle and get more involved and active after arriving home.

Government policy

Governments approach travel and tourism very differently. Some support by funded schemes, for example the so called holiday vouchers fall under this approach. Companies, trade unions, associations and even NGOs can apply for state (co)funded schemes from which their employees or members can receive holiday vouchers. These vouchers can be redeemed during holidays (in hotels, restaurants, etc.). Among other beneficiaries, spas or spa hotels can also benefit from this funded spending. Furthermore, governments through the state and enterprises, through the private health insurance funds and companies can also finance health treatments and even trips. These could aim at prevention, healing or recuperation. Health treatments based on natural assets can be heavily subsidied, therefore, a whole trip can cost relatively little. This is one of the main problems medical destinations face: the guest mix is dominated by segments with low-spending capacities. This leaves very little room for raising funds for reconstruction or upgrading.

As prices can differ from country to country, operators in a cheaper country try to attract patients from other countries. This is the issue which the European Union faces. In its Eastern European member countries' health related services are much cheaper, but this does not necessarily mean that patients should then go to a cheaper country. Political and economic interests are competing with each other, since state health insurance funds do not tend to finance treatments in another country. It could have a negative effect on the home countries' health sector.

Conclusion

This chapter has shown that there are numerous tools that can be used to enhance wellness in everyday life as well as many factors that have contributed to the growing need for wellness activities. As societies become more sceptical about traditional forms of medicine and therapy, they are turning to alternative sources of wellness, such as popular psychology or self-help books. Although less leisure time appears to be available, spending power has increased and the time-poor, cash-rich are prepared to spend large amounts of money to enhance their well-being and quality of life. In some cases, this may lead to downsizing or voluntary simplicity. In others, it may mean the integration of more spiritual practices into everyday life. Some may crave a sense of community to alleviate feelings of isolation or alienation in society. Others may feed their obsession with

Table 4.2 External and Internal Factors Affecting the Growth of Health Tourism.

External Factors	Internal Factors
Fashion and tradition	
Obsession with self and celebrity	
Fitness and sport	
Medicine	Search for community
Therapy and healing	Desire for downsize
Psychology	Towards new spirituality
Nutrition	Time-poor, cash-rich Élites
Government policy	Curiosity

Source: Smith and Puczkó

celebrity and indulge in expensive beauty treatments, even surgery. More healthy trends have led to a growing awareness of the close links between diet, exercise and wellness. Travel experiences are an integral part of this process, especially in cases where people need to engage in intensive programmes and workshops to change their lives (e.g. psychological or spiritual retreats), to rest and relax (e.g. spas or thalassotherapy centres), or to deal with stress away from the workplace (e.g. occupational therapy, Life-coaching).

Summarizing the factors discussed we can conclude that these driving factors can be grouped. In one group we can find those that tend to represent external issues and factors, while the other shows internal factors (Table 4.2).

Typologies of health and wellness tourism

Travel is more than the seeing of sights; it is a change that goes on, deep and permanent, in the ideas of living.

(Beard, 1901)

This chapter focuses on the different types of health and wellness tourism that have been developed in recent years. A spectrum of wellness destinations and attractions shows the broad range of products, services, and activities available. These range from those which focus on physical or medical healing, to those which have a psychological or spiritual dimension. Even within some of the diverse typologies of wellness tourism, there are many sub-sectors (e.g. within spa tourism). For the purposes of management and marketing, which are discussed in more depth in the second part of this book, it is important to make a distinction between products and motivations of tourists. In the past, wellness was used quite uniformly as a label for all forms of health-orientated services. This is no longer sufficient as demand for a diversity of services is growing and customers are becoming more discerning. The tourism offer needs to respond to the more sophisticated demands of tourists and to aim for an even clearer distinction between the products used and the labels used to market them.

A spectrum of health tourism

Table 5.1 uses some of the dimensions of wellness discussed so far in the book, but this time the connection to tourism is made more explicit.

Table 5.1 A Spectrum of Health Tourism.

Physical Healing	Beauty Treatments	Relaxation/ Rest	Leisure/ Entertainment	Life/Work Balance	Psychological	Spiritual
Medical spas/baths	Cosmetic surgery trips	Pampering spas/baths	Spa resorts with 'fun waters'	Holistic centres	Holistic centres	Meditation retreats
Mofetta	Hotel/day spas	Wellness hotels	Sport/fitness holidays	Occupational wellness workshops	Workshops (e.g. Hoffmann, psycho-drama)	Yoga centres
Surgery trips		Thalassotherapy centres				Pilgrimages
Rehabilitation retreats						

The holidays which take place within these environments would in some cases, be radically different from one another. There is little connection between a spa which deals specifically with physical or medical problems using water treatments and a spiritual retreat which focuses on meditation for the mind and soul. Depending on motivation, life-stage, and interests, tourists will select the form of wellness required, and this could be purely physical with a focus on sports and fitness; medical with a focus on the treatment of disease or surgery; mental or psychological with a focus on life-coaching or mind-control; relaxing and pampering in a luxury spa; entertaining and recreational in a purpose-built water park; or meditational and spiritual in a retreat.

It was, however, argued earlier in the book that wellness should focus on the balance of body, mind, *and* spirit if optimum health is to be gained. Kelly and Smith (2008) suggest that it is unlikely that the majority of visitors would be attracted by all domains of wellness simultaneously. Nevertheless, they argue that only holistic retreat centres attempt to provide visitors with the whole spectrum of wellness activities (except perhaps medical treatments). The concept of holistic tourism suggests wholeness and integration, implying that all of the dimensions of wellness could or should be included in the product. Unfortunately, one of the main barriers to optimum wellness, both in terms of lifestyle and holidays, is lack of time and money. Ironically, staying well is time-consuming and expensive, and the majority of people often cannot afford this luxury. It is also important to recognize which aspects of the self need attention at different stages of one's life. There are times when the physical body may need more attention (e.g. during illness or recuperation), but at other times, the mind (e.g. during times of occupational stress). Spirituality can help us to transcend both physical and psychological problems, but it is arguably the hardest aspect to cultivate, especially in secular societies. For this reason, the tourism industry is increasingly recognizing the need for segmentation *within* the wellness market (discussed in more detail in the following chapter), and a clear differentiation of products is needed.

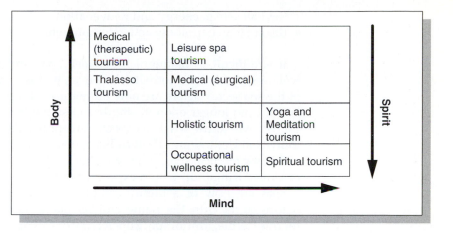

Figure 5.1
The Body-Mind-Spirit
Spectrum in Health Tourism.
Source: Smith and Puczkó.

It is interesting to consider that guests can use services in a direct or an indirect way. Direct would mean that they intentionally participate in an activity or looking for treatment, whereas an indirect way would be when they are 'just' sitting in thermal water, enjoy climate, or participating in Tai Chi for the first time ever. This differentiation can lead us to think that the spectrum of demand and supply in health tourism can range from 'soft-core' to 'hardcore', where softcore would mainly refer to spontaneous and hardcore to intentional decisions. It is not unknown that guests from both ends of the spectrum can be in the same place at the same time (Figure 5.1). This can leave management with serious problems (we will discuss these issues in Chapter Nine).

Spa tourism

> Tourism which focuses on the relaxation or healing of the body using mainly water-based treatments; such as, mineral or thermal pools, steam rooms; and saunas. Emphasis tends to be focused on curing, rehabilitating, or resting the body.

Spa tourism is arguably the best known form of wellness tourism and is sometimes treated as being synonymous with wellness tourism. ISPA (2007) defines spas as 'places devoted to enhancing overall well-being through a variety of professional services that encourage the renewal of mind, body and spirit'. ISPA also defines the key elements of the spa experience:

- Relax (e.g. stress management)
- Reflect (e.g. meditation)

- Revitalize (e.g. energy and rejuvenation)
- Rejoice (e.g. happiness and entertainment)

It is difficult to distinguish between spas and more general forms of wellness (e.g. holistic retreats); however, it also shows clearly the diversity of the spa sector. There are now numerous sub-sectors within spa tourism and it is no longer enough simply to use the label 'spa' and assume that tourists will know what to expect. Perceptions differ greatly, for example, tourists in Central and Eastern Europe are very familiar with the concept of historic medical spas, whereas other visitors (e.g. from the United States or United Kingdom) would expect something similar to a beauty salon.

Spas are now of a highly complex and diverse nature. This diverse nature starts with the name and its likely meanings. Bath, bano, bad, therme/terme, grotto, spa, kúpele, fürdő – all mean a thermal water-based spa, in various languages. The translation of the name from the original language often uses the term 'spa', but these establishments are not really always spas. Furthermore, their complexity lies in the fact that almost any service provider with some kind of health-oriented services can and does call itself a spa. Spas may differ widely in terms of what they offer, that is their services or treatment supply, however, they have one thing in common, which is the aspiration to improve health and well-being. Most spas have some form of water-based treatments; however there is a difference between mineral, thermal, and healing waters:

- *Mineral waters*: it has at least the set amount of dissolved mineral content which is minimum 500 mg/l or 1000 mg/l
- *Thermal waters*: natural waters that are at least 30°C or 32°C at source (this can vary country by country)
- *Healing waters*: the healing effects have to be proven, that is evidence-based

The International Spa Association (ISPA, 2007) has defined the 'ten domains of SPA' or segments of the industry as:

1. 'The Waters'
2. Food, nourishment, diet, and nutrition
3. Movement, exercise, and fitness
4. Touch, massage, and bodywork
5. Mind/body/spirit
6. Aesthetics, skin care, natural beauty agents
7. Physical space, climatology, global ecology
8. Social/cultural arts and values, spa culture
9. Management, marketing, and operations
10. Time, Rhythm, and Cycles

Not every spa contains every domain. The rejuvenation of the spa concept has generated several attempts to categorize spas. Since the modern concept of spas was established in the United States, one of the most comprehensive categorizations comes from the International Spa Association (ISPA, 2007 and the Spafinder Magazine, 2007):

- *Club spa* – is a facility offering primarily fitness services as well as a few other services rendered to daily users normally by spas in the broader sense;
- *Day spa* – is a facility offering beauty, fitness, and wellness programs without accommodation; and the duration of services varies between an hour and a full day;
- *Spa hotel* – a spa offering hotel accommodation and normally several days of all inclusive programs designed to ensure physical, spiritual, and mental balance;
- *Holistic spa* – a spa that offers alternative therapy and diet (for instance, vegetarian, or macrobiotic cuisine) in an effort to make positive adjustments to the mindset of guests;
- *Medical spa* – is a facility that offers traditional and complementary therapeutic and health protection treatment as well as other spa services and may also include health institutions;
- *Bath* – a spa constructed to utilize natural mineral, medicinal, or sea water located on site by offering hydrotherapy to guests;
- *Resort spa* – a resort in a remote location of beautiful natural setting normally detached from civilization, offering a wide array of wellness services and programs in an all inclusive arrangement to guests;
- *Sport spa* – an establishment offering spa services and special sports programs (the latter could range from golf through skiing and angling to training for running the Marathon);
- *Structured spa* – an establishment operating by strict rules, which offers guests the chance to attain a specific objective (e.g. weight loss).

ISPA represents the North American approach to spas. Based on their estimations the largest spa category (in North America) is the day spa (with some 13,300 spas). However, in Europe the same name 'spa' has a very different meaning. As the European Spa Association (ESPA, 2007) declares:

> *The European Spa Association's objective is to promote spas and balneology in Europe and to take care that the natural remedies based on mineral water, landscape and climate will be available to as great a number of citizens and visitors as possible.*

This objective is very much based on natural healing assets, especially healing waters while the North American definition lays its roots in health in a much wider context. Having more than 1,200 spas and health resorts in Europe (estimated by ESPA, 2006), many of which are medically respected health centres; these spas do have a somewhat narrower orientation, that is to provide physical healing to visitors who are often called patients. For example, historical medical spas in Central and Eastern Europe have a medical practitioner who oversees the care given to guests and tourists, many of whom visit based on a prescription from their doctor, and whose trip may then be funded by holiday vouchers.

Many European spas have natural, medical waters which are used for treating certain conditions such as locomotion or circulatory disorders. According to ESPA (2006) the following resources can qualify as curative assets:

- Springs with medicinal water for therapeutic use
- Healing gases
- Spas, spa facilities, and health resorts at the seaside
- Peloids in spas, health resorts, and spa facilities
- Bioclimatic/healing climate
- Kneipp therapy

Increasingly, purpose-built destination spas are becoming more popular in Europe as they are in the United States and elsewhere. These are mainly recreational or leisure-orientated and may combine water-based treatments with fitness and nutritional programmes, even including occupational wellness workshops. There is a new trend, especially in Central and South America, of adventure spas that are located in remote and tranquil locations and base their services on outdoor and adventurous activities as well as 'standard' wellness treatments and pools.

Case Study: Bad Blumau

Rogner Bad Blumau in Austria is an example of a purpose-built destination spa that offers a whole range of wellness activities and a very high-quality product and tourist experience. The unique design by the famous Austrian architect Hundertwasser gives the spa as fairy-tale appearance. It comprises of hot springs, hot indoor and outdoor pools, jacuzzis, saunas, and steam rooms, a range of massage types and beauty treatments. There are also medical and nutritional consultations on request, as well as a whole range of fitness activities. These include Nordic walking, spinning and skating, but also more holistic activities such as Tai Chi, Yoga, the 5 Tibetans and the 8 Treasures.

The hotel has conference and banqueting facilities where delegates are offered non-alcoholic conference drinks and an energy break with freshly squeezed fruit and vegetable juices. Merging into the realm of the business tourism sector, the spa offers seminar days on issues such as stress management, for example, and active regeneration breaks involving activities such as Qi Gong, drum massage, active brain balance, and individual relaxation units. This suggests that despite their ostensible focus on the body, this and other spas are sometimes aspiring to gradually become more than just centres for physical wellness. Indeed, many spas have high-quality accommodation attached (often in the form of hotel-spas or spa-hotels) and this allows for a different clientele catchment than that of the health tourism sector alone. Corporate clients are increasingly turning to coaching, stress reduction for employees, and other courses as away-day options. In addition, business and conference tourists may be more likely to choose hotels with spas, if their partners are accompanying them. This then raises the question of the primary motivations of the visitor/visitor group, where the focus on the body or indeed holistic well-being may be a secondary activity in some instances.

(Bad Blumau, 2007)

Leisure and recreational tourism

Of the many different spa types, although leisure (spa) tourism, by definition is not really part of health tourism, it should be briefly discussed. Although one can argue that leisure spas (e.g. fun waters, or even aqua parks) have a very distant relationship to health tourism, these facilities are forming an integral part of the supply. Leisure spas usually provide attractions and services to the whole family. The separated sections target kids with slides, baby pools and other fun elements, and parents with silent rest areas and pools, sauna park, and treatment sections. Most of the time, families with kids are not welcome in any health operation, since kids are not allowed to use the facilities, and families cannot necessarily pay the high entrance prices of luxury spas or spa hotels. This can leave a large segment out from health tourism. Leisure facilities in spas therefore often mix leisure guests from the local area as well as tourists, who can visit the spa especially. For example the H2O child oriented spa and hotel in Austria was built by the junction of the main motorway, in close proximity to three major medical and wellness destinations, in which kids are not allowed. With this development the region has become more competitive since it can give more to more segments. The Tropical Islands (near Berlin, Germany) wanted to create a stand-alone attraction with imitating a Tropical environment with pools, rainforest, beachfront, and Thai and Indonesian architecture, under the roof of a former air balloon (Zeppelin) hangar.

Leisure spas are typical representatives of themed attractions, since the major pool area is always following an Asian, Polynesian, or Mediterranean theme, for example. Kids love the pirate boat and parents also enjoy the exotic fauna and architecture. Leisure spas are like wellness supermarkets, except medical treatments they can provide something for the whole family.

Thalasso tourism

> Tourism that provides attractions by and services based on the sea. Water, algae, and salt are all used in the products.

In 16th century France King Henry III was advised by his doctor to take seawater treatments, and in 1750 the Englishman Richard Russell published his 'Dissertation on the Use of Sea Water in Affections of the Glands', thanks to whose success he was appointed physician to the royal household. After this time, seawater cures became widely accepted as being beneficial, and Thalassotherapy was founded in France in the late 1950s by Louison Bobet, a very popular champion who won the Tour de France several times. Today, there are around 70 Thalasso Centres along the French coast, mostly but not only on the Atlantic. Thalassotherapy can technically be found anywhere where there is a seacoast, but the most popular destinations seem to be France, Spain, Ireland, and increasingly North Africa and the Middle East (e.g. Dead Sea resorts).

Thalassotherapy comes from the Greek word for 'sea', and refers to a variety of treatments that use seawater and seaweed to revitalize the body and skin, to tone, moisturize, and improve circulation. Algae, mud, sea salt, and sand are also used in various treatments such as wraps and exfoliation scrubs. It is thought that seawater contains more than 80 basic elements in the same proportions that our cells need in order to remain balanced and whole, making it a highly beneficial medicine for supplying the body with essential minerals. It can be ionized with negative ions and then inhaled or sprayed. Thalassotherapy centres offer various packages, including underwater showers, mud baths, massage, seaweed, mud and algae wraps. Different forms of thalassotherapy have different effects, helping visitors to relax, including improving sleep quality; muscles can be toned; skin can be cleansed, toned, and moisturized; cellulite can be minimized. In addition, there are medical benefits, such as boosting the immune system, helping with circulatory problems, respiratory conditions, post-traumatic disorders, or chronic inflammations.

Talaso Pontiente (2007), a Thalassotherapy Centre in Gijon in Spain, describes a typical day in their centre:

> *Your day begins with a walk along the beach followed by your first seawater and seaweed baths. Then comes a session in either the dry sauna or the steam bath, after which you do some light exercise and receive a beauty treatment. A break for lunch in one of our various restaurants, which serve dishes to suit every taste, is the only interruption in the day's health programme. This is followed by time in the rest area before returning for a seawater bath to stimulate our body. The next and final stage is a session of sand therapy and massage which combine to produce the desired effect: our muscles are strengthened, the different organs in our body are stimulated, and we come out feeling toned up and full of energy.*

Definition and Criteria for Thalassotherapy Drafted by the European Spas Association

The ESPA drafted eight criteria to provide a uniform European definition of the term thalassotherapy in order to guarantee high-quality standards and to establish the term as a brand name. According to the ESPA's understanding thalassotherapy covers a wide spectrum, ranging from medical treatments to components of wellness programs. The term thalassotherapy can be used only if the following definitions and prerequisites are met and the following measures are offered or taken:

1. *Definition*: *Thalassotherapy* is an integrated plan for therapy, prevention, and health promotion. The plan shall be implemented for defined indications under medical care and with the participation of qualified expert staff.

2. *Therapeutic location immediately by the sea*: Thalassotherapy shall be carried out in places where the maritime climate has an immediate effect.

3. *Seawater*: The sea shall be used for bathing in natural waters. Suitable seawater, that is drawn locally shall be used for inhaling and/or bathing, for example in a bathtub or a swimming pool.

4. *Marine products*: It is possible to use mud or algae etc. for different applications.

5. *Low-allergen and clean sea air*: The quality of the air must warrant that extended stays in the open air will represent a relieving factor.

6. *Heliotherapy*: Natural solar radiation shall primarily be used for heliotherapy. In adverse weather conditions artificial UV irradiation may supplement heliotherapy.

7. *Exposure to the climate and motion therapy*: Exposure to the climate and motion therapy shall be carried out in fixed regimens in the zone close to the shoreline.

8. *Associated health-promoting measures*: Associated health measures, emphasizing relaxation, change of nutrition, and physical exercise shall be carried out to improve overall physical fitness.

(Visit European Spas, 2008b)

Case Study: Accor Thalassa Hotels

The Accor Thalassa programmes can be found in four (Ibis, Mercure, Novotel, Sofitel) of the many hotel brands managed by Accor. The other specialization of Accor Thalassa is thermal spas (Harmony and Purity). In Vichy, Dax, Saint-Lary, or Aix-les-Bains, visitors can enjoy the thermal spas during 'Fitness' break packages, combining pleasure with efficacy, by making use of the benefits offered by such waters. The pre-packaged short breaks can follow two streams: discovery formula and intense formula.

Packaging Thalassotherapy – Health for the Body and Enjoyment for the Senses

Accor Group which based its services on the exceptional qualities of the marine environment, operates in 14 destinations (such as Biarritz, Le Touquet) and uses the following elements:

- *Seawater* – The density of salt, high content of minerals and abundance of trace elements make seawater a source of new energy for the constitution. The seawater is heated to between 31°C and 35°C at which temperature healing qualities of the seawater can easily be transferred to the body via the skin.
- *Marine mud* – This comes from the mud collected at low tide. Such mud offers therapeutic benefits as it is saturated in oxygen, mineral salts, trace elements, vitamins and clay, and is capable of retaining heat and conserving water.
- *Seaweed* – This is freshly collected and incorporated in the thalassotherapy process (e.g. baths, wraps, masks or poultices). Seaweed has a high concentration of minerals and vitamins essential for the major biological functions.

- *Air and climate* – Extremely pure and naturally charged with negative ions. The air conveys the beneficial substances of seawater in the form of aerosols. The effect of the climate may be bracing, relaxing or soothing (depending on the coast involved).
- *Destinations* – To enhance the beneficial effect of its treatments sites located in the most attractive regions of France (and the world). Every stay involves a refreshing change of scenery and new cultural experiences.

(Accor Thlassa, 2008)

Holistic tourism

Tourism that provides the visitor with a range of activities and/or treatments which are aimed at balancing the body-mind-spirit.

A holistic retreat may be defined as a purpose-built centre which accommodates its guests for the purpose of learning/improving body-mind-spirit activities (e.g. yoga, pilates) and perhaps receiving complementary therapies or treatments whilst there. Group programming of classes is the norm. A retreat will usually have no other type of tourism/visitor activity besides that of a holistic nature. Table 5.2 gives an example of a typical holistic retreat centre programme and the ways in which most of the domains of wellness are included.

Table 5.2   A typical Programme in a Holistic Retreat Centre.

Time	Activity	Wellness Domain(s)
6.30 a.m. to 8 a.m.	Yoga	Physical, mental, spiritual
8 a.m. to 9 a.m.	Breakfast and Demos (Community meeting)	Interaction, socializing communication
9 a.m. to 10 a.m.	Karma Yoga (e.g. doing tasks)	Altruism, community-building
10 a.m. to 11 a.m.	Co-listening	Interaction, communication
11 a.m. to 12.30 p.m.	Course 1 (e.g. dance, painting, creative writing, singing)	Self-expression, creativity, fun
12.30 p.m. to 2 p.m.	Lunch	Interaction, socializing
2 p.m. to 4 p.m.	Free time	Creating personal space, relaxation
4 p.m. to 5.30 p.m.	Course 2 (e.g. life-coaching, dream workshop, relationships)	Psychology, interaction, communication
5.30 p.m. to 7 p.m.	Dinner	Interaction, socializing, fun

(Kelly & Smith, 2008)

This fairly intensive programme almost represents a microcosm of everyday life, in which participants try to achieve a balance of activities as well as socializing and relaxing. Experience suggests that it can be exhausting to try to achieve this balance every day, and few can aspire to this! On the other hand, we can be strong in several domains in parallel, especially where there is a proven link between domains (e.g. physical exercise can improve mood and decrease depression).

A comprehensive collation of data on holistic tourism operators was undertaken as part of Smith and Kelly's (2006) research. Over 450 operators were identified using various search terms related to the sector. Many of these were located in the United Kingdom, Spain, Greece, and Turkey, but a growing number were identified all over the world (e.g. in Australasia and the Americas, as well as much of Europe). The average cost of a holistic holiday was £520 (about 800 EUROs) and the average capacity of a centre was 16. The following case studies contrast the highly organized retreat centres identified in Smith and Kelly's (2006) research and the more 'ad hoc' destinations where holistic activities take place.

Case Study: Skyros

The two Skyros Centres in Greece were set up in 1979. Visitors stay for 1 or 2 weeks at a time and undertake a number of self-selected courses and workshops that are designed to balance body, mind, and spirit. Participants can take a range of psychological, therapeutic, creative, communicative, or active courses, usually two per day for 5 days. Participants are also encouraged to engage in morning *Demos* – a community meeting led by a different participant each day, *Oekos* – an open group discussion/listening forum, co-listening with one other participant, and work groups based on different collective tasks, and evening and weekend social activities. The aim of this structure is to create strong bonds between the community members, and to encourage an atmosphere of support, trust, and openness. None of the activities is compulsory, however, and participants have the freedom to plan their own time.

Skyros attracts a wide range of people. The majority are professionals (e.g. teachers, lecturers, doctors, nurses, business, and media people). Approximately 70% of participants are in their thirties or forties. Many also have 'life issues' to resolve or may be on the brink of burn-out. Glouberman (2004) describes the intention of Skyros to create a world that heals and to create a healthy culture: 'This culture must be one that encourages us to come home to ourselves, to honour our true selves in relation to others, and to commit ourselves to the most universal values we can find'. Thus, the ethos behind Skyros is to create more than just a holiday, which explains why many participants claim to find it so life changing, and repeat visitation is more than 30%. Skyros 'aftercare' is excellent, including a letter to all participants, invitations to reunions and social events, and website chat rooms and notice boards.

(Skyros, 2008)

Case Study: Goa

Goa could be described as an 'ad hoc' holistic destination where there are few specific 'centres' (except for one or two well-established yoga centres such as 'Purple Valley'). It tends to attract more backpackers and spiritual tourists than stressed out executives, but these are increasingly starting to be attracted to the region, as are mass package tourists. Tourists can choose from a range of holistic activities such as yoga, meditation, massage, but these often take place in the practitioners' house or on the beach. Cost is low by tourist standards, but many of the courses are designed for long-stay visitors (e.g. gap-year back-packers or hippies who return annually). Courses are advertized unofficially on billboards, lampposts, or trees in public spaces (e.g. markets, beach bars, shops), although many practitioners now have websites. Apart from some Ayurvedic practices, there appears to be no regulation of these practices, and the Government Tourist Office in Goa expresses little formal interest in this sector. The majority of practitioners are neither permanent residents in Goa, nor Goans or even Indians. The majority (apart from Ayurvedic masseurs from Kerala) appear to be Western travellers who are often semi-permanent residents. Some of them are well-qualified instructors (e.g. British Wheel of Yoga accredited teachers), but many appear to be merely experimenting with a newfound personal interest. As a result, the tourist experience could not be said to be 'authentic' in terms of local cultural or wellness practices, but the experience nevertheless seems to be an enriching one for most visitors.

(Smith & Kelly, 2006)

Yoga and meditation tourism

Yoga and meditation could be said to be sub-sectors of holistic tourism but also of spiritual tourism. Iyengar (1989) once said that 'yoga is not a religion but is meant for individual growth and for physical, emotional, intellectual, and spiritual balance'. Yoga and meditation are practices, which are ideally integrated into everyday life, but many people first discover them as part of a holistic holiday. There are many different forms of yoga, but the most popular forms currently found in retreat centres are hatha yoga with an emphasis on asanas (physical postures), breathing and meditation, and ashtanga yoga, which is more dynamic and requires physical strength to move from posture to posture in a pre-set sequence of an hour and a half. The latter requires much more knowledge of yoga whereas hatha yoga is suitable for beginners. Other forms of yoga are increasingly becoming popular, especially with more expert practitioners, but it is more likely that yoga is hybridized or merged with other forms of activity, for example, Tai Chi, Pilates, or dance.

Yoga was initially very popular in the 1960s and 1970s in Western Europe when the hippie movement was at its peak and more spiritual practices, especially from India were embraced. In the 1980s and 1990s it seemed that an aerobic fitness craze took over, but in recent years, yoga has been increasing in popularity once again, not least because of celebrity endorsement, for example Madonna, Sting and Spice Girl Geri. As stated by Hardy (2002):

> Yoga has returned to the limelight, coinciding nicely with modern man's feeling of spiritual emptiness and physical exhaustion, arriving just in time to rescue us from darkness in our higher charkas and rigidity in our lower backs. The image of lumpy leotards and boiled cabbage community centre classes is gone, replaced by a lean new version. Yoga has been repackaged as a mental and physical survival kit for the new millennium.

It is sometimes difficult for many Westerners to grasp that yoga is not a fitness routine, but instead a spiritual practice which can lead to self-knowledge and create harmony with others and the world around us. It is also considered to be a form of meditation, indeed Raja Yoga is a form of yoga where there are no physical postures, only breathing and visualization techniques. Other popular forms of meditation include Buddhist meditation or Transcendental meditation, which are being increasingly sought by stressed out Westerners wanting to achieve peace and calm in their lives. However, it is sometimes difficult to distinguish between a holistic or spiritual retreat and a yoga holiday. According to Yoga Holidays (2007):

> A yoga holiday is primarily an activity holiday. The time devoted daily to yoga usually won't exceed four hours, in one, or possibly two daily classes, and you will have time for other activities or just to relax and chill out. The location should reflect this, with a beach or other notable attractions nearby. The atmosphere is often relaxed, and it is usually a great opportunity to meet other like-minded people. On a retreat, on the other hand, the yoga schedule is likely to be more intense, possibly including some meditation, times of silence, etc. The main focus is no longer to enjoy yourself on holiday, but to deepen your yoga practice. Again, the choice of location should reflect this, with a quiet, possibly remote location. Retreats should be fully residential, the food vegetarian, and meal times carefully thought out to fit smoothly within the daily yoga routine. You will find more 'hard core' yogis and yoginis on retreats, and the overall atmosphere can be quite serious, with much less 'free' time.

It is recommended that beginners or those who are not so serious about yoga should opt for a yoga holiday rather than a retreat. More dedicated aficionados tend to head for yoga centres like Rishikesh in India.

Case Study: Yoga in Rishikesh, India

Rishikesh lies at the foothills of the Himalayas along the banks of the river Ganges, the first town that the river reaches on its descent from the Himalayas. Rishikesh is home to many yoga centres and ashrams, such as Sivananda, Osho, Vivekenanda, and Bihar school of yoga. It is world famous as a place to study classical Indian yoga and has a spiritual atmosphere which attracts many western visitors. Although class instruction in India often tends to be less precise and directive than in western countries, it is expected that the students will not be beginners in yoga. Rishikesh is also a pilgrimage centre for Hindus and wandering sadhus (holy men). Many people come to bathe in the sacred waters of the Ganges, as Hindus believe this can remove layers of karma. There is live temple chanting and religious ceremonies, or pujas on the river, especially at night time. As a holy city, it is fully vegetarian.

Rishikesh hosts an International Yoga Festival, which is held every year in the first week of March. In addition to daily yoga sessions led by expert teachers, visitors to the festival can learn more about yoga through a programme of workshops, lectures, and live demonstrations. With 350 and more attendees from over 30 countries, it has grown to become one of the largest yoga events in the world.

To stay in some of the ashrams students need to commit to 15 days or more and attendance at the morning and evening yoga and meditation classes is compulsory. Some of the centres offer three intensive courses a year and each course is of about 3 weeks duration. Asana (postures), Pranayama (breathing techniques), and basic Yoga philosophy are taught. Besides these 3-week courses, there are short workshops and ongoing 'general-classes'. Below is a sample of a typical yoga day in Rishikesh organized by Damask Rose Tours (2008) as part of an 11-day programme:

06.30–07.30:	Introduction to Pawanmukta-I groups of asana.
07.30–08.30:	Breakfast.
08.30–10.30:	Lectures on introduction to Yogic principles.
10.30–11.00:	Tea break.
11.00–13.00:	Introduction to Yoga Nidra (psychic sleep or yogic sleep).
13.30–14.30:	Buffet lunch.
15.00–16.00:	Introduction to Antar Mauna (inner silence-meditation technique)
17.00–18.00:	Singing of devotional songs.
20.00–21.00:	Dinner, overnight stay at the hotel.

Whereas yoga works for some people, others need a different type of activity to clear or control their minds. It is possible to learn meditation on a holiday, but it is usually recommended that beginners spend several days learning the basic techniques. One rather extreme version of a meditation retreat (at least for many uninitiated Westerners) is a Vipassana silent meditation retreat offered in countries like India and Thailand.

Case Study: Vipassana (Silent) Meditation Retreats

Vipassana which means to see things as they really are is one of India's most ancient techniques of meditation. It is a process of self-observation in which the individual focuses on the natural breath to concentrate the mind, and the ensuing meditation encourages mental purification which allows one to face life's tensions and problems in a calm, balanced way. The practice develops clarity of seeing which allows grasping, judgement, and fear to fall away. One discovers and cultivates qualities such as compassion, equanimity, wisdom, joy, and moral integrity (Vipassana Meditation, 2007).

The technique of Vipassana Meditation is taught at 10-day residential courses during which participants learn the basics of the method, and practise sufficiently to experience its beneficial results. Men and women are usually separated. Total silence is required – no talking, no books, no television, no music, and no writing. Spirit Rock Meditation Center (2007) in Canada describes a typical retreat day:

> A typical daily schedule starts at 5am and ends at 10pm. The entire day is spent in silent meditation practice with alternating periods of sitting and walking meditation. Meals are vegetarian and are prepared with health and nutrition in mind. Lunch is the main meal of the day, and a light tea is served in the late afternoon. The combination of this regular schedule, group support, silence, and instruction provides a beneficial environment for developing and deepening meditation practice.

Various travellers' blogs describe the experience in different ways, with some visitors unable to stay for more than a few days because they found the silence and workings of their minds maddening, whereas others found the peace and serenity they were looking for. De Palma (2007) describes how extremely hard it was to meditate for the first few days, he wanted to leave after four, but by the end found peace and calm and took his new practice back into everyday life feeling more engaged with his life and the world.

Spiritual tourism

> Tourism that focuses on the spiritual quest of the individual is leading to transcendence or enlightenment. This may or may not have a religious affiliation, but it is often likely to include rituals, ceremonies, and traditions that are derived from different religions.

Spiritual tourism can be either religious or secular or may combine elements of both. It is always difficult to make a distinction between cultural tourism and religious tourism, as many visitors to religious buildings (e.g. temples, churches, mosques, synagogues) have non-religious motivations. The same is true of spiritual tourists who may be seekers on a quest for enlightenment, and for whom religious buildings offer a calm sanctuary in which they can feel meditative and transcend everyday life. Those spiritual tourists who are predominantly secular or disillusioned with organized religion may journey instead to spiritual landscapes (e.g. mountaintops, deserts, oceans). De Botton (2002) suggests that people like to connect with the universe and infinity through 'sublime' landscapes. Others may simply attend courses which can lead to spiritual enhancement (e.g. yoga, meditation, chanting).

Increasingly, non-religious tourists are going on pilgrimages. The pilgrimage market can attract specific religious tourists (e.g. Muslims to Mecca), but increasingly it attracts a more spiritual market (e.g. Santiago de Compostela). Pilgrimage tourism became popular during the Middle Ages, which were marked by journeys to holy or sacred places. The most common destinations of the period were Santiago de Compostela, Czestochowa, and Rome. Pilgrimage is a physical journey, which often symbolizes and reflects the life journey of the individual (Devereux & Carnegie, 2006).

Case Study of Spiritual Pilgrimage: Santiago de Compostela

Recent years have shown a rapid increase in those who choose to walk, or ride by cycle, or horse to Santiago de Compostela, a medieval pilgrimage route from central France to the northwest tip of Spain. In 1987, 2,905 pilgrims walked, cycled, or travelled by horse to Compostela. In 1997, this number had risen to 25,179. In 2003, this had nearly tripled to 74,614. Of this number, 36.4% were between 16 and 30 years of age. A total of 69.9% of all pilgrims saw the main motivation for their journey as being a spiritual one (Registro de la Oficina de Acogida de Peregrinos, 2004).

The road to Santiago is not an easy one. From Le Puy-en-Velay to Santiago de Compostela is just over 1000 miles. Walkers who start from St Jean de Pied de Port on the French side of the Pyrenees still have 500 miles to walk before they reach Santiago. Many accounts talk of the worry and the excitement of a physical challenge and the preparation for it. Early on, most pilgrims experienced times when they felt the journey would defeat them. But very soon, many individuals ceased to be concerned with strict schedules and began to come to terms with what they had taken on. This sense of relaxing into the journey and becoming separated from the spatial and psychological status quo to which Carrasco (1996) refers, brings with it a heightened experience of the present. New communities become formed on the route both with other pilgrims and with people who live on the route or offer support or hospitality.

It is the closely bonded community all with the same goal of reaching Santiago, all experiencing physical and emotional challenges and all separated in a timeless present that makes the Camino so special. It goes beyond just physical well-being, towards a personal well-being engendered by being part of a pilgrim community with common goals and common motivation. In some cases, the effect of the pilgrimage brings about real life changes. The pilgrimage experience often builds an inner confidence and understanding of self, which becomes more apparent *after* the pilgrimage. The journey and community aspects coalesce to enhance wellness but also contribute towards the fulfilment of self.

(Devereux & Carnegie, 2006)

There is also a close connection between bathing and spirituality, for example, bathing was traditionally seen as a way of purifying the body, washing away sins, and being baptized or initiated into a faith. Many cultures still view bathing in healing waters to be a sacred or spiritual act and some believe that water absorbs and accumulates the vibratory pattern of words, healing thoughts, and intentions:

- Native American spiritual healers chant rhythmically and shake rattles over water to enhance its healing properties.
- Mayan Shamans place their hands above water and repeat their traditional prayers nine times to enrich and consecrate the water in which their patients bathe.
- Roman Catholic priests make water holy by ritual blessings prayed over it, and making the sign of the cross above the vessel containing the water.
- Incan priests and priestesses prayed as they immersed their hands in water which flowed through channels and into their temples to build up spiritual energy for ceremonial and domestic purposes.
- Today, in the Caribbean, priests and priestesses vigorously crush fresh herbs into water and infuse it with the herbal and spiritual energy. They even chew the leaves and spit into the water adding their ashe or spiritual power to the mixture.

(New Orleans Mistic, 2008)

Occupational wellness

Occupational wellness (or health incentive), as defined by the National Wellness Institute (2007) in Chapter Two focuses on the satisfaction and enrichment that people receive through work. This includes attitudes to work, the workplace and colleagues, the sense of belonging, involvement and challenge, career ambitions, and personal performance, but also the degree to which work-life balance is achieved. A report in the CBC News (2007) reported that as many as 30% of Canadians would say that they are workaholics, the characteristics of which are described as:

- Working more hours than average.
- Working more does not give a sense of accomplishment.
- Feeling stressed.
- Stuck in a routine.
- Inability to finish 'to-do list.'
- Exaggerated sense of work's role in life

We could assume that this is true for the majority of capitalist countries with long working hours, therefore, the market for occupational wellness could potentially be enormous. Workshops are increasingly being developed which focus on stress management, team building, balancing work with social life, family and other commitments, becoming a better communicator/manager/employee, etc. Life-coaching has emerged as a popular personal and professional development technique in recent years and involves client-focused goal setting, performance targets in business and personal achievement contexts, stress reduction, motivation and personal empowerment. In fact, it is now being offered at most holistic retreat centres. Neuro-Linguistic-Programming (or NLP) is also a growing practice and is a communication/visualization technique used to overcome psychological blockages and phobias and to help clients to achieve their personal potential. Practitioners often offer these two techniques together as part of a package.

It may seem somewhat paradoxical to suggest that occupational wellness holidays can be developed, as in the past, holidays were simply supposed to represent a break from work! However, these days busy managers and employees can scarcely afford to take breaks from the workplace, and even if they do, the ubiquitous email and mobile phone connections do not allow for total escapism. Many people have forgotten how to relax as they have lapsed into learnt patterns of workaholic behaviour from parents, colleagues, friends, or employers. As a result, burn-out is becoming a more common phenomenon. As documented by Dina Glouberman (2002) the founder of Skyros, the Baby-Boomer market, which is the key target market for wellness tourism is currently also the most prone to burn-out. For this reason, she developed the Skyros Centres as discussed earlier in this chapter.

Case Study: 'Destineering' – Luxury Life Coaching Retreats

Destineering is described as taking a fresh look at your life and focusing on what you really want to do with it. This involves exploring how to build on talents and passions and to pursue a meaningful sense of purpose. Using life-coaching, Destineering retreats claim to transform your life. Award winning coaches are employed who guide visitors through their transformative experience, giving them time to reflect in a stunning location. Destinations include the Canadian Rockies and mediaeval towns in Umbria. Retreat guests come from a variety of backgrounds, but most of them have in common the fact that they are very successful in their chosen field but are wondering what to do next. Some people may be thinking about switching careers whilst others just want to think more creatively about the future. Interaction with other guests is an integral part of the transformative experience, but the life-coaching is one-to-one and can continue after the retreat is over.

A summer weekend retreat in Whistler, Canada (2007) consists of the following:

- Two night's accommodation in a room with private bath or shower room
- All dining experiences including breakfast, picnic lunches in beautiful locations and three course gourmet meals at Brew Creek Lodge in the evenings
- The 'Destineering Experience' – a series of coaching activities and inspirational storytelling designed to inspire you around developing a highly meaningful sense of purpose in your life

- Access to 1:1 coaching during the retreat
- Guided hikes through the Whistler mountains and woods
- A host of Destineering surprises aimed at making you feel welcome and pampered during the course of the retreat

Testimonies from various retreat participants show that the role of the life-coach or retreat leader is especially important. One stated that:

> Denise's positive, non-judgemental feedback and reflection of who I am and my potential gave me the feel-good factor that maybe I'm not so crazy after all, but more importantly the sincerity that whatever I've come to do is within me and I can make that difference in my life should I choose to.

Many felt that they could change their lives on their return home:

> After my Destineering weekend I came away with a great clarity around my goal, and an action plan for realistic and meaningful results. I feel rejuvenated, and stronger for the experience.

And many just enjoyed the location, experience and the opportunity to take time out and reflect:

> Relaxation, fabulous food, beautiful surroundings and most importantly time ... time to focus on how you might leave your footprint on the world.

(Destineering, 2007)

Medical tourism

> Medical tourism can be defined as travel to destinations to undergo medical treatments such as surgery or other specialist interventions.

Often health tourism is used to label medical tourism and sometimes the other way around. Some writers have continued to use the phrase 'health tourism' to cover all forms of health-related tourism including medical tourism (e.g. Garcia-Altes, 2005), and some distinguish 'medical tourism' as involving specific medical interventions (Connell, 2006). Medical tourism, however, can have two major forms: *surgical* and *therapeutic*. There is a clear distinction between the two. Surgical, certainly involves certain operation(s), whereas therapeutic means participating in healing treatments. Surgical medical tourism has been a growth sector since the 1990s and is increasingly being assisted by the internet, agents, and brokers.

Medical tourism has been frequently described as 'First World treatment at Third World prices' as it tends to take place in locations of the world where medical (surgical) treatment is much cheaper than in the tourists' own country (e.g. India and Thailand). Waiting lists may also be too long or tourists may want to recuperate in more beautiful surroundings than home. Sometimes certain countries are perceived as being 'expert' in medical techniques (e.g. dentistry in Hungary or sex change operations in Thailand), or treatment is not available or illegal in the tourists' own country (e.g. abortion, euthanasia). As mentioned in the previous chapters, the pressure of the media is creating a culture of self-obsession and poor self-esteem, often to the degree that people will do anything to enhance their looks. This includes frequent and multiple operations to look younger, slimmer, and more beautiful. In the case of celebrities and some members of the general public, anonymity is also required as they do not want anyone to know that they were surgically enhanced!

In South America, countries such as Argentina, Bolivia, Brazil, and Colombia lead on plastic surgery medical skills as their surgeons have a wide experience of treating domestic patients. It is estimated that 1 in 30 Argentineans have had plastic surgery procedures, making this population the most operated in the world after the United States and Mexico (Balch, 2006). In Bolivia and Colombia, plastic surgery has become quite common. According to the 'Sociedad Boliviana de Cirugia Plastica y Reconstructiva', more than 70% of middle and upper class women in the country have had some form of plastic surgery. Colombia also provides advanced care in cardiovascular and transplant surgery.

There is clearly a spectrum of medical tourism which ranges from necessary surgery for life-threatening conditions (e.g. cancer), to more aesthetic but sometimes necessary practices (e.g. orthodontic dentistry), to physically non-essential but psychologically boosting cosmetic surgery. Many people are only just discovering medical tourism, as there were frequently concerns about safety, sanitation, professionalism, and insurance in countries like India or Africa. However, increasingly patients are being reassured that many of the institutions (e.g. hospitals and clinics) and the techniques and equipment used are of an even higher standard than they are at home. For example, in the United Kingdom where the super-bug MRSA is spreading like wildfire through hospitals and waiting lists are at an all-time peak, many people are more than happy to take their money and their health problems elsewhere!

There are naturally concerns about destinations where medical tourism is taking place, as it is inevitably becoming a private-sector dominated practice. This often means that the best doctors and surgeons are lured away from the public healthcare system as they can make more money from medical tourism. The most beautiful or accessible locations are being developed for medical tourism, therefore there might also be a 'brain drain' from rural and remote areas where medical facilities for local people are often the most needed. Ethical approaches to the development of medical tourism are therefore needed and governments should carefully regulate the practice.

Case Study: Surgeon and Safari, South Africa

Surgeon and Safari, whose slogan is 'Privacy in Paradise', first opened its doors in 1999 and had just one client from California. Clientele had increased to 10 by the following year, and the company has enjoyed growth of almost 100% every year since. Lorraine Melville, founder of Surgeon and Safari – a company that specializes in facilitating medical tours – reports that her company services up to 30 clients a month. The majority of her clients come from the United Kingdom and the United States. The average client is aged between 45 and 65 and is usually single. The most requested procedures are face and eyelifts, tummy tucks, breast reductions, and dental rehabilitation, including implants, crowns, and periodontic work. Clients can also choose from hair transplants, liposuction, chin or calf augmentations, ear surgery, brow lifts, botox, ophthalmic procedures (such as cataract surgery), and orthopeadic procedures like knee and hip replacements. Melville argues that the quality and professionalism of the services offered, from the surgeons to the hotels, are amongst the very best in the world, and the prices are highly competitive. The internet is used to create communication between client and surgeon on an ongoing basis. High medical standards are combined with true business ethics. When clients want to recuperate, they have the option of doing so on safari or going to the sea. Although many need to rest instead, some excursions take up most of the average 10-day visit, e.g. trips to the Waterberg or Pilanesberg Game Reserve. There are also day trips to Sandton City, cultural villages, Soweto, the Apartheid Museum and other touristic experiences.

(Witepski, 2005)

Therapeutic medical tourism is somehow different from surgical. It has similar elements, that is medical check ups and diagnosis, but its difference lies in the fact that it often require a long stay or a repeat visit to the destination. Therapeutic tourism tends to use some natural assets that have a healing capacity. This healing, however, cannot take place during one weekend, while dental surgery could, but requires series of treatments and checkups. Therapeutic trips can, however, be of a post-operational or recuperational nature, too, for example taking place in a sanatorium. Surgical trips necessitate the availability of a clinic or hospital; therapeutic trips can be based in a medical hotel. This form of medical tourism, interestingly, can cost much less for the guest than a wellness trip, especially, if health insurance is funding it.

Medical wellness, as a cross over product, has emerged recently in some European countries, especially in Germany, Slovenia, and Hungary. This really is a product halfway between medical and wellness tourism, since it provides the assurance by a specialized doctor to guests who do not consider themselves ill, but as people who want to preserve or improve their health. Since 'softcore' wellness visitors often choose treatments and activities randomly, medical wellness can provide them with some guidance and advice about what to do and how to do it. We can see arguments, however, that wellness visitors may not want to be associated with illnesses at all, and the on-site doctor and the name of the product, medical wellness, would have negative connotations.

Conclusions

This chapter has demonstrated that the health tourism sector is diverse and consists of a number of sub-sectors. This is important to realize for the management and marketing of wellness facilities. It is also interesting to see how ancient traditions have been re-packaged for contemporary lifestyles and travel experiences at the same time that new products and services are emerging. Although it is difficult to balance all domains of wellness within one holiday, many hotels, retreats, and destinations are trying to do just that. Whereas in the past, this was probably just true of holistic centres, it is becoming increasingly true of wellness hotels and spa resorts, which offer such a wide-range of activities and services that tourists can almost create their own wellness programme according to individual needs.

An international and regional analysis

From John Bunyan's Pilgrim's Progress to the ancient Chinese Dao, the Way, the physical act of travel has been used as a metaphor for humanity's spiritual quest for enlightenment.

(Chaline, 2002:12)

This chapter focuses on the supply side of health and wellness tourism in an international context. This involves examining the phenomenon of globalization and the fact that many wellness products and services are becoming ubiquitous, for example in wellness hotels and purpose-built spa complexes. For consumers, it can be beneficial to offer similar wellness services throughout the world; however, for most destinations differentiation will be required. For many tourists, the location for wellness is far from irrelevant, and evidence seems to suggest that there are still regional wellness products which are unique and attractive to visitors. These are often dependent on the climate and resources of the region. Destinations can make good use of the sea, mountains, lakes, clean air, sunshine, desert, or other local attractions and resources, such as food products or plant extracts. It is important that they do so in order to create sustainable development, but also to emphasize their uniqueness in an increasingly competitive market.

Western Europe

According to ESPA (2007) in Europe there are more than 1,200 spas and health resorts, which are medically respected health centres.

Many of these are located in historic towns which have traditionally served health and wellness tourists as far back as Roman times. This is true of Vichy (Vicus Caldius) in France, Baden Baden (Aquae Aureliae) in Germany, Bath (Aquae Sulis) in the United Kingdom, and Spa in Belgium amongst others. Many of these resorts had their heyday or golden era in the 18th or 19th century and subsequently declined as fashions changed and many visitors went to seaside destinations instead for sea water bathing and climatotherapy. This was particularly true of the United Kingdom in the 19th century. Bacon (1998) describes how this was mainly due to the failure of public and private investment to renew the British product (which was originally a pioneer and model for much of the rest of Europe) to a level at which it could compete internationally. State protection and regulation was not strictly enforced, therefore there was little proactive economic development and planning. Heavy industries sometimes encroached on health and leisure zones, and there was not sufficient public investment in new infrastructures (e.g. parks, roads) or entertainment facilities (e.g. theatres, casinos).

As a result, whereas in the mid 19th century there were around 200 operational spas, by 1919 this number had declined to around 60, by 1946 there were only 10, and in 1978 only one (Leamington Spa). In contrast, Austria still has over a hundred operational spas which are registered by the state, as well as numerous new purpose-built recreational and leisure spas, especially in ski resorts.

Case Study of Bath: Regeneration of an Historic Spa

In Bath (or Aquae Sulis as it was known by the Romans) there was archaeological proof of human activity around the hot springs as far back as 8,000 BC. This was followed by evidence of Celtic shrines around the springs, as the waters were deemed sacred. It was the Roman invasion in AD 43 which transformed them into a series of baths and bathing facilities. The complex contained at least five hot and cold baths, sweat-rooms and cold rooms. Following the withdrawal of the Romans, the early Christians largely rejected the idea of regular bathing, so the baths fell to ruin. This was also attributed to a possible earthquake. It was not until AD 973 that Bath's position as a centre for religion and healing was reconfirmed and pilgrims and invalids alike flocked to its waters, as well as travellers and writers. Various monarchs including Queen Elizabeth I in the 16th century made the baths available to the public as well as royalty and nobility (although facilities were often separated). It was noted that men and women bathed naked together, as well as animals of all kinds! In subsequent centuries, (i.e. 1700s onwards) it became a more sophisticated and glamorous resort for royalty and aristocracy with pumps rooms to drink water in, assembly rooms in which to gamble, dance and socialize, as well as parades, parks and promenades. It was thought that Bath influenced the development of many other European spa towns and resorts. By the late 1700s, however, the spa declined again because of economic recession.

The 19th century saw a new revival of the spa culture, this time with the creation of the complex called The Royal Baths complete with treatment centre and ladies' swimming pool. However, Bacon (1998) describes how Bath already began to go out of fashion in the mid-19th century, having being a pioneer for other European spas decades earlier. Patronage was largely transferred to seaside towns. The New Private Baths opened as a medical facility in 1889, and during and after the First and Second World Wars, many soldiers were treated there and National Health Service funding was provided. However, its withdrawal in 1976 meant the beginning of another decline.

Following a 25 year closure, Bath's new spa opened in 2006. For years, visitors could enjoy the buildings and the view of the hot springs, but they could not bathe. Like other United Kingdom historic spa towns, most visitors came to enjoy the heritage buildings and the town centre, but were not able to experience what the buildings were designed to achieve. This situation is similar to Spa in Belgium, where the original heritage spas are no longer functional, and only a new thermal centre can be used by visitors. A spa revival scheme was developed in the late 1990s based on National Lottery money via a Millennium Commission grant. This represents the seventh reinvention of the spa in its history. Five listed buildings were regenerated and a new modern spa – The Minerva Bath – was created. Although the architecture and facilities are completely contemporary (and maybe a controversial juxtaposition with the traditional buildings), the rooftop view from the pool over the whole World Heritage Site city demonstrates that the new can represent the multi-layering of history and heritage and not just its replacement.

(White, 2003)

With the shift to seaside health tourism, thalassotherapy also has a long history in Western Europe, especially in resorts on the Atlantic Ocean. It was especially popular in France. The importance of the sea air was also significant enough to draw large numbers of visitors, especially those who were from industrial cities. This was overtaken by the desire for sunshine in the 20th century. Visits to mountain areas were also common for rest, recuperation and the benefits of fresh air, especially the Alps. France also has approximately 100 active spas and some 40 thalasso centres. Mainly traditional forms of health tourism (e.g. thalassotherapy, hydrotherapy, climatotherapies) are available in France.

Although there are fears that the industry in German speaking countries (Germany, Austria, and Switzerland) is becoming somewhat saturated, the supply and quality of products has been prodigious in recent years. There are approximately 400 officially recognized spas and health resorts between the North Sea and the Alps: Over 300 modern health centres, more than 50 climatic health resorts, 48 seaside health resorts, 62 Kneipp hydrotherapy resorts and over 160 mineral spas and mud spas and a whole range of hotels and specialist wellness centres catering for relaxation, fitness and well-being. In Germany, the idea of cultivating a sense of wellbeing has a long history going back to royalty and artists in the 18th and 19th centuries who would meet up in German spa resorts such as Baden-Baden, Bad Kissingen, Bad Neuenahr and Bad Wildungen (The now Kempinski Grand Hotel Spa Heiligendamm Ambience Germany's first seaside spa resort was founded in 1793 by Grand Duke Friedrich

Franz I of Mecklenburg-Schwerin. The spa was used as a holiday destination by Tsar Nicholas I and his family because of the Baltic's 'curative' qualities.).

Germany also has more than 500 wellness hotels, which are constantly extending the scope of their relaxation programmes. The number of programmes on offer is particularly large in the coastal regions and in southern and south-western Germany. Although wellness breaks have long been popular with Germans, international guests are still in the process of discovering German resorts. An increasingly popular package is 'Peeling and Putting' – wellness and golf. This is an appealing combination, given that many regard golf as a form of outdoor meditation! (Germany Tourism, 2008). Although with an ever decreasing amount, the German health insurance system still supports treatments in medical spas, which is a fundamental element of domestic health tourism.

Austria and Switzerland are behind Germany only in the number, but not in the quality of establishments they offer. In all three countries, specialized facilities and destinations (e.g. biohotels or underwater music for relaxation) and themed spas with identical architectural design appear and complete the supply of traditional health, that is medical destinations. In German speaking countries the ritual of the traditional Finnish sauna was also a little bit 'upgraded'. The so-called Aufguss (or 'Pouring ritual' in English) has become a local tradition. Water is poured three or four times onto the hot coals, a towel is swirled around to raise the heat by the sauna master, and sometimes other substances (e.g. ice, honey, mint, or even beer!) can be applied to the skin.

Holistic tourism is also growing quickly in Western Europe, especially in the United Kingdom and the Netherlands. This includes yoga and meditation retreats and workshops, trade shows (e.g. 2–3 day Body-Mind-Spirit or Yoga Shows), and holistic festivals and events.

Central and Eastern Europe

Some governments (e.g. Hungary, Czech Republic, Slovakia, and Slovenia) have recently invested large sums in the development and upgrade of traditional medical resorts. Russia has been planning to invest in the upgrade and modernization of its medical tourism facilities (especially in and around Sochi, the host of the Winter Olympics in 2014). Through social and health policy the state is still providing large subsidizes for medical treatments (and trips). In many CEE countries spa trends have always been characterized by the overwhelming role of social tourism and prescribed cure trips (e.g. to sanatoria owned by trade-unions) in the last 40–50 years. On the other hand, the lack of investment for renovation and new projects is one of the major problems of the spas in other CEE countries, especially in those with delayed privatization such as Poland, Romania, and Bulgaria.

Both the Czech Republic and Slovakia have similar resources in health tourism, that is mineral and thermal waters and medical mud (plus in

Slovakia we can find climatic resorts, too). The historic spa destinations of Marianské Lázně (Marienbad), Karlovy Vary (Carlsbad) and Františkovy Lázně are the most famous of 37 health destinations in the Czech Republic, or Piešťany in Slovakia (of the 13 destinations). Recent developments in both countries target wellness visitors and younger generations. In these countries health or medical tourism is organized around natural healing assets and therapeutic services; holistic services, labelled as alternative health services have just recently been introduced to the market (Figure 6.1).

Poland enjoys a similarly long history of health tourism, destinations have been attracting health tourists since the 13th century. There are altogether 43 health resorts, most of which are 'sanatoria' type facilities. Visitors can find thermal waters, salt caves, medical muds, and even oxygen bars in Poland. Recent extensions and upgrades added beauty and cosmetic and some wellness treatments.

Most countries on the Balkan Peninsula (i.e. Slovenia, Croatia, Serbia, Romania, Macedonia, Bosnia and Herzegovina, and Bulgaria) have natural healing resources, for example thermal water springs, healing climates or caves, and the price levels are still under the levels guests from the sender countries may have to pay in their home countries.

- Romania has approximately 3,000 thermal springs and 70 medical destinations, many of which (e.g. Baile Felix, Baile Herculane, or Sovat) are quite famous in the region. The morphological resources, that is the Carpathian mountains make Romania a very competitive destination for health and wellness tourism, especially, if the essential tourism and general infrastructural development were completed.
- Bulgaria's over 800 thermal springs were already popular during Ancient Times, for example the first Thracian dwellers in the area in the 5th century BC, already preferred to locate their settlements around the hot springs. The Greeks built 'nymphaeums', while the Romans built 'asclepions' in these locations, all dedicated to the mystical or healing use of waters. Besides patients could enjoy the healing effects of the mountain and sea climate, too. Now, Bulgaria has been heavily investing in product and infrastructure development to enhance its health tourism supply.
- Slovenia, Croatia and Serbia share similar resources, that is thermal water and healing climate. The most developed of the three is Slovenia (with 87 thermal springs and several other natural assets, such as 2 peat sites), where many modern facilities were built recently, attracting not only medical but wellness tourists, too. Serbia and Croatia have also declared that health and wellness tourism development is an important way of creating a more competitive product portfolio, and started to move away from the so far medical orientation.
- Hungary has declared in its National Tourism Development Strategy that it wants to be the most important health tourism destination in Europe. The resources are quite significant from thermal waters, through medical caves to a mofetta (CO_2 bath). Historic spas (especially

Figure 6.1
Spas in Central-Eastern Europe (big circles: major spas (mineral water, mud and climate), small circles: other spas).
Source: Bachvarov, 2004; Jordan, 1999.

in Budapest), a natural thermal lake (Hévíz) or a unique natural cave bath (Miskolc-tapolca), plus recent investments in spas and hotel infrastructure are all supporting the achievement of this goal.

- The vast country of Russia is very rich (e.g. over 5,000 medical destinations!) in natural healing resources and traditions (e.g. banya). During the socialist system these resources were made available to everybody, which left the remains of some historic facilities derelict and at the same time overdeveloped by giant hotels or sanatoria. The healing orientation is still dominant, but wellness services are expected to be introduced in Russian spas, too.

Case Study: Caves and Salt Mines in Central and Eastern Europe

Halo (salt-based) therapy is performed in a special room, the walls and floor of which are covered by tremendous amounts of salt. These may be naturally occurring (e.g. a salt cave or mine) or artificially created. Medical research which focuses on the treatment of various respiratory diseases confirmed that Halotherapy resulted in improvements of the clinical state of most patients. Russia has become one of the world leaders testing the effectiveness of Halotherapy as a treatment for asthma, chronic bronchitis and the entire range of upper and lower respiratory tract diseases. The Russian Ministry of Public Health sanctioned the Halotherapy method in 1990.

The suggestion that air full of saline dust can have a curative function for patients with respiratory diseases was first developed by a Polish mining physician Feliks Bochkowsky. He noticed that workers in salt mines did not seem to become ill with lung diseases. In 1839 he founded the Salt Spa in Wieliczka near Krakow (Poland), which is still in operation. Originally it served for treatment of almost all diseases, and since 1958 it has been used for the treatment of diseases like asthma, chronic and acute bronchitis, upper and lower airway diseases and allergies. Nowadays, salt mines are known to be used for therapeutic purposes in many other countries, especially in Central and Eastern Europe, such as Ukraine (Solotvino, Artiomovsk), Austria (Solzbad-Salzeman), Russia (Berezniky, Perm), Romania (Slanic, Praid, Seiged, Sovata, Ocna), Germany (Teufelshohle), Hungary (Tapolca), Azerbaijan (Nakhichevan), Kirgizia (Chon-Tous) and others.

The Bochnia Salt Mine Bochnia (35 km to the east of Krakow) is the oldest one in Poland and simultaneously, the oldest salt enterprise in Europe, which has been working uninterruptedly since 1248. The 2.5 km tourist route runs at a depth of 290 m. The mine's largest cavern, the Ważyn chamber, has facilities for recreation and health treatment services.

Health holidays here are for everybody who wants to rest in the Bochnia Mine with its special climate, and who wants to regenerate and improve his/her physical condition, as well as to pamper his/her body and relax the mind. There are 7-days, 11-days and 14-days stays, with 2 medical examinations (on request there can be additional ones), treatments in the Rehabilitation and Biological Regeneration Centre, such as: pearl and brine baths with hydro-massage, flagellation, rotation bath for upper and lower limbs, negative pressure massage, hydromassage, classical massage, laser therapy, phototherapy, heattherapy, cryotherapy, magnetotherapy, electrotherapy, kinesiotherapy, and inhalation.

7 day holidays
Includes: 15 treatments and 5 visits of 3 hours in the Mine, 4 of them during the day and 1 at night.

11 day holidays
Includes: 20 treatments and 7 visits visits of 3 hours in the Mine, 6 of them during the day and 1 at night.

14 day holidays
Includes: 25 treatments and 10 visits of 3 hours in the Mine, 8 of them during the day and 2 at night.

In addition to medical facilities the sanatorium provides the visitors with opportunities for recreation: gymnasium, table tennis, sport-gear/deckchair rental, and a snack bar. It is also possible to arrange for conferences, seminars, banquets, weddings and other events to be held in the Ważyn chamber.

(Way to Poland, 2008)

Nordic and Scandinavian Countries

In Northern Europe, because of the lack of natural healing assets and tradition, people do not tend to believe in or trust the beneficial impacts of medical waters. This results in health and wellness (tourism) being based on relaxation and mainly includes fitness services, massages, (fun) baths with hot water and saunas. However, the first bath of the North was initiated in Stockholm by a medical doctor Carl Curman Sturebadet in 1885 to meet the '…desperately needed- swimming, exercise, and a road to better health…in 1899 there were 63 treatment areas with 43 bathtubs for soaking' (Sturebadet, 2008). The facility in 1902 was extended with a swimming pool in Art Nouveau with Old Norse and Moorish features. The first similar establishment was opened in 1928 in Helsinki, and the Yrjönkatu Bath ever since is a must visit attraction of the town (note: there are separate days for men and women!).

In Nordic countries, the sauna often represents an integral part of everyday life (especially in Finland) rather than being a luxury that is associated with wellness programmes (there are three forms of saunas: smoke, wood and electricity heated). It is well-known that Nordic people have a generally healthy attitude to life, and many of the fitness activities which are part of everyday life (e.g. Nordic walking) have now been exported to wellness centres and spas all over the world. The Queen of Norway even donated her hiking boots to a museum! Interestingly, the use of the term 'Swedish massage' is a misnomer, and although it is often attributed to Peter Henry Ling (1776–1837), he in fact developed a system of movements and gymnastics. The landscape is clean, the air is fresh, and the diet is rich in fish (particularly fish high in Omega 3 fats), rye and oats, root vegetables and berries. Denmark, Finland and Sweden ranked in the top 5 countries amongst 21 of the world's richest countries for children's well-being, according to UNICEF's Innocenti Research Center (2007). Nordic Well (2007) describes how:

> *The cold North is home to many traditions that are warming and soothing. Underpinning them are the ideas that relaxation and cleansing are every person's right, and that relaxation therapies can contribute to a better society. These traditions-some of them, a thousand years old-include sauna, water therapies, massage and herbal treatments.*

They also describe how design is modern, simple, clean, airy, light, calm, uncluttered, in harmony with nature, inviting, functional, and inclusive, as well as being combined with three influences: a Zen-like belief in the power of nature; a tradition of linking design to the wellbeing of all people; and a skill for choosing appropriate technology (e.g. the Serena Water Amusement Park in Korpilamp (Espoo, Finland) combines these factors, since it was carved into the rocks, guests can enjoy the pools, the slides as well as the sauna areas – all within the hill overlooking the ski slopes on the other side of the valley).

Julie Lindahl, a Swedish Wellness Expert and author of the book '*On My Swedish Island: Discovering the Secrets of Scandinavian Well-being*', describes how Nordic Wellbeing focuses on five lifestyle areas: design, food, gardens and herbs, outdoor life and relaxation. Her retreats include fitness and nature meditation; gathering and preparing food from nature; detoxing and relaxation techniques including sauna, herbal baths and massage; and a quiet opportunity to write paint or do needlework in an inspirational natural environment (Wellness of Scandinavia, 2007).

There are some interesting new developments in Finland which are based on natural resources, for example, the concept of 'Lake Wellness'. This is discussed further in a case study in the third section of this book. Cold water bathing is very common in Finland especially, and is a favourite winter past-time in Finland. The health benefits include relaxing muscles; reducing blood pressure; decreasing rheumatic symptoms; and strengthening immunity. It is expected to have further diversification of markets for rehabilitation spas in Finland in the future (i.e. post-veteran era). They also discuss the significant potential for lake-based wellness in Eastern Finland.

By contrast, people in Iceland recognize the benefits of hydrotherapy in hot water. The average Reykjaviker goes to a thermal pool about 15 times a year, enjoying not only the health benefits but also the social and psychological ones. One of the ultimate Nordic spa experiences is the Blue Lagoon of Iceland. Most of the visitors would necessarily know or find out, that this really stunning facility actually reuses the hot water from the nearby geothermal power plant. Theories include that hydrotherapy can detoxify the blood; stimulate blood circulation; enhance the immune system; improve digestion; and relax the muscles. Iceland's brand of hydrotherapy is unique in the world, mainly as a result of the fact that it is naturally endowed with a natural source of piping hot underground water. Official sources calculate that there are about 800 geysirs spouting geothermal water at an average temperature of about 167 degrees Fahrenheit. The largest hot spring in Iceland, Deildartunguhver, has a flow of 150 litres (40 gallons) of boiling water per second. It is recommended to sit in the hot water for 15, 10, and 5 minutes in hot pots of increasing temperature with breaks to cool off in between (Nordic Well, 2007).

Of the Baltic countries (Estonia, Latvia, and Lithuania), Estonia has the most significant resources in health and wellness tourism. The facilities are typically and traditionally healing oriented using therapeutic mud or the sea. However, in the most important health destination of Pärnu, new resort style spas have also been opened (e.g. Tervise Paradiis Spa Hotel & Water Park).

Case Study: Cryotherapy in Nordic Countries

There are several hotels in Nordic countries and regions (e.g. Finland, Lapland) which offer a treatment known as cryotherapy. For example, the most modern cryo-equipment in the world has been in operation since 2003 in Haikko Spa, situated 50 km east of Helsinki, Finland.

The benefits of dipping into freezing lakes or rolling in snow after a sauna are well-known throughout the region, therefore a logical extension of this has been to create cryotherapy chambers in many hotels and spas. Cryotherapy means natural treatment of human skin with extremely cold air (−80 up to −110°C or less) with numerous benefits to cell production, pain killing, treatment of injuries and inflammatory diseases and improving general health. Low-temperature cures may also help newborns who have been starved of oxygen during a difficult birth to get through their first vital days in the world, and researchers claim that subjecting athletes to temperatures as low as minus 120°C could improve their performance.

Cryotherapy can be administered in two ways: placing the whole body in chilled chambers or locally with cryo-instruments. The effect of the therapy is based on the speed and force of the cold impulse, on the impact of the 'nerve-kick'. In such a short exposure the body maintains its normal temperature. Only the surface temperature of the skin drops down to +3 ... +4 degrees during the cryo-session. The Univers Combi-system in use at Haikko Spa consists of a two-method-unit working with both electricity and liquid nitrogen (closed circuit), unique in the world.

Cryotherapy can be taken as

- pleasure inducing experience
- immunity improving therapy
- cure for pain or various disorders
- sports training
- treatment for cosmetic purposes.

(Haikko Spa, 2008)

Southern Europe

There are also a number of traditional historic spas in Southern Europe, for example Abano or Montecatini Therme in Italy, and well as in Spain, Portugal and Greece (e.g. Loutraki – The City of Waters). In Italy alone, approximately 200 destinations and 450 spas offer various services to guests, who can combine their stay with cultural and gastronomic delights. Some modern spas also exist, especially in mountain resorts which are used by skiers (e.g. in Andorra).

In addition to historic and thermal spas, the lifestyle and diet in the Mediterranean is one of the healthiest in the world. The existence of a good climate and the seaside has benefited residents and tourists for centuries. Thalassotherapy is offered throughout the region, for example, in Greece, Spain, France, Italy. Islands like Cyprus and Malta are increasingly positioning themselves as medical tourism destinations, capitalizing on their English language skills as well as their high quality clinics. Wellness hotels in the region are proliferating extensively and there are few countries which do not have a large number of spa and wellness hotels.

Although some parts of Turkey are technically in Asia, many visitors consider the country (especially the seaside) to be an extension of Southern Europe, therefore its assets are discussed here. Turkey is located on top of a major geothermal belt, therefore it is among the top seven countries in the world for quality and quantity of thermal springs with over 1,000, with temperatures ranging from 20°C to 110°C. Most are in the Aegean regions and because of their proximity to popular tourism destinations such as Izmir, Pamukkale, and Marmaris, public transport is easy. Many of Turkey's historical places developed because of their springs, like the ancient city of Hieropolis which was built upon the rich mineral springs of Pamukkale, and the ancient Lydian city of Kaunos, whose people took baths in the rich mineral mud of Lake Koycegiz (in Kangal Hot Spings the carbon-dioxide rich water is the home to small fish that actually bite the infected skin off of the guests sitting in the water!).

In addition, the Turkish bath or hammam is world famous and the concept has been exported everywhere. As well as being part of the Islamic ritual of purification, it was also a place to socialize or do business (an extension of the Roman tradition). Men and womens' bathing areas or schedules are separate. Many hammams were built during the Ottoman era and retain their unique style of architecture. Bathers are vigorously massaged and the skin is exfoliated after spending time in the steamy chambers, Cooling and resting areas are then recommended.

Many yoga and holistic centres are located in Southern Europe (for example, Skyros and Yoga Plus in Greece, and Cortijo Romero in Spain). This is largely because the landscapes and climate are so attractive to visitors and course tutors alike. Although such centres could technically be located anywhere, many of the lifestyle practitioners who choose to re-locate (especially from the United Kingdom) go to Spain or Greece. Turkey is becoming increasingly popular with yoga centres and retreats being located there (e.g. Huzur Vadisi).

The province around Granada in Spain has Arabic baths, the remains of thermal baths dating from the Roman period, water cisterns, fountains, natural swimming pools, and irrigation channels, all of which are evidence of the great importance that water had for the area. The most unique attractions are perhaps the Arab Baths, where the typical atmosphere of traditional Hammans has been re-created, which in the Andalusi period were the centres of social life. Visitors alternate between pools with waters at different temperatures. The baths include a Warm Room, with a pool at a temperature of approximately 36°C, a Cold Room, in which the water is at 16°C, and a Massage Room. They are beautifully decorated with mosaics, arches with fine lattice work, and exotic scents, music and warm light help to create atmosphere.

There have also been some new developments in the Canary Islands and in the Balearics. The Canary Islands have an all-year-round climate which is ideal for certain medical conditions and healing. Most of the spa facilities are located in large chain hotels and are seen as a complementary offer. The main focus is on relaxation and beauty. The Balearic Islands locate their spas within hotels or wellness centres, and offer a whole range of products ranging from thalassotherapy to ancient Greek baths to Chinese medicine to African traditions. Ideally, there needs to be unique regional health and wellness offers and signature treatments on these islands in order to compete with nearby African countries such as Morocco, as well as Spain.

Middle East and North Africa

In terms of natural resources in the Middle East and North Africa (MENA), there is mainly desert and sea, although as far as 3,000 BC people with eye problems could make a pilgrimage to Tell Brak (Syria) hoping that deities would perform miracles. Some wellness hotels offer products and services that are unique to the region, such as the Desert Sand-Herb Rasoul Scrub offered in Dubai. Hammams are indigenous to the region and consist of a process of sweating, exfoliation and cleansing of the skin, and massage administered by therapists. Special hammam hotels exist in countries like Morocco. Thalassotherapy is also offered in several hotels in Morocco and Tunisia, as well as Egypt and the United Arab Emirates. Indeed, large numbers of high quality spa hotels are being developed in the region, especially in the United Arab Emirates, or Oman where the distinctive local architectural features are particularly stunning.

However, it is perhaps the Dead Sea which attracts the majority of wellness tourists to the region. The Dead Sea is sometimes described as the world's largest 'Natural Spa'. It is located between the West Bank and Israel to the west, and Jordan to the east. It has year-round hot weather, an enriched oxygen atmosphere, therapeutic UVB solar radiation, a mineral-rich salt sea, mineral-rich mud, thermomineral hot springs and luxurious spas. Research has shown that the combined climatic factors have a long lasting positive therapeutic effect on dermatological diseases such as psoriasis, eczema and rheumatic or degenerative joint diseases. Thalassotherapy and Balneotherapy are carried out by bathing in the Dead Sea region's special mineral spring waters and provide temporary relief of arthritic pain. The pollen-free atmosphere and unpolluted air, higher oxygen content, high barometric pressure and low humidity soothe the symptoms of asthma, cystic fibrosis and certain lung diseases. Coronary function, depression and hypertension are treated by Climatotherapy and by Heliotherapy. This seasonal affective disorder syndrome generally affects individuals who live in northern climates where winter weather conditions are long, cold and cloudy with short daylight hours.

Case Study: Zara Spa Dead Sea

At the lowest point on earth there's a higher form of wellbeing at a Spa for the new millennium

Zara Spa in Jordan provides luxury accommodation for those wishing to enjoy the healing properties of the Dead Sea. The different minerals in the Dead Sea Water help repair skin damage, enhance skin metabolism, relax the muscles and facilitate breathing. Use is made not only of the saline water, but also the Dead Sea Mud which helps in clarifying, nourishing and retaining moisture, resulting in a fresher, healthier and more youthful appearance of the skin. It also helps balance the skin pH, and helps in firming and tightening the skin due to the presence of silicates. These elements are therefore ideal not only for medical conditions but also beauty treatments.

A typical 7 day package consists of:

1 ZARA Spa consultation
7 ZARA Spa Experiences
1 Dead Sea salt scrub
2 Dead Sea natural mud wraps
1 Thalgo facial
1 Thalgo eye indulgence treatment
1 Dead sea healing Mud facial
1 Reflexology
1 Full body aroma massage
2 Full body swedish massages
1 ZARA Spa hot stone therapy
1 Hydrobath with herbal essence
1 Affusion shower
1 Spa manicure and Spa pedicure
1 Hair conditioning treatment

The Zara Spa recommends a sequence of activities which are supposed to maximize the benefits of the experience, starting with a pool with a 3% salt concentration to allow the body to adjust to the unique climate and mineral rich waters. Visitors should then progress to a pool with 27% salt concentration (pure Dead Sea water), which helps eliminate toxins from the body and balance PH levels. 10–15 minutes in each pool is recommended with rests in between and plenty of water. There are also Thermariums, Tropical Showers, a Caldarium, a Laconium, and a Fitness Suite. Safer sunbathing is also possible, as the specially filtered UVA & UVB radiation in the Dead Sea region makes it one of the safest places in the world to sunbathe. At the end of the day, a float in the Dead Sea itself is recommended.

Zara Spa was the Golden Award Winner for Best Spa in the Middle East and North Africa (MENA Travel Award 2005) and frequently features as one of the world's top spas in specialist books and magazines.

(Zara Spa Dead Sea, 2008)

Increasingly, the Middle East is gaining a reputation for medical tourism, especially in the United Arab Emirates (e.g. Dubai) and Jordan, which is trying to position itself as the 'mecca' of medical tourism in the Middle East. Other countries like Iran are also boasting excellent doctors, high quality facilities and cheap healthcare. Although the Middle East mainly generates medical tourism, there is a growth market also *to* the region.

Yoga holidays are offered almost anywhere in the world, but increasingly in the Middle East and North Africa (e.g. in Dahab on the Red Sea, Egypt). Doing yoga in a desert setting, for example, can add to the spiritual experience. Sometimes yoga holidays are combined with belly dancing (e.g. in Hammamet, Tunisia). One yoga holiday in Morocco includes a Jimi Hendrix experience in Essouira or trekking with Bedouins in Egypt (Yoga Travel, 2007). Spiritual tourism does not tend to be combined with religious tourism in the Middle East, even though it is a major centre for pilgrimage tourism (with all Muslims being expected to complete the Haj to Mecca in Saudi Arabia). Spiritual and religious tourism are also common in Israel, but usually for different/separate religious groups rather than secular spiritualists. However, recently there has been a growth of spiritual or holistic festivals which appeal to younger residents and tourists.

Africa

Although luxury spas exist in Africa, this is largely in South Africa and on some of the islands, for example in the Seychelles or Mauritius. South Africa is the leading destination in Africa for spa tourism and use is made of the mountains and sea as well as the bush. As it is a major wine growing country, there is also a gradual increase in vinotherapy. The South African Tourist Board (2008) describes how the African spa has taken on a whole new meaning from the European concept, as nature is almost always used in products and treatments, as well as centuries of indigenous and tribal traditions of healing. They also promote the Spiritual South where guests can participate in 'wholistic' tourism, for example animal or eco-therapies (like 'Mingling with Meerkats'), 'Horse-labyrinth' or eco-psychology.

The African Day Spa has become almost a brand name (e.g. for product ranges) and the 'Bush Spa' is a common phenomenon, where tourists stay in a lodge in the African bush, experiencing natural and herbal treatments, often combined with safaris. The spa at Cape Grace in South Africa uses healing techniques and traditional remedies of the region's native San and Khoi tribes, who used massage, indigenous plants, and the spices introduced by the Indian Ocean traders en route from Asia to Europe. The signature African Cape Massage, for example, uses circular massage motions inspired by the spherical moves of healing tribal dances, along with moisturizing shea butter from the nut of the African Shea Tree, and snowbush oil, an anti-stress agent distilled from a local plant. The African Face and Body Treatment uses an algae mask to soothe the face, and neck and shoulders are gently massaged with colorful warmed beads, a tradition of the Xhosa people, to relieve tension (www.capegrace.com, 2008).

Kenya offers opportunities to combine safaris and spas, as well as centres like Wildfitness, where visitors can get fitter using natural habitats (e.g. sprinting in sand dunes, swimming in creeks, jogging through jungles).

Case Study: Wildfitness, Kenya

Wildfitness is a special kind of health holiday – more like an open-air fitness retreat than a spa (although massages and therapies are offered). It aims to help people rediscover their natural physical potential which they would have needed to survive in the wild. The concept is based on the fact that humans used to be hunter-gatherers in wild savannahs, nature provided everything they needed, and they were tall, lean, agile, fast, and fertile. These days, most people tend to resemble 'zoo humans' who live in an environment which is very different to the one they evolved for. As a result, physical, mental, psychological and spiritual health has suffered.

Wildfitness Kenya participants stay on the north coast near to Watamu, which is a small fishing village and was voted as having one of the top ten beaches in the world. It is a designated World Heritage Site because of its natural beauty. Activities take place on the beach and in its forest surrounds, where inmates spend their days swinging from trees, canoeing along mangrove swamps, running, jumping, weight-training and diving. Other activities include 5 mile runs on the sand, swims across the creek, hikes into the bush, yoga, Tai chi, and aerobics.

Expert fitness coaches cater for all ages and levels of ability. A typical programme lasts from nine days to three and a half weeks, and group size is limited to eleven people. Emphasis is placed on three main elements, which are:

- Wild Movement: For example learning proper techniques for physical activities like running and swimming, challenging oneself, enhancing performance, preventing injuries, strength training.
- Wild Eating: For example locally sourced raw and organic produce to ease digestive and other problems. Two menus are available: The Primate Menu (e.g. eggs, seeds, nuts,

fruit, non-starchy vegetables) and the Hunter-Gatherer Menu (the same but with the addition of meat and fish). There may also be cookery lessons and nutritional workshops.

- Wild Living: For example learning how to control stress through breathing, sleeping, relaxing, being in nature and studying physiological responses to these aspects of life. This also includes having fun and bonding with the small group as tribes would have done.

Wildfitness aims to be ecofriendly by employing local people wherever possible, making donations to national park and turtle conservation, using local produce, paying a fee to local communities if they are used in any way, and use of energy saving devices and biodegradable products.

(Wildfitness, 2008)

Medical tourism in Africa is also a growing phenomenon, especially in South Africa where surgical and cosmetic tourism has a good reputation. Increasingly, Kenya is also offering medical tourism, for example, heart transplant surgery. In addition, tourists can learn about traditional African herbal medicine and the Kenya government is registering and licensing genuine herbalists to practise alongside trained medical doctors. There is only a small growth in wellness tourism in East and West Africa at present, largely because of indigenous health problems and high poverty levels. Perhaps controversially, some tour operators (for example Victoria Safaris, 2008) offer HIV and AIDS tourism in Africa, where visitors are taken to East Africa to see the impacts of the pandemic. This includes visits to Kenyan slum areas, beaches along the coast of Kenya and the beaches on Lake Victoria.

Asia

Spa and wellness are gaining unprecedented growth and popularity across Asia. Luxury spas and spa hotels are being built throughout the region with some of the world's best being located in places like Bali, Phuket, Langkawi, and the Maldives. Even some of the less visited destinations such as Laos, Cambodia or Vietnam have an emergent spa industry. Various reports and estimates put the growth of the Asian spa at between 30% and 60%, annually, for the next 5 years, making this industry the fastest growing sector of the tourism and service industry (Asia Spa Festival, 2007). Some of the former Soviet Union countries, for example Kyrgizstan, offer tradtional, natural asset based healing services, for example treatments in salt mines.

Most of the Asia spas, even if they are located in chain hotels, include local signature treatments which can be very special and luxurious (e.g. Balinese coffee-peeling ritual). Another example is the Mandi Lulur, which is originally a bridal ritual from the royal palace in Java. This beauty and care treatment starts with a massage. Afterwards the body is embrocated with a paste consisting of rice flour, turmeric, sandalwood and jasmin. After the paste has dried, it is carefully rubbed off, cleaning the skin of any dead cells. A mask of yoghurt ensues, which has a cooling effect and restores the natural pH to the skin and moisturizes it. After a short shower a bath of blossoms is given and then the receiver is rubbed with an oil that especially cares for the skin.

In Japan, onsens (ritual bathing establishments that can be individual facilities or as part of a Ryokan, i.e. inn) are representative of tradition and heritage. Japan is very rich in hot thermal and vulcanic waters and visiting an onsen is a must to almost any visitor (e.g. in Jigokudani Monkey Park, snow monkeys are sitting in the hot spring!). The findings of the ISPA 2003 Japan Spa-goer study confirmed the important role spas play in the life of Japanese citizens. According to the data, not less then three in five Japanese residents visited a spa during a year. This meant 76.4 million spa-goers in 2003.

In Asia, the traditional health approaches and techniques (e.g. Thai massage, Chinese medicine, yoga, Ayurveda) have become globally exportable. However, for many tourists, especially holistic or spiritual tourists, an authentic experience can only really be gained in the country of origin. Thai massage is available everywhere in Thailand, but visitors can also learn the technique in massage schools which offer special training programmes. It is possible to experience yoga and meditation in numerous ashrams and retreats throughout India. Ayurvedic treatments are on offer throughout India, but most especially in Kerala where the practice originates. However, Nepal is also promoting Ayurvedic tourism:

Case Study: Ayurveda in Nepal

Nepal plans to increase health tourism investment in Ayurvedic tourism so that it can rival Kerala as a destination. Nepal has a long history of Ayurveda and it is thought that 75% of the population practises this form of medicine. There are around 4,000 traditional practitioners in Nepal and 623 qualified practitioners under the Department of Ayurveda. Indian health products major Dabur is one of the major enterprises that is involved in the cultivation of rare herbs and the manufacture of herbal products in Nepal targeting the growing interest in Ayurvedic products. Nepal is a source of rare Himalayan herbs and oils which could be used for wellness treatments and therapies. It is estimated that there are around 1,600 types of aromatic medicinal plants. The traditional system practised in Nepal has its origins in the Tibetan healing system. It therefore combines components of Buddhist religion, influences from Indian Ayurveda and Chinese medical traditions. In addition to the rich herbal heritage, Nepal plans to promote a more general wellness theme using healing through mantras, chanting and medicines prepared with a blend of herbs and metals, including precious metals and stones. Considerable investment in wellness tourism is needed in order to follow the successful examples of India, Thailand and Malaysia.

(Ayurnepal, 2008, Medindia, 2008)

Tourism Malaysia is launching an intensive campaign promoting the country's spirituality in response to foreign interest in religious diversity, as well as the large number of overseas tourists that already attend the country's spiritual events. Visitors will be invited to tour Islamic mosques, Christian churches, Indian and Chinese Temples, Sikh gurdwaras and other spiritual sites around the country, as different faiths, beliefs, celebrations and places of worship are an integral part of Malaysian life. Many religious ceremonies already attract foreign visitors, such as the Indian Thaipusam in the Batu caves. The last Thaipusam was heavily promoted throughout Hong Kong, Australia, and Singapore, resulting in a large increase of tourists. Other festivals celebrated in Malaysia, which tourists may wish to attend, include the Chinese Lantern Festival and St Anne's Feast, observed by the country's Christians (Just the Flight, 2006).

Medical tourism in Asia is also growing exponentially with India, Thailand, Vietnam, and China in particular attracting tourists from all over the world because of cheap prices as well as good service and extensive expertise. However, in 2007 Singapore won the Best Medical/Wellness Tourism Destination at The TravelWeekly (Asia) Industry Awards 2007. China has just entered the international tourism market and already has become one of the fastest growing destinations for medical surgical trips (e.g. dentistry in Hong Kong).

Australasia and the South Pacific

Spa tourism in Australia is very much in line with the North American approach, where speciality spas are dominant. In Australia the spa sector is dominated by mostly small to medium sized business operators. There is a growing number of day spas, destination spas and resort spas in Australia. Research in 2006 found that Australia has 503 day spas, destination spas and resort spas. This research shows Australia has increased 129% in spa facilities since 2002 (Intelligent Spas, 2007). Spas are differentiated by the length of stay, that is day or destination spa; the natural assets based on which services are provided, for example natural or hot spring, and spas focusing mainly on beautification, for example nails are grouped separately (Figure 6.2).

In the case of Australia, Victoria is being positioned as the leading destination for spa and wellness tourism, incorporating the state's natural attributes, including mineral springs, geothermal waters and world class spa resorts and facilities. Three of Australia's top 15 destinations for domestic spa visitation are located in Victoria (Daylesford/Hepburn Springs, Melbourne and Great Ocean Road). For the spa and wellness tourism sector to have increased appeal to the international market, spa/wellness destinations may need to explore opportunities to source and include products that are indigenous to the area, for example Hepburn Springs and Daylesford Naturals products. This can include raw products used in treatments that are sourced in the local area, or those that have been or are currently being used by Australia's indigenous Aboriginal

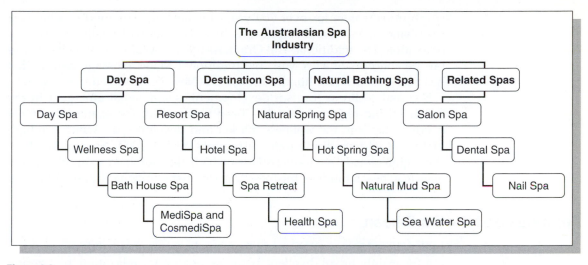

Figure 6.2
Structure of the Australian Spa Industry. *Source*: Australian Spa Association, 2006.

communities. For example, the spa menu at the Daintree Eco Lodge and Spa in Queensland has been collated out of respect and with approval of the local tribal Kuku Yalanji Elders and aims to integrate the wisdom of ancient cultures, medicines, spirituality, and healing.

Australia also has a growing number of holistic retreats, especially around Byron Bay. Examples include Gaia Retreat near Byron Bay (where Olivia Newton John is one of the owners), Golden Door Spas in the Gold Coast hinterland of Queensland, Elysia in the Hunter Valley, Sebel in the Yarra Valley Wellness Retreat Program, Samadhi Spa & Wellness Retreat near Daylesford, and Authenticity Health and Wellness Retreat.

New Zealand is a spa destination where spa services are based on the assets of the natural environment making bathing in natural hot springs a key attraction. Hanmer Springs in the South Island is a place where people can enjoy hot springs surrounded by mountains. The spa industry in New Zealand is a developing one, but there are essentially three types of spas available: hot spring spas; destination spas or retreats; and day spas. Combinations of all three are also available. The Polynesian Spa in Rotorua is the best known, as it combines geothermal, cultural and health & spa experience. It was voted a World Top Ten Spa (medical and thermal spas) by Condé Nast Traveller magazine for the past few years.

Another is Hell's Gate Wai Ora Spa, which is home to New Zealand's most active geothermal field, including a large variety of volcanic features including exploding waters, steaming fumaroles, pools of boiling mud, the only accessible mud volcano and the largest hot waterfall in the Southern Hemisphere. Within this active geothermal reserve is the Wai Ora Spa and Wellness Centre-where visitors can experience the unique geothermal muds and sulphurous geothermal waters in a traditionally Maori-themed environment. Maori have been bathing in the geothermal muds and sulphurous waters for over 700 years for healing. The mud can be used to enhance the skin and sulphurous spas with hot water falls are used for relaxation. The traditional Wai Ora massage is also offered, which is based on the concepts of Miri Miri, the traditional Maori massage regime that has been practiced for hundreds of years (New Zealand Tourism, 2007).

Spa and wellness tourism development is somewhat emergent in the South Pacific region, but it has been recognized, for example that Fiji needs to tap into the wellness market and develop spas, which are high yield and add greatly to tourism receipts (SPTO, 2007). Several hotels in the region already have spa facilities which are combined with other packages (e.g. beach tourism, business tourism, honeymoons, and weddings).

Americas and the Caribbean

In the United States and Canada there are large numbers of day-spas catering for mainly urban dwellers, who are looking for relaxation, pampering and stress relief. These include club spas, cruise ship spas, day spas, destination spas, medical spas, mineral springs spas, and resort/hotel spas. The listings of the Spafinder Magazine confirms the fast development and proliferation of the supply. Whereas in 1987 forty-six destination spas and 80 hotel/resort spas were available, by 2008 this category did not even exist anymore. It was replaced by 39 new categories from Adult Only Spas to Yoga Programmes (Loverseed, 1998 & Spafinder Magazine, 2008). Observing the proliferation of wellness services in the area made The Caribbean Resort & Day Spa Association set guidelines (Chambers, 2006) to help owners and developers to make the distinction between a facility that offers spa services, and a true spa.

The Canadian Tourism Commission produced a Business Strategy for Spa Health and Wellness Tourism in Canada in 2005. ISPA estimates that there are about 2100 spas in Canada, with 75% of them categorized as day spas. Canada's spa, health and wellness tourism sector is relatively young by global standards, given that most spa facilities are just over a decade old. Health and wellness programs in Canada focus on hydrotherapy (water based therapeutic treatments), algotherapy (all forms of the use of algae in therapeutic treatments), fangotherapy (warm mud therapies), sudation (sauna), exfoliation, pressure therapy and several message techniques. Fitness programs, wellness assessment, and nutritional counselling are other services offered.

In the United States and Canada, the concept of Therapeutic Recreation is well-established. It is defined by the Canadian Therapeutic Recreation Association (2007) as:

> *A profession which recognizes leisure, recreation and play as integral components of quality of life. Service is provided to individuals who have physical, mental, social or emotional limitations which impact their ability to engage in meaningful leisure experiences. Therapeutic Recreation is directed toward functional interventions, leisure education and participation opportunities. These processes support*

the goal of assisting the individual to maximize the independence in leisure, optimal health and the highest possible quality of life.

Spa vacations are ideal for people who are living with lifelong disabilities or debilitating conditions.

Many indigenous traditions are derived from the Americas and are being exported to spas all over the world. One the best known is Lomi Lomi massage from Hawaii, which is usually offered as a 2 hour treatment in European spas and is a gentle wave-like or rocking technique. Native American Indian rituals are also used increasingly in holistic and spiritual retreat centres. These are now quite globalized, but in the United States, Canada, and Mexico, some more 'authentic' experiences can be had in holistic or spiritual retreats. 'Sweat Lodges' (Native Indian ceremonial saunas) are becoming more popular in spas and retreat centres. In Mexico, Temazcals are similar, and they are also offered in other Central and South American retreats and spas. In countries like Peru, the consultation of local Shamans can be offered to visitors, for example, a ceremony involving drinking shamanic medicine which is said to expand consciousness (Sylge, 2007). However, there is controversy over the increasing use of the term 'Native Shamanism', which is not based on purely traditional teachings, but is a packaged blend of studies which include bits of Native American ceremonies along with Wiccan spells, New Age spirituality, and Eastern medicine (Native American Healing Traditions, 2007).

Goldsmith (2008) gives numerous examples of how indigenous American traditions are being used in spas and retreat centres. The Willow Stream Spa at the Fairmont Scottsdale Princess draws from the Arizona Native American tradition of 'purifying' the spirit in its desert purification ritual, which includes burning sage. Mii Amo a destination spa at Enchantment in Sedona, Arizona, offers Inner Quest, developed by local tribal elders of the Yavapai-Apache Nation. The treatment includes a simulated sweat lodge experience. Skana, the Spa at Turning Stone in Verona, New York, offers a genuine sweat lodge experience presided over by a Lakhota Sioux leader and an Oneida tribal drummer and fire-tender. At Auriga, the spa at Capella Pedregal in Cabo San Lucas, a *curandera* or Mexican folk healer is available for treatments and rituals based on local Mexican folk healing traditions. Auriga has four signature treatments that correspond with the lunar phases such as New Moon: The Beginning, a treatment with juniper, rosemary, and fennel to rouse the spirit; and Waxing Moon: Sowing the Seeds, a therapy with white jasmine blossoms and salt exfoliation to release creative energies. In Ivins, Utah, Red Mountain Spa offers Four Directions, inspired by the indigenous Dakota and Lakota tribes. This healing treatment embraces the four directions of the Medicine Wheel and includes animal totems, smudging, and sacred herbs, plants, and stones. The Aspira Spa at the Osthoff Resort in Wisconsin, is using the waters from Elkhart Lake, which the Potawatomi, Menominee, and Ojibwa tribes consider sacred, in its Sacred Waters Massage.

In South America there is a long tradition of baños, which are similar to historic baths or spas in Europe. As stated earlier in the book, plastic surgery and other forms of cosmetic tourism are extremely popular in Central and South America, especially in Argentina, Columbia, Brazil and Bolivia. Certain forms of dance that are indigenous to Central or South America are frequently offered as core products, such as salsa dancing in Cuba or Capoeira in Brazil (an Afro-Brazilian dance-like martial art, first practised by African slaves in the 16th century during Portuguese colonial rule).

Hiking, biking, kayaking and rock climbing. Gourmet cuisine and fine wines. Facials, massages and pedicures. These elements and more can be found at an adventure spa. By definition, an adventure spa offers spa treatments, healthy gourmet food and an abundance of outdoor activity. Adventure-spa goers are looking 'for learning or advancement in outdoor skills … and are active vacationers who want a healthy and active' trip. Guests typically want to combine adventurous, outdoors activities by day (e.g. rock climbing, kayaking, hiking, biking, yoga) with pampering spa services and luxury treatments by night (Pascarella, 2008). Central and South America have the perfect landscapes for adventure spas, from the wildlife-rich jungles, to the rugged mountain chains, to the numerous hot springs, beaches, lakes and rivers. There is also a keen emphasis on ecospas which aim to preserve and protect these natural resources.

Case Studies: Adventure Spas in South America

Tierra Atacama Hotel and Spa in San Pedro de Atacama in Chile has an adventure-spa philosophy. The high Altiplano of the Atacama Desert has rivers, green canyons, lakes, geysers, salt flats with flamingos, sand dunes and natural hot springs. They believe that guests want to experience the outdoors actively and adventurously and then be welcomed back to the hotel with a variety of relaxing options ranging from a simple nap to one of their professional spa services: Their motto is: *Get dirty|Get clean|Get rested|Have fun|Be happy*

(Tierra Atacama Hotel and Spa, 2008).

The Island Experience Adventure Spa in Brazil is located on the island of Ilha Grande and promises a complete mind and body makeover. The seven day programme offers a sequence of yoga, rainforest hiking, sea kayaking, snorkeling, daily massage, spa treatments, and Brazilian spa cuisine specially designed to detox the body. The day starts with outdoor yoga followed by a healthy organic breakfast. Next, there may be a hike through the rainforest down to a quiet cove, where guests kayak near a secluded beach. Snorkelling is also possible. After a vegetarian lunch there may be a rest and later a massage or an optional second yoga class. Creative activities may also be offered, such as painting or learning the basics of Brazilian rhythms, for example samba, bossa nova, or capoeira. A special detox dinner is followed by Brazilan cultural events and entertainment. A typical package includes:

- Six nights of lodging (Sunday Night to Saturday Morning)
- All meals and snacks everyday

- More than 6 hours per day of supervised activities (trekking and kayaking)
- Daily yoga classes (two per day)
- Daily full body massages
- Various recreational activities (snorkeling, Brazilian music, art and dance)
- Brazilian cultural entertainment activities
- Round trip to/from Rio International Airport.

The Adventure Spa in Brazil believes that people can change their life in just 1 week. Facing their own limits, beating whatever challenge is waiting for them, learning to manage their fears and frustrations, opening ourselves to new cultures, thoughts and beliefs. The Island Experience was created by a group of friends who share the same devotion for adventure, healthy habits, outdoor sports, wildlife and environment.

Their motto is: *Breathe … Disconnect … Live a healthier life … Go for the experience!*

(The Island Experience, 2008)

Case Studies: Ecospas in Central America

Eco Spas in Central America aim to offer the traveller a design and philosphy which complements the rhythms of nature. The treatments and food integrate indigenous plants and rituals. For example, Spa Uno in Costa Rica's treatments involve products using fresh local ingredients like avocado, mango or banana. They also offer jungle-resistant wedding make-up! Maruba Spa in Belize calls itself a 'jungle spa' as it is located in a 1,000 acre jungle reserve. The spa makes use of natural ingredients from the jungle to develop the Maruba Therapy product range. This includes different 'mood muds'. Their philosophy is to offer a balance of health and rejuvenation through fitness, beauty, nutrition, relaxation and nature. In addition to pampering and relaxing health and beauty treatments, activities include hiking in the medicinal rain forest, touring Mayan ruins, going on photographic and nature safaris, birdwatching, horseriding, diving, and snorkelling.

(Spa Uno, 2008; Maruba Spa, 2008)

Arashá, a Tropical Forest Resort & Spa in Ecuador offers more than the exotic and delicious fruit of the region, which was the inspiration for the name of the facility: '*Arashá is an experience that appeals to all senses*'. It is located less than 3 hours from Quito in the middle of the most bio diverse 'Hot Spot' on the globe. Arashá offers ecologically sensitive bungalows and services from stress-relieving aromatic massage, to participating in any one of the many educational eco-tours, to making chocolate out of cacao seeds. It has been recognized with many awards as the finest resort in Ecuador. The wide varieties of programmes visitors can choose from are as follows:

- Chocolate Workshop (e.g. chocolate fondue visitors can make from natural cacao seeds)
- Artisan's Workshop (e.g. making earrings, collars, rings)

- Health benefits of natural juices and exotic fruits workshop (learning about the local tropical fruits and the health benefits their juices provide)
- Medicinal Plants workshop (understanding and learning about the medicinal plants in the forests)
- Complete body & spiritual cleansing with a Colorado Shaman
- Ecologically friendly 18 holes mini pitch-and-putt golf course
- Oriental meditation
- Sangay Theater (Eco-educational and classic films)
- Exotic Tropical Forest Flowers arrangement workshop.

(Arasha Resort, 2008)

In the Caribbean, health and spa tourism are recognized as important sectors, so much so that there have already been three symposia focusing on Health Tourism. For example, the following issues were discussed in 2007:

- Standardization and Accreditation of Caribbean Health and Spa Tourism Sector
- Integrating Indigenous Healers into the Health Tourism Domain
- Financial Institutions marketing to the Health and Spa Tourism sector
- How to Market Caribbean Health Tourism Overseas
- Developing private label products for hotels and spas
- Promoting Health Tourism effectively via the Internet
- Health Tourism Domain Integration
- Health Tourism Education and Training
- The use of natural foods in treatment modalities.

The Caribbean Resort and Day Spa Association provides help, guidelines and coordination for those interested in health tourism development. Rather than focusing on medical tourism, it was thought that the public facilities in the region are very limited by comparison with places like Asia. Cuba is an exception, since beyond the newly built resort spas, it can build on its thermal waters. There are a couple of spas offering therapeutic services and patients can have various medical surgical treatments as well in the Cuban hospitals and clinics. The best opportunities for the Caribbean are therefore likely to be in the niche of 'wellness', ie, spas, luxury resort spas (e.g. in St Lucia), recovery treatments, herbal or traditional healing, as well as some special medical facilities such as dialysis and fertility clinics. The need to add some special local ingredients was recognized (such as the wider knowledge of the healing properties of many spice and herbal remedies) to make the Caribbean 'brand' of wellness products unique and truly attractive. The English-speaking Caribbean has a huge language advantage over Latin America when it comes to dealing with Americans, the natural landscape and scenery are beautiful and the weather is warm all year round.

Table 6.1 Typology of Global Health and Wellness Facilities.

Regions	Main Sending Markets		Prominent Approach to Health Tourism			Notes
	Domestic	International	Advanced	Traditional	Under-developed/minimal	
Europe						
Northern Europe	✓				✓	Mainly leisure and recreation
Western Europe	✓✓✓	✓✓	✓			All forms available
Central and Eastern Europe	✓✓✓	✓✓✓	✓	✓		Medical therapeutic orientation; Introduction of global wellness treatments and leisure and recreation
Southern Europe	✓	✓	✓	✓		Traditional and new approaches and services co-exist (e.g. historic spas and resort spas)
Americas						
North	✓✓✓	✓	✓			(Re)discovering medical services as well as proliferation of products and segments
Central	✓✓	✓✓	✓		✓	New approaches and services capitalize on local resources (especially resort or eco-spas)
South	✓✓	✓	✓		✓	New approaches and services capitalize on local resources (especially resort or adventure spas)
Africa	✓	✓	✓		✓	New approaches and services capitalize on local resources (e.g. traditions)
Asia						
Middle-East	✓	✓✓	✓	✓		Traditional and new approaches and services co-exist (e.g. hotel spas and hammams; and medical services)
South-East	✓	✓✓	✓	✓		Traditional and new approaches and services co-exist and blend
Far-East	✓✓	✓	✓	✓		Medical services attract foreign tourists, domestic tourism builds on local traditions
Australia, New Zealand, and South Pacific	✓	✓	✓			New approaches and services capitalize on local resources (e.g. traditions)

Key: the number of ✓ refers to the relative role of the given market; and indicates the most prominent approach(es).

Source: Smith and Puczkó.

Conclusion

This chapter has demonstrated the regional diversity of wellness tourism, indicating that despite trends towards globalization and standardization of facilities and services, there are unique products in different areas of the world which are worth travelling for. This might mean natural resources (for example, medical and mineral waters in CEE or hot springs in New Zealand or Iceland), spiritual traditions in Asia (e.g. massage, yoga or meditation), thalassotherapy treatments in a specific location (e.g. by the Dead Sea), real Turkish baths in Turkey, traditional Arab Baths in Spain, Finnish saunas and lakes – the list could go on. Even in cases where the surroundings seem irrelevant (e.g. for yoga or holistic holidays, fitness-based or nutritional programmes, medical and beauty tourism), it seems that certain destinations are more attractive than others. Visitors are sometimes looking for specific resources, sometimes a beautiful, inspiring landscape, maybe a good climate or healthy food. More often than not, they are also looking for the chance to feel special, looked-after, and pampered. The provision of a quality, customized experience is therefore an essential selling point for any destination regardless of location, as the chapters in the following section will demonstrate. The following table gives a summary of how health and wellness tourism looks in the discussed regions (Table 6.1).

PART 2

Managing and marketing health and wellness tourism

CHAPTER 7

Demand, motivations, and profiles

*More spiritual adventurers exist today than most people think.
They travel unknown seas and they are the ones who, in the end,
without knowing how, suddenly change the winds of history.*
(Arias, 1999:19)

Relatively little research has been undertaken about the profiles and
motivations of the so-called health visitors. Instead, there has been
a focus on the different sub-sectors, such as spa tourists or spiritual
tourists. Whilst it is useful to establish typologies of health tourism
and tourists, as stated by Dann and Cohen (1996:303) 'Typologies
are still only heuristic rather than explanatory devices'. Typologies
often serve merely to indicate collective trends and do not take
into consideration individual behaviour and proclivities (Sharpley,
1994). As well as being rather general, many traditional tourism
typologies are at least a decade old, thus they fail to reflect current
lifestyle trends and values. Swarbrooke and Horner (1999) suggest
that academic typologies should be combined with market segmentation to build up a clearer understanding of tourist profiles.
This may combine geographical, socio-economic, demographic,
psychographic, behaviouristic or life-style factors. As discussed in
the previous chapter, there is a strong link between peoples' lifestyles and their propensity to engage in wellness tourism.

Profiling wellness visitors

Table 7.1 gives a general indication of the types of visitors who
use the current range of wellness products and services. This is
by no means definitive, but it shows some of the trends in different regions of the world.

Table 7.1 Profiling Wellness Visitors.

Type of Wellness (Product/Location)	Typical Activities	Wellness Domain(s)	Typical Visitors
Traditional spas (e.g. Central and Eastern Europe, Japan, Italy)	Sitting in mineral waters, massage, sauna, steam room	Physical, curative, medical	Older people with specific diseases or complaints
Hotels and day spas (e.g. UK, USA, Caribbean, South East Asia)	Beauty treatments, relaxing massage, aromatherapy, jacuzzi	Cosmetic, relaxation	High income visitors, business tourists, more often women
Purpose built recreational spas (e.g. Austria, Germany)	Swimming pools, thermal but not medical waters, themed saunas, and steam rooms, jacuzzis, fitness activities	Physical, relaxation, fun	Skiiers, hikers, couples, sometimes families with children
Seaside resorts and thalassotherapy centres (e.g. France, Israel, Greece)	Hydrotherapy, salt inhalations, salt scrubs, seaweed wraps, tanning	Physical, curative, cosmetic	High income hotel guests, older visitors
Holistic retreat centres (e.g. Greece, Spain, USA, Australia)	Yoga, massage, creative, spiritual, and psychological workshops	Physical, mental, psychological, social, creative, spiritual	Mainly 'baby boomers' aged 35–55, more likely to be women
Yoga centres (e.g. India, USA, Cananda, Europe)	Yoga, meditation, chanting	Physical, mental, spiritual	Most likely professional women aged 40+
Meditation retreats (e.g. Thailand, India)	Meditation, fasting, chanting	Mental, spiritual	'Baby boomers', backpackers, 'hippies'
Pilgrimage centres (e.g. Spain, France)	Visiting spiritual landscapes, religious buildings, walking pilgrimage routes	Physical, spiritual	All ages but increasingly under 30, not necessarily religious
Medical centres (e.g. Hungary, South Africa, India)	Operations, cosmetic surgery, dentistry, special treatments	Physical, cosmetic	Western Europeans and Americans for whom treatment is cheaper abroad, mainly 30+

Source: Information based on various sources: including ISPA data 2003–2008, Puczkó and Bachvarov (2006), Devereux and Carnegie (2006), Smith and Kelly (2006), Lehto et al. (2006), Monteson and Singer (2004).

From Table 7.1, we can see that there are a high number of women and people over 30 involved in wellness activities, but relatively few men and young people. The reasons for this have not been explored in great depth, but of course women have always been far more interested in physical appearance, weight issues, make-up, and haircare than men. This is partly due to social expectation, fashion, media pressure, and so forth, but it has meant that day spas and beauty salons are more regularly frequented by women. Women are also more open to discussing their feelings and emotions in a public forum, according to popular psychological research (e.g. Gray, 2002). Women traditionally played the role of carer in many families and therefore took primary responsibility for the health and well-being of family members, for example, medication, and nutrition, even encouraging exercise and relaxation. Although many women now work full-time and cannot devote as much time to supporting husbands and children, it is still often expected that women should somehow hold families together and play a nurturing role. It is well-documented that working mothers have very little time to themselves for leisure activities and relaxation, as they still tend to do the majority of domestic work and childcare. It is not surprising therefore that more women crave or need specialist wellness services and time out from busy schedules to look and feel better.

In comparison, men may prefer different modes of relaxation, some of which have a wellness dimension such as sports or fitness activities. The labelling that is used to target men needs to take a different form, as it is unlikely that beauty or pampering would sound appealing. For example, spas can sell their services to men, but as tools for relaxation or stress relief. Popular activities would include massage, saunas, steam rooms, and gym facilities. Young people (e.g. 18–25), on the other hand, would not see the need for wellness when they are often in peak physical condition, suffer relatively little stress and have few responsibilities compared to the over-30s. They would not be attracted by any kind of services that imply sickness or disease and which primarily attract elderly visitors (e.g. medical spas), and luxury spas or beauty salons are usually too expensive for them. However, there are rising levels of depression in young people aged 18–25 especially men in many Western countries (Mullholland, 2005). This could be attributed to many factors, such as peer pressure or media pressure to be attractive, rich, and successful; the loss of a clear gender role with the increasing emancipation of women; or too much stress and competition within education or the workplace. For marketing purposes, words like 'fitness', 'chilling', 'escape', or 'fun' can be more attractive than wellness for young people, even 'rehab' which has become trendy amongst celebrities who need to de-tox after indulging in party lifestyles for too long!

Typical consumer research focuses on a number of factors, some of which have already been discussed in Chapter Three. Demographic segments are clearly important such as age, gender, income level, life stage, geography, religion, or education. In addition, psychographic segments become even more important for wellness tourism analysis such as lifestyle, values, occupation, personality, and hobbies. Clearly, the life stage of individuals or the aspiration of being part of 'tribes' makes a difference to their needs. For example, young people may have relatively few physical health problems, will be unencumbered by family responsibilities, tend to have more free time but will have less spending power. They are most likely to travel with friends seeking fun (e.g. in aqua parks or fun waters), to enjoy music festivals perhaps with chill-out zones, or in some cases to backpack in spiritual destinations (e.g. India) and try out yoga, meditation or other practices which are associated with a 'cool', hippie-like identity. Busy middle-aged executives tend to have very little spare time because of long working hours and family responsibilities, but have high spending power and a willingness to pay for short-term pampering and luxury (e.g. day or weekend spas and massage) or work/life balance courses and stress management (e.g. life-coaching). Elderly travellers will have less spending power but more time, and they may suffer from more physical health problems. Therefore medical spas or wellness cruises may provide the best form of relaxation.

Case Study of a Child-orientated Spa: Sonnentherme and Hotel Sonnenland

The Sonnetherme (Lutzmannsburg, Austria) was reopened in 1999 introducing brand new services. The facility serves as a leisure and recreational bath targeting families with kids specifically. This means that all the services in the bath complex and in the hotel Sonnenpark attached to it caters for the needs of kids and their parents. The complex has five clearly separated sections: Baby World (shallow pools and baby sauna) for babies and toddlers, Funny Waters (slides and other fun elements) for children, the Silent Dome (relaxation pools), the Sauna World and the Beauty and Massage sections are for adults. Children under 14 cannot enter the Silent Dome and the Sauna World. The Baby World provides sleeping room, free buggy loan, walking schools and see-saws, free baby swimming trial and regular baby swimming courses from 3 months up plus baby lagoon pool, baby kitchen, bubble pool, breast feeding zones, changing dome, and shady outdoor loungers.

All facilities of the (four star) Hotel Sonnenpark cater for kids of all ages, including large play area with toys, a feeding room, and small kitchen, cots and baby alarm in the rooms, childrens' menus and 'Sunnybunny' who comes during dinners and provides entertainment for the young guests. Kids, following Sunnybunny can slide down from the dining area directly to the playroom.

(Sonnentherme, 2008)

Segmenting health and wellness tourists

Segments for health and wellness tourism are closely related to segments for health services. It is very interesting to refer to some research by the Natural Marketing Institute in the USA (Forgen, 2005) on health personalities. Talking about the segments and targets in health and wellness tourism, it makes sense to analyse the attitude and practices the segments represent towards health (and not towards tourism). The study revealed that the American society can be categorized into five groups according to their health personalities:

- Food actives (26%): Who believe in creating healthy lifestyle through balance of diet, exercise, and nutrition.

- Well-beings (23%): Who focus on achieving good health through all means, e.g. diet, nutritional supplements or changing lifestyle.
- Eat, drink, and be merrys (21%): Who know that they probably should live a more healthy lifestyle, but are not that concerned about it.
- Fence sitters (18%): Who are neutral about health issues, knowing what to do, but would not do it.
- Magic bullets (12%): Who are looking for the one pill, diet, procedure, etc. that would solve a particular health issue.

Certainly, the first two personalities could make the base for permanent demand in health tourism, wherereas the 'Eat, Drink and Be Merrys' and the 'Magic Bullets' could form the impulse demand, who, for whatever reason, may become guests. But their interest does not stay for long.

The global market research company, GfK started a so-called Socio-Lifestyle research project a couple of years ago. The objective of data collection was to identify the main types of lifestyle and the corresponding characteristics. Although questions about health tourism demand were not included in the survey, these lifestyle categories could give us some directions as to who may become a customer and why for the different forms of health tourism. Note that market studies on motivations and drivers are more regular in other industries than in tourism, that is travel and tourism can learn a lot from segmentation-oriented studies carried out in the service industries. This information can also provide the necessary links to and with accompanying industries, e.g. cosmetics, travel gear, transportation.

According to the European lifestyle categories (Figure 7.1), it can be expected that:

- The 'Metamorphosis' oriented customers (e.g. 'Crafty World' or 'Cosy Tech World') can show significant interest in holistic tourism and spiritual or psychological activities, whereas the 'New World' segment may find adventure or eco-spas attractive.
- The 'Mirage' style people could be the major market for luxury spa hotels, spa resorts or destinations.
- Medical tourism and services can attract the peoples belonging to 'Steady World'.

Following the information search about the main drivers, ISPA ran a joint USA–Canada spa-goer and non-Spa-goer consumer study in 2006. It may not be very suprising, that the findings of this study correspond to the model of Plog (1974). In Plog's model visitors can fall under one of the three major categories, e.g. allocentrics, who are open to new experiences, and place; psychocentrics, who like safe journeys, well-known circumstances; and the majority of midcentrics, who want a little bit of both extremes. The analogy from the ISPA's study means that a relatively small segment is the 'Core' spa-goers, who feel that learning about and going to spas are important to their lives (e.g. demand for therapies). At the other end of the spectrum are the 'Periphery' spa-goers, who enjoy going to spas but otherwise show little interest in them (e.g. demand for indulgence

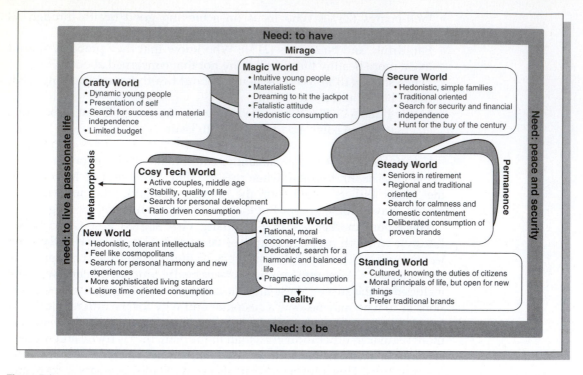

Figure 7.1
Euro-socio-style®. *Source*: GfK Lifestyle Research, 2005 with permission.

and cosmetics). The so-called 'Mid' spa-goers try to achieve a balance between pure pampering and transformative mind, body, and spirit experiences. The drivers for non-spa-goers are the same, but they typically fulfill these motives through experiences they can provide for themselves (ISPA, 2006a, b). However, 'Work' is everywhere in non-spa-goers' everyday life and receiving an authentic and trustworthy experience is key for non-spa-goers.

When operators and organizations define their targets and targeting strategies and tactics, it is essential to know what benefits existing and prospective customers may associate with a health trip. An in-depth survey for the Destination Spa Group (2005) provides insight on the destination spa goer as compared to the general vacationer. Respondents of the survey listed many positive benefits from a destination spa trip, that is:

- Energy level and mental ability increase, and destination spa goers:
  - Are more alert and have improved ability to concentrate
  - Feel more creative
  - Feel better able to handle everyday life and have an increased ability to relax each evening
  - Have more energy when they awake in the morning

- Appear to have a very high ability to resolve challenges
- Seem to handle business affairs better
- Physical fitness improves and spa-goers:
  - Feel more physically fit and have more endurance
  - Feel more agile
  - Are more happy with their body image
  - Exercise more enthusiastically
- Interpersonal skills and connections improve and spa-goers:
  - Feel more connected to and cared for by family, friends and work associates
  - Have a greater understanding of self
  - Family and friends see a definite positive change.

These findings support the idea that the general theme that characterizes positioning in health and wellness tourism is benefits (and to a lesser extent user or competitive positioning themes).

The attempt at segmenting health tourists has evolved from being mainly a brand or site related issue to a national or even international one. We refer to a couple of recent studies that collected information about visitors and guests. The findings of The Leading Spas of Canada (2006) study revealed and also confirmed that spa-goers in day and resort spas are quite different from those of medical spas, for example. The key findings of the 2005 Canadian Spa Goers Survey summarized that compared to individuals who did not visit a spa in 2004, spa goers:

- Are younger;
- Are students;
- Are employed full-time, part-time or self-employed;
- More frequently have university and/or postgraduate education;
- Have a greater annual household income;
- Use the Internet as their primary source of income.

Another study, organized by the Hungarian National Tourist Office in 2002, however, revealed that the Hungarian medical spa-goers:

- Are older;
- Are pensioners;
- Average or little above average university education;
- Have average or lower than average annual income;
- Do not use the Internet.

The National Tourism Authority in Ireland (2007) produced a Health and Wellness Strategy in which they note that in the UK and Ireland, indulgence is one of the main reasons people visit a spa. Research shows that there is an increased need for consumers to feel better. This desire is driven by a hectic commuter culture, stress-related health problems and a tiring pace of life. Irish Spa goers have two main reasons for visiting spas: to pamper and indulge themselves and to escape. They also identified six discreet segments for health and wellness:

- *Fun seekers* (going away with friends and enjoying themselves. Not spa regulars or experts)
- *Occasional pamperers* (taking time out from a busy, stressful schedule. Spas are a rare treat)
- *Relaxers* (seeking rest and time out. Spas as escapism)
- *Serenity seekers* (seeking peace, understanding and self-acceptance. Wellness as lifestyle)
- *Beauty queens* (interest in looking good and being glamorous)
- *Help seekers* (looking for change in their lives)

Lifestyle segmentation may also draw on the geography, topography, or culture of a country or region. For example, for Wellness Tourism in Eastern Finland where there are many lakes and forests and the emphasis is on outdoor recreation, Kangas and Tuohino (2007) suggest the following segmentation:

- *Careless of holistic well-being*: Mostly men, under 35 years old, little interest in mental well-being, sport, or fitness. They enjoy sleeping and sauna (note that saunas are an integral part of life for most Finns and not a luxury spa activity!).
- *Work and health-orientated nature people*: Over 85% women mainly 35–44 years old, interested in sport, fitness, health, and nature, as well as mental well-being and balance. Tend to eat healthy food, go to the gym, and do Nordic walking.
- *Seekers of mental well-being*: A third of respondents were men, a third of respondents had children. Over 60% are aged 25–44. They are most interested in domestic life, mental well-being and balance.
- *Cultural appreciators who exercise in nature*: Interested in nature, health, and sport rather than domestic life. Almost 75% were women mostly aged 45–65. One-third lived alone, one third has children, and 25% were empty nester couples. They tend to enjoy cross-country skiing and winter swimming.
- *Family-orientated*: Love and family are the most important things in life, but nature, sport and health are also rather important. Spiritual and mental well-being were less important. 75% of respondents were women, aged 18–44. They tend to enjoy downhill skiing.
- *Home-orientated*: Enjoy domestic activities, cooking, and handicrafts. Mostly 45–54 year olds and empty nesters if they had children. Less interest in gyms than in walking or outdoor recreation.
- *Spirituality and nature appreciators*: 72% women, mainly 55–65 years old, many of whose children have left home. Walking is a popular activity.

Many of these segments could be used in other contexts, but the wellness activities chosen by the participants such as cross-country skiing, Nordic walking and winter swimming (e.g. in Lakes) are very typical of the region and would not be relevant elsewhere (e.g. the Mediterranean,

Asia). While this is an excellent cluster analysis and the methodology could be used in a more international context, the factors will vary according to geographical and cultural context. There is clearly a need for research at national level in most countries or regions which want to develop wellness tourism in order to identify clusters or segments. It is not enough to focus on general consumer behaviour or lifestyle trends – the research should also include travel and tourism patterns.

Demand and motivations of health tourists

Götz (2008) raises an interesting idea about why many people like to bathe in waters. He refers to the two theories of evolution. One (the more accepted one) bases its approach on savanna-theory or Darwinism, while the other one assumes that water monkeys were the predecessors of human beings. Some ethnologists believe that some humanoids had to adapt to a lifestyle that was very much based on sea and sealife. This would explain the propensity of almost all civilizations and societies, ancient and modern, to engage in some form of water-based activites for health and well-being.

The Austrian Ministry of Economy and Employment (Austria) collected the major factors that guests may look for when they decide where to travel. The ministry wanted to collect those factors that can provide developers and managers with help and directions. The study (BMWA, 2002a) enlisted the following major factors: geographic location, basic offers, ambience, atmosphere, information, fitness areas, changing and wet areas, sauna, relaxation areas, massage, cosmetics, nutrition, qualified personnel, programmes for groups, accommodation supply and its price level, and products taking into account the different needs of women and men.

In terms of demand, wellness and holistic tourists are likely to be 'Active Health Seekers' (House of Lords Report on CAM, 2000), who are highly motivated and determined to play a role in their own health. They frequently choose alternatives to orthodox medicine and are not afraid to experiment. Sociological research carried out by Cleaver and Muller (2002) into the tourism behaviour of 'Baby Boomers' bears relevant findings for the wellness sector. The Baby Boomer market (now the late 30s to mid 50-year-old groups) is a key target for wellness. These consumers are often at their peak earning potential, have high education levels, enjoy greater freedom from debt, have more time for travel and greater desire for 'self-fulfilling' activities (Cleaver & Muller, 2002). Psychographic analysis of census and other data in Australia by the Ray Morgan Research Centre (1997) has resulted in the development of a 'lifestyle typology' for the Baby Boomer population containing 10 categories. In terms of value segments, they appear to occupy a place somewhere between 'visible achievers' and 'socially aware'. Dickman (1997) describes 'visible achievers' as those who are generally over 30 and earn above average income. They are in control of their lives, but want personal recognition of success. They tend to have a strong focus on themselves and their families. They are likely to be 'inner-directed' (Middleton & Clarke, 1998), educated, mature, self-confident, with strong cultural, aesthetic and creative aspirations, and a desire for self-realization. Interestingly, this may also be the group which Glouberman (2002) identifies as most likely to experience burnout. The second group are 'socially aware', community minded and environmentally friendly. They are likely to be progressive and open-minded, and take a global view of the world and political issues. They also tend to be early-adopters of new products.

According to the findings of the Wellness Lifestyle Insights study (Hartman Group, 2007), the key life stages and situations that make people in the USA interested and motivated in wellness were the following:

- High school athletics
- Going to college
- Pregnancy/having kids
- Aging/milestone birthdays
- Personal/vicarious health experience

Most wellness tourists have the motivation to optimize their physical and mental health. Depending on their personal circumstances, they may be seeking escapism from stress; rest and relaxation; a spiritual experience; to be in nature; self-development or improvement; meeting like-minded people and forming communities; and emotional or creative expression.

In terms of wellness or 'well-being' tourists' behaviour and travel patterns, Tourism Australia's (2007) research shows that:

- Well-being is addictive! well-being travellers take this experience often.
- On average well-being travellers have been on seven well-being trips in the last 5 years.
- Travellers prefer to take well-being experiences domestically rather than overseas.
- Travellers don't want to deal with airports or a different culture when they are travelling for well-being.
- Longer well-being experiences are taken overseas, but there are usually other reasons for the trip.
- Domestic well-being travellers stay on average 5 days, 4 of which are for a well-being experience.
- Those who travel overseas take 16 days with 8 days for well-being.
- Some specific offers are also taken overseas (i.e. meditation in India).
- Pampering, spa treatment trips are especially limited to a maximum duration of 5 days.
- There is a greater need to add other experiences (or go overseas) when the duration is increased.

For most wellness tourists, there are emotional needs which trigger the desire for certain kinds of experiences on a trip from which the results are ideally taken home (Table 7.2).

Overall, it is difficult to give an overall profile of wellness tourists therefore it is better to return to some of the sub-sectors identified so far in the book in order to focus in more depth on the different demands and motivations of tourists.

Table 7.2 Emotional Triggers for Wellbeing Trips.

Emotional Triggers	Trip Focus	Take Home Result
'My life lacks meaning'	Learning and finding the direction	Renewed self through awareness of direction
'I know the goal, but I'm stuck'	The goal: to detox, get fit/ healthy, enhance spirituality	Renewed self through progress towards the goal
'I am worn down by everyday life'	To replenish their own needs	Renewed self through enhanced well-being
'My relationship with my partner is worn down by everyday life'	One another and the relationship	Renewed relationship
'I need a reward/to celebrate'	Indulging themselves	Renewed self

Source: Tourism Australia, 2007.

Spa tourists

ISPA (2007) estimates that there are nearly 100 million active spa-goers worldwide. This includes research from 12 countries – Australia, Austria, Canada, France, Germany, Italy, Japan, Singapore, Spain, Thailand, UK, and the USA. Spa visitors are mainly female in professional and executive jobs (often 70%+), however, men account for more than 40% of spa-goers in Australia, Austria, Germany, Japan, Singapore, Spain, and Thailand. Baby boomers dominate this market: 60% fall into the 30–49 age group. Those 50 years and older have decreased from 23% to 17% in the past 5 years. An encouraging finding is that younger spa users (<30 years old) are increasing in number. This group accounted for 13% of the resort-based spa-goers in 1992 and 17% in 1997 (ISPA, 2003). Women continue to make up 74% of this market. Many people go to spas mainly for stress relief, but at least half value time to be alone. Most Americans and Canadians visit spas alone (ISPA, 2006a). The most popular treatments for women tend to be massage, facials and manicures, whereas men prefer steam, sauna, massage and exercise machines. Interestingly, physical shape, fitness, losing weight, nutrition and appearance were NOT important motivations, instead the top reasons for going to spas were feeling stressed, wanting a small indulgence, the desire to 'splurge', to feel better, rest and relaxation, and pampering. Interestingly, the US spa-goers (63%) are more likely to travel out-of-town to visit spas, but this is true of only 49% of Canadians (ISPA, 2006a), however when Canadians do travel to spas they are likely to stay longer.

Interestingly, Euromonitor International (2008) found out that Japan sold the most spa packages in the world in 2006 via travel retailers (Table 7.3).

Table 7.3 Number of Spa Packages Sold Worldwide 2008.

Spa Packages	USD (million)
Japan	4,360
USA	2,432
Italy	2,387
Canada	1,077
United Kingdom	846
Switzerland	636
Germany	607
France	404
China	360
New Zealand	347

Source: Euromonitor International, 2008.

Spa goers' profiles are likely to differ – sometimes radically – according to which countries they come from. For example, ISPA's (2003) study of the Japanese spa market shows that 60% of Japanese residents had visited a spa in the past 12 months compared to 21% of Americans. Day spas are the most popular, followed by mineral springs (39%). Unlike in the USA where 69% of spa visitors are women (ISPA, 2006a), equal numbers of Japanese men and women tend to visit all categories of spas. Steam baths/sauna are the most frequently requested treatment (48%), followed by massage (27%), but the Japanese prefer reflexology to manicures and pedicures. The average age of a spa visitor is 45, similar to the USA, where it is 44 (ISPA, 2003).

ISPA (2006b) makes a useful distinction between segments in spa tourism:

- *Core* (Most involved)
- *Mid-level* (somewhat involved)
- *Periphery* (least involved)

These reflect the degree to which consumers approach their spa experiences as part of a holistic, long-term orientation towards health and well-being, rather than just engaging in escape or mere indulgence. Core spa-goers are more committed to larger wellness lifestyles and see their spa treatments as part of that, whereas peripheral spa-goers see spa treatments as a (rare) indulgence and have not made the connection with wider wellness or health issues. Consumer visits to spas usually incorporate one of the following drivers:

- *Indulgence* (pleasure, fun, appealing to the senses)
- *Escape* (i.e. relief from the pressures of social life)
- *Work* (individual work related to self-improvement, i.e. physical, mental, and emotional)

Day-spas tend to target city dwellers with limited leisure time (Crebbin-Bailey et al., 2005). Azara et al. (2007) showed that the average age of typical visitors to the Devonshire Spa in the UK was 41 for men and 45 for women. Although the spa is visited by many local people, national and international visitors were also present (44% for men, 71% for women). Most people were looking for relaxation, escape, a new experience, and personal/individual fulfilment. Many liked to be alone there, especially women. Men in particular emphasized the stress-relief aspect.

Increasingly, we can see a number of new and purpose-built recreational and leisure spas in countries like Austria, Germany, and Switzerland. Most of these are of a very high quality with a diverse range of thermal facilities and treatments. Some are located in mountain and ski resorts and are frequented by skiiers or hikers. Excellent provision is usually made for families and children, even if the childrens' facilities are physically separated from the adult ones. Such centres are more likely to attract equal numbers of men and women, and especially couples (romantic packages can be purchased, for example).

However, the profile of medical or health spa visitors, for example in Central and Eastern Europe may be radically different from recreational, day or beauty spas. Referring to the research by HNTO (2002) it seems to be the case that medical spa visitors are from a higher age group (e.g. 55+), there are often as many men as women. In some ways, it is perhaps more helpful to look at the profile of medical tourists to gain an insight into who visits these spas, as their profiles can tend to be radically different from wellness spas.

Holistic tourists

Eliade (1971) sees the internal and external quest as homologous, and Graburn (2002:31) suggests that 'the relationship between an inner and outer metaphor may be the key to understanding tourists' motivations, expectations and satisfactions'. Holistic tourists' inner journey will be equally if not more important than the outer one, and they are focused on a sense of self rather than 'Other'. Holistic tourists are often interested in 'finding' their true selves. In this context, as stated by Seaton (2002:162) 'Tourism is at least as much a quest *to be* as a quest to see'. De Botton (2002) cynically suggests that we are largely unable to escape from ourselves and our persistent worries, and Edensor (2001:33) questions whether we are truly able to 'transcend the mundane'. Holistic tourism perhaps affords opportunities to do just that, but it is arguably more than a mere escape route. Holistic tourists appear to crave the enhancement rather than the avoidance of self, and many go away to confront the very problems that other tourists are only too happy to leave behind. Given the apparent de-differentiation of tourism and everyday life (McCabe, 2002), it is not surprising that tourists are increasingly using tourism as a means of improving their home life, rather than merely escaping from it. For this sub-sector, the link between lifestyle and tourism is especially strong.

A continuum of interest/experience can be referred to with regard to holistic tourists/participant travellers. At one end are tourists who have little prior knowledge of yoga, Tai Chi and so on, but who are willing to 'try it out' by way of a relaxing holiday. Further along, are those who perhaps attend classes at their local gym sporadically or who may have attended a one day workshop on reflexology, reiki or some other complementary therapy. These tourists may wish to participate in a holistic holiday to rejuvenate themselves and/or their interest and motivation in 'better living' when they get home. At the extreme end of the visitor continuum are those who are regular, committed advocates of yoga, Tai Chi (or whatever the chosen activity of their holiday is based upon). Such visitors often already incorporate healthy diet and exercise into their daily lifestyles and as such, are not looking for *new* skills but, rather to re-locate the activities they enjoy, temporarily to different, warmer, more pleasant, surroundings.

Analogies to eco-tourism are useful in this discussion of the emerging holistic tourism sector. Swarbrooke and Horner (1999) refer to the spectrum of ecotourist types in terms of 'shades of green', ranging from 'light green' to 'totally green'. Purple is often used as a central colour in alternative therapies, therefore an analagous reference could be posed in relation to holistic tourists.

• Little prior knowledge/practice of holistic activities • New experience • Self-contained/One-off holiday • Unlikely/may lead to integrative 'better living' upon return home • Seeks comfortable surroundings, guided instruction, scheduled programme	*Lilac* (Experimenters)
• Sporadic/occasional practitioner of holistic activities • Renewed/lapsed/motivational experience • May become regular holiday type • Likely to *renew* better living upon return home • Seeks a range of surroundings/accommodation types • Requires some guidance and a choice of activity programming	
• Regular practitioner of holistic activities • Continued/re-located experience • Typical holiday choice • *Reinforces* and consolidates home-based lifestyle/behaviour • Seeks simple surroundings (less relevant than the quality of activity) • Requires advanced instruction and space for self-directed practice	*Deep Purple* (*Purists*)

Source: Smith and Kelly, 2006.

The following quotations selected from the Internet sites of various holistic centres gives some idea of tourists' experiences of a holistic holiday and the motivations that led them there or might encourage them to book a holistic holiday in the future. For many, the location is an integral part of the experience; for others it is the presence of a charismatic group leader or teacher; some enjoy the relaxation or social elements; and others take parts of the experience back home into their everyday lives.

> *Now here I am back home and I still carry all the blessings of those two weeks around with me. I look forward to the next time.*
>
> (Sacred Journeys, UK)

> *I feel more present in my moment-to-moment experiences, and I feel enriched by the lives and stories of the other women here.*
>
> (Hawaiian Retreats for Women)

> *I've actually forgotten what date it is. Actually I have lost all track of time. Thank you for the most amazing and well spent three days of my life.*
>
> (Little House of Avalon, Ireland)

> *Few dreams are so well conceived, fewer so impeccably executed.*
>
> (Serrania Retreats, Spain)

> *Magical gardens and stunning landscapes, with such a sense of freedom to roam.*
>
> (Oxon Hoath, UK)

> *Sandra, you are a true inspiration giving time to everyone.*
>
> (Sacred Journeys, UK)

> *So good to find a retreat with a bar!*
>
> (Oxon Hoath, UK)

Yoga tourists

Yoga tourists are perhaps a sub-sector of holistic tourists in that true yoga enthusiasts do not see yoga as a fitness or exercise programme, rather as a spiritual path which aims to balance body, mind, and soul. Ideally, yogic thinking should be integrated into everyday life including asanas (physical postures), breathing practices, meditations, and nutrition (ideally vegetarian and organic). The kind of visitors who choose yoga holidays are those who already tend to practice yoga at home, although some beginners are also attracted to yoga holidays because of positive press and promotions. Research is sparse, but Lehto et al. (2005) demonstrate that the profile of yoga tourists tends to be mainly female with a high level of education and a professional job, aged 35–54 years old, spiritual but not religious, and interested in vegetarian and organic food as well as complementary and alternative medicines. Yoga is generally seen as a lifestyle rather than a sporadic hobby. They list the top five motivations for yoga holidays as:

- 'to renew myself'
- 'to relax'
- 'to be more flexible in body and mind'
- 'to let go of stress from a busy life'
- 'to help me gain a sense of balance'

Although more women than men tend to practice yoga, there are large numbers of male yoga teachers and spiritual gurus. This could help to encourage men to become involved in certain forms of yoga. In general, it is believed that men are drawn to more physical and strenuous forms of yoga, such as Ashtanga, which involves moving from one posture to another in a 90-min sequence. Men are perhaps more likely to get involved in martial arts and practices that are perceived to be more 'masculine' such as Tai Chi and Qi Gong. Interestingly, women-only classes are a rarity in Tai Chi and it is generally beneficial to have a mix of Yin (female) and Yang (male) energy within a class (Tai Chi Finder, 2007). Retreats exist which focus just on Tai Chi and Qi Gong, but these practices are also included in many holistic holidays.

New age tourists

Johnston and Pernecky's (2006) work on the profiles of New Age tourists, demonstrates how specialization indices can be created for such niche sectors. In their research on a New Age Festival, the New Spirit Festival 2004 in Auckland, New Zealand, specialization based on tourists' skills, knowledge, and involvement was measured, resulting in respondents being categorized as low, medium or highly specialized individuals with respect to three aspects of New Age tourism – spirituality, motivation, and consumer needs. Distinctive profile characteristics emerged, showing differences in levels of preference for organic food, alternative healing treatments and religious beliefs.

Nine questions within the survey were used to create an index of specialization. The questions fell into three general categories: experience, centrality to life and investment. *Experience* measured the respondent's New Age practices and skills. Questions were asked concerning lifetime number of trips to New Age sites/events, number of trips to New Age sites/events annually and ownership of New Age items. *Centrality to lifestyle* measured the respondent's knowledge of New Age/spiritual places, the number of New Age/spiritual courses completed, and involvement in New Age/spiritual activities. Lastly, *Investment* measured the respondent's monetary expenditures on New Age products and services over both specific time periods and throughout their lifetime.

The analysis of the returned surveys showed that the respondents had the following demographic characteristics:

- Most (98%) were from New Zealand, from Auckland and from different regions of the country.
- Most were women (82%).
- Most (92%) were between 31 and 70 years of age. Only 21% were between 21 and 30 years old.
- The majority (82%) identified themselves as New Zealand European; there was only a small percentage (9%) of Maori and/or Asian representation.
- By contrast, income and education levels were diverse.

About 50% of the respondents said they were 'Non-believers' who had no religion. 'Believers', the remaining half, divided themselves into Christians and 'other'; the latter included self-reference to identities such as 'Pagan Witch'. 69% of the sample believed or behaved in ways that made them *high* specialized New Age tourists. A further 22% scored as *medium* specialized, while only 9% of respondents were *low* specialized.

Overall, the research showed that people who participate in the New Age phenomenon should not necessarily be homogenized into one group, suggesting that even within sub-sectors of niche tourism, there can or should be further segmentation. It is also difficult to use labels such as 'New Age' because of possible negative connotations. In this research, for example, data analysis showed there seems to be a sub-group of people who live out New Age lifestyles but do not self-identify as New Agers.

Spiritual tourists

Cohen (1996) differentiates between different tourist motivations and experiences, categorizing them as recreational, diversionary, experiential, experimental, and existential. While the first three categories of tourist are largely 'escaping' routine, boredom, or alienation, they are not necessarily expecting to find meaning elsewhere. In contrast, experimental tourists seek spiritual centres in different, alternative directions; often sampling and contrasting 'authentic' life or rituals in an attempt to find themselves. In many cases, they tend to be younger, 'postmodern travellers' hanging out in ashrams or Kibbutzes for some length of time, but can also include aging hippies from the 1960s and 1970s who never left the destination, or increasingly, 30-something, burnt-out recuperating professionals. Cohen (1996) is slightly cynical about this type of tourist (the eternal 'drifter') for whom the search itself can become a way of life. Existential travellers, on the other hand, tend to commit to one spiritual centre, residing there permanently or visiting periodically on a kind of personal pilgrimage. Mundt (1994) refers also to 'ecotourists' in the context of younger, often environmental tourists who are dabbling in alternative lifestyles and who seek peer accreditation for 'right on' behaviour. Spiritual tourists are often both experimental and existential in that they are usually on a quest for

Table 7.4 Spiritual Tourists Differ in Many Ways from Religious Tourists.

Religious Tourism	Spiritual Tourism
• Affiliation to specific religion or religious group • Interest in quest for religious enlightenment • Enjoys visiting specific religious sites and landscapes • Empathizes with other religious tourists, pilgrims, and local communities • Engages in ritualistic behaviour • Ultimately seeking religious union or salvation	• Likely to have 'multi-faith' empathy • Interest in personal, spiritual development • Enjoys visiting spiritual or mystical landscapes • Seeks interaction with local and indigenous communities • May engage in rituals and ceremonies • Hoping for reconciliation of body, mind, and spirit

Source: Smith, 2003.

a spiritual place (internal or external), even if they have to visit multiple centres before they find what they are looking for (Table 7.4).

Spiritual tourists seem to have in common the fact that they believe in a power beyond themselves, but not necessarily a specific 'God'. They tend to choose trips which take them on an inner as well as an outer journey; seeking peace, calm, and transcendence. Simple, natural environments are sought where accommodation and food may be basic. They are often willing to endure hardship to reach a spiritual goal, and may join communities where basic manual or agricultural work is required (e.g. in communes or ashrams), or may even be altruistic enough to assist in conservation projects or helping the poor. This is particularly true of pilgrims (Devereux & Carnegie, 2006).

Medical tourists

Medical tourists can be any age but are most likely to be older or retired people from Western developed countries where prices for medical treatment are high and waiting lists are long (e.g. USA, Britain). Assenov and Suthin (2007) estimated that in the UK in 2004 over 41,000 people were expecting to experience a waiting time of 6 months or more to have various surgeries. In the USA, medical insurance is particularly expensive so many people are uninsured or under-insured, and therefore cannot afford treatments there. Richards (2006) also notes that about 7% of China's 1.3 billion population travels to other Asian cities for medical tourism. The motivations of visitors vary according to what kind of treatment is needed. For example, as stated by Henderson (2004) tourists may travel for reasons of illness or wellness within the context of medical tourism. There is a spectrum of medical tourism which ranges from serious operations such as heart bypasses, through medical, but non-surgical and asset-based treatments, to dentistry, cosmetic surgery, even sex change operations in countries like Thailand. Many of these patients prefer discreet treatments and services, since they would not necessarily want to show themselves in public just days after the operation. Witepski (2005) notes that in the case of companies like the South African 'Surgeon and Safaris' (which focuses mainly on cosmetic or non-essential surgery) the majority of her clients come from the UK and the USA. The average client is aged between 45 and 65 and is usually single. In terms of motivation, recuperation in a beautiful setting is an added attraction to the cheaper prices, not to mention the medical skills of practitioners (e.g. it is thought that high numbers of skilled dentists can be found in Hungary).

Targeting new markets

It should be recognized that there is a great deal of untapped potential for health and wellness services and tourism. The Spa Association (2005) surveyed a sample of residents in the USA of whom 19% were male and 81% were female to find out why people did NOT go to spas. 63% said they never went mainly because it was too costly. Other reasons included a lack of understanding of what a spa is, uncertainty about treatments, it was too time consuming or there was no spa in their local area (Figure 7.2).

85% had never been on a spa vacation and were only somewhat likely to visit a spa in a hotel they were already visiting. Although 65% said they preferred to visit a spa near their home, 35% would seek a spa whilst travelling. Therefore, although not always a primary motivation for tourism, spas can do much to attract 'incidental' wellness tourists within an existing destination. ISPA (2006b) suggest that spas need to overcome

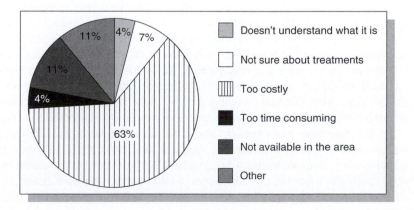

Figure 7.2
Reasons for Not Visiting Spas. *Source*: SPAA, 2005.

negative impressions and stereotypes that spas are 'self-indulgent', 'just for women', or 'too expensive'. ISPA (2004) suggests that core consumers tend to be the most catered to in terms of communication, menu designs and available spa treatments, but they represent the smallest percentage of the overall spa population. Positive and trustworthy experiences need to be created for first-timers so that they become repeat consumers, and non-spa-goers should be offered incentives such as discounts or free samples of products.

It can be seen from the various analyses above that the wellness market (at least in Europe and the USA) is still dominated by the over 30s and women. This is perhaps inevitable, although we see slow but sure shifts towards more men enjoying spas or stress management workshops, however the need for more men-only spas and male-orientated treatments may be needed more in the future. Young people may go to spiritual retreats or on pilgrimages. Teenagers in the USA and Canada are visiting spas more and more frequently for massages, facials, manicures and pedicures (ISPA, 2006a). Whilst it is desirable for most wellness centres to attract more visitors, they should not fall into the trap of trying to attract all markets simultaneously (e.g. a common mistake in under-visited spas). Elderly medical visitors would not appreciate being disturbed by young people or children amusing themselves in 'fun waters'; many women find it difficult to share bathing, relaxation or sauna areas with men, especially where nudity is enforced (e.g. Germany and Austria); visitors looking for relaxation, pampering and beauty do not want to be surrounded by sick people or feel like they are visiting a hospital; those who are interested in healing the physical body will have little interest in psychological or spiritual practices, and so forth. Common sense should prevail when developing, managing, and promoting spas.

Case Study of New Markets: Mens' Wellness

Directly or indirectly the majority of customers and service providers believe (or accept?) that wellness, spas or health are terms only women find interesting. Visiting spas or having a treatment is not considered 'manly'. This is rapidly changing, though. We can see various trend reports in which researchers and practitioners forecast men to become the future 'women', or more precisely, men will show a growing demand for various wellness services.

Even in the beginning of this century, this concept of 'men and wellness' was seen as joke material as Whittal at MenEssentials reported back in 2003. He quoted a spa manager from British Columbia (Canada) saying that ' … she had no interest in such things; spas were a woman's domain … and if men wanted in they had to tolerate the frills and lace'.

As we can see from survey and visitation figures (e.g. ISPA's), men now account for almost half of all spa customers. Whittal also said that, 'If a guy can change a bed and wash poopy diapers without feeling that his masculinity is under siege, then a facial and mud bath ain't gonna kill him either'. Taking this sarcasm aside, the wellness industry is more and more opening up for men. Developers and managers can make a huge difference if they take the following recommendations into account:

- *Avoid 'Men Welcome' spas*: This usually means that the owners or managers recognized the growing momentum of the men's market but have not developed a men's treatment menu.
- *Try crossover spas with a partner*: These spas originally catered to women, but they brought along their partners. This required the businesses to adapt to their new customers' needs (as one owner summarized: 'The rugged look is still in, but why not save it for later? Much later'. (Debra Pender, Beyond Wrapture, British Columbia)
- *The hybrid salon/spa ('Grooming Salon') opened up*: A modern twist on the traditional barbershop, the hybrid is actually a men-only version of the woman's beauty salon in decidedly masculine surroundings.
- *The men-only spa arrived*: While in Europe there have been a few such establishments (e.g. The Refinery in England and Nickel in France), the first men-only spa was opened in New York in 2002 (designed as a submarine!), then in San Francisco.

Gradually almost all forms of health tourism and types of facilities started to approach men. Search engines, hotel chains, day spas, etc., all created a link or special site for male visitors. For example Premium Spa Resorts offering, e.g. treatments and golf training together, addressed men in the following way:

> *Attention all men! These offers have been especially designed for you! Don't let stress and the daily grind get the best of you. Come let us pamper you with our wonderfully relaxing & revitalizing massage treatments. Your overworked muscles will thank you for it – guaranteed!*
>
> (Premium Spa Resorts, 2008).

The motto of why spas are more for men too was that 'Given that the ravages of aging and the need to relax and repair are increasingly less gender specific concerns, it is no surprise that more and more men are regularly partaking in spa treatments'. Foss (2008) mentions another reason why men-only are getting more fashionable: 'While I have never been shy about visiting a spa, but it does get uncomfortable sometimes when there are nine women for each man (that's why it might make sense to go with a woman). Most high-end spas now, therefore, have separate lounges but some mid-range ones don't'.

Not all products and communication even when they use the same vocabulary mean the same thing, though. The gay community has also discovered the male- or men-only spa phenomenon. Gaywired, for example, collected a list of 'hot' spas 'Global grooming hotspots for the guys from all around the world' (Wells, 2007). The compilation, including 316 Club Bar Spa in Chicago, Spa Europa in Calgary or H_2O Spa in Dubai does not necessarily list gay-only facilities, but it is anticipated that gay guests may find companions there.

One of the main gay-oriented websites (www.gay.com) compiled a Guide to Spa Travel for gay men to gay-friendly spas, specifically. There are only a limited number of exclusively gay spas (and a couple of minispas in a handful of gay resort guesthouses), therefore they warn visitors to check what a spa may offer 'Before dropping your towel'. Barr (2005) did an intensive analysis of one of the world's first gay-only spas in Palm Springs (USA), the East Canyon Hotel and Spa. Palm Springs is the home of many natural mineral springs and the Betty Ford Clinic, plus over-40 gay hotels. Many of them also cater for lesbians in women-only gal-ranches. The question, 'Why a gay-only spa?' may become easier to answer considering what a guest said in East Canyon: 'Because I don't want raised eye-brows if I check in with another man and I don't want the masseur to make small talk with me about my non-existent wife and children. I totally relax here because I know everyone else is gay. I don't have to deal with anybody else's issues about my sexuality'. Although it is a gay-only spa, the treatments' names do not overdo and do not want to sound as macho, like 'Tequila Slammer Pore Unjammer'. It does not enforce sexuality, as many gay-only gyms or saunas do (e.g. there is no gym, and this is not a clothing-optional, i.e. naked facility) and does not use names for treatment such as 'rub 'n' tug', either!

Popular gay and lesbian destinations like Bali, Las Vegas, Thailand, The Algarve/Portugal, etc., all tend to provide more and more gay-only day spas, which provide a gym, sauna(s), pool(s) and a bar.

Case study: Turtle Cove Gay Resort and Spa (Australia)

Turtle Cove is located between Cairns and Port Douglas (North Queensland) and has been serving gay and lesbian travellers for almost 15 years. This makes Turtle Cove one of the very first gay and lesbian-only resorts of the world. The resort provides opportunity to enjoy the beach and the ancient rainforest at the same time. In Turtle Cove visitors can:

- Experience the great outdoors.
- Relax and rejuvenate with Australian Holistic Spa Therapy.
- Meet new friends from all over the world.
- Sun themselves on the absolute private beach.
- Enjoy a cocktail by the pool, or kick back in the jacuzzi.
- Dine at the Sandbar, the beachfront restaurant overlooking the Coral Sea.

(Turtle Cove, 2008).

Conclusion

It is clear that more research is needed on the various sub-sectors of health tourism to identify which segments or clusters should be targeted. Increasingly, lifestyle factors are becoming the most important determinants of segmentation, but these are complex and specific to different age groups, genders, even societies and cultures. As discussed in Chapter Four, there is a clear link between the way people conduct their everyday lives (e.g. their propensity to integrate health practices or not) and their travel behaviour. The growth of customized service and the experience economy also means that visitors are becoming more discerning and demanding, so destinations and attractions have to focus on tailoring their products not only to segments but to individuals. This is challenging, especially when visitors also expect to experience something indigenous or local to a destination. Thus, health tourism needs to become even more diverse and unique in its product development, targeting new markets at the same time as satisfying ever more demanding exisiting ones.

Planning and development

Creativity is the hallmark of the world of spa which has incubated some of the most important new ideas in health, beauty, wellness and style.

Ellis (Spa Finder President, 2006)

Introduction

This chapter analyses the way in which health and wellness tourism is developed and planned for. It is recognized that multi-level planning is the most effective and sustainable approach. This involves the integration of national health tourism strategies, regional developments, and local destination and site management. It is important to be aware of the impacts of health tourism development and to follow principles of sustainability and eco-friendliness, especially as health tourism is often based on fragile natural resources and assets. Locations of facilities need to be carefully chosen and building should be closely regulated. A development philosophy needs to be created which infuses all aspects of the planning process, from the selection of the site or location through to the training of staff and the delivery of services. This is a complex procedure for all forms of tourism, but especially for health tourism which can be resource intensive, as well as attracting visitors demanding high quality and luxury products and experiences.

Planning

Planning defines objectives and allocates the instruments and the methods to achieve them. Planning is one of the most important tools in national, regional, and local authorities: conscious planning means the task of preventing or decreasing the negative impacts of tourism to the minimum level and to facilitate and strengthen the positive ones (Rátz & Puczkó, 2002).

There are two major types of tourism development (Pearce, 1989):

- Spontaneous development: When the destined tourism goes from one developed level to another by itself or the components of a tourism product developed by themselves.
- Planned development: All activities are motivated by well-defined objectives of a destination (of any level).

These general observations are also true for health and wellness tourism, too. We can see various cases for either of the above-mentioned types.

Case Study: Health and Beauty Tourism (Moldova)

The Republic of Moldova has spa water treatment centres or sanatoria and resorts that provide health and beauty tourism services. These are located in attractive and peaceful surroundings, where various treatment services are offered. The customers of these establishments are the local population and a small number of regular foreign visitors. The most important centres and resorts are categorized by spa water treatments and rest and recreation.

Those in greatest demand are those located close to rivers or open water: Vadul lui Voda, Ghidighici and Costesti. Here there is potential for international tourism development. The Republic of Moldova is the proprietor of a series of spa water treatment centres and resorts located in the territory of the Ukraine. The Republic of Moldova's favourable climatic conditions permit the offer of various methods of treatment in spa water centres: heliotherapy, aerotherapeutics, thalassotherapy, terencurotherapy, ampelotherapy, peloidotherapy, balneotherapy, etc. Mineral springs with curative qualities in the Republic of Moldova (over 47 springs) represent a major resource for beauty and health tourism development.

The major deficiencies are:

- Lack of coordination and regulation by the state of sanatoria activity.
- Accommodation facilities are mostly old fashioned and do not meet international tourism requirements.
- Medical inventory and furniture are old.
- Lack of staff proficiency in foreign languages.
- Technical state of buildings and adjoining infrastructure are deplorable.
- Lack of additional recreational facilities (swimming pools, tennis courts, etc.).
- Catering structures do not provide a diversified cuisine to meet tourists' needs.
- There are no quality promotional materials produced in major international languages.

The government strategic directions therefore are as follows:

- Elaborate a governmental programme for health and beauty tourism development.
- Accredit spa water treatment centres and resorts and classify their accommodation units.

- Undertake a survey of mineral water resources in the Republic of Moldova and of their qualities from the balneal standpoint and elaborate investment projects for promotion in international markets.
- Ensure the implementation of a training programme for the managers of health and beauty establishments with the objective of developing efficient management and marketing.
- Implement a marketing programme both on a national level and for separate attractions.
- Include statistical reports on spa water treatment centres and resorts in the system of statistic surveys.
- Develop resort areas to conform to international standards.

(Moldova Tourism, 2008)

Impacts of health and wellness tourism

Planning at any levels in short, aims at achieving objectives, maximizing positive and minimizing negative impacts. Health and wellness tourism and the related services have similar impacts on the host environment as any other type of tourism; however some specific impacts can also be identified.

The impacts of tourism are grouped into three major categories, that is economic, socio-cultural, and environmental impacts. The product specific impacts of health and wellness tourism can be as follows (after Mathieson & Wall, 1982; Rátz & Puczkó, 2002).

Economic impacts

It is anticipated that the beneficiaries of and those adversely affected by impacts can either be the population and entrepreneurs, the central and local municipalities, and the tourists as well (Table 8.1).

Health and wellness tourism as we could see it so far have some special qualities that are manifested in the form and type of economic impacts:

- *Employment*: Any form of health and wellness tourism and facility need better skilled employees than, for example, mass tourism facilities would. While this is a favourable impact, in reality sites where the development takes place may have a limited supply of workforce with the needed skills and experiences. This leads to the import of skilled staff from other areas or countries (where it can lead to shortage of staff). In Central European countries, where the differences between the capital and the regions can be really significant, operators often need to offer higher wages to attract employees to the countryside. Since health tourism demand tends to be less seasonal than mass tourism (or at least multi-seasonal), fluctuation of workforce causes less problems.
- *Economy*: Guests tend to spend more than other types of tourism, since they either stay longer (for some weeks in medical resorts) or stay in hotels at the higher end (at least three star quality). Furthermore, the

157

Table 8.1 Economic Impacts of Health and Wellness Tourism.

Impacts On...	Positive Aspects	Negative Aspects
Employment	Skilled workforce	Imported workforce (from other cities or even countries)
	Limited seasonal fluctuation of employees	Migration
Economy	Multiplier effects (especially employment multiplier)	Formation of dependence
	Higher than average per capita spending	Spending concentrated in health and wellness facilities
	Complex spending structure	Increase of regional inequalities
	Imported technology and products	Imported technology and products
Living conditions	Proliferation of services offered	Mono-cultural supply
	Image of settlement develops	Prices may increase
	Infrastructure developments	Differences between the tourist and non-tourist areas

After Rátz and Puczkó (2002).

services they use are very human resource intensive, such as personal services (e.g. treatments or high quality accommodation). This can mean a higher employment multiplier than other forms of tourism (Horváth, 1998). Because of a more complex nature and likely better returns, entrepreneurs invest in related services, and that can lead to mono-cultural development and even to over-dependence on one single activity. The imbalance of supply can question the long-term sustainability, since any change in economy, health finances or fashion, can have an instant impact on destinations and operators. For example even 1% change of state support on medical treatments can mean either very good or very bad news to many destinations. On the other hand, the development of Alpine Wellness in Austria or Switzerland, for example, was an answer for dependence on winter tourism. Less developed destinations are happily taking technology and processes that are not available locally, but this can lead to the exclusion of local makes as well (e.g. visitors trust beauty products with known brands, therefore local brands, even with the same effects and lower price, can be avoided).

- *Living conditions*: The economic impacts have direct implications on living conditions. Local population are positive when infrastructure like roads and sewage pipes are developed, but oppose those developments that favour only a part of the settlement. Many places become known because of an important source for health tourism, for example thermal spring or climatic resort. Popularity may attract more and more visitors as well as investors and can lead to the increase of prices, which is a positive thing when locals want to sell, but a negative thing when they want to buy (e.g. property).

Socio-cultural impacts

Health and wellness tourism has substantial impacts on the local socio-cultural environment (Table 8.2). Most of these impacts, however, are relevant only to those destinations that are populated. Greenfield or enclave developments, for example seaside spa resorts, in unpopulated islands have very limited implications:

- *Cultural heritage*: Locations where listed or ancient buildings host the health and wellness facilities, for example historic spas, can benefit from the rediscovered popularity. However, architectural styles, and milieu can be destroyed by the introduction of new building styles and keeping balance between the needs of conservation and expectation of visitors and operators can be hard. For example the Colonnades in the historic Czech spa towns of Marianske Lazne or Karlovy Vary, mainly serve as tourist attractions of architectural beauty and not as facilities for drinking cures.
- *Population*: Even in remote spa resorts, the growth of the local population is almost inevitable. The immigration of employees can mean a signification change to the local population in terms of their number, age, language, race, or education. One of the major problems popular destinations face is the blending of temporary or permanent citizens. Many visitors, after enjoying their stay in a spa or retreat home, may decide to buy a summer or holiday home there. Often the owners of holistic retreat or yoga holiday facilities are not from the given region or even country. In small settlements the appearance of new locals can mean the bringing back of life; on the other hand, holiday home owners do not necessarily understand the everyday problems of the community. Many traditional spa towns in Hungary, for example, have a whole new part with holiday homes (e.g. in Mezőkövesd in North East Hungary). The municipality is left with the obligatory tasks, for example street cleaning and lighting or litter collection for 12 months, whereas home owners turn up only a couple of weekends in a year.
- *Employment*: From the local economy and population point of view the introduction of health and wellness services mean positive impacts in terms of new jobs and income opportunities. This can be true for large scale spa resorts or wellness hotels, but is less likely relevant for retreats where even the cooking and cleaning is done by the visitors themselves (as part of the healing process). The local workforce can find it difficult to cooperate with the top management, especially in chain development, where the management represents the owner(s) or the management company. Certainly, the management can think the same about the local workforce (e.g. The management of Danubius Hotels, one of the largest hotel companies specialized in spa hotels, found it unexpectedly difficult to incorporate the employees of the newly acquired Czech facilities, since the work ethic was so different from the standards in the other member hotels).

Table 8.2 Socio-Cultural Impacts of Health and Wellness Tourism.

Impacts On...	Positive Aspects	Negative Aspects
Cultural heritage	Revitalization and protection of traditional architecture	Mismatch in style and overuse
Population	Growth of population	Imported workforce (from other cities or even countries)
	Presence of holiday home owners	Facility and holiday home owners do not consider the destination as their permanent home
Employment	Generation of new jobs and income opportunities Skills developed	Competition with workforce outside the settlement
Community	Revitalization of social, cultural life Increase of the community's pride in their settlement Transformation of social stratification Learning languages, education	Costs of impact management Growth of the proportion of seasonal residents Demonstration effect Suppression of local language

Source: Smith and Puczkó.

- *Community*: Local assets used in health and wellness tourism can make local communities more sustainable, since through employment opportunities and developed services the whole local community can benefit from tourism. Enclave developments have no such impacts and the related impacts of retreat homes or ashrams are limited, too. The introduction of new services or the arrival of new people, for example a yogi, can cause all sorts of issues. Locals may find it difficult to understand and absorb these new things because of religion, tradition, or lifestyle issues (e.g. the locals of the Greek island to where Skyros organized its first holistic trips in the 1970s, thought that those visitors were simply mad!). People with skills that are demanded by operators can rise very quickly and this is not welcomed by those who were left out. Young people will aspire for those valuables and values they see from visitors and this so-called demonstration effect can lead to major arguments between family members or groups of the local community. On the extreme side, in relatively poor countries, such as India more and more people illegally sell their kidneys for hospitals that take foreign medical patients.

Environmental impacts

In comparison with mass tourism, health and wellness tourism tend to have a different set of impacts on the environment. Theoretically, health

Table 8.3 Environmental Impacts of Health and Wellness Tourism.

Impacts On...	Positive Aspects	Negative Aspects
Vegetation and wildlife	Conservation of habitat Parks and gardens	Pollution Introduction of new species
Elements	Infrastructure developments	Waste (solid and water) management Change of landscape Emissions (gas, vapour, fumes) Thermal, healing water (drilling)
Land use	Change in land use	Growth of built-up area Change in hydrological and other natural systems
Buildings and milieu	New architectural styles Conserving local styles	Growth of built-up area Wear and tear Introduction of new styles

Source: Smith and Puczkó.

and wellness facilities cannot accommodate such crowds, but an aqua-park, for example can easily be categorized as a mass tourism attraction.

Environmental impacts can come in two major groups, on the natural and the built environment (Table 8.3). Health and wellness tourism can have impacts on both groups and are especially important if tourism was built on a local natural asset, for example healing climate:

- *Vegetation and wildlife*: Vegetation and wildlife are especially important if we are talking about a healing climate, cave, lake, or mud. These healing assets are part of a habitat, therefore any development and use has a direct impact on vegetation and wildlife. The conservation of vegetation and wildlife are, therefore, especially important, since any detrimental modification of the natural environment can alter the asset itself. (The Tapolca medical cave (Hungary) lost its water due to a nearby bauxite mine. When mining was discontinued, the water level rose slowly again.) For standalone resorts or retreats, it is essential that the neighbouring environment remains intact, since that is part of the attraction itself.
- *Elements*: Apart from the 'standard' impacts of tourism on elements, for example emissions or waste, the most significant impacts of health and wellness spas is the excess water. Water used in spas could be hot and full of minerals. These waters, theoretically, should all be treated, since warm water rich in minerals means an unnecessary load to natural waters. The rise of temperature results in the disappearance of species and the minerals are deposited in the waterbeds.
- *Land use*: Health and wellness developments may mean significant change in land use, for example building new and large buildings.

161

These developments can mean the introduction of new styles and can make a destination densely built-up.

- *Buildings and milieu*: The responsibility of developers and authorities are especially important in natural settings, where any building can change the whole atmosphere.

The various impacts of health and wellness tourism can differ from site to site; it would be a generalization to say that the above-mentioned impacts occur everywhere. The planning processes should set boundaries and limits within which developments can take place, and facilities operate (e.g. treatment of used thermal waters, use of reusable energy sources, etc.).

Planning at national level

There are several and a growing number of countries, for example Czech Republic, Hungary, Thailand, India, etc., that declare on a national level the importance of health tourism (e.g. the Hungarian Government awarded 147 million Euros as subsidy for almost 100 health tourism projects between 2001 and 2004). This means that in these countries the planning for health tourism is established at a national level. This is mainly manifested in the form of a national health tourism strategy or development plan. In these documents national institutions that surprisingly tend not to be the ministries of health, but are more likely the ministries responsible for regional development and/or tourism, define the main objectives, goals, and actions.

Certainly, strategies on a national level are prepared in those countries where some (or more) assets are substantial:

- Natural assets that are used in evidence-based medicine, e.g. waters, mud, climate, cave.
- Good health education, e.g. for surgeons, dentists, balneotherapists.
- Favourable overall and health specific price level.
- Sufficient supply of complementary services, e.g. attractions, landscape, culture, sea.

For example in the tourism development strategy of Slovakia, the government declared that: The central forms of tourism for which Slovakia has the best conditions and which will need to be supported, developed and qualitatively improved over the course of the coming years are:

- Urban and cultural tourism
- Spa and health tourism
- Winter tourism and winter sports
- Summer tourism and waterside holidays
- Rural tourism

(Slovak Government, 2005)

Consistent government support can be essential to support the development of a successful health tourism industry, as indicated in the case of Jordan.

Case Study: Medical Tourism in Jordan

Since 1927 hospitals in Jordan could be run by the private sector and to date there are over 50 of them (more than 50% of all hospitals and clinics, but they are mainly small and medium sized facilities with up to 150 beds). Arab patients started to come for medical treatments during the 1970s. As a result of the increasing number of Arab patients seeking treatment in Jordan, the Ministry of Health established an office at Queen Alia Airport in 1998. By the turn of the century, revenues generated by medical tourism become approximately two-thirds of the total tourism revenue. A study by the Ministry revealed that the private hospitals try to keep the average length of stay to a minimum, since the most income is generated during the first 2 days of the stay, that is, this is the time for the operation. Patients tend to be accompanied by at least one member of the family who represent additional sources of income. The main sender countries for medical tourists are those where the doctor/population ratio is lower (e.g. Yemen, Sudan, or Libya), and the medical skills of doctors are perceived to be lower, or where the price of medical services are higher than in Jordan. The Ministry made an effort to invite all the involved parties, that is from health, spa and tourism industries, to set up a National Medical Tourism Cluster.

However, there are fears that there may be a regressive trend in Jordan's medical tourism market. Despite the ambitious strategy written by the Medical Tourism Directorate in 2004, there has not been enough support from government and medical tourism no longer seems to be a priority for the Health Ministry. This means that there was a rapid reduction in visitor numbers in 2007 compared to 2008.

(Jordan Times, 2008; Competitive Team, 2008)

The success of national level planning is based on the tools and resources it can dedicate to achieving goals. If the national plan or strategy was supported by funds and mechanisms (all set in the national development plan), the likelihood of success can be very high. Otherwise plans and strategies exist on paper only.

Planning at regional level

Planning at regional level has two objectives:

1. It has to ensure the high level of satisfaction of tourists with the given attractions and services (meaning that tourism as an economic activity is successful within the given region).
2. The development of tourism should bring beneficial changes in financial, in socio-cultural, as well as environmental aspects. Since the development of tourism has positive impacts only in a couple of cases, this is why one should try to keep the balance of impacts positive, meaning that predominantly the beneficial changes should be perceived by residents.

Planning at regional level is very similar to planning at national level. It has to be noted, though, that the word 'region' can refer to rather different things from a region of a country (the Alps in Germany) to a region formed by countries (the Alps from France to Austria).

Regional level planning can mean different things region by region, depending on how centralized or decentralized the region is (e.g. setting objectives at a project level versus at regional level). Regionalization, as we will see in Chapter Nine in health and wellness tourism can have two major forms:

- Destinations can define very specific goals, especially, if the destination management organizations (DMO) had authority and power from planning to implementation. They can equally influence investors' decision making or the targeting and segmenting activities of the destination. The Destination Management Gastein (Western Austria) is responsible for three settlements in Gastein Valley (Dorfgastein, Bad Gastein, and Hofgastein). The organization has been having an impact on planning activities, which helped to achieve that all the three villages have their own identity and product portfolio (active and sport; leisure and wellness; leisure, wellness, and medical tourism, respectively).
- The cooperation is not as closely defined in clusters as in destinations. They can work together to define and to achieve goals and it is more likely that the planning will influence communication than product development activities.

Burgenland (Austria) provides us with an interesting case for direct and indirect coordination of developments at regional level. The region (or 'land') has five major spa destinations and all the four have a different specialization. The Sonnentherme specializes for families with young kids, Therme Stegersbach offers services for older children and their parents, Bad Tatzmannsdorf is a destination for leisure and recreation, while Sauerbrunn specializes for men and Jennersdorf for women. Altogether these are forming an integrated destination.

Planning at local level

Planning for health and wellness tourism at local level depends very much on the intentions of the local government.

'Organic' versus planned development

If a local council applied a very liberal approach, then tourism could be considered as an overwhelmingly market driven industry, in which the public sector plays a minimal role. This approach can lead to 'organic' development of the destination or settlement. Organic, in this case, refers to non-controlled development, when the various stages and elements of development have not been harmonized. Investors could develop more or less whatever they wanted to.

Regulations by a local or national institution could have some counterproductive impacts on the facility. Regulations could easily ruin spontaneity and even atmosphere.

There are a number of destinations which seem to have emerged like that over several years or decades because of their spiritual quality or easygoing atmosphere. Goa in India is perhaps a good example of this (see Smith & Kelly, 2006) where numerous holistic practitioners settle or visit regularly to offer courses and classes to backpackers and long-term travellers. Chiang Mai in Thailand is similar, as many tourists visit to enjoy Thai massage courses, Vipassana (silent meditation) retreats or Tai Chi (e.g. on the Tai Chi Thailand 10 day programme). It is the spontaneous development of such locations and the ever-changing mix of supply that makes them interesting and appealing to visitors.

Case Study of Organic Development: Byron Bay, Australia

Byron Bay is an example of what could be called an 'organic' wellness tourism development. It is often described as 'the alternative and spiritual capital of Australia'. Located in New South Wales just south of the Queensland border, Byron Bay is a small town which for years has been seen as the place for alternative lifestyles. In the early 1970s, a group of festival organizers (of the Aquarious Festival) approached the local aboriginal elders to seek their permission to hold a festival in Nimbin. It signified an important step. The new thinkers' respect for the indigenous people, their land and their culture was not only fundamental to the value systems of these people, but also to the genesis of reconciliation. Students and hippies flocked to the area for the festival in 1973 and many just never left. Two decades of new settlers and alternative lifestylers began to repopulate the area, and another set of pioneers established themselves around Mullumbimby and Mainarm. The commune, legally known as a multiple occupancy or 'MO', was conceived.

Many of the hostels in the area function as communes with a number of long-staying residents, and there are options of staying in tents, tepees, and wagons as well as dorms and rooms. There are daily programmes of yoga, dance, and hula-hoop classes, as well as fire-juggling, drumming, or making your own didgeridoo. The weekly roving markets of the Byron area are famous for their range of new age and holistic products.

There is an Ayurveda College where visitors can have treatments and health and lifestyle consultations, as well as a Naturopath Bodyworks Clinic which offers de-tox and cleansing programmes in addition to massage. The Ambaji Wellness Centre has free meditation at lunchtimes and many of Byron's best healers and therapists are represented there, such as reiki, psychic, and tarot readers. Therapies such as iridology are available at the Quinessence centre and all kinds of naturopathic and homeopathic consultations are found in Cocoon nearby.

(Virtual Byron, 2008)

Organic development can be successful in the long run, but in practice this approach has more risk elements than the so-called integrated approach. The term of double integration in tourism planning (Inskeep,

1991) draws attention to the importance of these relations. Integrated planning and double integration means the following:

- Tourism must be integrated with its (social, cultural, economic, physical, and political) environment, and tourism must have its place in national and regional plans.
- Planning must include all the components of the system of tourism as demand and supply are interrelated and influence one another.

There are a number of wellness tourism destinations which have been purpose-built (e.g. whole resorts or a selection of hotels clustered around a central resource such as a healing spa or lake), which applied the above-mentioned integration. Visitors may not identify the benefits easily of the integration, but they can definitely see the aesthetic results, that is the atmosphere and milieu of the destination was left intact or was developed in an applicable way. Almost all historic spa towns and facilities from England through Germany to Romania struggle to keep the harmony alive, which can easily be lost with only one wrong decision (e.g. allowing developments without a sufficient amount of parking places or permitting a non-matching architectural design).

In the healing process or in the creation of well-being, the atmosphere and the surroundings are crucial. This is supported by the recommendations of World Federation of Hydrotherapy and Climatotherapy (FEMTEC/FITEC) (Kaspar, 1992) about how a destination can become or call itself a medical destination:

- During operational hours at least one resident doctor should be available. Resident doctors should know and understand all possible illnesses and statuses for which the healing asset can be used. Facilities should be fitted with necessary diagnostics and other equipment that are applying the healing capacities of the site.
- Other accompanying medical services, e.g. emergency, patient transport should be available.
- Accommodation facilities directly in connection to and with the medical facilities should meet the highest hygienic expectations and in the meantime these should create a cosy and comfortable atmosphere.
- The catering provided should be able to offer any diet that was prescribed by the resident doctors.
- The location and the atmosphere of the area should aim for total relaxation.
- Transportation infrastructure cannot disturb medical services, all main roads should be located around and not within the medical destination. Through traffic is not permitted and the centre should be pedestrianized.
- Infrastructure should be of the highest quality and supply, all polluting activities (e.g. industry) should be banned or minimized on site and in the vicinity. The protection of the environment should be of paramount importance.
- The architectural regulation should aim for the provision of the permanent relaxing atmosphere as well as harmonious appearance.

There are a number of medical destinations that did apply the integrated approach and in spite of their often complex history, they still deliver an intact experience: services and atmosphere (e.g. Baden-Baden in Germany).

Case Study: Planning at Spa Town Level

Baden-Baden (Germany) versus Héviz (Hungary)

Baden-Baden (Germany) is considered as the 'king of spas' as they are traditionally understood in Europe. The town has always been proud of its heritage and traditions. For centuries, Baden-Baden was the meeting place for the noble, important, and rich. In Baden-Baden 800,000 litres of soothing, healing thermal waters flow from 23 springs each day. Facilities and services were all developed to meet the expectations of this segment (e.g. a casino, promenade, exclusive hotels, festival hall, theatre, Kurhaus). Now, the town which refers to itself as 'the green town of short distances', fulfils all the criteria of what Femtec/Fitec (mentioned earlier in the chapter) set to become a medical destination. Product developments kept a very close eye on the combination of the preservation of what made the town unique as well as the diversification expected by the market (e.g. programmes such as 'Fitness for Executives' or 'Golf and Health'). The town centre is pedestrianized and full of cafés, restaurants, shops selling branded products (e.g. jewellery, watches), and luxury hotels (e.g. The Brenner's Park Hotel and Spa, for instance, has a 'Spa Suite' and the world's only 'Bulgari Cabin'). Besides the health facilities of the individual hotels and clinics, there are two baths. Friedrichsbad, or the Römerbad (Roman Bath), represents history and tradition, while Caracalla Therme is for the new demand, with pleasure and wellness services (e.g. sauna world). While Friedrichsbad does not want and cannot cater for large numbers of visitors, Caracalla Therme does and can. The two facilities are located separately and not linked with each other. The town management and planning has proved to be successful, since it could keep the historic charm as well as develop.

Héviz (Hungary) has one of the world's wonders: a lake with natural healing thermal water which is not too warm to bath in. The lake is a home for water-lilies that makes swimming in the lake as well as the healing effects even more special. On the lake visitors can find a bathhouse still keeping its original architectural style from the end of the 1800s. However, as soon as visitors leave the promenade from the main entrance leading towards the new bath and the town, the feeling of history and heritage disappears very quickly. During the socialist system, the tradition of conservation was not much cultivated, that is original architecture disappeared or was extended by a new 'ward' in an incompatible style. The town by today has lost its charm and character and is not able to match the already mentioned Femtec/Fitec criteria (e.g. the bus station is right next to the lake, and a road also passes through it). One can observe all the architectural styles of the last 50 years in Héviz. This architectural mismatch is now completed with shops selling very cheap and kitsch products, the eateries beside the major car park sell very fattening and unhealthy foods. The hospital and the medical hotels have invested heavily in developing wellness services, but these efforts cannot be supported by the lost appearance and milieu of the town.

Table 8.4 The Development of Spa Destinations and the Related Impacts.

Stages	Economic Impacts	Socio-cultural Impacts	Environmental Impacts	Behaviour and Attitude of Tourists	Transport System
	Level	Level	Level	Level	Level
0 Discovery Isolated area and assets	0 Minimal	0 Mirage or refusal. May feel as intrusion to everyday activities	0 Limited, scattered impacts	0 Lack of knowledge versus specialized interests	0 Transit or isolation
1 Engagement Pioneer facilities, hotel	1 Local/family run enterprises. Local employment	1 Observing. First local enterprises	1 First trauma, the most violent reactions	1 General perceptions versus growing demand	1 Opening up – the first entry points
2 Development Multiplication of facilities	2 Increase of income. Spread of services, changing employment needs	2 Infrastructure development servicing facilities. Commercialization of the personal relationships	2 Increase in built-up areas, development of infrastructure. First signs seasonal congestion. Changing of landscape	2 Progress in perception and knowledge of assets and benefits	2 Increase of transport links
3 Consolidation Organization of the holiday space. Beginning of hierarchy and specialization	3 Multiplying impacts. Arrival of regional, international enterprises. Local businesses lose out	4 Segregation. Demonstration effects, dualism	3 Full range of impacts. First efforts to change situation	3 Spatial competition and segregation	3 Diversifying modes of transport
4 Stagnation and decline Completion of hierarchy and specialization, saturation	4 Building up complete range of services. Dominance of few large enterprises	4 'Total' tourism, plans for breaking out	4 The degradation of physical environment. Regulations, best practices	4 Disintegration of perceived space. Departure of certain types of tourists. Forms of substitution. saturation	4 Maximum connectivity

Source: Rátz and Puczkó (2002) after Pearce (1989), modified.

Spa destinations can locate themselves in the Stage/Impact Matrix that summarizes the observed stages and associated likely impacts. The life-cycle of spa destinations does not differ greatly from that of other destinations with high number of visitors. The differences, however, can be identified (Table 8.4):

- In discovery and engagement stages the arrival of tourism can be very shocking to local people, who may have been using the natural assets for many generations already. The development of new facilities around or on the asset may be translated as 'occupation'.
- The behaviour and attitude of tourists can remain two-fold. Many of them believe in the healing capacity of the site, whereas many of them may visit it because of its historic importance, architectural or natural beauty or image and fashion. Certainly the range of services and impacts of these groups are rather different and sometimes conflicting, too (e.g. medical visitors or more likely patients find the presence of healthy visitors disturbing, and so the mixing of visitors does not work the other way around either).

Planning and development at site level

Supposing that there are applicable national, regional and/or local plans, site-level planning is much more related to business objectives than general goals. Regardless of what facility we want to develop, the existing assets, location, architecture and the service portfolio to be offered can make all the difference.

Development concept

The development concept combines all the above-mentioned elements into one and is crucial to the success of the project. The development concept can easily be translated by any developer, that is 'What do I want to achieve and how I am going to achieve that?' Developers can give very different answers to questions like that. If we talk about public sector developers the objectives can be rather mixed: leisure, social, health, regional development, employment creation, and tourism objectives can all be incorporated into the project. Whereas private sector developers can focus on one or only a few objectives, for example developing a financially lucrative project – in this case, in health and wellness tourism. In both cases, the responsibility of professional advisors can be very significant, since most developers do not really know what they should be developing.

Development philosophy of Rogner (Austria)

We could see that many hotels have spa facilities and may have become a member of a wellness hotel accreditation system. However, there is only a handful of hotel chains (e.g. Accor Thalassa, Danubius Hotels) that are specialized in health and wellness. One of the trendsetters is Rogner Hotels, the hotel chain coming from Austria.

According to the philosophy of this family run business: 'Success is not a matter of mere good fortune. Ultimately, it must be based on a philosophy, or at least a concept'. Rogner's approach is unambiguous: everything stays in the owner's hands – the concept, planning, construction and operation. Besides, they believe that 'don't redo successful ideas too often', that is each and every project must be tailored to its purpose and setting. Landscape, cultural traditions, climate and economic aspects are just some of the factors that need to be taken into account. Individual creativity and painstaking research simply ahead of the planning stage proper are as essential to Rogner's recipe for success as the constant challenge of finding new solutions to old problems.

The developments are both architectonical masterpieces and fountains of well-being which can truly be called unique wellness paradises that are surrounded by a large natural area or park. Without doubt Rogner Bad Blumau, Therme and Spa is the chain's flagship property, which was designed by world famous Austrian architect, Friedensreich Hundertwasser. His approach to architecture, that is 'The absence of kitsch, makes our life unbearable. You can't do without romance' applies very well what Rogner defined as his philosophy: 'At Rogner Bad Blumau, as a hotel with soul, well-being of every individual has top priority. Below its green covered and colourful roofs, its varied shapes and flowing lines activity is combined with a relaxed and laid-back feeling'.

Rogner bases its developments on natural healing resources and the key specialization is on wellness, with the optional supply of medical services. In a Rogner hotel 'Wellness is more than just well-being', Rogner's spa and wellness philosophy is based on the elements of water and man.

The wellness hotels are designed to cater to couples, therefore:

- There are king-size beds in the bedrooms.
- The therapies/treatments are also available for two guests treated parallel.
- The restaurant layout offers tables for two and not for more.

According to the Rogner's understanding of wellness, the health orientation should drive the whole operation and this is also expected from all suppliers, that is raw foods. Quality of all services is not only measured by the Austria-based Best Health Austria seal, but also the owners own mystery shoppers in every quarter.

They believe that special touches such as paying a short visit for 30 min after check in by the guest relation manager to the new guests and asking them about first impressions and offering help and information, can make guests feel really special. There are rituals and unexpected gestures that guests can enjoy: fruit is offered twice a day to guests in the rest areas or incense rituals are carried out in the pool area. Rogner understood the need of guests for private space, therefore the kingsize beds by the pools can be booked in advance (which certainly provides an extra source of income, too). Wellness treatments offered are under continuous renewal, for example every 6 months at least one new treatment or ritual is introduced. This besides its novelty value reconfirms visitors' loyalty, that it is really worth coming back again.

Rogner believes that to make a successful wellness hotel, it has to have its own full-size wellness facility. The hotel should not build on any existing nearby bath or spa that caters for walk in guests.

It is understood that the fifth star in the hotel rating is the employees. To make employees comfortable and to master their skills, the hotel organizes various training programmes, for example language, offering and selling. Members of staff can use the hotel's facilities between Sunday and Thursday for free and also with a partner every year they can spend one night in the hotel.

(Rogner, 2008)

The concept of interdependence and synergy of nearby facilities is well known among developers. Often developers, however, want to create a thermal bath only, which is almost not possible to run profitably. A very good example of applying the synergy approach can be observed in Stuttgart (Germany). The SI-Centrum Stuttgart accommodates the following modules under one roof: VitaParc (Schwaben Quellen, one of the largest thermal spas in Europe), Relax & Vitalcenter (beauty spa), Body & Soul (fitness club), Schlemmer Oase (Feast Oasis), conference centre, theatre, hotel and long-term rent apartments.

Location and assets

Assets based on which a development can take place, as we could see earlier, can be thermal/medical waters (for bathing or drinking), climatic conditions, medical caves, medical mud, a shrine or a spiritual site. Although these assets are very different by various parameters, they share one common quality, that is they are site specific. This makes them almost impossible to be moved or relocated. All natural assets are prone to external impacts and developments, and this makes them easily vulnerable (e.g. sea pollution can be detrimental to seaweed, which is a fundamental element of thalassotherapy).

This location-specific quality makes asset based development very complex and often full of constraints:

- *Thermal/medical waters*: The curative qualities of the water and the capacity of the well(s) limits development options. This is especially true for medical waters that can cure only certain illnesses; therefore the main demand would come from only those who suffer from that illness. Everybody else would come only for a 'dip' and these visitors may not form part of the targeted segments (since they do not stay overnight and do not demand medical treatments either). The temperature of waters can vary and the site may need to dilute it with colder thermal or fresh water to make it suitable for guests' use. Private developers can find it problematic that thermal/medical water springs are either in national or local government's ownership. Apart from authorities responsible for environmental protection, building permits or water bodies overview the developments since the developers have to gain a permit for taking the water itself. Municipalities, in order to protect the often council-owned bath (spa) may limit or refuse to give access to medical waters. Developers can have access to thermal springs only.

- *Climatic conditions*: Healing climates can be found primarily in mountain and seaside areas. At the age of climatic changes, the longevity of assets is not so sure anymore and that leaves owners and developers in an unstable situation. The key asset in these cases is the clean (and salty) air, as well as the view that comes together with it. This view can become under threat when developers go for maximum build in ratios erecting buildings that would obstruct or dominate the views (buildings can even obstruct natural airflows).
- *Medical cave*: Caves with healing capacities are very rare and date back thousands of years. The special cave climate, often rich in minerals complete with stable temperature and humidity make these caves very vulnerable. This vulnerable status means a very strict constraint and limit to the use of the caves. The number of guests at any time is maximized and the variety of activities and services in these caves are rather limited. The treatment is to stay in the cave for a couple of hours every day at any time, therefore the stay itself can mean very little stimuli. For example the Gastein Curative Tunnel is a small train that runs for approximately 2.5 km into the heart of the mountain. Both the warmth and humidity will cause the body temperature to rise to a level between 38°C and 39°C, which enables an increased absorption of radon. The radon as an inert gas, exercises a short-term radiation effect and thus stimulates cellular metabolism.
- *Medical mud*: Medical mud is a little different from the above-mentioned other natural assets. This difference lies in the possibility of transport, that is the mud can be used either on site where it was extracted or almost anywhere else, since the mud can be transported (and reheated on location again). Often the original site is neither attractive nor suitable for any type of service development (e.g. river or lake bank), therefore the mud is transported anyway. The application of the mud, for example, for body wraps leaves the facilities with a significant amount of (e.g. radioactive) waste, the treatment of which requires special attention and technology.
- *Shrine or spiritual site*: A shrine or other spiritual sites that can be a rock, a river, or a mound, etc. can often inspire and attract visitors who are looking for inspiration and transcendence. In terms of development the limits and boundaries for planning are less straight forward than in the case of the other location-specific assets. Often the ownership of the site is in the hands of someone other than who want to visit the place, therefore the interests can be very conflicting. Since the core of the asset is intangible, worshippers and visitors may even be considered as 'abnormal', which does not make planning and development easy. In some cases, the location in question is not even aware of the asset, for example one of the Earth Chakras was found in Hungary and that may have a very significant impact on the community.

Many spas and spa hotels are located in or near to ski resorts. The main reason for this trend is either the objective of extension of the main season or the competition of the product supply. These developments are of rather different qualities and styles. Many are fairly standardized (e.g. Tatralandia, Slovakia), but offer good quality relaxation, pampering and healing facilities for those who need a rest from physical exercise. Others, especially through innovative architecture and interior design provide an enhanced experience (e.g. on top of the breathtaking mountains).

One of the main advantages of historic (mainly medical) spas is their location, that is the spa is part of the historic city fabric. This makes the facility appealing for even those who would not consider themselves as medical or wellness tourists. Historic spas from Bath (UK), through Baden-Baden (Germany), Baden (Switzerland), Vichy (France), and Marianske Lazne (Czech Republic) to Osaka (Japan) capitalize on their location. However, this is not really easy, since most of the visitors are not patients, therefore their needs and interests are very different from those of traditional guests.

Architecture and design

A well-designed spa should be aesthetically pleasing, comfortable, and functional (D'Angelo, 2006). Nordic Well (2007) states that design is one of the key factors in inducing a feeling of wellness:

> Modern, simple, unassuming, clean, airy, light, calm, uncluttered, in harmony with nature, inviting, functional, inclusive. These are the values and senses that Scandinavian designs have emphasized over time. They are the combined result of three influences: a Zen-like belief in the power of nature; a tradition of linking design to the well-being of all people; and a skill for choosing appropriate technology …. An idea of design that promotes creativity, intimacy, personal calm and sense of meaning.

These days environmental consciousness should pervade spas and wellness facilities. Many spas already use natural resources such as thermal or spring waters, geysers, seawater, waterfalls, or caves. Naturally textured woods, bamboos, or cork are popular as they are eco-friendly and also sustain moisture. Many designers try to use features that are in keeping with the local architecture and cultural styles so that the spa or wellness centre is integrated into the environment in which it is located. Sometimes design needs to be adapted to different markets, for example, men may prefer less feminine environments and prefer minimalist styles. Spas that want to attract families with children tend to use brighter colours and motifs that capture the imagination. The location of certain features is also important. Some spas especially in Asia use the principles of Feng Shui in their design. This allows the maximum amount of energy or 'Chi' to flow freely, balancing Yin and Yang or masculine and feminine energies; using lighting to enhance dark corners, and strategic placement of objects to break up long corridors. Thompson (2007) suggests ways in which the principles of Feng Shui can be implemented in a design context (Table 8.5).

Table 8.5   Feng Shui Colour Basics and Feng Shui Elemental Decor.

Colour	Theme	Good For...
Red	Energizing	the dining room to keep guests energized and excited
Orange	Joy	family rooms, playrooms, use softer shades for more relaxed fun
Yellow	Happy	dens, kitchens, offices, wherever creativity is needed
Green	Balance, renewal	living rooms, bedrooms, halls
Blue	Healing, calming	wherever you want to relax
Indigo	Healing, relaxing	childrens' rooms, healing rooms
Purple	Richness, transformation	spiritual rooms, feelings of abundance

Strive for balance between the five elements. Are any of the elements below missing from the room?

Water	Wood	Fire	Earth	Metal
Fountains glass	Wood furniture	Fireplace red accents	Browns earthtones stone	Chrome mirrors stainless

Are any of the elements above dominating the room? Balance it with the complementary element below.

Earth	Metal	Water	Wood	Fire
Browns earthtones stone	Chrome mirrors stainless	Fountains glass	Wood furniture	Fireplace red accents

Source: Thompson (2007).

Noise control is important especially if some areas are open plan. Ease of transition is also a major consideration so that the flow from one facility to another does not involve long walks in cold or draughty corridors or the climbing of numerous stairs. There should be a centrally located reception with information provision and a welcome desk, in addition to well-placed relaxation areas with reading materials, herbal teas, small snacks, and perhaps chill-out music or nice scents from oil burners or incense.

Service portfolio

In health tourism, services can involve a certain amount of associated and real risk. Treatments and programmes are dealing with bodies, minds and spirits, therefore guests want services and staff that look safe and are safe, but are also interesting and can enhance health and experiences. Besides the location and the design, the offered service portfolio (and its price level) can make any health tourism facility successful. Certainly, these success elements should be considered as separate factors, but more like part of the 'one-for-all' strategy. No spa or a spa hotel can be successful, even having architecture never seen before, if what they offer does not match the architecture and the whole service concept. When a wellness hotel (Marianske Lazne, Czech Republic) allows guests to visit the one pool during an allocated (but not discussed) time-slot of 30 min a day (!), guests may not want to repeat their stay, regardless of how beautiful the historic spa town actually was.

Visitors expect services that are either well known or not at all known to them. The first group reassures them, while the second group can create a unique experience. Furthermore, the assets, the architecture and the interior can and should articulate expectations. Providing very unhealthy foods in a medical spa or medical hotel, as is the case in numerous facilities in Central and Eastern Europe does not fit the promise and is counterproductive.

The range of offered services is essentially important considering those who are accompanying a guest with a health interest and motivation. Remote spa resorts on an island, mountain retreats or medical hotels are all facing the challenge: what can guests do when the 'official' programme or treatments are finished? This question is especially true for those who would not use those services anyway, for example kids or other family members. Facilities where other attractions, for example a town, a festival, ski slopes, a golf course, mountains, the sea, etc. are in close proximity, are in a relatively easy situation, since the service portfolio offered on site should not be very wide. However, spa resorts may prefer to keep their guests within the 'fence' at all times. This approach is at least questionable from the point of view of sustainability.

Conclusions

This chapter has shown clearly that the most successful developments are those which are planned or regulated in some way, ideally combining national government intervention and support with private sector creativity and vision. Although some 'organic' resorts can flourish, these usually have a relatively long history of alternative and holistic lifestyles which would be disturbed by the imposition of too much structured development or regulation. However, the same is not true of spas and resorts which make use of fragile natural or cultural resources. These developments need to be monitored for adverse impacts and controlled to avoid despoliation of the environment or local traditions and lifestyles. In addition, some attention must also be paid to the provision and presentation of facilities for visitors down to the smallest detail. This includes not only services, but experiences too. The following chapter expands on some of these points, demonstrating the need for sound management principles to accompany sustainable development philosophies.

Managing destinations and sites

Spas are entities devoted to enhancing overall well-being through a variety of professional services that encourage the renewal of body, mind and spirit.

(ISPA, 2006b)

Introduction

This chapter focuses on the management of spas and other health centres and facilities. This includes some of the generic management issues that are common to all forms of health tourism, and those which are specific to different sub-sectors. Important issues include the location, design and atmosphere of health environments, as well as more fundamental issues relating to organization, HR, operations and quality of service. The need for proper qualifications and training, regulation of practice and attention to health and safety issues are extremely important. Whether the service is medical, holistic, psychological or spiritual, it can have a powerful impact on the individual concerned. Although it is possible to have a relaxing, pampering spa break, many people now go on wellness holidays with the express intention of changing their lives. This can be a significant step and requires careful management.

Management of health and wellness tourism

The management of health and wellness services can be analysed from two different angles, that is geography and asset or site level.

Geographical aspects

Health and wellness services and therefore tourism can be managed at national, regional and local level. At *national level* both national and voluntary organizations can play a role in the management of health and wellness tourism:

- State authorities and offices often support and control health and wellness services with the preparation of national health, wellness or medical tourism strategies and development plans. In these, the main directions for development are defined. State organizations, such as a department of health can certify and monitor services providers in health and wellness, furthermore, state institutions define parameters based on which, for example, a spring or a cave can call itself a medical asset. To complete the management process, national tourist organizations run research projects and promotion campaigns supporting the image of the country (or region) and its health oriented destinations. Besides in some countries schemes are in operation (partially) financed by the state or by private health insurance companies providing support for health oriented trips.
- Voluntary schemes are also run in many countries, through which service providers team up and set up associations. The associations can be responsible for certification processes (e.g. Wellness Hotels Deutschland), lobbying for more recognition or support, or for co-operation in promotion and running a booking site together.
- Governments should also be responsible for protecting and conserving national resources and assets from over-development or unsustainable tourism. This process can also be aided by national or even international voluntary organizations.

Case Study of Mismanagement of National Health Resources: Pamukkale, Turkey

The health-giving properties of Turkey's natural hot springs have been well known since antiquity. The ancient city of Hierapolis was built on the site of the rich mineral waters of Pamukkale, where the hot waters created enormous circular basins in the earth as it flowed down the mountainside, resulting in dazzling white calcareous rock. For thousands of years visitors, including pilgrims, have enjoyed the healing powers of Pamukkale's calcium-rich hot springs and bathed in the white terraced pools, as well as swimming in the Sacred Pool. The Sacred Pool is where the springs that feed Pamukkale's mineral pools originate in a depression among the cultural artefacts of the ancient Romans, and columns and capitals can therefore be found under the water.

In the 1970s and 1980s visitors could still come to the little town outside Denizli, take a cheap room, walk to the springs and enjoy the pool. However, larger hotels built at the site of the spring to service increasing numbers of tourists and irresponsible tourism itself caused the spring to almost stop producing water, and the originally white pools started to turn grey. Visitors walked with their shoes on and even bathed using soaps and shampoos.

Locals also disregarded the site and rode motor bikes up and down the slopes causing destruction. UNESCO was called in and Pamukkale was given the World Heritage Site status in 1988 and the additional protection this requires. Hotels that diverted the spring water were torn down. Trails were set up through the pools, and bathing in them was not allowed. (There have since been some unconvincingly 'fake' pools built for tourists to enjoy themselves in with water pumped in at certain times of day.) As a consequence, the pools have returned to their pristeen whiteness, and are once again a worthwhile tourist destination.

(CTG Heathcare, 2008)

The phrase 'regional management' requires a short discussion about what would constitute as 'region'. The term region can be based either on geography (e.g. a valley), on administration (e.g. country) or on culture. From tourism or tourists' point of view a region can be different from the previously mentioned ones, since visitors consider areas as a region based on their attractions and related services. How these are organized, however, would not interest visitors too much. Management at *regional level* is important especially in German speaking countries, e.g. Germany, Switzerland and Austria, where health destinations are managed by a special destination management organization, the so-called 'kurdirektion' or 'kurgemeinde'. These organizations are responsible for the various management aspects of health and wellness services, such as all elements of marketing, from market research, through co-operation to promotion. The partnership is found by the local/regional government and the actors involved in service supply, e.g. hoteliers, spa/bath and other attraction owners, catering providers, etc. The operation of the 'kurdirektion' is financed from the membership fees paid by members, the tax levied on staying visitors (so-called 'kurtaxa'), and the services the kurdirektion provides for customers.

Another way of managing regions is by creating clusters based on a certain activity in which all interested parties can be involved (e.g. from public, private and voluntary sectors, and local communities).

Case Study: Well-being Cluster (Austria)

Aims
The long-term aim of the Well-being Cluster is the fortified positioning of Lower Austria on the health and wellness market and ultimately, the establishment of Lower Austria as THE health and wellness destination in Central Europe.

Target groups
Companies, institutions and players from the areas of:

- Health and wellness tourism (health and wellness hotels, spas, thermal springs spas, day spas).

- Preventative medicine (physicians of preventative and complementary medicine, health centres, rehabilitation centres).
- Natural products (in particular, organic food, natural cosmetics, natural remedies).
- Complementary medical service providers (healthy nutrition, exercise/sports, psychosocial health).
- Research and educational facilities.
- Suppliers (in particular regional vendors).

(Well-being Cluster, 2008)

Asset and site specific aspects

As we could see earlier, the assets or attractions for health and wellness tourism are numerous, ranging from site specific assets (e.g. sea climate or medical mud) to assets that can virtually be provided anywhere (e.g. massages or self-development programmes). The management at site or asset level is therefore more related to physical evidence, to cost structures, to service portfolio or to quality assurance or the management of seasonality.

Visitors to any health service or provider, even to medical services mainly build their initial decision on trust. This trust is often based on only a reference by a friend or some pictures and short description of a website. As we will see in the Marketing Chapter the management has to deliver at least up to the level of the promised quality and experience. Should that not happen, visitors or patients may never come back.

The range of facilities in question can be quite wide, which translates to very complex management issues. Furthermore, it should also be recognized that many facilities can have more than just one focus, for example a thermal spa can at the same time be visited by local customers (as leisure) and wellness tourists. Some common issues that somehow affect every facility can be identified:

- *Demand for skilled staff*: Most of the services and treatments offered in these health institutions require special skills, trainings and maybe years of experience. Certainly, there are huge differences; a retreat may be delivered by one person, whereas a surgical clinic needs a high number of qualified and experienced staff.
- *Seasonality of demand*: Although health tourism is not as much prone to high fluctuation as 4S tourism, the high and low seasons also need special (marketing) management actions. The main season, however, can be different from the summer, that is spring and autumn can be equally popular seasons for visiting health services. On the other hand, medical tourism has relatively low seasonality since both demand and supply can be more easily harmonized, for example with appointments, prescribed treatments or even with waiting lists.

- *Guests with little previous experience*: Many guests visiting health services have little or no knowledge about what he or she is supposed to do during the visit. This can include problems with procedures and processes or understanding of what a treatment may actually mean or do.
- *Development and running costs*: Especially water-based facilities and hospitals have to face the risk of high running, maintenance, renewal and replacement costs. Thermal or medical waters can quickly plug up pipes, which then need either regular cleaning or frequent replacement. Excess waters are also seen as hazardous waste (because of temperature and mineral content) that needs special treatment.

Creating memorable experiences

D'Angelo (2006) notes that spas need to cater for people who are seeking inclusive approaches to health, beauty and wellness. Balance and harmony are important factors to counteract stressful lives. As mentioned earlier in the book, there is something of a renaissance in the interconnectedness of body, mind and spirit. With this in mind, spa directors and managers need to provide an environment which is infused with this sense of harmony and integration. In the past, many spas (especially in the USA, Australia and much of Western Europe) were mainly focused on beauty, pampering, weight loss, and fitness. Now there is a shift back to more natural healing methods, relaxation and spiritual principles. It is common to see a blend of Eastern and Western philosophies and the integration of alternative, traditional and holistic practices. In addition, there has been a revolution in anti-aging products and technology. Cosmetic surgery and age management have become more mainstream services. Concerns about the health of the skin have also increased with the higher incidences of skin cancer. In some countries, the healthcare system is deemed inadequate with long waiting lists and poor or expensive facilities. The idea of wellness as preventative healthcare is becoming more common, therefore spas can play a key role. It is sometimes reported in the UK that it would be cheaper to spend the rest of one's days in a spa hotel than to go to a residential nursing home!

The idea of a wellness or 'lifestyle' centre is becoming more common. These take a holistic approach to health, blending spa therapies with nutritional counselling and programmes, exercise and fitness regimes, alternative medicines and complementary therapies, yoga classes, massage and psychotherapy. Many wellness hotels are now trying to infuse the whole business with holistic principles, especially in Germany, Austria and Switzerland or in many parts of the USA where wellness-based lifestyles are well understood.

There are some generic issues which can be relevant for all wellness facilities or destinations, as discussed below.

Atmosphere

Creating a relaxing, clean and pleasant environment is of paramount importance for all wellness facilities, but most especially for spas and spa or wellness hotels, which may also need a touch of luxury (spiritual or holistic tourists may accept more basic facilities). The use of design, colour, lighting, location of furniture, degree of natural light, greenery, views, music, or scents can all contribute to creating a harmonious atmosphere. Certainly, most of these qualities are determined during the planning process. The management may face difficulties when the services and/or the surrounding environment do not support or accompany each other. These mismatches certainly result in sub-optimal satisfaction and consequently lower the optimal revenue level.

Spas or baths to create special atmosphere tend to apply the concept of crossover, that is blending local and unusual or far away styles and concepts. The spa (Taunus Therme) in Bad Homburg (Germany) for example, mixed Asian and European bath approaches and now offers a Feng Shui sauna. Since saunas have become a standard element of any wellness facility an 'Asian style sauna' can be surprising and therefore inviting and memorable.

Facilities can create unique experiences introducing little (as well as cheap to run), but unexpected rituals, for example lighting a couple of incense sticks during the afternoon around the rest area can create a very special atmosphere (not only in a yoga retreat but even in a pleasure pool). Certainly, the outfit worn by the member of staff carrying out the ritual can make a difference: just compare the image that was created by an outfit of T-shirt, shorts and flip-flops and an Asian style gown completed with leather sandals. Also, working together with other local businesses, offering seasonal fruit to visitors can be taken as a nice thought or gesture.

Atmosphere or more precisely experiences can be created by other means than architectural design. In any visitor attraction, wellness visitors also consume the provided services based on their previous experiences, knowledge and expectations. One of the main criteria of interpretation (see the works of Tilden, 1977; Beck & Cable, 1988; Puczkó, 2006) is to define the main message of the visit in such a way that can be translated and understood by most of the visitors. This is not different in wellness facilities either.

Managing visitor's expectations and experience

Visitor's expectations of a wellness centre or spa will differ greatly according to which country they come from, their language and their experience of wellness facilities generally. For example, the British or Americans would have a very different understanding of what they would expect to find in a spa (i.e. luxury, pampering, beauty) from a Central or Eastern European (i.e. healing waters, physical health checks, medical treatments). Information provision and marketing is therefore extremely important in managing visitor expectations. In some cultures, nudity in spas is the norm or even a requirement in some areas (e.g. saunas and steam rooms). This is true of Austria, Germany and some spas in CEE and Scandinavia. However, for some visitors (e.g. Americans, British, Asians, Southern Europeans) this can be unexpected and even embarrassing. In some cultures (e.g. Finland, Japan) men are separated from women when using sauna or spa facilities. In other cultures, mixed nudity is accepted. Some nationalities are used to doing activities in groups and are not used to enforced silence (e.g. Southern Europeans). This can create a certain amount of tension in countries, where spas and wellness centres are seen as quiet, restful, sometimes even spiritual spaces (especially in saunas and steam rooms).

Help may also be needed to guide visitors around spas, as it could be their first visit or rituals and traditions may differ from those in their home country. Language may be a barrier where there is little or no translation, especially in countries where language can seem completely unfamiliar (e.g. Finland, Japan, China). Visitors sometimes have problems knowing which entrance to use if there is more than one, which tickets to buy when there are many options, and might not understand the cloakroom system (e.g. in Hungary, where a cloakroom attendant usually has to be approached for a locker and key) or the new technology (e.g. in Austria where the locker system can be operated using a wristband). Knowing just how long to stay in medical, mineral or thermal waters is not clear to the inexperienced. Even if 20 min is the recommended time, bathers need to know how long to rest or whether they should go to a cool shower after. Just a small information panel outside a bath, sauna or steam room can be enough to inform visitors, what the recommended length of time should be.

Spa etiquette

Resorts and hotels: Let you sample a little bit of everything – from golf to tennis to sightseeing to horse back riding to water sports to spa treatments. But sometimes these activities don't mix well, and so it helps to know some of the etiquette, even on vacation. The suggestions below will help you to get the most out of your time at a resort or hotel spa.

Advance booking: As resort and hotel spas often fill up fast, book as far in advance as possible.

Medical conditions: If you have any type of medical condition, be sure to mention it when you book an appointment. Certain treatments may not be advisable for you. Also, tell the technician if you are wearing contact lenses before you have a facial.

Mixing activities and spa-going: On the day of treatment, try to stay out of the sun and avoid alcoholic beverages. Also don't schedule a physically demanding endeavour after a spa appointment.

Valuables: In order to avoid all worries and stress, leave all jewellery and valuables in the hotel or resort's safe and don't bring them with you to the spa.

Punctuality: Ideally arrive 15–30 min early so you can enjoy an unhurried transition into the spa.

Exploring the facility: Most resort and hotel spas have more amenities than the average day spa. On arrival at the spa, check out the activity schedule, so you won't miss anything that might be of interest.

Therapists: If you prefer either a male or female therapist, but the spa fails to ask, don't hesitate to let your choice be known. Also, if you have enjoyed the services of a particular therapist on a prior visit, feel free to request that person.

Nudity: The idea of going *au naturel* is very scary to some people, but don't let that stop you from enjoying the spa. If modesty is an issue, call the spa in advance to discuss its policies and suggestions.

Attire: In addition to a swimsuit, bring attire for other activities you plan to enjoy: light, comfortable attire for fitness classes, gear and boots for hiking, and sneakers for exercise class along with another pair of comfortable shoes.

Cancellation: Unexpected things do happen, and sometimes it's impossible to keep an appointment. If you must cancel, give the spa as much advance notice as possible.

Communicating your preferences: Be sure to speak up. All aspects of treatment can be modified to your taste: amount of light, kind (or absence) of music, room temperature, and whether or not you choose to have a conversation or enjoy the treatment in silence. If you want the therapist to give you a deep massage, or be gentler, let him or her know. Also, feel free to ask questions.

Shaving: If you must shave, do so at least 2 h before your scheduled appointment, particularly if you're a man receiving a facial or a woman receiving any kind of scheduled bodywork.

Eating and drinking: Try not to eat for at least an hour before a treatment, and avoid the consumption of alcohol on the day of a treatment. Drink plenty of water before and afterward, especially if you plan to take a fitness class or enjoy heat therapy, such as a sauna or the steam room.

Using shared facilities: Before entering a soaking pool, swimming pool or whirlpool; always shower. When enjoying the sauna or steam, always sit on your towel and wear the plastic shoes provided by the spa. Women should not shave their legs in the steam room.

Perfume: Because the emphasis should be on relaxation and because others may be allergic, it's best not to wear perfume to exercise classes.

Smoking: For the most part, smoking is not allowed at resort/hotel spas. If it is, there are usually designated areas where you can smoke.

Children: A spa is a great place to get a little alone time, so it's best to not to bring children under 16.

Pets: Some animals are welcome at certain resorts but should not be brought to the spa.

Cell phones: Leave phones and pagers at home or in your room; or turn them off before entering the spa.

Conversation: In the relaxation room and elsewhere, keep conversations at a low volume.

Gratuities: Ask if gratuities are included, though that is not usually the case. If not, about 15% is customary.

Eco-awareness: Being respectful of your environment is part of the spa experience. Use only the number of towels necessary (Spa Finder, 2008).

Even more sophisticated would be a recommended programme of activities in a sequence, including cooling down, rests and water breaks. Below is an example from Friedrichsbad in Baden-Baden.

The 17 stages to well-being

The 17 stages follow the Ancient Roman bathing traditions. Visitors are presented with a map upon arrival, so they can anticipate the elements and stages of the visit. Some of the stages are delivered by a member of staff, that is the given treatment would take exactly the length of time promised (the numbers in the list below indicate the location of the given treatment during the visit).

1. Shower (5 min)
2. Warm (air) bath (5 min)
3. Hot (air) bath (5 min)
4. Shower (5min)
5. Soap- and brush-massage (5 min)
6. Shower (5 min)
7. Thermal steam bath (10 min and 5 min)
8. Shower (5 min)
9. Thermal fullbath (10 min)
10. Thermal jacuzzis (5 min)
11. Thermal movement bath (5 min)
12. Shower (5 min)
13. Cold water dip
14. Drying-off with warm towels (4 min)
15. Cream treatment (8 min)
16. Rest and quiet area (30 min)
17. Reading room (30 min)

Service management

As in all tourism businesses, service in wellness centres or spas should be professional, friendly, welcoming and helpful. Service approach is especially essential in any health operation, since most visitors (or patients) hand themselves over to the staff (either physically or mentally). Tourists also expect a certain level of knowledge or expertise about the treatments that they are paying to receive. Receptionists and support staff should be able to inform visitors about treatments available and advise them what might be suitable. Equally, staff working in restaurants and catering should be able to help guests make healthy food choices according to their individual dietary requirements. The increasing customization of spas and wellness services means that every individual should be made to feel special and cared for. They should not be neglected or made to wait for long periods in a reception area, or be left feeling uncertain about spa etiquette (i.e. what should be done once in the spa). This might be difficult to achieve in a large, chain hotel, therefore most wellness (and medical) hotels tend to be small(er) and run by the owner (family).

Fralix (2007), gives a rather easy clue to spa managers, when she defines the so-called SAUCE approach to human resource management.

According to SAUCE members of staff can be categorized into four groups:

- *S Personalities*: The 'S' person is driven by Specific factors and is process and methodology oriented. This person would not generalize and justifies with facts, figures and specifics, therefore managers need to use data and specifics in communication.
- *A Personalities*: The 'A' person is driven by Action, get things done quickly, and task and result oriented. They are often in a hurry and often late. They love teamwork, but only if they are in charge. Managers need to get to the point in communication with them.
- *U Personalities*: The 'U' person is driven by Understanding, that is finding things out as well as being understood. They are intuitive, visionary and change oriented. Managers should allow time for processing ideas and thinking out loud and they should expect questions, challenge and disagreements from them.
- *C Personalities*: The 'C' person is driven by Connection, that is they are group, relationship and team oriented. They do not like arguments and management has to check in with them often (so they know that everything is ok).

Obviously there are many combinations of personality: especially among managers the 'S/A' person often is the most typical; the 'A/U' people are the rebels and may soon start their own competing business; hiring some 'A/C' people means that the owners actually understood the importance of good management; and the 'S/C' person should not do anything else but dealing with human resources. In spas or more like in health facilities, managers may find 'S' and 'C' personalities easier to manage than 'A' or 'U' types, since the close connection with guests and patients and the often delicate matters of these connections requires a workforce that can follow methods as well as show capabilities of connection.

A certain level of sensitivity is required on the part of those people administering services, treatments or courses. Massage therapists should preserve the modesty of clients at all times, as many people feel very vulnerable before and during a massage, especially one that requires nudity. Psychological counsellors need to ensure that clients do not go away feeling too exposed and emotional. Yoga and meditation teachers need to recognize the sometimes powerful spiritual impact of their work and ensure participants do not feel confused or upset. Spiritual leaders and gurus especially in India have often been criticized for preying on the vulnerability of tourists who are drawn to charismatic practices without really understanding them (Brown, 1998). In some cases, certain medical processes or fitness programmes could result in pain or injury, therefore practitioners need to deal with both the practical (first-aid elements) and any personal distress caused. Some holistic centres (e.g. Skyros) recommend that visitors do not make any major life-changing decisions when they return home (e.g. leaving their jobs or partners or going to start a new life) for at least 2 months. This means that the potential impact of some wellness holidays can be extremely powerful.

Service quality

The (marketing) management aspects of service quality can be best high-lighted by referring to the Service Quality GAP model (e.g. Parasuraman et al.,1985). The seven gaps identify the most important problems in delivering services, for example, in tourism. As we mentioned on many occasions, health and wellness tourism is more prone to service delivery and production problems than some other forms of tourism.

Gap No.	Description	Causes	Typical Situation in Health and Wellness Tourism
1	Customers' expectations versus management perceptions	Management does not understand what their customers want	Providing Ayurveda and Thai massage everywhere when customers look for local experiences
2	Management perceptions versus service specifications	Management knows what consumers want, but either unable or unwilling to develop and provide it	Saving money on skilled staff or number of employees (e.g. from therapy department)
3	Service specifications versus service delivery	Management understands what needs to be delivered and appropriate specifications have been developed, but employees are unable or unwilling to deliver the service	Missing customer orientation, unmotivated and inattentive stuff by the pools, treatment rooms, etc
4	Service delivery versus external communication	Company promises more in its external communication than can be delivered	Labelling a bathing establishment as a spa or a medical hotel as a spa hotel
5	The discrepancy between customer expectations and their perceptions of the service delivered	Based on previous experiences customer perceptions are altered	Modified service supply or interior design and calling it 'upgrade', that is globalizing a local service provider
6	The discrepancy between customer expectations and employees' perceptions	Staff does not understand what their customers want	Cultural, age differences or differences in health condition between guests and staff
7	The discrepancy between employees' perceptions and management perceptions	Management does not understand employees	Managers expecting their employees to treat patients as average guests

Adapted from Parasuraman et al. (1985).

Service quality and regular monitoring of service quality in health tourism is the focus of many organizations all around the world. Various, mainly voluntary quality assurance initiatives are available for use, for example:

- www.Spaaudit.com recommends the ways in which owners or managers can do quality checks on their own. The do-it-yourself secret shopper is a self-administrated system that overcomes a common challenge faced by spas; how to accurately assess team performance when most of the service delivery happens behind closed doors (Spa Audit, 2008).
- The European Spas Association (ESPA) has started its own international quality seal, the so-called EUROPE SPA. These criteria '... focus on safety, hygiene and the therapy infrastructure. Aspects such as service, therapy, wellness, accommodation as well as kitchen and food safety are addressed in around 400 audit questions' (European Spas Association, 2007). A mystery shopper assigned by ESPA carries the audit out, which then will be awarded for 3 years (and the seal costs the site 1,250 € per year).
- The European Tourism Institute (Germany) that works together with the European Wellness Institute analysed the medical spas and destinations of Germany and provided mainly researchers and operators with the comparative evaluation of service quality, operation and management (European Tourism Institute, 2008).

Wellness Hotels Deutschland: Wellness Tree

The 'Wellness Tree' symbol, since 1997, has acted as a mark of quality and a guarantee of ensuring that the label wellness is only used by those hotels which can uphold the standards required. Every hotel is checked every year. Since 2006, the process of quality management and assurance has been certified by the TÜV Rheinland, the quality assurance organization. The main goal of WHD is to contribute to the overall satisfaction of the wellness guest. Every hotel that aspires for the quality seal, has to fulfil the following criteria:

- Tranquil locations in exceptionally beautiful natural surroundings.
- 4–5 star quality with boundless hospitality and a clear emphasis on the wellness guest
- Attractive well-kept spas and wellness areas (with pool, saunas, beauty treatments, sport and relaxation zones, amongst other features).
- Fully qualified, friendly staff in all hotel areas.
- Gourmet standard *Wellness-Vital* cuisine (for those guests who are interested).
- Cultural and experiential offers (for those guests who are interested).
- Non-smoking rooms and a restaurant which is completely non-smoking.
- Environmentally friendly hotel management.
- A guaranteed commitment on the part of the hotel to ensure and enforce quality in all areas.

WHD categorizes offers under the following categories:

- Active and fit
- Golf
- Well and care
- Time for us
- Beauty
- 4 seasons (Wellness Hotels Deutschland, 2008).

The rapid development of the market also forced the British Spa Association to strengthen its quality criteria. 'The Waves of Excellence' is an accreditation system developed to indicate that a spa is offering products and services that the consumer can enjoy with confidence, such as quality of service, ambiance, satisfaction with therapies and treatments, value for money, professionalism of staff, range of services available, etc. (British Spa Association, 2008).

Visitors, besides the various seals of quality, can learn about sites and destinations from various sources, for example from:

- The many 'World's Best Spas by Readers Awards' by SpaFinder Magazine, Concierge.com or Condé Nast Traveller, etc.
- Travel diaries by previous guests, which they share in on-line virtual communities (e.g. tripadvisor.com, lonelyplanet.com, igougo.com, etc.).

Training and regulation

Although we said earlier that skilled people are of paramount importance, many staff are lacking proper qualifications in the field of wellness tourism. It is actually possible to 'qualify' as a yoga teacher, massage therapist or life-coach after a series of short training programmes, sometimes lasting only a month or a few weekends. The British Wheel of Yoga in the UK is now therefore only accrediting yoga teachers who have completed a 2-year intensive training programme approved by the Sports Council of Britain. The Government of India insists that true Ayurvedic practitioners train for 3 years. These are, however, rare examples. Some practitioners have no training whatsoever, for example, those individuals who set themselves up in destinations like Goa as yoga or meditation teachers. It seems that many tourists neither know nor care about the lack of qualifications or regulations (e.g. Smith & Kelly's (2006) research showed that people only cared about whether or not they liked the teacher!). This is quite a dangerous pattern, as irreparable damage can be done to body, mind or spirit through neglectful or uninformed practice. In the case of medical tourism, it is absolutely imperative that doctors are properly qualified.

Case Study: Unregulated Yoga Holidays

Rew (2007) describes an experience of a yoga holiday in the Canary Islands which demonstrates clearly some of the problems of the unregulated holistic and yoga sector. There is a clear gap between the brochure and reality, which promises something such as 'a sanctuary of solace', whereas in actual fact the resort is uncomfortable, noisy, unprofessional and largely unregulated. Sometimes retreats are not even properly finished by the time guests arrive, meaning that they are driven elsewhere (often involving an arduous journey) to practise yoga as there is no suitable space in the retreat itself. Many visitors drop out of the yoga classes, leave the retreat and ask for compensation. This report is based on numerous testimonies of the same story. Rew quotes Lisa Jeans, who runs luxury bootcamp The Complete Retreat, who says that 'There have always been people running hippy-style yoga retreats with no qualifications, but I've noticed a lot more cowboys open in the last few years. Some of it is people setting up retreats for purely commercial reasons, some of it yoga fanatics lacking the skills to run successful holidays'.

The main problem is that many of the people who set up retreats are not qualified in business or management. The Association of British Travel Agents expressed concern that in the last 5 years literally thousands of similar holidays had been set up without the necessary skills, resources or manpower to stop things going wrong. Many instructors or retreat managers are not even properly qualified in yoga. Unlike most sports and fitness holidays and courses, anyone can legally be an instructor on a yoga holiday with no qualifications or experience at all! People rarely think to check their teacher's qualifications, especially when they are going on holiday. They are particularly vulnerable if they have not done any or much yoga before, and may not have heard of the governing bodies in their home country (e.g. the British Wheel of Yoga in the UK). Even if the teachers are qualified, the company may not have the necessary experience to act as a tour operator.

Choosing a teacher registered with a national governing body can guarantee a reasonable standard of instruction at least. The website of the European Yoga Union has links to the sites of member countries' governing bodies, and the BWY in the UK has 3,500 registered teachers, all of whom have at least 4 years experience and have annual quality reviews. Its website has lists of teachers and people can ring up to verify qualifications. Ideally, the operator should also be a member of a trade association like the Association of Independent Tour Operators (AITO) or the Association of British Travel Agents (ABTA).

It is often difficult to identify the relevant qualifications for a 'spa therapist' as they may specialize in one service only (e.g. massage, beauty), but it is becoming more common for therapists to multi-task as this is more economical for spas and wellness centres. Thus beauticians might extend skin care and make-up expertise to manicures and pedicures. Many massage therapists become aroma therapists or learn different massage techniques. Yoga teachers can offer meditation or Thai massage (sometimes dubbed 'the lazy man's yoga'). Life coaches may learn different psychological therapies to help clients (e.g. Neuro-Linguistic-Programming). New accreditations and qualifications may be needed to accommodate the cross-over skills that are being developed, as many require a separate diploma and licence.

It is rather difficult, however, to assure visitors that the staff are actually skilled and experienced. Of course, 'big labels', that is well-known brand names can help visitors to overcome lack of trust. Wellness facilities and treatments located in international chain hotels (e.g. JW Marriott, Shangri-La or Sheraton) or signature spas (e.g. Elizabeth Arden's Red Door) or branded wellness centres (e.g. Holmes Place) are less prone to risks associated with inadequate training or skills. Facilitators, trainers or therapists without a 'good' brand often emphasize the location of their training (e.g. trained by a guru or at a famous location), refer to the products they use (especially in beauty spas), the number of years of experience or refer to famous clients such as celebrities (and soon they will make their own brand).

Health and safety

Crebbin-Bailey et al. (2005) discuss some of the most important health and safety aspects for spas, which are equally important in other health facilities, too. These include the health and safety of employees and guests alike, and they need to comply with the different laws and regulations of a given country. There is a need to assess the risk of injury or illness, hygiene issues are paramount, filtration, purification and disinfection of waters and facilities are crucial and chemicals need to be stored safely. Consider only the risks a water-based facility might mean, that is from the floors of the changing rooms to the poolside tiling.

Food provision also needs to be given health and safety considerations. Spa employees should be trained in first aid and know what to do if a guest has a problem or injury. Typical accidents may be caused by slipping on wet floors, poor or non-swimmers getting out of their depth in pools, diving in shallow waters, drinking alcohol before treatments, misuse of equipment, illnesses caused by over-exposure to hot temperatures, infections from under-sterilized waters, long hair or body parts being caught in water outlets, amongst others.

Quality management systems

The Dostwell project is a European project which shows some of the current weaknesses in the quality systems relating to wellness tourism. This includes lack of common standards and quality criteria, lack of existing qualifications, lack of efficient co-operations, missing knowledge about trends in wellness tourism, lack of know-how concerning the expectations, needs and wishes of potential wellness guests and misuse of the term wellness (Kögler, 2007). There are some examples of quality systems that have been put in place in Europe, for example the Alpine Wellness label (covering currently more than 40 hotels in Austria, Germany, Switzerland and Italy), Wellfeeling Switzerland (a Swiss hotel network), which are more like marketing tools, and the possibility to use existing quality models such as ISO (International Organization for Standardization) or the

European Foundation for Quality Management (EFQM). These operate more as management systems focusing on organizational and operational processes. Customers often have to know about the system to appreciate the wellness operator's achievement, but arguably such schemes give wellness centres, spas and hotels something to aspire to, clear guidelines for good practice, and enhances their competitive advantage (e.g. Rheinland TÜV of Germany has developed a quality assurance system for wellness hotels and ESPA created a similar system for spas).

Specific management issues for different kinds of spa

D'Angelo (2006) differentiates between types of spas for the purposes of developing business and management strategies. Clearly, the way in which spas are managed will vary somewhat depending on whether they are day spas, destination spas, hotel spas, resort spas, medical spas or leisure spas. However, ISPA (2006b) suggests that spa-goers on all levels expect that their entire spa visit will be tightly structured, especially important during transitional points in their visits, when many spa-goers regularly feel uneasy. Being 'transported' out of normal waking consciousness is a key marker of a quality spa visit. Mid-level and Core spa-goers value opportunities to customize their spa visits as much as possible to suit individual desires and preferences. Products are not top of mind for spa-goers, but services are.

The following represents some of the categorizations that are typically used in the US or Asia, supplemented by discussions of those spas that are more common in Europe (e.g. medical, historic).

Destination spas

Destination or resort spas usually offer all-inclusive spa therapy or wellness programmes, therefore all elements of the holiday need to have a healthy dimension to them, including the food and drink offered. The staff would typically include a number of medical and healthcare professionals, various therapists (e.g. massage, beauty) and fitness instructors. The connection between all elements of the visitor's package needs to be understood and integrated. Guests may stay for several days or weeks. ISPA (2006b) notes that spa-goers tend to equate destination spas and resort/hotel spas in their minds. They need help to link the intentions of their destination spa visits to their everyday lives, and may even seek life-altering changes at the destination spas. Escape is a strong motive to visit destination spas, but social and economic pressures often undermine a spa-goer's ability to escape.

In a destination spa the whole stay is characterized by the various elements of the wellness supply. The location of the facility could be rather remote, that is the guests cannot easily do anything else, but staying in the spa (e.g. Tabacon Thermal Water Resort, an adventure spa in Costa Rica). However, they may not even want to do anything else, but stay on-site.

This leaves the management with the major problem of how to entertain the guests all day long, for many days. The solution is of course easier in a retreat type of spa, where the number of guests is relatively low at any time (e.g. up to 40). It is much more difficult to do with a large facility with hundreds of guest, where various cultural programmes should be organized, for example.

Resort spas

Resort spas may not be so orientated towards complete health and wellness programmes, but will offer the chance to relax and unwind using some spa facilities, sports and leisure activities. In general, such spas are mainly targeted at people who want to enjoy leisure facilities rather than curing specific medical conditions or health problems. The atmosphere should therefore be one that focuses on fun and entertainment rather than creating a sanitized, medical environment. ISPA (2006b) suggests that the perception that resort spas are expensive leads to expectations of high quality experience and risk of poor value. Most vacationing tourists and business travellers do not organize their trips around resort spas, and business travellers may even want spa experiences that are removed from vacationers and vacation culture.

Wellness, medical and spa hotels

Wellness, medical and spa hotels can follow two different strategies. One would mean that the whole facility serves one purpose, that is the better health of visitors, whereas the other may mean that some services were added to a 'standard' hotel facility. Certainly, it is easier to manage the first approach since the whole facility (from fittings down to heating technology) was planned and built at once. Hotel managers can have a wide range of tools with which they make the stay of visitors special, that is textiles and beddings can be eco-friendly or use all-natural materials; drinks and food in the minibar can only or mainly present healthy ranges; meals can offer healthy and locally grown options, etc. The room minibar in AquaDome Hotel (for example, Langenfeld, Austria) has no alcohol beverages, but fruit drinks and fruit yoghurts. The minibar is filled up every day and free of charge. In the room (and in the sauna area) locally grown fresh fruits are offered every day and chocolate, for example 'Mozart Kugel', as a national speciality, is also a standard element of the fruit basket.

It is anticipated that wellness visitors may represent higher than average spending patterns. In many countries the average room rate achieved in a 'wellness' hotel can be higher than that of standard hotels. This, however, can be counterbalanced with the higher running, and more frequent replacement costs, especially in those facilities that have their own pool and sauna area. The running costs of pools and saunas are quite significant since the water has to be at a certain temperature and the saunas and steam rooms should be warmed up regardless of the number of guests using them. In small hotels, therefore, management limits the period during which pool and sauna facilities can be used or they alter the use of these facilities by allowing men and women at different times.

Specialized hotel facilities often face the problem, which can be described using the 'have-or-not-to-have' dilemma, that is should they offer the services on-site or should they just 'use' the services available at a nearby spa. To make this question more complicated they have to make a strategic decision about allowing (or not) walk-in guests into the hotel's spa facility. Certainly, opting for more guests sounds like a 'pro' in theory, but this may lead to managing visitor groups or segments that may not fit (e.g. by spending capacity, preferred activities, age groups).

One of the key issues in a hotel is how to estimate and manage dining demand. In destination or resort spas, guests may not have much option to dine anywhere else, but a spa hotel can have a whole town or many other hotels and restaurants in the neighbourhood. One of the popular solutions is to provide packages with either full- or half-board. This can especially be typical for medical hotels, where the meals can be a part of the whole medical programme, although in other hotels too, where meals can be themed, for example introducing local cuisine. The range of dishes provided, however, should fit the services and the travel package. Any inconsistency would devalue the experience and the impact of the stay significantly.

PKF Hospitality Research (PKF-HR) carried out a survey about the financial performance of hotel spa departments of resort and urban hotels (Mandelbaum & Lerner, 2008). PKF-HR Hotel Industry database stated that treatments such as massages, body wraps, and facials are the largest revenue (51.3%) for hotel spas. Interestingly clothing and merchandise sales grow the most (20.4%) during 2006. Not so surprisingly, due to extensive labour requirements, spa departments achieved profit margin ratios less than the average for all other operated departments (31.1% and 40.8%, respectively).

It should be noted that retreat and holistic centres provide on-site accommodation to guests. This forms part of the whole experience. Accommodation needs can range from very basic to lavish facilities, and the personal involvement of guests can also range from active involvement in meal preparation and clearing up after, to no involvement at all.

Purpose-built recreational spas

Purpose-built recreational spas are often built in areas where there is a need to provide leisure services or fitness facilities for local residents. It is likely that they will be visited by local people and tourists alike, but usually for 1 day only or for a few hours. Many such spas do not offer accommodation and they do not provide different packages. The usage is mainly recreational, therefore few or no medical treatments will be offered. Massage facilities and other therapies may be available, but it is more common that different pools, jacuzzis, saunas and steam rooms are the main form of activity. In Germany, Austria and Switzerland such spas often exist in mountain areas and ski resorts, therefore relaxation is a primary motivation. There may be a separation of facilities for those who would like quiet relaxation time (e.g. a 'sauna landscape or temples' with many different types of sauna and steam experiences) and more family/ children orientated facilities with 'fun waters'. Recreational spas are easily consumed by even those who do not speak the local language, so they tend to be very popular among tourists.

Spas, however, almost anywhere face a major problem, that is, unless they are extremely unique (e.g. architecture), it is almost impossible to run a facility profitably. This is due to the high development and running costs that cannot be repaid or covered from guests' spending. That is why many of the spas are managed together with hotel facilities (and the entrance fees are included in the hotel room). Revenue management is as crucial in spas as in other visitor attractions. Guests can spend money not only on the entrance ticket(s) but also on catering, renting (e.g. beds or rubber rings), treatments or products with the spa's very own label.

A crucial tool in the management's hand is the definition of opening hours. Many segments, such as prospective guests working long hours, cannot visit the facility during the standard opening hours (9 a.m.–6 p.m.). These opening hours would not fit families either. Therefore more and more spas stay open until 10 p.m. or even later, especially on Fridays and Saturdays. There are a handful of developers and operators, for example VAMED in Austria, or Starwaters in Germany that specialize in leisure and recreational spa operations.

Medical spas

ISPA (2006b) suggest that many spa-goers maintain unfavourable and inaccurate images of medical spas, which are seen as 'last resorts' for attaining physical states that are seemingly unachievable through conventional spa treatments. Medical spas are perceived as posing short-term risks and long-term unanticipated consequences. ISPA's view is very much different from that of ESPA since medical spas are well established and accepted forms of medical facilities in Western, Southern and Central and Eastern Europe. However, medical spas face major challenges, since the often hospital or sanatorium-like feeling and atmosphere tend to be less and less appealing and competitive. This of course means the need for service and architectural developments.

Medical spas are often dependent on government or national health insurance provided support. In many countries national health insurance (partially or totally) finances the so-called evidence-based medicine, that is medical waters or mud based treatments. Most of the medical spas were built in the last 50 years and have been providing services for hospital and walk-in patients. Since almost in every country national health insurers face financial challenges, less and less is available for supporting treatments in spas. This leaves the management of spas, that are often not private but municipality led, in financial constraints. The running costs of medical spas can be especially high, since the availability of medical (trained) staff is essential so are various equipment (e.g. for under-water massage).

Those visitors, who are not ill and their visit was not prescribed by a doctor may find it surprising that most of the medical waters have an identical smell and colour. This is because of the mineral content. This smell can be rather unpleasant and could stay on the skin for many hours after the visit. Therefore sufficient showering facilities must be provided, since the demand for getting rid of the smell can be very high. Healing waters may not be transparent and are dark (brown, yellow or black). Most visitors associate unpleasant experiences with anything that is not transparent and they would preferably avoid bathing in these waters.

Med Spas operate under the full-time supervision of a licensed health-care professional that offer clinical-grade aesthetic enhancement and spa treatments (e.g. plastic surgery). Treatments blend state-of-the-art medical therapies with a relaxing spa experience. Not to be confused with a Med Spa, Medical Spas provide comprehensive wellness and preventative care that may adhere to traditional Western medical concepts, complementary/ alternative philosophies, or a combination of the two. Spa treatments are incorporated into wellness programs as a beneficial way to reduce stress.

Withman and Fadra (2007) have compiled a short list of what can really make the management of these Med Spas more efficient:

- Room utilization: Define hours per day occupied for services.
- Room productivity: Estimate room's revenue per day.
- Staff productivity: Calculate revenue by staff members versus their salary and any ratio less than two should be questioned.
- Marketing metrics: Any marketing cost that generates <1.5 times, its costs should be dropped.
- Public relations: Make plan for actions and allocate funds.
- Inventory: Use computerized inventory management systems and plan actions for those situations when material used during treatment exceeds 7% of service revenue and make sure that your mark up on products for resale is at least double.
- Marketing: Be aware that in the first year of operation, marketing costs can reach up to 20% of projected revenue and may stabilize at 10% after.
- Revenue per square foot/meter: Use benchmark data from similar facilities.
- Payroll: Target your payroll around 35–40% of revenue.
- Rent and overhead: Consider sub-leasing space.
- Think outside the box: Look beyond your core products and services.
- Hours: Chart your revenue hour by hour and consider opening earlier and closing later on some days.
- Internal benchmarks: Establish benchmarks for various metrics that are vital to efficiency, review and disseminate results on regular basis
- Cost structure: Financial and Med Spa consultants can significantly change your financial situation.
- Cut the fat: Your operation can always be more focused in terms of number of lines or number of suppliers you use.

Historic spas

Historic spas may need to consider issues of heritage management or conservation, as they are often hundreds of years old and cannot accommodate large numbers of visitors or necessarily provide for all kinds of visitors, especially if their buildings are listed and there are restrictions on development. They may not be able to support intensive leisure usage, therefore visitor numbers at any one time may be limited and children may not be allowed to enter.

The ITER-CADSES (2005) European Union financed project highlighted the main problems for historic spas:

> Italy, Austria, Hungary, Romania, Bulgaria and Greece share a common cultural heritage: historic spas. Starting from the Ancient Greek and Roman times, these facilities were built in areas where 'the waters' were thought to have healing properties. Through history kings, popes, emperors, and the nobility made grand entrances to spa towns, which became also extremely important from an artistic and cultural point of view. Nevertheless little has been done to protect this remarkable cultural ensemble of cultural and landscape elements or in other words an extraordinary combination of archaeology, architecture, craft and landscape. In the last years spa tourism has come back into fashion and underwent a radical transformation into a new market product called 'wellness'. This health oriented mass exploitation has not been equally accompanied by a policy for the identification, knowledge and protection of the concerned historic buildings, conservation areas and landscape.

Historic spas can certainly vary and some representatives still can be found in the following countries, for example:

- Austria, Hungary: Neo-classical
- Hungary: Art-nouveau
- Italy, Germany: Roman-style
- Japan: Zen (onsen)
- Turkey: Oriental (hamam)

Historic spas are often located in listed buildings and that means constraint for any development. Heritage protection agencies rarely support the introduction of any new facility or technologies if that necessitated the modification of the building structure or even a wall or floor (this may include the introduction of lifts, too!).

Day and beauty spas

Chambers (2006) describes The Resort and Day Spa Association's guidelines which help consumers to make a distinction between a facility that offers spa services, and a true day spa:

- A clean, safe, calming and nurturing environment.
- Private treatment rooms for each client receiving a personal service.

- Showering and changing facilities for women and men.
- Spa robes and shoes for all sizes.
- Business licenses: professional, licensed aestheticians and therapists on staff.
- Professional spa products for which aestheticians and therapists have received training in their use.

In addition, a range of massages, body and facial treatments, steam, sauna or hydrotherapy, as well as a private fitness trainer, nutritionist or spa cuisine.

Monteson and Singer (2004) describe how day spas should operate and what kind of facilities they should have, for example dry treatment rooms for massage and facials, wet treatment rooms for body wraps, scrubs, etc., hydrotherapy rooms for baths and hydromassage therapies, a salon for hair, make-up, nails and an exercise or fitness room. There may also be a retail area or shop. A day spa should provide a staffed reception area where the staff are dedicated to making customers feel individually welcome and cared for. There should be separate mens' and womens' changing rooms, and often separate facilities such as sauna, steam room, hot and cold pools. There is a need to provide customized service to encourage visitor's loyalty and repeat visitation. The whole experience is thought to be more important than individual treatments, so the atmosphere, service, quality, cleanliness and professionalism will all count for as much. Special packages and incentives are ideally created and men may need to be targeted differently from women.

Especially in North-America, the concept of Medical Day Spa, or Med Spa, which differs from Day Spas by the nature of its services, that is the medical orientation has recently become more and more popular.

Case Study: Ecospas

The organization of Ecospas aims to give guidelines for environmental management to the spa industry. As well as encouraging clients to take good care of their bodies and their inner selves, their main goal is to help preserve and revive the planet.

Information is provided about ecologically-oriented day spas, resort spas, destination spas and cruise spas. Information is available on products that support, rather than destroy the earth. Those products include natural cosmetics, hair and nail care, biodegradable and recyclable products, cleaning agents that protect the earth. Links are given to spas that have created an ecologically oriented environment, as well as to resources that will help managers to create a spa environment that ensures harmony for clients and for the earth. There are also links to organizations that support the 'green movement' and support spas turning 'green'.

Some examples of eco-friendly spa practices include the following:

The Sports Club Co./Splash Spas
  Uses biodegradable sandals in all locations.

The Spa at Post Ranch Inn
Uses a grey water system to recycle laundry water for use in its landscaping.

Rancho La Puerta
Has organic gardens to supply organic, healthy spa cuisine.

Echo Valley Ranch and Spa
A safe habitat for a wide array of species, including native birds. Recycling is a major focus here. The Doves hope to teach by example, demonstrating that luxury and environmental responsibility needn't be at odds with each other.

Hidden Creek Ranch
The goal of owners Iris Behr and John Muir is to inspire guests to tread lightly on the earth and to learn green living practices during their stay.

Spring Creek Ranch
A luxury resort with a conscience, Spring Creek has buildings constructed of native woods. Fruits and vegetables harvested from a nearby organic farm. As well their extensive spa menu includes numerous energy treatments.

(Ecospas, 2008)

Managing holistic centres and spiritual retreats

A holistic centre or retreat may be defined as a purpose built centre which accommodates its guests for the purpose of learning or improving a body–mind–spirit activity (e.g. yoga, meditation) and perhaps receiving complementary therapies or treatments whilst there. Group programming of classes is the norm. A retreat will usually have no other type of tourism/visitor activity besides that of a holistic nature, but it is likely that they will vary the programmes, courses and workshops that are offered throughout the year. Whereas holistic centres usually offer 1–2 week holidays, spiritual retreats sometimes offer programmes lasting several weeks, even months. Visitors can be resident in the retreat and help with the operational aspects (e.g. cooking, cleaning, cultivating in the garden, maintenance). Holistic centres charge relatively high prices, whereas spiritual retreats often ask for a minimal amount or just accept donations.

A continuum could be said to exist in terms of level of organization and structure for holistic centres and retreats. At one end, 'ad hoc' retreats offer relatively unstructured courses and workshops which are low cost. These typically exist in Asian countries (e.g. India, Thailand, Sri Lanka). Although the management and operational aspects are fragmented usually relying on individual practitioners, the practices tend to be more spontaneous and authentic. This kind of experience might suit a backpacker or spiritual visitor whose primary motivation is the practice itself (e.g. yoga, meditation) as well as the context. At the other end of the spectrum are purpose-built retreat centres which are aimed more at the middle-aged, middle-class, urban 'burn out' market who are seeking ways of re-evaluating and re-balancing their lives. They are willing and able to spend large amounts of money on holistic holidays, which are still simple (e.g. the Atsitsa Centre in Skyros accommodates people in small outdoor huts which are often shared), but which are well-organized, carefully programmed and staffed with highly qualified people. The location for such centres is largely immaterial as the practices are generally 'global' but favoured locations are beside the sea, in mountains or in quiet, pretty villages

Smith and Kelly (2006) collected details on around 450 holistic centres and retreats which were then placed in a database. An in-depth questionnaire about the management and operations of the centre was sent to a sample of 400 centres (those which had electronic addresses). Although there was only a 10% response rate, these came from all over the world. Questions were asked about the centre itself, products, motivations for establishment, problems and challenges, regulatory issues, finance, marketing, tourism, local engagement and sustainability. In terms of motivation for setting up a holistic centre or retreat, the answers could be grouped as follows:

- *Locational motivators* (e.g. 'I wanted to live in Italy', 'I was tired of London')
- *Practitioner motivators* (e.g. 'because we love yoga')
- *Altruistic motivators* (e.g. 'to help people find themselves')
- *Personal discovery motivators* (e.g. 'an to fulfil my dharma', 'I had a chronic illness and went on a spiritual journey')
- *Business development motivators* (e.g. 'I saw a population that was lacking in targeted services')

In terms of entrepreneurship, management and operations, most practitioners got no financial or advisory assistance. They merely decided to go with the establishment of a centre based on lifestyle issues and a strong instinct that it was their destiny to do so. There was a varied response to the idea of 'regulatory issues' with many centre managers unconcerned about the regulation of staff and their qualifications. Instead, they claimed to understand something of health and safety and insurance. Many centres also offer aftercare to guests, but it is variable in quality. Marketing is largely web-based and word-of-mouth, and not all centres use tour operators, in fact, many do not see themselves as part of tourism at all! As stated by one practitioner: 'Tourism generally does not understand the essentials of what we do'. Many centres operated almost in isolation from the local area, especially when the centre managers were foreign (a frequent phenomenon), which meant that the degree of sustainability was not high:

- Use of local food/drink – 27%
- Cultural excursions – 22%
- Use of local transport – 16%
- Employment of local staff – 20%
- Cultural courses – 15%
- (e.g. language, cookery, handicrafts)

The challenges of running a centre include the problem of seasonality, the high staff costs if hiring trained experts, the administration office often being located outside the centre, the limited capacity of most centres, the expense of marketing and increasing competition.

Conclusion

This chapter has demonstrated clearly the complexity of managing health and wellness tourism from the protection of natural assets through to the regulation of staff and services. It is often easier to develop health and wellness products and to promote them, than to manage the quality of facilities and resources. There is a need for a degree of national level intervention for the conservation of national assets as well as regulation of the tourism industry and health practitioners. Regional quality assurance organizations and networks can help to standardize provision and to share examples of good practise. Resort and site level management is often dependent on private individuals or companies, who/which may or not be experienced in health tourism management. However, visitors in this sector need to be provided with high quality experiences and safe products, whilst being cared for and nurtured by well-qualified and trained staff. This is the main goal of health tourism destinations and businesses otherwise their long-term prognosis will be anything but healthy!

Reaching customers

Rich fat man has become an oxymoron, and poor and fat have become synonymous.

(Pilzer, 2008:18)

Introduction

The marketing of health tourism is almost like any service industry's marketing, with one exception: it involves some kind of health element, which is one of the most personal, therefore sensitive aspects. This has an impact on the demand, the supply, and the intermediary side too. This chapter does not follow the textbook marketing approach, for example does not necessarily follow strictly the logic of Ps or Ss. We introduced the major characteristics of demand in Chapter Seven (e.g. segmenting).

As we could see many times earlier, health tourism specifically builds on trust. Guests trust the healing natural asset. Participants trust the guru. Patients trust the surgeon. And all of them expect a little more than just nice experiences and memories. They want better health, nicer teeth, nicer curves, or a more stable frame of mind. The real and perceived risks associated with health services during the trip, therefore can be much higher than in the case of other types of trips. This results in a wide range of techniques and approaches which service providers and marketers use to reassure existing and prospective visitors.

Based on the above mentioned qualities of health tourism it is crucial for any facility, operator or organization to apply quite different marketing approaches. This is certainly new to those facilities that intentionally or unintentionally started to receive tourists from other parts of the country or of the world, for example clinics, medical spas, or small-scale retreat homes. The whole concept of marketing can be very new to those spas and spa hotels that were operating in a market-free environment in Central and Eastern Europe or in Russia or to hospitals that now want to open to foreign patients. Facing the same market challenges that all other entities do, and adapting to a new situation is not easy (especially given that most of the medical spas still rely on substantial amounts of state or local government subsidy every year). This highlights another aspect of health tourism marketing. Many facilities are two-faceted: on the one hand, they provide health services; on the other hand, they want to attract visitors who pay the market price for the treatments. These two major types of demand make marketing complicated, since in the first case we cannot even talk about a 'market' as such, whereas tourism is one of the most competitive sectors.

Marketing communications

Holloway (2004) and others (e.g. Kotler et al., 2005) summarized the determinants for marketing communication strategies and tactics as follows:

- *The nature of the product.* Tourism products are not homogeneous and this is particularly true in the case of health and wellness tourism. Products are not well known and even similar labels may mean something rather different. Brochures, websites, DVDs, fairs make attempts to introduce services and facilities, but to understand all the complexity, more and more attach a guide or manual to their products facilitating better understanding e.g. Spa Week Media Group created a video library that was 'designed to promote the spa lifestyle to a new generation of spa-goers'. The library under the brand name of Spadcast introduces procedures, treatments, and products. The categories from which customers can view short films are Non-Invasive Cosmetic Procedures, Plastic Surgery, Beauty, Anti-Aging, Male Grooming, Teen & Ween, and Wellness – www.spaweek.org/spadcast/.
- *The target at which the communication is aimed.* Both 'push' or distribution channel-oriented; and 'pull' or final customer-oriented communications are heavily used in health and wellness tourism. In many countries, based on the relative novelty of the product, dealers, retailers, or doctors still can be motivated (push), and customers can also be relatively easily attracted by buzzwords such as 'experience', 'ritual', 'self-realization', 'escape', or 'sanctuary' (pull).
- *The stage in the life cycle in which the product is to be found.* This determinant has very close links with the 'nature of the product'. It is almost impossible to create a global promotion mix for health and wellness tourism, since the products are at very different stages in their respective life cycles. We could see before that may be luxury spa resorts can face similar life cycle positions everywhere. Therapeutic medical tourism, however, is relatively new to North America, while it is one of the fundamental forms in Central and Eastern Europe, or Asia.
- *The situation in which the marketer finds him or herself in the marketplace.* Health and wellness tourism, especially those forms that are not

site-specific, are highly competitive and the market, especially in the luxury segment, is the whole world. In this case personal and personalized services, attractive and unique architecture, the location etc. can become the focus of communication (or USP). The site-specific providers highlight their assets, experiences, the healing impacts, prices, and personalities involved in the procedures.

- *The budget for the promotional strategy.* This determinant, as in all forms of tourism, very much depends on the available resources, the strategy objectives and the media selected.

Not only a well-known site with global coverage, but also country-specific ones can be popular. Arizona SpaGirls (www.arizonaspagirls.com), for example claim 'combining yellow page practicality with insider information'. The site positions itself as an information site for women almost exclusively and this is also manifested in the style of language they use, for example 'Simply put, Arizona SpaGirls is your little pink book to looking and feeling your best!'.

As we will see in the various cases we refer to, the messages can come at three different levels. Discussing the regional and thematic similarities and differences of health and wellness products and related communication it seems that at all level marketers have to face challenges (Table 10.1).

The world's largest search engine Google, lists (in March 2008) spas under 'Speciality Travel'. Interestingly the geographical and thematic coverage is not complete, since Africa (with 2), Asia (with 6), Europe (with 35), North America (with 56) and Oceania (with 3 links) listed, but South America is not. The other related links include 'Fitness' and 'Beauty' but these are under 'Health' and not under 'Travel'. Interestingly 'Speciality

Table 10.1 Marketing Challenges in Health Tourism.

Levels	Challenges for Health and Wellness Tourism
Cognitive level (i.e. making customers aware of the products and services)	*Fading labels* The proliferation of use and the erosion of the term wellness devalues original products and confuses customers
Affective level (i.e. creating an emotional response to messages)	*Demolishing barriers* A significant part of the market takes with a pinch of salt anything that is called wellness and believes that it is not for him or her, but for the rich and famous (and often they are right, too)
Behavioural level (i.e. making customers act in the aspired way: to make a purchase)	*Compound segmentation* Segmentation takes place based on numerous factors; from basic factors such as age or gender (e.g. men or young people), to very complex ones such as lifestyle

Source: Adapted from Holloway (2004).

Travel' can take us to 'Medical Travel' too, under which 'Disabled' (with 220), 'Fasting and Cleansing' (with 13), and 'Holistic' (with 34) categories can be found. For those who are looking for other major portals a wide choice of service providers can be found in 10 'Guides and Directories'. Only two of which, however, introduce country-specific information, for example 'Spas in Thailand' and the 'Royal Spas of Europe'.

TripAdvisor, one of the popular on-line communities polled 3,000 at the beginning of 2006. Interestingly, spa vacations were ranked only behind sightseeing and shopping as reasons to make a trip. TripAdvisor also experienced an average annual growth rate of 20% in the number of spa locations over the last 8–9 years.

Case Study: Royal Spas of Europe

Eight historic spa towns (used to be nine with Loutraki in Greece) with very different, but still somehow similar characteristics joined together and started the Royal Spas of Europe partnership. The members are

- Archena (Spain)
- Baden-Baden (Germany)
- Bad Neuenahr (Germany)
- Bayreuth (Germany)
- Budapest (Hungary)
- Marienbad (Czech Republic)
- Naantali (Finland)
- Sárvár (Hungary)

These European spas and health resorts are rich in tradition: emperors, kings, members of the high nobility, and famous heads of state were among their guests, making them famous. The Royal Spas return visitors to a time when European spas were to enjoy wellness in sublime elegance. The initiative's aim is to promote both the long tradition as well as the modern facilities of baths and thermal centres. The communication highlights health services and facilities that are complemented by attractive packages of cultural and historical heritage.

The Royal Spas of Europe initiative aims to meet the highest quality requirements. For this reason a set of criteria were set, which has to be met by any member, for example health, wellness and fitness services, thermal facilities, medical care, infrastructure, standards of hotels, and cultural events.

Interestingly the alliance refers to spas, but the members are spa towns, except Finland, where a spa hotel became a member. This may leave room for misunderstanding for anyone who visits the website or reads the brochure. The information provision of the alliance does not really go further than providing one platform from where the individual members can be reached.

(Royal Spas, 2008)

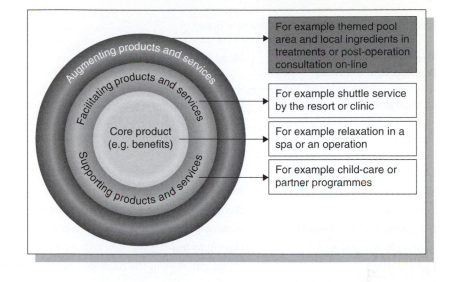

For example themed pool area and local ingredients in treatments or post-operation consultation on-line

For example shuttle service by the resort or clinic

For example relaxation in a spa or an operation

For example child-care or partner programmes

Augmenting products and services

Facilitating products and services

Supporting products and services

Core product (e.g. benefits)

Figure 10.1
Links between Health Product Development and Targeting. *Source*: Smith and Puczkó.

When a place or destination targets prospective customers, the major trend is to go beyond the introduction and communication of the core product, for example relaxation at a spa. The facilitating and supporting services and products tend to have more and more importance, let alone talking about the so-called augmented elements (that really can make the product different). Considering the fierce competition in health and wellness tourism, service provider's focus on the augmented services and products, since very little room is left for creating something different in the core, supporting and facilitating factors. The above chart lists some examples of how the product development and targeting is linked (Figure 10.1).

Concerning the various available levels of product, it is revealing to refer to some research carried out by the Small Luxury Hotels (SLH) hotel chain in 2005. They collected what their visitors like and dislike when in a spa. From these two lists any (hotel) spa can see which parts of the products offered can fall under which product level categories (e.g. 'small talk' with staff may seem to be a facilitating service, but guests would prefer not to have it, etc.) (Table 10.2).

There are a great number of sources from which visitors can find out more about health and wellness services and destinations. The printed and on-line sources, for example SpaFinder, Beautifulbreak, Relax-Guide, Spa Index, etc. use very extensive lists of categories introducing their partners (and advertisers). These categories represent the given source's segmenting and targeting strategy as well as the listed partners' positioning strategy. From the compilation of these categories, it is quite clear that as the market saturates new segments and categories are emerging continuously. The lists are very long and items often do not really represent clear differences from other items. These clarifications are, of course, provided by the given supplier (e.g. the Connoisseur Spas are 'The crème de la crème of spas, this elite collection was chosen using strict criteria such

Table 10.2 Customer Likes and Dislikes in Spas.

The Top 10 Most Commonly Booked Spa Services	Most Disliked Experiences
Aromatherapy massages	Having to appear naked for treatments, or to use a mixed sauna without bathing suits or being bathed by strangers
Facials	Receiving hard-sell tactics to spend more on spa or beauty products
Local 'signature' therapies	Treatments derived from chocolate or other dessert ingredients
Manicures	Any evidence of lack of cleanliness or poor hygiene
Pedicures	Being ushered out speedily once their treatment is over
More 'creative' treatments	Pretentious spas which seem to prefer clients with perfect bodies
Ayurvedic massages	Having to make small talk with over-familiar staff
Reflexology	On arrival, finding the hotel spa fully booked with locals
Body wraps	
Hydrotherapy programmes	

Source: SLH (2005).

as extraordinary ambience, luxurious accommodations, high staff-to-guest ratio, exceptional spa services, outstanding cuisine, and industry awards and recognition') (Table 10.3).

Operators are also aware of the quick proliferation and sometimes misleading use of the terms, therefore those that find informing their customers important, often create lists, glossaries, A-Zs, etc. of wellness and health services. Besides, almost all printed and on-line magazines (e.g. SpaArabia, SpaAsia, American Spa Magazine, AVIDA Magazine, asiasmedicaltourism.com, medicaltourism.com), association publications and websites (e.g. australianspaassociation.com, federterme.it, leadingspasofcanada.com, or visiteuropeanspas.com) or portals for communication (e.g. spasofamerica.com and spafinder.com) provide help and guidance for their readers or visitors about what certain treatments and forms of health tourism and health services may mean. There are many beautifully presented books on the market using amazing images, for example, Spa Style series that can lure even those who have never been in a spa before.

The Small Luxury Hotels, the chain of independently owned, luxury hotels compiled a list featuring spas provided by its members: 'The Spa Book'. One of the main reasons for this compilation was summarized by the managing director of SLH as follows: 'Spas are a notoriously unregulated business. We have now extended the benchmark of quality that SLH represents to cover the centres of therapeutic well-being that exist within our already qualified, pre-selected, luxurious hotels, offering consumers a reliable source and global seal of approval; one that has not existed in

Table 10.3 A Comparison of Online Health and Wellness Services.

Types of spas or packages

Destination Spa Group	spasofamerica.com	SpaFinder Magazine	spaindex.com (lifestyles)	Beautifulbreak.com
Corporate retreats	Resort	Adults only spa	Adventure spas	Wellness and relaxation
Detox	Beach and spa	Adventure spa vacations	African American owned day spas	Beauty, spa, etc.
Luxury vacation	Ski and spa	Boutique size spa	Airport spas and spa kiosks	Health and harmony
Medical	Ayurveda	Casino spas	Bed and breakfast spas	City and wellness
Personal coaching	Weight loss	Comprehensive/integrative spas	Casino spas	Romantic for two
Spiritual retreats	Urban spa	Connoisseur spas	Cruise ships with spa facilities	Ayurveda and thalasso
Stress management	Golf and spa	Day spas	Dental spa centers	Active, golf, spa-summer and winter
Weight loss	Thalassotherapy	Dental spas	Detox programs	Fasting and detox
Women only	Medical spa	Destination spas	Eco-Friendly/holistic spa facilities	Men's only
Yoga	Anti-aging	Going solo spa	Family oriented spa facilities	Family fun
		Hablamos Español (bilingual spas)	For armed forces	Classic cures and therapeutic stays
		MedSpas: Cosmetic	For breast cancer patients	
		Medical spas: Wellness	For cancer patients	
		Men-only day spas	For sportsmen	
		Mineral springs spas	For teenagers	
		Mobile/home spas	Juicing, fasting, colonics, and cleansing programs	
		Spa lifestyle real estate	Maternity/pregnancy programs	
		Thermal waters spas	Medi-Spas	
			Mobile spa services and mobile spa parties	
			Pet-friendly spas	
			Ranch style spas/Dude ranch spas	
			Smoking cessation Programs	
			Vinotherapy	
			Wedding and honeymoon spa packages	
			Weight management programs	
			Wine spas	
			Women only	
			Yoga programs and retreats	

(Continued)

209

Table 10.3 (*Continued*)

	Destination Spa Group	spasofamerica.com	SpaFinder Magazine	spaindex.com (lifestyles)	Beautifulbreak.com
Types of Services and Programmes	Aquatics Biking Canoe and Kayak Cooking school Creative arts Cultural activities Dance instruction Educational workshops Fitness programs Gardening Golf programs Guided hiking Health assessments Labyrinth Nutrition education and counselling Outdoor adventure Personal training Skiing Specialty cuisine Tai Chi and pilates Tennis programs Walking		Affordable spa vacations Detoxification programs Inclusive-pricing Vacation Kids/family-friendly vacations Luxury spa vacations Male-oriented vacation programs Mommy and baby programs Mother and daughter programs Nudist spa vacations Pet friendly spa vacations Pre- and Post-natal programs Romantic/Honeymoon Senior friendly spa vacations Sleep-health consultation Smoking cessation programs Spirituality programs Stress management programs Teen spa vacation programs Wedding/event programs Weight-management programs Winter-sport spas Yoga programs	Afternoon tea at the spa Chinese medicine Hot Springs and Mineral Springs Threading With golf, sports, hiking	

Source: Destination Spa Group (2005); Beautiful Break (2008); Spas of America (2008); SpaFinder (2008); Spa Index (2008).

the past'. Following the trends SLH highlights in its communication, the signature treatments offered by the members such as green tea facial (Huntington Hotel), rainforest mist massage (Hotel Hana Maui), maple sugar body scrub (Mirror Lake Inn), or traditional Malaysian warrior treatment for men (SLH, 2005). SLH also revealed that over one in three guests spend more on treatments than food and wine!

Branding

Branding is seen as essential to any operator or organization in making their product different from others. It is not uncommon in health and wellness tourism that brands are seen as either only logos or a term. Certainly, a brand can be a name, symbol, term, or combination of all these and brands should reflect the product or service and the benefit customers may have from the consumption. Brands with strong and well-managed personalities and pillars can give better returns (Table 10.4).

Case Study: Spa Chakra Brand Philosophy

Spa Chakra integrates elements of conventional and holistic methods to create the renowned Transformational Healing™ approach to health and wellness. All spa therapies are customized, beginning with a comprehensive Self-Assessment Questionnaire. This tool reveals the primary stress affecting the client's well-being, be it nutritional, emotional, electromagnetic, or physical. This vital information helps therapists devise a personalized course of treatment.

Each therapy features a customized product blend tailored to the client's personal needs and preferences and applied with the exclusive Guerlain Méthode – patented facial and body massage technique proven to provide exceptional results through enhanced product infusion and lymphatic drainage. In 2003, Guerlain also selected Spa Chakra as its partner to provide design, consulting, and management for the new Guerlain Spa network of luxury flagship destinations. Spa Chakra exclusively utilizes Guerlain's world-renowned skincare and fragrance in each personalized therapy and offers the complete array of Guerlain products in spa retail boutiques. In the name of the brand the word 'chakra' refers to the seven energy centres of the body, and is taken from the Sanskrit word meaning 'wheel'. Three brands are managed under Spa Chakra: Spa Chakra, Guerlain Spa, and Private Label Collection.

(Spa Chakra, 2008)

Anybody considering branding activities should consider some key elements in brand positioning. This may seem to be easy, but it has to be noted that there not too many brands with high brand equity (i.e. for which customers are ready to pay high prices) in health and wellness tourism.

Table 10.4 Branding Considerations for Health and Wellness Tourism.

Key Elements	Meaning	Examples from Health and Wellness Tourism
Benefits	What can it offer?	'Healing' (functional benefit) 'Escaping'(emotional benefit)
Values	What does it stand for?	'To create innovative and enriching experiences in a sustainable environment' (Six Senses)
Personality	The behaviour of the brand	'Our girl with local experiences' (Arizonaspagirls.com)
Reason to believe	Evidence – why this is better?	'Evidence based healing effects' (Hungarian National Tourist Office)
Brand essence	What is it about – in one line	'Limitless Well-Being' (European Spa World)

Source: Smith and Puczkó.

Major international brands, especially hotel chains (e.g. Four Seasons, Marriott, and Hilton) all stretch their existing and well-established brands over new products, that is spas and wellness centres.

Branding, such as planning or management, can take place at national, regional, local, and site level too.

Branding at national and regional level

As was mentioned earlier, many countries have entered the competition in health and wellness tourism at national or regional level. Countries such as Thailand, the Philippines or Singapore, Jordan or UAE, Bulgaria, Hungary or Romania, all try to position themselves as medical or wellness destinations. National tourist offices and NGOs publish promotional leaflets, operate websites and participate in health-oriented fairs and exhibitions to promote the service providers of their respective countries. They run campaigns and themed years in which special attention is given to health and wellness, plus the complementing services and products.

In German-speaking countries, branding (and product development) in health and wellness tourism has developed in much wider directions than we can see in, for example English-speaking countries. The deeply rooted 'bad' or bathing tradition in German-speaking countries is not only supported by the wide choice of available services, but also by the names of settlements. One can find well over a hundred places called 'Bad *something*', many of which have become very famous and popular. Interestingly in all three countries there is a place, that is Baden (Switzerland), Baden-Baden (Germany), and Baden-bei-Wien (Austria) that actually represents the historic spa concept and tradition itself in the respective countries.

Visitors may either think that every 'Bad *something*' has something similar to offer, for example a bath (spa), or may think that this is just one-of-a-dozen. These assumptions and perceptions, of course, mean challenges to marketers.

The market is very much segmented nowadays, therefore the service providers also position and brand themselves more diversely. There are a handful of expressions or labels that cannot even be translated to English (or they would just be called 'spa'). Introducing some of the sophisticated labels from German:

- Medical tourism
  - Kurpark (cure park)-Historic spas and spatowns tend to have a so called 'Kurpark', which provides resting and walking opportunities for guests before or after the treatments in the spa (e.g. Königlichen Kristall-Therme am Kurpark in Schwangau)
  - Kurzentrum, Kurhotel, or Kurhaus (clinic or medical hotel)
  - Gesundhotel (health hotel)
  - Kompetenzzentrum (medical centre)
  - Heilbad (medical bath), heilklima (climatic resort), heilstollen (medical cave)
- Wellness tourism
  - Wohlfühl or Wohlsein-Oase (well-being oasis or hotel)
  - Wohlbefinden (well-feeling)
  - Vitalhotel or vitalbad (vitality hotel, bath)
- Leisure and recreation
  - Thermenhotel (spahotel)
  - Bad, Warmbad, (Römer) Therme or Quelle (bath or spring).

The best way to compare national and regional branding efforts is to compile the most typical examples. We collected communication (and positioning) messages from many countries all around the world. Some of them have been communicating their health services for many years, therefore we show the changes, where it was possible. Interestingly, many countries that really are strong in health tourism, for example Czech Republic, Ireland, or New Zealand, do not provide separate communication for this product. In these countries health and wellness tourism related information are available about the existing services and locations under the country brand, and no special 'health' oriented brand is communicated (Table 10.5).

We can see that most of these messages revolve around the same words: wellness, health, life, and feeling good. This generalization leaves prospective travellers with the problem of not being able to identify and link the messages to and with the given countries (hint: try to name the countries reading the messages only...). Although Switzerland appears to have a somewhat uninspiring label in Table 10.5, it actually provides excellent and extensive information about its health tourism-oriented national brand and its family brands.

Table 10.5 National Marketing Slogans for Health Tourism.

Country	Messages	Year
Austria	'Europe's No. 1 Spa Destination' 'Feel good in Austria' (for non-German speakers) (or 'Schlank und Schön') 'Wohfühlen. Lebenselixier' ('Well-feeling. The Elixir of life') and 'Kuren. Entspannungen' ('Cures. Relaxation') (for German speaking countries)	2008
Bulgaria	'Waters of Wellness-Refreshing. Bulgarian Spas'. 'Open doors open hearts. Balneology and SPA Tourism'	2007 2008
Croatia	'To Croatia for Strength and Health' (iconized by a red apple) 'The Way of Life'	2000 2008
France	'Harmony and Well-being. Are you looking for de-stress or feel revitalized?'	2008
Germany	'Everything but Stress' 'Germany has everything your heart and soul could desire. Here you'll discover new meanings of happiness. Welcome to a world of well-being'.	2000 2008
Hungary	'Hungary Keeps the World Healthy'	2002
India (wellness)	Wellness: • Ayurveda: 'A gateway to Indian Medical Heritage' • Yoga: 'Communion of soul with the universal soul or God'	2008
Italy	Wellness: 'In search of wellness' Treatments: 'Salutary effects' Spas/treatments: 'Naturally Regenerated'	2008
Jordan	Leisure and Wellness: 'A Place to Rejuvenate and Restore Your Mind, Body and Soul'	2008
Poland	'Natural Choice (for Health and Beauty)'	
Serbia	'Spas and Health Resorts in Serbia' 'Legendary Mineral Springs and Mountain Air. Since the Roman Empire travelers have sought the rejuvenating effects of the region's forests and waters.' (wellness) 'Springs of Life and Vitality' (health resorts)	1999 2008
Slovenia	'With Nature to Health' 'Wellness – tailor-made for you'. 'Wellness is not a remedy, but a healthy way of life'.	1999 2008
South Africa	'Spiritual: The Sacred South'	2008
St. Lucia	'Health & Fitness: A holiday on St. Lucia is a total refreshment for your mind, your body and your spirit'.	2008
Switzerland	'Health Destination'	2008
Thailand	'Health Tourism Hub of Asia'	2003
The Philippines	'Island of Wellness'	2007

Source: National Tourist Offices and Spa Associations' Brochures and Websites.

Case Study: Branding Switzerland

Switzerland enjoys excellent resources for all types of health and wellness tourism, for example natural assets, high-quality services, good image, exclusivity, accompanying services and attractions, all completed with high prices. The Swiss Tourist Office pays special attention to the positioning and communicating of the available services and facilities from pampering city spas, to taking time out from daily life in the seclusion of the mountains. The major brand pillar is the 'total nature', that is 'fresh mountain air, tranquility, idyllic landscapes, and magnificent mountain scenery'. The brand elements are as follows:

- *Health Destination* – Breathe in and chill out. (Healthy diet is not enough: the skin needs special care, like nurturing treatments using Far Eastern traditions and oriental rituals, and techniques using local plants and herbs)
  - Land of health (Uniquely unspoilt nature or healthy climate)
  - A label that guarantees quality ('Alpine Wellness' for health and beauty means regional cuisine, herbal treatments, and construction materials of local origin)
  - Mountain oases and southern sunshine (High alpine spas many with hamams, completed with Mediterranean flair and the lush natural beauty)
- *Active wellness* – Get high and get happy. (Nature is the finest wellness oasis of all, accompanied by the hotel: with seductive scents, relaxing baths, restorative massages)
  - Some like it cool (hotel wellness areas)
  - Some like it hot (1,001 possibilities for hitting a natural, healthy high, e.g. challenging sports)
  - Some like it green (golf and gourmet kitchen)
- *Private Spa* – Relax and reconnect. (Private experiences for two enjoying exotic treatments and rituals from all around the world)
  - All the time in the world (sensual atmosphere and the feeling of having all the time in the world for one another)
  - Regional delicacies (inner wellbeing comes about above all through balanced nutrition)
- *Design Spa* – Look and linger. (good taste has come to Switzerland)
  - Young, beautiful and fit (feel young and surprised by stylish design; by colour schemes that are blissfully soothing; by lighting that flatters your complexion; by scents, materials, and water features that work together to create a satisfying completely. You feel beautiful, surrounded by a refined aesthetic that also has an effect on your inner wellbeing. In addition, you feel fit because you have spoilt yourself with nothing but the best – for body, skin, and soul.
  - A new world of wellbeing (opening up for the youth, e.g. Lenkerhof in Lenk, uncompromising style and innovative design, e.g. Waldhaus in Flims or new aesthetic of wellbeing in Bergoase ('mountain oasis') in the Tschuggen Grand Hotel in Arosa, Graubünden.
- *Day Spa* – Drop in and bliss out. (try it)
  - The business of pleasure (Always mix business with a dose of pleasure)
  - Shop but don't drop (extend shopping with wellness experiences
  - Spas for a short break (Try 'Alpine Wellness')

(Swiss National Tourist Office, 2008)

It is clearly shown that both Switzerland and several other countries (and later we will see that operators too) tend to focus on the so-called emotional brand pillars (e.g. 'Design Spa'), which is also supported by rational pillars. The latter ones are more often used in the communication for medical tourism, since evidence-based medicine can and should support its healing promise with data or facts (e.g. what percentage of guests achieved improvement during a 3-week stay, etc.).

Branding can take place at regional level, too, which can either mean co-operation between countries or branding for a region or country of a single country. For example, the 'See Wellness' (Lake Wellness) is a trademark of Carinthia the province of Carinthia in Austria. This initiative is a perfect example of product development at regional level. The 15 member hotels build on the natural energies of Carinthia's lakes. 'See Wellness' is actually a research project that aims at identifying the beneficial impacts of the natural energy flows of lakes and the Sub-Mediterranean climate. These energies should improve the well-being of visitors (see Wellness, 2008). See also the Lake Wellness concept development in the Finland case study, in Part Three.

One of the most advanced initiatives for a regional brand is the Alpine Wellness.

Case Study: Alpine Wellness

'Breathe again – Recharge your batteries – Move mountains'

Medical studies have shown that the simple fact of being over 1,500 m above sea level has a positive effect on bodily health. Visitors are invited to treat themselves to a bit of good: whether gently relaxing, taking in physical fitness or partaking of medically supervised health care – member hotels in Bavaria (Germany), Austria, Switzerland, and South Tyrol (Italy), quality certified by independent auditors, are categorized into different specialist areas and are ready and prepared to welcome you with an individually tailored programme to meet personal relaxation requirements.

Alpine Wellness Philosophy does not just mean the positive effect of the alpine altitude and the climate, the use of alpine materials in the architecture and interior furnishings, alpine cuisine and the rediscovery of alpine healing formulae. Alpine Wellness also refers to a return to grass roots, and rediscovering the knowledge associated with the nature, culture, and life quality in the region. The effect of natural displays and the original charm of the alpine environment do their bit to make the special sensuality of the Alps and unique and exclusive experience.

The Alpine Wellness brand is managed by the Alpine Wellness International (AWI) GmbH. Their main objective is to redefine 'superior tourism'. The idea of this project is to promote the Alps worldwide as one of the most attractive and effective regions for wellness. The unique quality philosophy of Alpine Wellness approaches each guest's requirements sensitively, offering a matchless range of packages from relaxing programmes to preventative health and fitness – all with that unmistakeable alpine character.

The specialist areas or sub-brands of Alpine Wellness are (using the same logo in different shades):

- *Alpine Relaxing* (in dark red) – Topping up on vitality, feeling the sensuality of the mountain landscape, taking refuge in nature (saunas with a view, purifying whey baths and aromatic hay baths, natural resources for treatments and food)
- *Alpine Fitness* (in green) – Nature provides inspiration through its spiritual power and Alpine Fitness means outdoor activities.
- *Alpine Health* (in brown) – Tailor made Medical Wellness packages for preventative health, alleviation of symptoms, healing using natural resources of the Alps (for spinal trouble, burnout syndrome, asthma or allergies).
- *Alpine Character* (in blue) – It is reflected in the hotel architecture, as well as in the room furnishings and the decor in the relaxation areas, establishments are characterized by free access to Nature, a particularly peaceful and idyllic location, as well as the use of healthy home produce in the kitchen and cellar.

(Alpine Wellness, 2008)

Branding can take place in smaller regions and in a less complex way, too. This can aim for creating a joint platform for communication (e.g. on the web, in brochures and at fairs), but the members do not take the co-operation further, that is they would not develop new products together. The European Spa World project includes four members, one country and three regions (Slovenia, Burgenland and Styria of Austria, and Pannonia in Hungary) provide guests looking for relaxation new dimensions in Wellness, beauty, sports and health: 'Against the backdrop of a countryside which has no parallel in all Europe'. The joint promotion site and brochures offer four major products: Health & Healing; Wellness & Pleasure; Sport & Movement; and Pleasure & Nutrition (European Spa World, 2008).

Theming, that is creating and developing a brand based on a theme is a well-known technique in branding. Themed attractions, e.g. parks, restaurants, hotels, or routes can be found everywhere. As we could see earlier (Chapters Eight and Nine), theming in health tourism is also known and used. Visitors can enjoy many themed spas or spahotels, and even cruises. Health tourism-oriented routes, however, are very rare, and only in a handful of cases were developed so far. One example is the Wellness Route 'Salz und Sole' in Germany, which links salt flats between Neckar, Hohenlohe, and the Swabian hills. The thematic route includes hotels and wellness hotels, pools and sunbathing areas, cities, and attractions. Salt and sunshine are used to offer a rich diversity of sporting activities, accommodation and pampering treatments for body and soul (Salz und Sole, 2008).

The Jordan Tourist Board also offers themed routes with 3-, 5-, or 8-day itineraries which were developed for visiting leisure and wellness locations as well as historic and heritage sites in Jordan, for example a 5-day programme includes:

- Day 1. Dead Sea-Overnight at The Dead Sea
- Day 2. Ma'in Hot Springs-Overnight at Ma'in
- Day 3. Petra-Overnight in Petra
- Day 4. Aqaba-Overnight in Aqaba
- Day 5. Amman

(Visit Jordan, 2008)

Branding at local and operator level

It seems to be a little easier to create and maintain a brand for a site or for an operator. It only seems that way though. We could see that customers are not yet that experienced in health and wellness vocabulary and do not yet know as much about destinations either, as they may know of sun and sea destinations. This can cause a lot of problems for operators or for local organizations.

As we could see in Chapter Eight, health destinations often have their own organization responsible for destination management and marketing. If not in an exclusive resort, guests (and accompanying visitors) can easily find it a little claustrophobic to stay in the same facility all day (i.e. between treatments that are rather short), therefore destination management organizations' (DMOs) main objective is to offer and introduce the available additional services and attractions in the area. In Europe, mainly historic spa towns or towns with an established clinic or major spa tend to label themselves as health or wellness destinations. In other parts of the world, the health element typically is only one of the many image making elements or strengths.

International spa and hotelchains, however, have made progress in creating their own brands, based on health services, for example:

- *Starwood Hotels & Resorts Worldwide* (managing brands such as Westin, Le Meridien, W Hotels, Sheraton, St. Regis and The Luxury Collection) defined its own principles for the Starwood Spa Collection brand, called The Seven Pillars of Well-Being. These principles (or pillars) are
  - Beauty: The esthetic
  - Life balance: The spiritual (practices)
  - Harmony: The body (massages)
  - Aqua: Life flow (spa)
  - Vitality: Energy (fitness centres and pools)
  - Nature: Environment (the natural beauty of the location) and
  - Nutrition: Nourishment (food)

(Starwood Spa Collection, 2008)
- *Six Senses* has created a family of brands, Soneva, Six Senses Hideaway, Six Senses Latitude, Six Senses Destination Spa, and Evason, plus Six Senses Spas are operated in our resorts as well as at third-party properties.

- Spas at *One&Only Resorts* are '...in blissful sanctuaries of tranquility, where the body is resorted and the soul is soothed'. Just as each One&Only resort is individually designed and inspired by its local surroundings, so too is each One&Only Spa, where guests can enjoy a whole concept of 'Pathway of Wellness.'
  - ... to Vitality – A tonic for body and soul
  - ... to Inner Peace – Balance and re-enter
  - ... to Love – An awakening for togetherness – ideal for two.
- Each pathway includes:
  - A 90-minute spa treatment
  - A 60-minute class, and
  - Spa cuisine

(One&Only Resorts, 2008)

- *AMresorts* in Central America developed three brands for health and wellness visitors:
  - Secrets Resorts & Spas (adults only)
  - Dreams Resorts & Spas (scenic locations, full service spas and fitness centres – Unlimited Luxury)
  - Sunscape Resorts & Spas (families, couples, friends – Unlimited Fun)

(AMresorts, 2008)

Marriott and *Renaissance* also offer wellness services in many of their hotels all around the world. They call the wellness department 'Wellness Zone', they label spa trips as 'Spa Gateways' and they highlight signature treatments as 'QUAN spa' in the communication. What makes the marketing of the Marriott's a little different from its competitors is that they pay special attention to gastronomy: 'Marriott Spas' culinary philosophy pairs the fundamentals of great ingredients with the principles of wellness. Flavour balanced with health, freshness enhanced by technique, our spas aspire to indulge you with what is good for you. To emphasize this element even more, the website of Marriott recommends Spa Wellness Recipes (e.g. 'Spa-in-a-Glass', pomegranate-key lime brewed tea on ice).

Danubius Hotels

The largest hotel chain in Europe specialized mainly in health-oriented hotels (Danubius Hotels Group), has recently re-branded some of its hotels. Members of that hotel chain which are located primarily in medical tourism-oriented destinations in Hungary, Czech Republic, Slovakia, and Romania, were labelled as 'Danubius thermal' hotels in Hungary and 'hotel balnea' in Slovakia. The new brand (for nine properties in four countries), 'Danubius Health Spa Resorts' or DHSRs, following the upgrading and diversifying of the on-site health facilities in the hotels, fits more the expectations of the demand and can represent the brand assets of the hotel chain. The six elements of the brand are Natural Resources, Medical

Expertise, Therapeutic Treatments, Well-being & Relaxation, Fitness & Beauty, and Spa Cuisine. The hotel chain has opened its membership based on fitness centres under the brand of Danubius Premier Fitness (ten properties in two countries), whereas the beauty and cosmetic unit is branded with The Emporium Wellness & Beauty label (four properties only in Hungary).

(Danubius Hotels, 2008)

We can conclude that focusing on emotional elements of the brand really is the most often applied strategy of operators and marketers, regardless of which part of the world the given attraction happens to be in, for example

- 'The Power of Contrast' (AquaDome, Langenfelden, Austria)
- 'S.O.S. Package. Transform a hectic life into a good life.' (Stay Overnight and Spa, Vintage Hotels, Ontario, United States)
- 'The Crossings offers their guests moments of welcome, focus, discovery, meditation, surprise and delight' (Austin, United States)
- 'Soulful Sanctuaries' (The Golden Door, California, United States)
- 'We've Spent 40,000 Years Creating the Day Spa of your Dreams.' (Li'tya Spa Dreaming, St Kilda, The Caribbean)
- 'Enjoy a Whipped Cocoa Bath, a Chocolate Fondue Wrap or a Mojito Sugar Scrub' (The Spa at Hotel Hershey, United States)
- 'The Kurotel. Longevity Center and Spa' (Gramado, Brazil)
- 'Thermal Village' with thermal walks, geyser or dipping in the communal bath (Whakarewarewa, Rotorua, New Zealand).

We can see a somewhat different branding approach in holistic and spiritual tourism. As was mentioned before, these forms of health tourism heavily build on either the spiritual leader or a key person (e.g. a yogi or guru), or a site-specific quality (e.g. Earth Chakra). Since these operators do not compete with each other as for example spa resorts do, and since the business orientation is often missing from the operation itself, the branding, in whatever form it takes place, can differ significantly from other forms of health tourism. The same very selected branding and communication can be observed in the surgical form of medical tourism too.

Mass communication is very typical of spas, hotels and cruises, however, festivals, clinics, or ashrams use very well selected and much more focused channels of communication. The internet is certainly the ever-growing channel to inform customers and web surfers, and most service providers and destinations publish brochures too. Holistic and spiritual destinations tend to be marketed via special interest groups (e.g. yoga groups), specialized magazines or direct mails.

We have to refer briefly to the branding practices for the upcoming market of *men*. We discussed this phenomenon in Chapter Seven, but here some references to branding should be made. Both straight and gay men visit more and more health and wellness service providers, but the communication they accept is certainly different. Every destination and attraction wanting to increase the number of men in their facilities should bear in mind that it is very easy to send misleading or unclear messages to these segments. Just compare these slogans. It is difficult to distinguish between the promotion of gay compared to straight facilities, which could lead to either embarrassment or disappointment:

- Straight
  - 'Men's only – To be selfish is good!' (Beautiful Break, 2008)
  - 'The most stylish spas in the United Kingdom – the ones which demonstrate outstanding service and attention to detail (men-only day spas or men's clubs)' (Spagasm, 2008)
  - 'Get a golfer's massage. If this spa doesn't rejuvenate you, the entertainment in the Lobby will!' See the game of the day, with Keep Your Shorts on Day package. (you'll get a t-shirt and shorts instead of the typical robe) Wow! sign up for your Sports Massage! (Sonwai Spa at The Hyatt Regency, Scottsdale, United States, 2008)
- Gay
  - 'A spa with men in mind' (Hiranyikara, 2008)
  - 'House of Male' (House of Male, 2008)
  - 'Colour your Holidays' (Bali Romeo, 2008)
  - 'Welcome to Singapore's Most Exciting, Versatile & Complete Men's Spa! Unwind after a day's work, or rewind after a night out-club One Seven is the place to refresh, renew and release! Catch up with old friends or make a few new ones!' (One Seven, 2008)

Twelve Marketing Tips (for Reaching Men)

There is more to market to men than extra-large robes and tacking the word 'executive' onto your basic facial. The International Spa Association (ISPA) collected some helpful tips on marketing to potential male clients.

1. Advertise in men's magazines.
2. Create special golf/spa and tennis/spa packages.
3. Offer bachelor parties.
4. Reward double 'referral points' to customers who refer new male clients.
5. Create special promotions encouraging women to bring in their spouses and boyfriends.
6. Host a men's-only night.
7. Highlight men's treatments on the service menu.
8. Develop signature treatments for men.
9. Use warm, earthy colors throughout your spa.
10. Offer more athletic-type fitness classes.
11. Choose different color robes for the sexes.
12. Hire a mix of male and female therapists.

(American Spa Magazine 2008)

The advertisement of health and wellness tourism services, destination or brands does not really differ from the practices of any other form of tourism. However, we can see some typical and product-specific advertisement approaches:

- Hotel and resort spas, and spa lifestyle communities are featured in upmarket (both for women and men) lifestyle, on-board flight and spa-oriented magazines (and their respective on-line versions) and in TV programmes (e.g. see 'Stars and spas' at TravelChannel).
- Medical tourism advertisement uses healthy or luxury lifestyle-oriented magazines and websites, and doctors' waiting rooms (e.g. cosmetic surgery ads can be found in luxury lifestyle, while medical wellness treatments in healthy living magazines).
- Holistic and spiritual tourism is not mass advertised, but more likely to use direct mailing (e.g. newsletters), specialist magazines and via special interest classes, clubs, and societies.

One would imagine that if the labels and tags used were not specific enough, then the images applied would be. This may not be the case. Very easily we can play similar games with images used for seaside or skiing promotion. Usually we can see the following advertisement concepts (adcepts):

1. Natural feature (e.g. cave, lake)
2. Parts of the historic building(s)
3. Part of the interior
4. The views from the facility (overlooking the sea, mountains, a valley, a historic town, etc.)
5. Somebody just having treatments and he/she is almost in a transcendent mood (facial expressions)
6. Tanned people around the pools and in saunas
7. Young women in bikinis lying around or in the thermal/medical pools and the poolside 'striking a pose' (especially in ads from Central and Eastern Europe)
8. Elderly people sitting in dark waters
9. Person with an amazingly white and full set of teeth

Apart from the first four elements it is practically impossible to locate the given country, location, or site to anyone (including domestic visitors or even local citizens!). Combining these images with already discussed standard health and wellness vocabulary, the result is that visitors make their decisions on supplementary factors or parameters (e.g. distances from nearest airports) that are secondary to the main benefit, that is some form of healing.

Packaging, distribution, and pricing

The way in which, or even the extent to which wellness tourism products are packaged depends very much on the typology of wellness tourism and the intended target market. As a general rule, wellness tourists seem relatively happy to purchase pre-selected packages within which there is some flexibility and freedom of choice. For example, spa visitors may select a pampering and relaxation package to which they can add further treatments or fitness activities. Holistic tourists may opt for a week in which certain courses are offered, but usually they select only a small number of those or can even choose to do something else (e.g. relax on the beach or go on an excursion).

Most packages seem as if they are customized to the visitor's needs and take into consideration individual needs. Even if the transport and accommodation and food provision is the same for everyone, few health, and wellness tourists like to travel in groups or feel as if they are being treated *en masse*. For this reason, health and wellness holidays (with the exception of state-subsidized medical tourism) tends to be more expensive than average holidays, and are more in line with other special interest tourism trips where groups are small or individuals are offered tailor-made packages.

Quality is another issue that is of extreme importance to most health and wellness tourists, especially if they are receiving treatments which are physical or psychological. Although the qualifications of the practitioners may not be known to them, they need to feel cared for and safe. Therefore, the packages may need to include some pre-care (e.g. advice about treatments or preparation for treatments) and some after-care (e.g. the means to ask questions about recovery, or the chance to be part of an on-line community in the case of holistic retreats). One of the most sophisticated systems would require the potential visitor to give details of their profiles and needs and for a package to be recommended. Even if the operator or hotel only has two or three packages available, visitors would feel special and catered for as individuals. Accor Thalassa, for example, pre-packaged its services in the following ways (Accor Thalassa, 2008):

- Fitness La Cure by Accor Thalassa
- Slimming
- Anti-stress
- Young mother
- Refreshed legs
- Marine beauty
- Men's tonic

The recommended 6-day specific treatments are classified as

- Health
- Personal coaching and/or sport
- Duo
- Exclusive (sleep, golf, anti-aging, anti-smoking, etc.) treatments.

A typical spa package from a wellness or spa hotel tends to offer visitors their accommodation, full or half board, a welcome drink (either fruit juice or champagne, or fruitbasket), use of all facilities on site or the spa adjacent (e.g. pools, saunas, fitness programmes), and maybe one or two treatments (e.g. a massage, facial, manicure). Transport is not usually included and other treatments have to be booked on arrival or in advance and paid for as extras. Holistic centres also include accommodation, full or half board, and two to three courses or workshops per day. Within a typical package, there would be some freedom of movement everyday and time for rest and relaxation (e.g. 2–3 hours in the afternoon). Too much programming or a tightly timed schedule can make a wellness visitor feel as stressed as he or she would at home!

It has been estimated that there are over 100 different forms of yoga (Yoga Magazine, 2007) therefore the choice of holidays and activities can be somewhat overwhelming for the beginner. However, for more experienced yoga enthusiasts there are growing numbers of exciting new products and combined packages. As well as offering specific types of yoga such as Astanga or Kundalini, many yoga holidays or retreat centres combine yoga with meditation, dance, creative activities, nutrition, music, and mantras. In terms of packaging, yoga can be combined with skiing, wildlife safaris, dancing, surfing, diving, etc. Combined packages are appealing to those people who are not 'hard-core' yoga aficionados but may want to use yoga to warm-up for other sports or to use yoga to relax at the end of the day. For more dedicated yogis and yoginis, there are numerous deep and spiritual yoga-based retreats being offered all over the world. Holidays for yoga practitioners and teachers are increasing all the time too, and numerous centres offer the chance to intensify knowledge of one form of yoga or to acquire knowledge of a new form. Some yoga teachers may want to increase their repertoire and introduce some massage, dance, or martial arts to their practise. Yoga festivals are also becoming popular, as are fairs and trade shows which are open to the general public.

Case Study: Ananda Retreat and Spa in the Himalayas, India

Located in the foothills of the Himalayas, Ananda is considered to be one of the best destination spas in the world. A restored Viceroy's Palace, Ananda is a spa dedicated to restore, balance and renew the mind, body and soul through a holistic approach of Ayurveda, Yoga, and innovative spa techniques. The following package gives an example of what is included in a five night 'Wellness Bliss' package:

- One Ayurvedic and wellness consultation (duration 30 minutes)
- One wild rose salt glow (duration 45 minutes)
- One Aromatherapy massage with the choice of grounding, detoxifying or invigorating blended oils (duration 85 minutes)
- One reflexology session (duration 55 minutes)
- One stress-busting hot and cold stone therapy (duration 85 minutes)
- Two personalized Yoga sessions (duration 60 minutes)
- Two personalized meditation sessions (duration 30 minutes)
- One Swedish massage (duration 55 minutes)
- One Ananda royal facial (duration 85 minutes)
- One Ananda touch, a signature back-treatment (duration 30 minutes).

(Haridwar Tour Packages, 2008)

Tour operators and health insurance companies tend to have a varying role in the packaging and distribution of health and wellness tourism products and services. Travellers can find information about health and wellness offers via the following distribution channels:

- General tour operators that diversify their existing product portfolio with mainstream spa-type services
- Some independent and smaller tour operators specialized in wellness tourism or medical tourism (e.g. FIT Reisen, Mondial or Thermalia Travel in Europe, Iran Gashttour or Tours and Virtus Tours and Travels from Arabia, ThaiMed Associates, or GoIndia Medical Tourism from Asia).
- Specialist operators that are often linked to the service provider itself (e.g. retreat) and offer additional products (e.g. essential oils or books), package holistic, and spiritual trips (e.g. Skyros).
- Health insurance companies, because of better prices, more efficient or faster treatments, may cover treatments that are not at the home place of the insured. This can encourage people to take both domestic and foreign trips. Of course, medical doctors can also act as part of the distribution channel recommending a site for a certain set of treatments.
- Both general travel search engines (e.g. Yahoo!Travel) and specialized ones (e.g. Spas of America, or SpaFinder) offer, promote and introduce destinations and operators, as well as websites and publications of national, regional, and local tourist offices.
- General and specialized fairs and exhibitions
- Lifestyle clubs and societies of the trainer or leader can be a source of information about where-and-what to do.

Major or international tour operators (e.g. Thomas Cook/Neckermann and TUI in Europe, Classic Vacations or Pleasant Holidays in the United States) with many brands can either programme health services into the 'standard' packages or have one that is specialized in health and wellness. General tour operators, as part of diversifying their package portfolio may publish a brochure or create a link on their website for health and wellness offers. Certainly, the titles of these brochures and websites follow the global trend: TUI calls it 'Vital' or 'Fit&Gesund', Thomas Cook/Neckermann labels it with 'Care' or 'Wellnesswelten' by DERTOUR. Since the various forms of health and wellness tourism do not tend to enjoy similar market position in all countries managed by the tour-operator, these special publications may be available for certain markets, only.

It is quite interesting from a communication and positioning point of view, how tour operators label their packages:

- TUI introduces packages such as: Natürlich and Gesund (Natural and Healthy), Kuren and Wohlfühlen (Cures and Well-being), Gepflegt and Schön (Treatments and Beauty), Verwöhnen and Enstpannen (Pampering and Relaxation)
- Thomas Cook/Neckermann compares facilities by wellness/pool areas, beauty and cosmetic services, treatments, gastronomy, hotel ambience, fitness and sport services

- Pleasant holidays offers spas linked with outdoor activities
- Classic vacations group packages by geographical locations/countries or resort and hotel brands, and not by activities

The following example from Kuoni shows the kind of language that is used by general operators in their promotion. It is obvious that the spa services are merely an add-on benefit to the mass tourism product, and very little specialized vocabulary is used:

Case Study: Spa Holidays by KUONI

Unwind, relax, and pamper yourself in one of Kuoni's specially selected spa resorts and experience a wide range of luxurious treatments in a choice of exotic worldwide locations. Choose from ancient Asian rituals and exercise to balance your mind and body, traditional massages to invigorate the senses or refreshing facials and saunas to while away the stresses and strains.

- Indulge yourself with some pampering whether it's beside the beach or in your own private room under the ocean, you will enjoy every second
- Look out for hotels that include spa treatments within your holiday offering the perfect excuse for some rest and relaxation.
- Choice of spa treatments available in most destinations with many offering local alternative therapies

Add to this sun kissed beaches, palm trees swaying in the breeze and stunning scenery and you really are on a perfect relaxing holiday, so much so you won't want to go home!

(Kuoni, 2008)

Medical packages tend to be very complex and all inclusive, even providing services for the accompanying passengers, especially for ill guests who may require door-to-door transport. In some cases, accommodation could be booked separately, but this is not appropriate if visitors are having operations or medical treatments which require extensive supervised rest. However, it is quite a recent phenomenon that medical tourism trips are packaged by tour operators, and it is often the medical spas, hospitals, or clinics, which arrange all the treatments. As they do not tend to be experts in tourism, the links between the medical providers and tourism services are becoming more extensive and formalized. Especially surgical trips require very detailed preparations, since all the details of the operation should be prepared and agreed well in advance. Buying a dental package, very likely will contain everything from organizing a check-up at home, through transferring existing medical data and X-rays between the dentists back home and the destination, to leisure and cultural programmes in the location.

The US-based MedRetret, for example, provides services for corporate employers, which can include medical trips in the health insurance packages they offer for their employees (MedRetreat gives a hint: consider a medical trip only if the costs in the United States were higher than 6,000 USD [MedRetreat, 2008]). Another example is GlobalChoice Healthcare, which provides all medical travel-related services for patients from the United States from scheduling client's procedures, transferring medical records, arranging travel and accommodations, and providing access to on-the-ground local assistance for the duration of clients' stay (GlobalChoice Healthcare, 2008).

We can consider what the MICE (Meeting, Incentives, Conferences and Exhibitions) industry tends to apply more and more as a special packaging approach. In an application for a MICE bid, organizers and destinations incorporate health and wellness services as well and they consider it as an added bonus, and competitive advantage. It is quite interesting to follow up what happens to the marriage of MICE and spas, since congress, conference or corporate meeting delegates' time is often completely full with the official programme. When will they have time to use the spa, in that case?

In health and wellness tourism, various pricing strategies can be observed. We can estimate that at least one third of spa operators transmit the 'we-are-not-for-everybody' message to prospective visitors. Associations and co-operation with other luxury brands, the way in which they promote themselves and the language they use in the communication, all support the upmarket pricing (and vice versa). This is one way to select visitors and to create the necessary image. There can be, however, a huge gap between the prices of wellness and medical services. Surgical trips to Asia, Central America, or Central Europe become competitive because of the relatively low costs of medical and tourist services there. Some might argue that this is a risky and short term strategy to base competition on price levels, though, but both intra-regional, for example within the Middle-East, or global tourism can also be boosted by better prices.

In many countries medical tourism or medical services offered during trips, form a close part of national health services, and prices are, at least partially, subsidised, that is consumers receive standard medical services (e.g. balneotherapeutic treatments) for free or at very low prices. This form of tourism can constitute a significant part of domestic tourism in numerous Central and Eastern European countries.

We can see some atypical pricing practices as well. For example in the Alpine region, winter is the main season. That is when most of the guests arrive to ski. The summer is the second most important season, that is, for hiking and trekking. Autumn and spring are considered as low seasons. This situation leaves hotel operators with no other option than to apply lower prices than they can do during winter. Visitors can achieve very good deals in four-five star spa hotels for trips in the summer, which is their main holiday-taking period. This pricing can make mountainous areas with high-quality spas very competitive with the seaside.

Conclusions

Reaching for health and wellness tourists can differ from standard approaches in tourism. The very personal and sometimes very risky nature of the services makes the selection of applicable communication strategies and tactics challenging. While in North America both segmentation and product development seem to have been reaching very sophisticated levels (e.g. Dude Ranch Spas!), other parts of the world have not yet applied similar approaches. Although consider what the following title may mean to an average customer: 'Optiwell-Fitbalance' as the marketers labelled a lifestyle and fitness day sponsored by a global breakfast cereal brand… .

Destinations and service providers tend to build on emotional brand elements and benefit-focused positioning themes. Still, this means limits to marketers (may be that is why there so many new words and expressions in the German language). It is really very difficult to brand and communicate a whole country as some type of health destination, especially globally. We could see that the understanding of terms and messages can vary country-by-country. This may slow down the globalization of marketing in this field (i.e. the simple copying and not adapting of what marketers say about health and wellness tourism may become less standard than in other types of tourism).

CHAPTER 11

Product development

The journey's end is only the beginning of another journey: the rediscovery of both home and ourselves, our perceptions of which have been subtly or dramatically transformed by our absence.

(Chaline, 2002:285)

Many forms of health are derived from ancient traditions and practices that have existed for centuries in some cultures and societies, yet in others they seem new and unfamiliar. The globalization of health has meant that many health activities and techniques can be easily exported. This is true of most forms of massage, spa and beauty treatments, medical processes and fitness regimes. Multi-media communications and mobility in the form of travel and tourism have revolutionized international product development. However, there is also a growing 'postmodern' flexibility and creativity in the way that products are packaged. For example, yoga can be packaged with almost any activity provided it is attractive to the target market. Consumers seem to be increasingly more open to trying 'old' activities in new contexts (e.g. Ayurveda, Chinese Medicine, Thai massage), or buying packages that combine existing interests with new ones. Advancements in technology and the growing importance of the experience economy means that there is also a quest for completely new products and activities which have not existed in previous cultures or contexts. Although these are harder to conceive, they are arguably what makes destinations unique and give them a competitive edge. This chapter explores the way in which health and wellness tourism products are changing in order to adapt to the increasingly diverse needs of consumers and other factors which influence their development. This includes the growing need to balance out different elements of body-mind-spirit products within one package or destination.

The globalization of health and wellness tourism products

The proliferation of spa and wellness hotel developments around the world means that it is possible to experience a large number of health and wellness products almost anyplace where there is a reasonable infrastructure for tourism. Products can include national and regional assets and resources, such as mineral waters, mountain chains, seas, or rivers, indigenous and local traditions and treatments, or site-level facilities and packages. Although many countries do not have natural sources of medical or thermal waters, swimming pools, saunas, steam rooms, massage and fitness facilities can be created anywhere. This is unproblematic if health is the secondary motivation of tourists (i.e. they are business or conference tourists who may just use the facilities if they have time, or sightseers for whom spa facilities are an added bonus). However, for more dedicated health tourists, the expectation is likely to be higher and the search for some form of uniqueness or local features may lead to disappointment if it is unfulfilled. They may be satisfied if the health resort or destination can offer an extremely diverse range of products (e.g. ten different massages, a whole range of fitness activities, a multi-cuisine buffet). An especially high quality experience could also count in the destination's favour. Competitive pricing is less of an incentive as most wellness tourists are happy to spend large amounts of money on pampering and relaxation. One exception is the cost of medical treatments where tourists travel long distances for cheaper prices than at home and/or proven healing effects of natural assets.

The location for holistic or occupational tourism is largely incidental, although centres are likely to be in a beautiful mountain village or beside the sea as an added attraction. However, the experiences gained within a holistic centre could just as easily be created elsewhere. Many holistic practitioners such as yoga teachers or life coaches work in different locations throughout the year offering the same workshops and courses. Skyros Centres in Greece and Thailand attempt to create some local experiences, such as language or cookery lessons, but these are fairly limited and most of the experience is 'global' or 'placeless'. Occupational wellness workshops often seem to take place in good quality chain hotels as this is what the business market has come to expect.

On the other hand, spiritual or New Age tourists often visit very specific landscapes or choose pilgrimage destinations which have a special significance. Some holistic/spiritual tourists are keen to go to Rishikesh in India for yoga, to experience Ayurveda in Kerala, or to learn Thai massage in Thailand. Visits to ashrams or meditation retreats also tend to take place in countries of perceived heightened spirituality, but it is now perfectly possible to visit such centres in the United Kingdom, United States or most other Western countries. In many cases, it suits foreign visitors better as the forms of yoga or meditation are adapted to Western bodies and lifestyles. Holistic or New Age festivals can technically take place anywhere, although the experience is no doubt enhanced if the destination has some kind of spiritual significance.

Medical, mainly surgical tourism usually takes place in countries which are perceived as being cheaper than the tourists' own country. This means that India, Thailand and other Asian destinations are the preferred locations at present. Many Western people (especially in the United Kingdom) are used to being treated by Indian doctors after many years or immigration and the tendency of Indian people to excel in the medical field. For Middle Eastern patients, India is a short flight away. Thailand has a reputation for tolerance and openness, therefore extreme operations like sex changes are popular there. Some Central and Eastern European countries have their specialities, such as dentistry in Hungary or certain forms of eye surgery in Russia. The language skills, professionalism, cleanliness, and friendliness of the people will also largely determine where people go for medical treatment.

Most day spas which offer cosmetic and beauty treatments could technically be anywhere, except in cases where they use products which are derived from local plant or flower extracts. Even signature treatments can soon become globally available with the 'help' of international brands in cosmetics and beauty. Purpose-built spas in countries like Germany, Austria, and Switzerland are of an extremely high quality and offer a diverse range of international treatments, but some of them do not offer many products that are indigenous to the area. An exception might be those offering Alpine wellness, where hay baths may be offered or other local treatments. However, such spas do make use of local organic foods and the landscape around the spas. Many spas in ski resorts are fairly standardized, but offer good quality relaxation, pampering, and healing facilities for those who need a rest from physical exercise.

One of the problems, even for historic spas, is that it is difficult to compete with similar historic spas elsewhere. For example, Czech spas cannot offer (in theory) much that is different in terms of products and experiences from the spas in Slovakia or Romania. The architecture can be different, but the facilities and service levels are likely to be similar. On the other hand, Austrian and German spas (also regional competitors) have had many more years of investment in facilities, better service training, and have a greater understanding of the links between lifestyle practices (e.g. fitness, nutrition) and wellness. As a result, even though the heritage buildings in Hungary and the Czech Republic are often more beautiful, it is hard for them to compete in the international market for wellness visitors. Hungary and the Czech Repulic attract large numbers of 'incidental' wellness visitors (i.e. those who come primarily to sightsee), but regional spas still rely largely on a domestic market.

Case Study: Problems of Product Development in Budapest – The Spa Capital

Budapest or the area has been renowned for its baths for nearly 2000 years. From tribal periods to the former bathing buildings and the barracks of the 2nd Roman legion in

Acquincum (part of the province of Pannonia). Already back to 1178 the present area of the Lukács and Császár thermal baths was used by the order that Saint John created to cure the sick, which founded a bath and hospital here.

The next era of development was brought by the Turkish who occupied most of Hungary for 150 years. Community buildings were built on the healing waters, and incorporating a culture of individual bathing. Still today, visitors and citizens can enjoy these historic baths.

The third period of developments dates back to the first half of the 1700s (e.g. studies about the healing impacts of the Buda hot springs). In 1772, a decree was issued by Maria Theresia, Empress of Austria stating that all mineral waters should be analysed and recorded in a list at the expense of the Treasury.

In the early 1930s, Budapest, as the capital possessing the most healing thermal water springs in the world, was awarded the title 'Spa City' and initiated by the Budapest Spa City Association, the first International Balneological Congress was organized in Budapest in 1937.

Today the city has bathing establishments in various styles: neo-classical, art-nouveau, turkish or baroque. The architecture is so unique that many films used the spa buildings as locations (even if the film suggested that the spa was actually in Paris!). The Budapest Spas Corp., however, or consequently faces lots of problems, that is how to introduce new services, how to renovate heritage buildings, and how to upgrade existing facilities under the rooves of listed properties with lots of limitations. Most of the regulations prioritize the conservation of the existing buildings and that leaves tensions between the involved parties. One of the new initiatives is to open one of the heritage spas for young visitors (The Rudas), who can participate in the programme called 'Cinetrip', where they can enjoy films and music from the thermal water.

The Tourism Office of Budapest has been placing a lot of emphasis on the communication of the rich spa heritage. The positioning of Budapest is very much based on the spa culture, highlighting the unique mix of spa types.

(Budapest Tourist Office, 2008)

The attempt to create unique or 'international' experiences, such as including Thai massage or Indian Ayurveda in historic spas is arguably displaced and merely represents a standardization of product development rather than innovation. On the other hand, Austrian and German wellness hotels and spas are now reaching saturation point and there is a need to limit the number of new developments or to diversify existing products.

Overall, it seems that there needs to be some differentiation of destinations on a national level, especially if they are trying to market themselves specifically as health, spa or wellness destinations. This might mean promoting their unique physical resources (e.g. hot springs, mineral waters, lakes, mountains), or even claiming to have the 'largest', 'longest', 'highest', etc. of these. Countries like Slovenia have been quite successful in their marketing of health and wellness tourism recently even though they use many images that are related to their diverse landscape and cultures, rather than to specific health products. Signature treatments can be promoted in hotels around the world, but it is debatable as to whether tourists would travel specifically for a massage. More likely they would pay for a long, leisurely package of several hours or days which is unique and makes use of local traditions or indigenous ingredients. Medical tourism is somewhat different in that most visitors require a stay of several days or weeks to recover, rehabilitate or rest. Their choice of destination may be more influenced by their doctor's prescription than their own personal travel motivations in the case of medical spa tourism, but those opting for private surgery may have far more independence in their selection of destination, hospital, even surgeon. Holistic and yoga retreats are often located far away from the spiritual home of the products they sell, but it seems that landscape plays a major role in tourists' decisions, as they crave beauty and tranquility. Sometimes, it is also the packaging of products that makes the difference.

Case Study of The Spa of Colonial Williamsburg

The Spa of Colonial Williamsburg in the United States was opened in spring 2007 and it adopted a unique approach. It uses a 21st-century interpretation of five centuries of health and healing practices from European, African and American Indian cultures in a so-called 'continuum of wellness'. The menu of services are in keeping with the Foundation's mission of learning from the past:

Seventeenth century: Cleansing Hot Stones Experience: the Powhatan Indians employed wellness tactics involving heating their bodies with hot stones in sweathouses followed by cold water plunges. In this modern-day interpretation, the body is warmed by hot stones, and then wrapped in herb- infused, steaming linen to encourage the natural release of toxins. During the heated wrap, cool aromatherapy cloths are applied to refresh the brow. The experience concludes with full-body, hot stone massage using oil containing lavender, cypress, juniper and rosemary.

Eighteenth century: Colonial Herbal Spa Experience: the 18th century marked the beginning of the assimilation between cleanliness and health, with doctors realizing that dirt on the skin prevented the essential process of perspiration. Thus, individuals began mixing baths of herbal and apothecary ingredients, a ritual adapted for the modern spa patron with a cleansing foot bath, followed by an orange-ginger body scrub, herbal body wrap and signature Williamsburg massage. Historic-inspired components of the experience include a variety of colonial herbs.

Nineteenth century: Root and Herbal Spa Experience: African traditions during the 1800s focused on the use of herbs for healing purposes. The Spa translates this into the experience by incorporating body exfoliation and an herbal bath with a 'strengthening' full-body massage. The exfoliating High Road Powder helps to boost spirit and energy before guests soak in an invigorating herbal bath steeped in Ritual Bath Tea and undergo an invigorating massage.

Twentieth century: Williamsburg Water Cures Spa Experience: Developments in medicine, health care, fitness and wellness in the last century highlight the importance of the

20th century in the continuum of wellness. The development of technologically advanced spa equipment, coupled with the history of bathing rituals inspired this experience. The Williamsburg Water Cures consists of a full-body, dry-brush exfoliation, followed by a hydrotherapy Vichy shower 'rain' massage and concluding with a traditional Aqua Latte bath to seal in the skin's moisture.

Twenty-first century: Skin Rejuvenation Spa Experience: Late in the 20th century and into today, the popularity in laser treatments and microdermabrasion has grown significantly, so this experience draws on new technology and products geared for anti-aging to address rejuvenation on two fronts. A deep pore cleansing and skin analysis prepares the face for a particle-free, ultrasonic exfoliation. This is followed by an enzyme-rich mask specific to skin type and an oxygen treatment to brighten the skin. Finally, an antioxidant serum and vitamin-rich moisturizer conclude the Skin Rejuvenation for results similar to, but more gentle than microdermabrasion, with immediate results.

The Spa's designer Sylvia Sepielli, who is recognized worldwide as a spa visionary, assisted in the facility design concept and was retained to create signature treatments and amenities. She is known for creating a completely unique look for each spa she designs, making it an expression of its location. She creates a signature for each spa that reflects the personality and culture of the area, and is known for doing extensive research into each location to create treatments that reflect that area, fitting perfectly into their settings. This spa represents a blend of the history and heritage of America, with its indigenous traditions and colonial influences, as well as contemporary features of modern global living and technology.

(Spa of Colonial Williamsburg, 2008)

Towards an integrated approach to health and wellness product development

In Western Europe, the focus has traditionally been on physical and medical wellness. This is especially true of Central and Eastern Europe where medical tourism in spas was subsidized in part by the state. The pursuit of physical wellness goes back to Roman and Greek times with the construction of baths dedicated to the cleansing and purification of the body combined with arduous fitness regimes. Similar facilities also traditionally existed in parts of Asia, such as Turkey or Japan, but they often had a more spiritual dimension. For many Westerners, yoga is seen as a physical activity, especially as it is often regulated by Sports Councils (e.g. in the United Kingdom). It is only on further practice that the spiritual dimensions are recognized and experienced. The same may be true of Tai Chi. In Asia, these practices are seen to be spiritual from the outset and are usually not offered as part of a fitness or sports programme. Many of the day and hotel spas in Europe, the United States and increasingly in Asia and the Caribbean tend to offer beauty and fitness facilities and cater for visitors who are mainly interested in physical wellness. However, there are growing numbers of purpose-built recreational short or long-stay spas and wellness hotels especially in Austria and Germany, which offer the whole range of facilities, including thermal waters, fitness and nutritional programmes, massage, and beauty treatments. It is also common for spiritual practices to be integrated into the product range (e.g. yoga, Qi Gong, meditation).

Some retreat centres offer programmes or products mainly for the health of the mind, psychology and emotions, but this is a relatively new phenomenon and the products are not necessarily aimed at those people seeking rest and relaxation. Instead, they must want an active participation in self-development and changing their lives. This may (increasingly) be paid for by their employers as a form of occupational wellness or an incentive trip, but more often than not, it is well-paid, exhausted executives who are willing to pay high prices to improve their mental health or to leave the 'rat race'. This form of product development can include advice on stress management or downsizing one's life, as well as recognizing the benefits of a less material life. However, help may also be needed to improve physical health which may have suffered as a result of overworking or allowing a degree of spirituality to enter the space left by the reduction in working hours or decreasing of material possessions.

Although spas are becoming more multi-functional, only holistic retreat centres consciously attempt to provide visitors with the whole spectrum of wellness activities (except perhaps medical treatments). The concept of holistic tourism suggests wholeness and integration, implying that all dimensions of wellness could or should be included in the product. Smith & Kelly (2006) define holistic tourism as 'tourism that provides the visitor with a range of activities and/or treatments which are aimed at developing, maintaining and improving the body-mind-spirit'. The number of holistic activities that are available in retreat centres around the world is truly diverse. The following list represents some of the more unusual product offers of one retreat centre in Snowdonia, Wales (Trem Y Mor, 2007), but there are hundreds more offering equally diverse programmes:

Examples of Holistic Retreat Products

- Retreat with Introduction to NLP (Neuro-Linguistic Programming) (learn to motivate yourself and others. It will give you a better understanding of the effect and impact of communication)
- Angel Workshop for the 21st century
- Psychic Retreat (discover your psychic awareness and tap into your gifts to help others. It also includes an Indian head massage and meridian facial)
- Retreat with Past Life Regression
- Discover Auras Retreat (Learn techniques to enable you to sense and see other people's auras)

- Discover the Power of Self-Hypnosis Retreat (Learn how to harness the mind to achieve what you want rather than responding to old patterns of negative belief and behaviour)
- Sound Therapy Workshop and Retreat
- Retreat with Chakra Therapy
- Chanting to Relieve Stress Retreat
- Retreat with Tree Oracle Workshop
- Four Elements Workshop and Retreat (different healing tools including crystals, smudging, walks, chanting, meditation and angels)
- Retreat With 3 Point Therapy Workshop (Discover how the use of Reiki, Reflexology, and visualization can profoundly change your life.)

The following table suggests a way of categorizing holistic tourism products, many of which may be offered separately or in combination with two or three others. It is, however, rare and arguably undesirable or impossible to offer all of them within one holiday or centre.

Categorization of Holistic Retreat Products

- Physical (e.g. massage, dance, Pilates, Alexander technique)
- Therapeutic (e.g. massage, aromatherapy, acupuncture, kinesiology)
- Medicinal (e.g. Ayurveda, herbalism, Chinese medicine, Bach Flower remedies)
- Mental (e.g. NLP, dream workshops, psycho-drama)
- Spiritual (e.g. meditation, yoga, Tai Chi, Shamanism)
- Healing (e.g. reiki, aurasoma, colour therapy)
- Creative (e.g. painting, photography, cookery)
- Expressive (e.g. singing, drama, comedy)
- Esoteric/New Age (e.g. tarot, crystals, angels, astrology)
- Personal development (e.g. counselling, stress management, life coaching)

(adapted from Kelly & Smith, 2008)

Body-mind-spirit dimensions can be difficult to integrate in one product given most peoples' propensity towards one dimension or other. Not all wellness tourists are seeking healing and/or renewal of body, mind *and* spirit. Indeed, a visitor with strong interests in yoga for example, would not necessarily want life coaching. A typical spa visitor may not want a psychological or spiritual experience. A spiritual tourist in a meditation retreat would not want a physical fitness programme, and a visitor learning about life coaching or NLP may have little interest in yoga or Tai Chi. Therefore tourism providers have to understand which elements of the body-mind-spirit product range are compatible, and more importantly, which of them are the most attractive to different target markets. Some centres try to offer a balance of body-mind-spirit products, as the following case study shows:

Case Study of Holistic Tourism Packaging: Cortijo Romero, Spain

Cortijo Romero is a holistic retreat centre near to Granada in Spain, which aims to help clients 'find themselves' and change their lives. This is a centre that tries to cover a range of body-mind-spirit activities and even categorizes its programmes into: Bodywork, Creative/Arts, Meditation, Fun and Laughter, Nature, Music, and Psychological, with each category offering a range of courses, which are delivered by experienced, professional practitioners from around the world.

The majority of visitors to Cortijo Romero come alone and are technically aged 18–80, but on average, tend to be 40+. One or two main courses are chosen per week plus additional activities are offered (totalling up to 20 hours per week) with an average of 10–18 participants per course. Additional facilities include gardens, pool, mountains, excursions to nearby villages, and vegetarian, healthy food. Examples of courses include The Alexander Technique, Bodywork, Circle Dance, Living The Dream, Story-Telling, Massage, Opening The Heart, Re-Shaping Your Life, Tai Chi, Voice And Movement, Yoga.

A typical daily programme for this and other retreat centres would consist of the following timetable:

- 7 a.m.–8 a.m.: Yoga or meditation
- 8 a.m.–9 a.m.: Breakfast
- 9 a.m.–10 a.m.: Free time or Karma Yoga
- 10 a.m.–12.30 p.m.: Course 1
- 12.30 p.m.–1.30 p.m.: Lunch
- 1.30 p.m.–3.30 p.m.: Free time
- 3.30 p.m.–5.30 p.m.: Course 2
- 6.30 p.m.–7.30 p.m.: Dinner
- 7.30 p.m.: Social activities (usually organized by the group)

Such a programme would run for 4 or 5 days per week with a possible rest day mid-week or an organized excursion. Most of the courses are self-selected, but advice might be given on request about creating the right balance for body-mind-spirit.

(Cortijo Romero, 2006; Kelly & Smith, 2008)

However, it should be recognized overall that the main barriers to optimum wellness both in terms of lifestyle and holidays is lack of time and money. Ironically, staying well is time-consuming and expensive, and the majority of people cannot afford this luxury. It is also important to recognize that different aspects of the self may need attention at different stages of one's life or even at different times of the year. There are times when the physical body may need more attention (e.g. during illness or recuperation), at other times, the mind may need calming (e.g. during times of occupational stress). Spirituality can help people to transcend both physical and psychological problems, but it is hard to cultivate, especially in secular societies.

Product innovation and new experiences

The proliferation of spa hotels and purpose-built spas around the world has been exponential in recent years, therefore there is a growing need for new product development in order to give destinations and businesses unique selling propositions. Even historic spas are gradually being regenerated in order to attract new markets, especially those which traditionally catered to veterans or elderly medical tourists. Although some of the new products are not always strictly compatible with local, historic traditions, they represent innovation and exciting experiences for visitors.

Case Study: The Golden Door: Historic Innovation

The Golden Door is a destination spa, offering treatments and products rich in tradition, yet executed with a modern interpretation. Packages mean a weeklong customized stay, and guests can achieve 'a deep, meaningful rapport with nature and a meaningful reconnection to the innermost self'. Altogether maximum 40 guests can stay at any time. The facility provides everything a wellness visitor may need and want from private grounds, through spa facilities, Asian-inspired architecture and fitness facilities.

Founder Deborah Szekely was already at the birth of her and her husband's first camp in Rancho la Puerta called Essene School of Life (1940). Learning from the exemplary experiences in 1968 they developed a unique philosophy of personal health and fitness.

The philosophy of Golden Door is inspired by that of ancient Japanese Honjin inns, places where royal and affluent travellers could stop to rest, rejuvenating body and spirit at the hands of attentive servants. The path to a transformative experience begins the moment you walk through the legendary doors. Golden Door was designed to serve as a portal to mental and physical well-being, and set the standards for the entire industry in North America. All Golden Door spas (altogether 5) are private enclaves, designed to each fit seamlessly into their individual environments. They are retreats of reflective and timeless serenity and beauty – a journey on a path to discover true tranquility and reach a 'perfect balance' of mind, body, and spirit. Signature services are offered, designed to reflect the distinctive surroundings of each particular day spa retreat.

Golden Door is truly the 'luxury daughter' of Rancho La Puerta, the very first spa and basis of the Golden Door philosophy created. First innovations at Rancho La Puerta were:

- First organic garden on the West coast of America – Golden Door has had an organic garden since its origin.
- Exercising to music
- Implementing chair exercises
- Practising reflexology
- Conducting various forms of herbal wraps

Successful innovations in Golden Door include:

- First spa to have a men only week (1960)
- First spa to have a labyrinth (1998)
- First United States spa with Japanese architecture/gardens, with Zen philosophy
- First United States spa to use a Jacuzzi as water massage
- Creators of water volleyball
- First exercise program created to exercise to Jazz music
- First to serve 'nouvelle' cuisine
- First spa to serve food portions to 'fit the size of the individual' depending on age/size/activity
- Created an exercise philosophy to 'live in your body'; a seven day planned exercise program, where all parts of the body had been exercised and stretched
- Inspired a health philosophy that does not end at the spa, since the 1950's guests take their customized program home with them
- Crafted a spiritual philosophy to gain spiritual health as well as physical health. Guests are encouraged to meditate with rosary beads using the mantra 'Every day, in every way, I get better and better'.

(Golden Door Spa, 2008)

What features make a spa or wellness centre exceptional?

In her book about the world's most exceptional destination spas, Napier (2002) emphasizes spas which have stunning designs or amazing locations or a range of special or signature treatments. For some spas, the location and natural features are the main attraction, for example, the Blue Lagoon in Grindavik, Iceland, which makes use of geothermal waters and may offer a glimpse of the Northern Lights in winter. Canyon ranch in Arizona, United States has an impressive desert and mountain setting with outdoor yoga and hiking opportunities. Les Sources de Caudalie in Bordeaux, France makes use of vinotherapy as it is a wine growing region. This includes a line of skincare products made from grapes which help to fight free radicals which are responsible for much skin damage. The anti-oxidant properties of red wine are also promoted. Barrel Baths are offered which contain spring water, grape extract and essential oils, wraps containing wine yeast extract, and massages with grape seed oil.

The Thermae del Parco in Sardinia is a thalassotherapy spa with five pools that are visited in rotation. The waters are so beneficial for joints and bones that even Russian astronauts come to recover from voyages into space. Underwater massages are offered, for example the increasingly popular watsu or underwater shiatsu. There are also eighteen restaurants. Some spas such as Chiva Som in Thailand offer formal education classes on nutrition, cooking and healing with Bach herbal remedies, along with some more esoteric topics, such as aura balancing, hypnotherapy and carved-fruit sculpture. There are exceptional medical spas such as Clinique La Prairie in Switzerland offering specific treatments for menopause, as well as a range of cosmetic surgery. The Somatheeram Ayurvedic Beach Resort in Kerala, India has won awards for the Best Ayurvedic Centre in India and offers not only tailor-made Ayurvedic packages, but also yoga, Indian dance, literature, music, and philosophy classes.

Daintree Ecolodge and Spa in Australia makes use of the landscape in an environmentally sustainable way as well as consulting local tribal people and using their healing methods and products. The most famous is the Secret Sacred treatment just for women, which is described as a once-in-a-lifetime experience never to be forgotten. It involves walking to a sacred waterfall to bathe and engage in a symbolic, meditative ritual to celebrate the female body, spirit and soul. In El Tamarindo in Manzanillo, Mexico there is a Temascul ritual in an igloo-style sauna. This is a pre-Hispanic tradition that invokes the healing powers of water, plants, air, earth, and fire. It lasts for two and a half hours and guests anoint themselves with scented mud containing coconut, cucumber and papaya before taking a dip in the sea and afterwards drinking fragrant herbal tea. There are then three 20-minute steam sessions in the Temascul hut. The Ulpotha sanctuary in Sri Lanka is another eco-friendly development in a rural, organic farming village with no electric lights or hot running water. The village is a magnet for some of the world's best yoga teachers and many types of yoga are offered, as well as meditation and various treatments in the native healing centre depending on which therapists are available.

LeSport in St Lucia in the West Indies offers the ultimate 'body holiday' with the mantra 'Give us your body for a week and we'll give you back your mind'. Packages tend to be all-inclusive making it a money-free zone and unusually for spas, alcohol is unlimited. Numerous sports and fitness programmes are offered, but visitors can also opt for a 'stress management' package including consultations, talks and lectures on reducing stress, yoga, tai chi, qi gong, and meditation. Some of the world's most beautiful spas are located next to or in skiing resorts, especially in Austria and Switzerland, but also in Canada and the United States, for example, the Wyndham Peak Resort in Colorado.

Attention to very small details can make a big difference to the visitor's experience, such as complementary aromatherapy products in the bathrooms, natural sea sponges, scented candles, a choice of different aromatic pillows, pot pourri, and fresh flowers. Unusual therapies can capture the imagination, such as the 'Stoned Cow' Native American full body massage using smooth hot and cold stones in Babington House, Somerset in the United Kingdom. Spas which develop new products all the time are appealing and encourage repeat visitation. Fresh, natural ingredients like yoghurt, honey, herbs, fruit, flowers and oats can have added appeal. True luxury and comfort can be a motivating factor. For others, it might be the availability of special or romantic packages, or childcare facilities for families.

One company which is especially focused on the small details which can enhance the wellness experience is the 'Six Senses' chain of resorts, which operate in South East Asia. They are careful to use local and indigenous features, as well as being sustainability orientated:

Case Study of Six Senses

Six Senses main objective was '*To create innovative and enriching experiences in a sustainable environment*' (this is supported by the compilation of The Little Green Book for Spas in which the sustainable spa concept and recommendations are introduced). Six Senses is a Resort & Spa Management and Development Company, established in 1995, which manages resorts under five brand names, besides Six Senses Spas:

- *Soneva (Intelligent Luxury)* are holistic spas offering top luxury in an environment that cultivates the indigenous feel in design, architecture, cuisine and service (ingredients from the resort's own organic gardens). Any Soneva resort has a limited number of accommodations, furnishings and finishes are crafted from renewable and sustainable sources.
- *Six Senses Hideaway (Redefining Experiences)* is the boutique interpretation of the brand; attention to detail and focus on the reality of the destination is the driving force (the personal attention offered to every guest is exemplified with butlers). A Six Senses Spa is a key component of a Six Senses Hideaway and accommodations consist of exclusive villas with a private pool.
- *Six Senses Latitude (Redefining Experiences)* tends to offer a greater number of accommodations than Six Senses Hideaway with unique and diverse design personalities.
- *Six Senses Destination Spas (Enriching Life)* offer structured and personalized programmes that blend holistic fitness activities, organic fishetarian spa cuisine, wellness education, self-discovery classes, relaxation and renewal. Preventative wellness is a fundamental component, combined with sound nutritional and naturopathic knowledge.
- *Evason properties (Redefining Experience)*, with a greater number of accommodations than Six Senses Hideaways and Latitudes. A blend of innovative concepts, together with a Six Senses Spa, makes them fashionable urban oases and desirable destinations in themselves.

As the company summarizes 'The pyramid of six spheres used to identify Six Senses Spas, represents the philosophy that is fundamental to the human experience':

> '*The foundation spheres represent the three primary senses of sight, sound and touch. The second level balances upon this foundation by satisfying the more acute senses of taste and smell. The apex sphere symbolises a sense of elation discovered only by balancing the first five – the unique experience of all senses elevated beyond expectations. It is our mission to deliver spa experiences that are both unique and memorable, and very much beyond expectations*'.

(Six Senses, 2008)

Contemporary developments in spas

The International Spa Association (ISPA, 2007) lists some of the new trends that exist in spas (Table 11.1). There has clearly been a shift in some of the thinking behind wellness enhancement towards more holistic and

Table 11.1 What's Hot, What's Not in Spas.

In	Out
Adventure spas	Fitness retreats
Ayurveda	Aromatherapy
Choreographed treatments	Treatments without purpose
Multi-function machines	Walking on the treadmill
Exercise	Cellulite treatments
Feldenkrais	Meditation
Free weights	Weight machines only
Heart rate monitor training	The fat burning zone
Hiking outdoors	Spending hours on the Stairmaster
Hydrotherapy baths	Kurs
Integrative medicine	Alternative medicine
Japanese-themed spas	European-themed spas
Long tights, flared bottoms	Thong leotards
Loose leaf tea	Tea bags
Mind body	No pain, no gain
Pilates	Crunches
Challenge courses	Power walks
Self-defence classes	Makeovers
Spas that are feng shui' ed	Spas that aren't
Steambath	Sauna
Strength training	Circuit training
Studio cycling	Rowing
Tae/kickboxing	Step aerobics
Thai yoga massage	Swedish massage

Source: ISPA, 2007

spiritual practices, including more experiential approaches. The influence of Eastern wellness (e.g. Feng Shui, Ayurveda, Japanese-themed spas, Thai massage and martial arts) is clearly becoming more pervasive. Fitness programmes are becoming more focused on body-mind connections, as well as stamina and posture, rather than painful repetitions (e.g. Feldenkrais – a form of movement therapy designed to isolate separate muscles, to promote flexibility, release tension, and enhance balance. It is also more popular to exercise in the fresh air than in a stuffy gym (e.g. Nordic walking, cross-country skiing).

It is clear that the majority of wellness and spa hotels and centres are including more and more ancient traditions as selling points. This can range from the design of the hotel (e.g. using principles of Feng Shui or Vasati) to the range of massages and treatments offered. The most common include yoga, Tai Chi, Thai Massage, and Ayurveda. Besides it is very typical nowadays to create special packages (and consequently new brands) combining skiing and golf with spas (e.g. we can see products such as well-skiing!). Golf condominiums or golf course developments would not now be complete without a spa or wellness centre in the clubhouse or in the main building of the complex. The rationale certainly exists for supporting this trend, since after doing sports the relaxing and soothing impacts of spas can be well received by guests. Plus, indoor facilities provide something to do for those who cannot or do not want to ski or play golf, or when the weather is bad.

Selfness and mindness: A new wellness trend?

Dsyli (2008), the CEO of Private Selection Hotels and Wellness Plus Hotels in Switzerland describes how the needs and expectations from a Wellness hotel are extremely varied and individual. Whereas 5 years ago we were talking about new awareness of the body and taking care of physical wellbeing, buzzwords like 'Work-Life-Balance' have gradually become pervasive, and other terms like 'selfness' and 'mindness'. Although these terms are mainly used in German speaking countries, they clearly have an important meaning for wellness product development everywhere, as they reflect the trend towards integration and wholeness. Selfness refers to the spiritual search for oneself and mindness is closely connected, referring to feelings and emotions. Mindness accompanies us in every situation in our lives, including our hopes, fears, and relationships with family, friends, colleagues, acquaintances (Table 11.2).

A wellness hotel should contain the following elements: movement/fitness, water, warmth, beauty, nutrition and relaxation, but not only as infrastructure, also in the philosophy of the whole organization, which

Table 11.2 Comparing the Concepts of Selfness and Wellness.

Selfness	Wellness
Mind oriented	Body oriented
Goal: self-development	Goal: rest and relaxation
Influences whole way of life	Happens in free time
'I develop further'	'I do myself good'
Active, forward-looking	Passive, accepting
Individual	Mass
Motto: 'Find yourself'	'Enjoy yourself'

Source: Parádai, 2007

should be guided by the mindness principle. This means, for example, including group lectures about meditation techniques, Qi Gong, Yoga, breathing exercises, Feldenkreis, and not only for guests but also for employees. All hoteliers should convey clearly what this means and what is expected from their staff. Three types of product offer are given:

- *Wellness light*: Hotels with Wellness facilities
- *Wellness plus*: Specialized integrated Wellness hotels with professional infrastructure and philosophy
- *Medical Wellness*: Medical and psychological aspects are added to the infrastructure and philosophy

An interview was carried out with Daniel Heller (2005) about the 'Selfness Center' which had opened in the Eiger Grindelwald Hotel in Switzerland, where he was Manager. He quoted the research of Matthias vom Horx from the Future Institute (Zukunftsinstitut), which suggested that the trend towards selfness was based on four main principles:

- Knowledge of one's own health.
- Work-Life balance.
- Experience and achievement levels.
- Abiliy to decide what is best for oneself.

Interviews with guests had shown Heller that they wanted to take more responsibility for their own life and wellbeing and to fulfil their potential. The Selfness Center offers guests the chance to put together their own personal programme, including aspects of wellness, fitness, health, communication and motivation. Specialist literature, lectures, workshops, and discussions are offered to help them. Products like 'Motivation training on the mountain' or 'Stress management through Nordic Walking' are created to allow space for new ideas to emerge in relation to self development. Special training is given to staff, who need to be interested in the concept and philosophy, as well as bringing their own knowledge of fitness, wellness, psychotherapy or other skills. The Selfness Center is fully integrated into the hotel rather than being a separate facility, and the concept pervades the whole organization, including the way that rooms are themed or the way the menu is designed.

New niche products in health and wellness

One of the most recent products in tourism is the development of wellness or holistic cruises. Many of these depart from American ports and tend to cruise the Caribbean. The facilities on board include spas, saunas, steam baths, massage rooms and beauty salons, healthy and organic food, yoga, and meditation classes, and a variety of specialist lectures and workshops. One example is 'Holistic Holiday at Sea' which describes its 2008 cruise as 'a body pampering, relaxing, and educational vacation.... A perfect combination of luxury, fitness, knowledge and entertainment'.

Case Study of Spas on Sea and Holistic Cruises

Spas have become huge business at sea, with ships eclipsing land-based spas in size and variety and fitness areas including everything from Pilates reformers to full-size boxing rings. Nearly every cruise line has incorporated low fat and sugar-free selections and heart healthy choices, along with seminars in everything from reducing body fat to healthy hair. The minimum 7 nights wellbeing cruises are focused on getting in shape while visiting outstanding destinations, with special menus, experts on board to offer seminars and Thai and Balinese massage, pressotherapy and more, in addition to the usual treatments.

Italian-owned MSC Cruises has joined the ranks of the lines offering special fitness cruises and a VIP class with special access to the spa. A 16,000-square foot Aqua Spa wellbeing centre is designed with a thermal cave, steam room, and sauna, Turkish bath, glass-fronted relaxation room overlooking the ocean and warm, atmospheric treatment rooms. State-of-the-art fitness equipment fills the gym, where classes from aerobics to yoga will be offered. Beauty treatments blend ancient and modern practices, using natural minerals, healing salts, and aromatherapy along with techniques including electronic stimulation. Thalassotherapy, aromatherapy, anti-wrinkle facial treatments, and massage incorporating shiatsu, reflexology and sports therapy are among the most popular offerings. The full service salon has everything from pedicures and hair colour to waxing (Green, 2008).

A Taste of Health, a federally approved non-profit educational foundation specializing in relaxing, educational, and spiritual vacations in the United States, has been organizing Holistic Holiday at Sea cruises since 2004. Departing from Fort Lauderdale, guests visit exotic Western Caribbean ports, including Key West, Cozumel, Ocho Rios, and Grand Cayman. They are provided with healthy food, attend lectures and workshops taught by world-renowned teachers and healers, and practise yoga and meditation. The main focus is on health and happiness, and the subjects of the lectures vary from learning the principles of feng shui to understanding the benefits of macrobiotic cuisine. Cookery classes and massage courses are also offered. There is even a Holistic Holiday talent show and several social events.

Prices begin at $1,095 per person for double occupancy, and include specially prepared organic/natural meals, lectures, yoga classes, meditation classes, workshops, cooking classes, nightly entertainment and the use of all basic spa/health club and onboard facilities. A Taste of Health reported that after the first cruise in 2004, nearly 25% of the guests from the first cruise signed up for the next year.

(A Taste of Health, 2008)

A number of destinations are offering massage holidays, either for those people who are already masseurs and want to learn a new form of massage, or for those who want to learn massage for the first time. Although there is some controversy about whether a person can become qualified as a massage therapist in a few days or weeks, for many people it is just an opportunity to learn a new skill rather than a new vocation. It is common for visitors to Kerala to experience and want to learn Ayurvedic massage, for example (even though the official training takes 3 years). Ayurvedic holidays are increasingly being developed especially in the South of India and Sri Lanka, including training courses for those wanting to learn more. A typical Ayurvedic holiday would consist of yoga classes, learning about ayurvedic treatments specifically tailored to the needs of the individual, for example, massage and a special diet, as well certain beauty treatments. Ayurveda can be used to treat many physical conditions such as allergies, urinary diseases, nervous diseases, stress disorders, muscular diseases, arthritis, and so forth. Many visitors to Thailand choose to learn Thai massage in one of the many Massage Schools (e.g. Wat Pho in Bangkok or International Training Massage School (ITM) in Chiang Mai). Courses usually range from 30 to 120 hours tuition and can include some theory, philosophy and yoga exercises as well as massage practice. Teachers' training holidays in yoga are also becoming more common, for example, the Sivananda Yoga tradition runs month-long 'boot camps' for prospective yoga teachers all around the world, including in the United Kingdom, Canada, Spain, France, the Bahamas, India.

There are numerous retreat centres which now offer special dietary programmes, not only vegetarian but also vegan, organic, 'live' and raw food. Raw Food Planet (2007) lists over 70 ashrams and spiritual centres around the world offering raw food or special dietary holidays. Typical programmes include fasting, meditation and yoga as well as some creative activities. Raw foodism (the tenets of which were first researched in the 1900s) is a lifestyle promoting the consumption of uncooked, unprocessed, and often organic foods as a large percentage of the diet. Depending on the type of lifestyle and results desired, raw food diets may include a selection of raw fruits, vegetables, nuts, seeds (including sprouted whole grains), eggs, fish, meat, and unpasteurized dairy products (such as raw milk, cheese, and yogurt). It is believed that enzymes are released in the mouth when raw food is chewed, and that these enzymes interact with other substances, notably the enzymes produced by the body itself, to aid the digestion process. Raw foods are said to have higher nutrient values than foods which have been cooked and to include health benefits such as a stable weight, clearer skin, more energy, and a better immune system. As discussed earlier in the book, de-toxing through nutritional changes and control has become increasingly popular in recent years.

Case Study: De-Tox Retreats In Austria

The Viva Mayr Health Resort in Southern Austria runs de-tox holidays under the supervision of doctors who follow Mayr therapy, the belief that the reduction of food is the best stimulator for the body's self-healing powers. A typical day starts at 7 a.m. with an Epsom salt drink followed by body brushing with alternating hot and cold showers, 7.30 a.m. breakfast, then a consultation with a de-tox specialist doctor using kinesiology and a breath test to check imbalances. Lectures are given about digestive disorders and their causes, as well as nutritional advice – for example, eating little in the evenings, no liquid with food, no raw foods after 2 p.m., chewing properly, etc. As well as a strictly controlled, customized diet, Kneipp therapies are used (water treatments which dissolve and remove matter-containing disease from the body), Nasal Reflex Therapy (acupuncture combined with aromatherapy to unblock nasal passages), Phytomer detox algen packs for de-toxing the body, hydroxeur herbal baths, and Elektrolyse foot baths to increase circulation, rebalance, and stimulate different organs, and allow tissues to eliminate acidity, toxic burdens, and other pollutants. Patients are given massages, reflexology, manipulation of digestive organs, and are asked to apply a liver pack every evening to allow the liver to detoxify. Yoga and relaxation are an important part of the package as de-toxing can make participants feel depressed, angry, tired, high or induce headaches depending on what dietary changes are required.

(Mayr Centre, 2008)

Art therapy has a long history among the practices of psychotherapists. Recently, however, different forms of art therapy, for example music, dance or painting has found its way to tourism, too (the first World Congress on Art Therapy was in 2003 in Budapest, Hungary). Art therapy can either be part of holistic retreats, where participants can learn about local painting styles, or part of medical tourism, where treatments are used to rehabilitate certain conditions or cure illnesses (some may argue that a painting holiday in Italy can also fall under the art therapy category). Art therapy can be used for those who suffer from drug addiction or alcoholism, for example, to enhance creativity and to let (sing, dance or paint) out traumas. Art therapy requires a team of experts representing experiences from psychology and psychiatry as well as artists or dance teachers.

Resonance therapy, under which we can find, for example, music therapy, dates back to Ancient Times. During prehistoric times they already used sounds of nature for stimulation. In Ancient Egypt sacral dances were used as well as music for healing. The same was true in China and India (e.g. mantras). During the therapy, resonance should reset the personal rhythm of the organ or tissue. It has three forms: active, when patients actively form part of music, for example singing. Passive music therapy refers to when patients listen to the music, taking the resonance of a specifically selected piece of music through associations and experiences. Dance therapy is the third form of resonance therapy, in which movement and music are combined.

Many health and wellness products have traditionally used animals to assist healing, for example swimming with dolphins, whale music for relaxation, animal spirit guides in Native American traditions. Therapeutic riding can also be used almost anywhere.

Case Study: Hyppotherapy or Therapeutic Riding

Within a Therapeutic Riding programme the focus is on hyppotherapy and recreational riding. 'Hyppo' is the Greek word meaning horse. A 'Hyppo' programme works on and develops riders physically, emotionally, and cognitively.

- *Physically*: The horse's movement during the walk provides input to the rider's trunk and pelvis that closely resembles the movement seen in the normal way of walking or running.
- *Emotionally*: As a participant they will overcome fears and conquer challenges in the riding arena. They will increase their self-esteem and self-worth. Example: some of these riders will never have the opportunity to drive a car, yet they will have the ability to control such a powerful animal.
- *Cognitively*: Because the horse is such a positive motivator, a single lesson causes the rider to work on memorization, following directions, maintaining focus, and task analysis.

The other type of riding may be recreational riding where work is done more on socialization, behaviour, and creativity.

- **Socially**: Most of the lessons are made up of two or more students, side-walkers, and horse handlers. This enables the rider to interact with many different people throughout the course of his/her lesson.
- **Behaviour**: Riders must behave in an acceptable manner in order to participate in equine activities. the motivation to ride is usually enough to maintain that level of behaviour.
- **Creativity**: The equine environment provides many opportunities to engage in creative activities. Imagination is called upon to transport riders to a new location as they ride.

There is not a rider who is not transformed by the power and spirit of the horse.

(Crystal Wood Stables, 2008)

There are many other new products being developed in the health and wellness sector, especially for a wider market. For example, Chapter Seven describes the growth of gay and lesbian spas. There are also spas developing which are specifically designed to accommodate disabled visitors, as the following case study shows.

Case Study of a 'Para-Spa'

The complex of Djerba-les-Bains and Le Grand Hotel des Thermes is the first of its kind in Tunisia. At the beginning, there was a water spring, exploited since the Roman era, with very good water quality rich in chloride, sodium, and magnesium, and the developer's wish to serve the needs of the handicapped. Associating hydrotherapy and tourism for the handicapped led to developing the health spa and the four star hotel. The complex was designed observing strict building and development standards, which led to significant overspending. However the challenge was met. The complex was perfectly developed to meet the needs of the handicapped and the first visitors came from Germany in 2000. Each room is designed using the smallest detail to ensure guest comfort and convenience. There is a synthetic carpet leading to the sea and the swimming pool, which is designed to take account of guests' physical ability. Swimmers can use special equipment to easily and safely swim. Many other sports and activities are offered which have been adapted for use by the less able bodied. The treatments are also designed to help ease certain physical and medical conditions. Numerous specialist staff are employed to help and advise guests.

(Djerba-les-Bains, 2008)

Conclusion

It can be seen in this chapter that although health and wellness products are becoming more standardized and globalized on the one hand, there are also numerous new and unique products being offered in a range of health and wellness destinations and centres around the world. Although innovation and new experiences are difficult to create in a competitive, even saturated market, it is important to tap into new leisure and lifestyle trends and to understand the changing needs of contemporary consumers. This may mean importing products from elsewhere in the world which are new and attractive, or developing signature treatments which make use of local traditions or ingredients. In some cases, a natural resource or landscape will be enough to attract visitors, in others, there may be a need for some creativity in design or product development. It is also important to employ effective marketing strategies and to ensure that the destination is as accessible as possible, otherwise even the most innovative product development will be wasted.

Conclusions: The future of health and wellness tourism

I have travelled so much because travel has enabled me to arrive at unknown places within my clouded self.

(Sir Laurens Van der Post, quoted in 1994:99)

This final chapter offers a summary of the main global and regional trends in health and wellness tourism and draws on industry data to make future predications for supply and demand. It is cl ear that health tourism is by no means a new phenomenon as we saw in the first chapter, but travelling to enjoy health destinations and services has grown exponentially in recent years. In some countries, the sector is in its infancy in terms of international tourism development (e.g. CEE) whilst in others (e.g. Austria) the market is becoming saturated according to recent reports. Of course, human beings will always crave wellness, but the activities they choose to achieve this can vary greatly as we could see from the previous chapter about new product development. Like with all forms of tourism, visitors will eventually seek diversity and difference, new destinations and activities, better quality facilities and services, or cheaper prices. The chapter about leisure and lifestyles suggests that it is important to take note of major social patterns, which are likely to impact on travel decisions and behaviour. This chapter discusses the likely future of health and wellness and makes recommendations for development and research.

A summary of contemporary global and regional development in health and wellness tourism

The following table provides a summary of the main health and wellness resources and assets to be found in the different regions of the world, the way in which they are used, and the main places where they tend to be offered. As it is difficult to generalize about whole continents, it is indicated if only one or two countries within a region can offer a certain resource. The focus is also on those countries that really use their assets for tourism purposes (i.e. with a complete infrastructure, targeted promotion, etc.) (Figure 12.1).

Many countries have natural healing assets such as medical, thermal and mineral waters, special muds, caves, climate, etc. These countries tend to have a long history of medical tourism and are often only just starting to move into more leisure-based wellness tourism. There can be some problems with the upgrading of traditional, historic baths and resorts, as well as the difficulties of increasingly incompatible markets (i.e. medical versus wellness guests). This is especially true of European countries, especially Central and Eastern Europe. Those countries listing indigenous healing traditions are those which still have existing indigenous peoples (e.g. Australian Aborigines, New Zealand Maori, Native American Indians, African tribes), those which still use the rituals and treatments of ancient civilizations (e.g. Incas, Aztecs, and Mayans in Central and South America), and those which have been retained and adapted for modern usage (e.g. India Ayurveda, Thai Massage, Chinese medicine). There is something of a revival of interest in natural, herbal, and indigenous healing methods and ingredients, so much so that luxury spas often include such products as their signature treatments. These are unique and give a local flavour to the spa or retreat centre's offer. Medical services are becoming almost ubiquitous, especially surgery of all kinds. It is most likely that the cheaper countries of the world are attracting the most tourists because of price differentials, but even in Europe there is quite a lot of intra-regional travel, especially for dentistry.

Nature plays a significant role in health and wellness in many countries, especially those which have a sea coast and can offer products like thalassotherapy (common in Europe). Mountains are another feature which have always attracted health visitors, especially the Alps in Europe. Jungles and national parks (e.g. in Central and South America, Africa) make ideal locations for adventure and ecospas, which is a growing trend. To a lesser (but increasing extent) deserts (e.g. in the Middle East or North Africa) are being used as locations for yoga and meditation holidays, but at present, the Dead Sea is the main natural healing asset in the Middle East. Spiritual traditions refer mainly to those practices which are ancient but not affiliated to one specific religion (e.g. yoga, meditation). These are mainly to be found in Asia, at least those which are starting to be exported to other countries around the world. There can, however, be close links between spiritual and indigenous healing traditions, sometimes including natural assets too (for example, Native American Indians believed that hot, healing springs were sacred).

	Existing assets for health and wellness tourism						Use of existing assets				
	Natural healing assets	Indigenous healing traditions	Medical services	Nature	Spiritual traditions	Leisure and recreation spas	Medical (therapeutic) Hotel, Spa or Clinic	Medical (surgical) Clinics or Hospitals	Medical wellness centres or spas	Holistic retreats	Hotel and resort spa
Europe											
Northern	(♦¹)					♦					♦
Western	♦		♦	♦		♦	♦	♦	♦	♦	♦
Central and Eastern	♦		♦	♦		♦	♦		♦		♦
Southern	♦			♦		♦	♦			♦	♦
America											
North	(♦²)	♦	♦	♦		♦	♦			♦	♦
Central	♦	♦	♦	♦				(♦³)			♦
South	♦	♦	♦	♦		♦					
Africa	♦	♦	♦	♦			♦	(♦⁴)			♦
Asia											
Middle-East		♦	♦	(♦⁵)			♦	♦	♦	♦	♦
South-East		♦	♦		♦		♦	♦	♦	♦	♦
Far East	(♦⁶)	♦	♦		♦		♦	♦	♦	♦	
Australia, New Zealand, and South Pacific	♦	♦		♦		♦	♦			♦	♦

¹ Iceland only
² Caribbean
³ Cuba
⁴ South Africa, Kenya
⁵ Jordan, Israel
⁶ Japan

Figure 12.1
International Analysis of Health and Wellness Assets. *Source:* Smith and Puczkó.

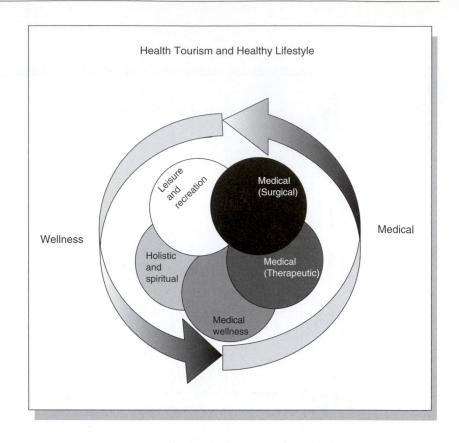

Health Tourism and Healthy Lifestyle

Figure 12.2
Whirl of Health Tourism and
Healthy Lifestyle. *Source*:
Smith and Puczkó.

Although many countries have a sea coast, for example, the tradition of Thalassotherapy is most common in Europe, but is increasingly being offered in North Africa or in Middle Eastern spa resorts. Leisure and recreation can mean different things in different countries, but here it refers either to outdoor fitness and sports (particularly common in Northern Europe, North America, Australia and New Zealand, but also in adventure spas in Central and South America, for example), or to water-based attractions. Natural healing assets can be used for leisure purposes, which is especially well embodied in the francophone concept of 'thermo-ludisme' (having fun in waters), but it is more likely that thermal rather than mineral waters will be used, and the wellness centre is more likely to be purpose-built rather than traditional. On the other hand, the range of medical services varies according to location. Medical surgical tourism, as discussed, tends to be offered in developing countries. Medical wellness has a big following in Germany in particular. Medical therapeutic tourism is common to many countries, especially those with natural or indigenous healing assets. In North America, the concept of Therapeutic Recreation is especially well developed. Holistic activities can technically exist anywhere, but the most common visitors to retreat centres are stressed-out, middle class people from western, developed countries. Although they may be keen to visit traditional ashrams in India or Buddhist retreats in

Thailand, it is more likely that they will go to a purpose-built centre in a pleasant location to enjoy a range of global and hybrid experiences. Many of these are based in Western and Southern Europe, North America and Australia. The most global, all-encompassing use of assets clearly occurs in hotels and resort spas everywhere in the world. These can blend anything from natural healing assets to cosmetic surgery to the use of indigenous ingredients to spiritual traditions.

Directions of development

We refer back to the chart in Chapter One, in which we introduced the forms and services of health and wellness tourism. Considering all we talked about so far, we believe that it is almost inevitable that the future of health and wellness tourism has two main directions. One, in which very specialized, often small scale developments open up (e.g. Sukko Cultural Spa), servicing either the upmarket or the 'hardcore' holistic demand. The other main and, at least in the short term, more influential trend will be the blend of services and forms (Figure 12.2).

Case Study: The World's First Cultural Spa

Have you ever imagined living life like in the pages of a history book or as a myth told throughout the centuries? The freshest concept of spa in the world has emerged in Thailand, the kingdom rich in cultural civilization – this is the 'cultural spa'.

Sukko Cultural Spa & Wellness is the world's first cultural spa with the unique Thai cultural service and design of an architect derived from the ancient capital of Siam, with three categories of rooms and 160 treatment beds in the new five-star day spa in Phuket with a more than 12,000 Sqm. spa area and full wellness facilities. Sukko provides individual spa packages based on the philosophy of Thai Ayurveda and other ancient wisdom descended through the generations, and they can be tailored to fit visitors' requirements, including weddings, honeymoons, outdoor sports, etc. Visitors will not only experience time-honoured wisdom straight from the pages of history books and relax with life aesthetics and various ways to nourish their happiness, but they will also be spiritually enriched by the spa superior cuisine, traditional Thai cookery, elegant clubhouse with traditional Thai martial art and exercise regimes, Salon of the legendary angel with secret techniques passed down from Thai ancestors, the kid's club with a range of rewarding activities and traditional Thai plays, and many other services and cultural attractions.

The Sukko Spa's qualities they believe give competitive advantage are: Treatments steeped in time-tested traditions, traditionally natural products and 800-hour trained staff.

(Sukko Spa, 2008)

This new 'well-blending' tourism, however will face challenges. Operators and marketers will find it more and more complicated to differentiate themselves and to create their own identities. New labels and words will appear and visitors will need to invest an increasing amount of time to find out what a given label may actually mean. It is expected that 'well-blending' tourism will become the new form of mass tourism, not to the same extent as the seaside, but very much like skiing has become.

The next table shows the likely future trends in the use of resources and assets, indicating where certain practices or facilities are likely to increase (▲), where they are likely to stay the same (►), and where they are non-existent or hardly developed (no symbol). The second column denotes the way in which certain practices and products are being exported around the world. It is clear that there is a growth in the use of global spa products, but also some traditions or spiritual activities which are indigenous to somewhere else (e.g. the exporting of Thai massage or Indian Ayurveda to European Spas or holistic centres). Psychological activities are increasingly being used everywhere, especially in the field of occupational wellness and business tourism (e.g. stress management, life coaching) (Figure 12.3).

New Age and complementary therapies are complex, in that some of them form an important part of spa or holistic tourism, but there is still scepticism about their effectiveness as healing methods. For example, Harrison (2007) describes Professor Dwakin's attack on all New Age therapies, stating that ' alternative remedies constitute little more than a money-spinning, multi-million pound industry that impoverishes our culture and throws up new age gurus who exhort us to run away from reality'. His research included faith healers, psychic mediums, angel therapists, aura photographers, astrologers, Tarot card readers and water diviners. This does not, of course, mean that the public does not want them! On the contrary, with the decline of traditional religion and the lack of faith in conventional medicine, more and more westerners are turning to so-called New Age therapies. However, there are many 'alternative' or 'complementary' practices (e.g. acupuncture, reiki, ayurveda, Chinese medicine) which have a long history in Eastern countries and are now being exported.

Natural resources are, of course, geographically specific, therefore healing waters, for example, cannot easily be exported except in the form of mineral water to drink (a common practice in many historic spas in Europe, for example). Mud or salt (e.g. from the Dead Sea) can more easily be transported and used in cosmetic or healing product ranges around the globe, and the same is true of herbs, plants, flowers or oils (e.g. African Bush products). By contrast, fresh air or a good climate can only be enjoyed in the location. This means that anywhere with very unique conditions and resources is likely to maintain its health tourism appeal. If too much from a location is exported, it gives visitors little incentive to visit. On the other hand, it can raise awareness and arouse interest in the destination. Spiritual practices like yoga and meditation are now being offered in the majority of western countries, but many visitors still seek ashrams or retreats in Asia to experience the 'real thing'. The same may be true of Thai massage or Ayurveda, but these are less likely to be primary motivations for tourists.

Holistic retreats offer everything from massage to yoga to psychological counselling, so these are often the best places to gain a whole range of healing experiences within one holiday. However, for many visitors the

	Trends in the use of existing assets/resources						Imported resources and practices			
	Natural healing assets	Indigenous healing traditions	Medical services	Nature	Spiritual traditions	Psychological activities	Spiritual traditions	Global spa products and procedures	Indigenous healing traditions	New Age and complementary therapies
Europe										
Northern	(▲[7])			▲	▲	▲		▲	▲	▲
Western	▲			▲		▲		▲	▲	▲
Central and Eastern	▲		▲▲	▲		▲	▲	▲	▲	
Southern	▲		▲	▲		▲	▲▲	▲	▲	▲
America										
North	(▲[8])	▲	▲	▲	▲	▲	▲	▲	▲	▲
Central	▲	▲	▲	▲		▲		▲		▲▲
South	▲	▲		▲		▲		▲		▲
Africa	▲	▲	▲	▲			▲	▲		
Asia										
Middle-East	▲	▲	▲	▲		▲		▲		▲
South-East	▲	▲	▲	▲	▲▲			▲		
Far East	▲	▲	▲	▲	▲			▲		
Australia, New Zealand, and South Pacific	▲	▲		▲	▲	▲	▲	▲		▲

[7] Iceland only
[8] Caribbean

Figure 12.3
Trends in the Use of Resources. *Source*: Smith and Puczkó.

New Age/ hippy association with the label 'holistic' or 'spiritual' may lead them instead to wellness spas, hotels and resorts. These may similarly offer body-mind-spirit products (e.g. 'mindness' and 'selfness' in German or Swiss hotels) but differently packaged and promoted. Sometimes the exporting of Eastern traditions needs to be 'softened' with a Western flavour. This arguably undermines their authenticity, but makes the product eminently more saleable. Medical services can technically be offered anywhere, but visitors will need reassurance of professionalism, regulation, and good sanitation (a former problem for some developing countries). As discussed earlier, certain countries may have a better reputation for certain forms of treatment (e.g. dentistry in Hungary and the Middle East or sex change operations in Thailand).

We believe that hotels and spa resorts are likely to grow everywhere. This is developing already to the point where people want to experience spa lifestyles everyday and will no doubt increase. Holistic tourism is also a growth sector in most parts of the world. Not all countries will include health and wellness as part of their leisure and recreational product base, but most will develop some form of medical tourism. There will always be a need for the treatment of disease and illness, so medical tourism is here to stay! But this is likely to be preventative rather than curative, and there is a shift from traditional forms of medical tourism (i.e. doctor-led) to a greater sense of self-responsibility (i.e. medical wellness). Cosmetic surgery is also a large growth sector in our image-conscious, media driven societies (Figure 12.4).

Future use of assets and resources							
	Leisure and Recreation Centres or Spas	Medical (Therapeutic) Hotel, Spa or Clinic	Medical (Surgical) Clinics or Hospitals	Medical Wellness Centres or Spas	Holistic Retreats	Hotel and Resort Spas	Spa Lifestyle Communities
Europe							
Northern	▲				▲	▲	
Western	▶	▶		▲	▲	▲	
Central and Eastern	▲	▲	▲	▲	▲	▲	
Southern	▶	▶		▶	▲	▲	▲
America							
North	▲	▲		▲	▲	▲	▲
Central		▲	▲	▲	▲	▲	▲
South	▲		▲		▲	▲	
Africa							
			▲		▲	▲	
Asia							
Middle-East			▲	▲		▲	▲
South-East		▲	▲	▲	▲	▲	▲
Far East	▲		▲			▲	
Australia, New Zealand, and South Pacific							
				▲	▲	▲	▲

Figure 12.4
Future Use of Assets and Resources. *Source*: Smith and Puczkó.

One of the major concerns in the future for many destinations is that everything will be available everywhere. Although some spa hotel and resort chains make an effort to include signature, indigenous and local traditions (e.g. in Asia), or to reflect local architectural styles (e.g. in the Middle East), many of them could be located anywhere. If they are based on natural resources and assets, this will give them a unique selling point, but if they are offering the whole spectrum of global wellness products, their lifespan and appeal may be limited. This has already started to happen in Germany and Austria where there is an over-supply of (albeit top quality) wellness hotels and spas. Visitors have started to lose interest and are already searching for alternatives. The spa sector is growing exponentially in Asia, but this is perhaps at the expense of more 'organic' spiritual developments, for example Thai islands which were once backpacker havens and retreats are now becoming over-developed with spa hotels for package tourists, and it is only a matter of time before Goa in India goes the same way. On the other hand, in North America, Australia and Western Europe, there is something of a return to indigenous and spiritual traditions, for example, the largest growth sector in the United Kingdom appears to be holistic tourism rather than luxury spas, albeit in high quality retreat centres. The business market may well embrace the growing number of spa and wellness hotels offering stress management and life coaching workshops, but the leisure tourist may require something more reasonably priced and fun. As peoples' lifestyles become healthier, life expectancy increases, and the rate of serious illness decreases, it is more likely that wellness facilities will be visited for enjoyment and entertainment, rather than medical reasons.

Figure 12.5 indicates the interrelationship between spas and the other forms of facilities. It is anticipated that some sort of spa and spa treatments and services will be available in almost any health and wellness tourism, from mobile spas and residences through festival and cruises to clinics and hospitals.

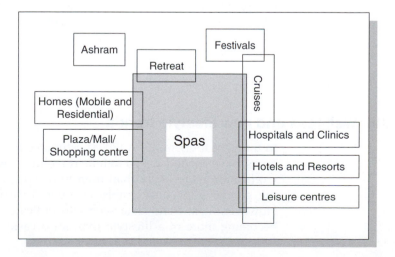

Figure 12.5
Inter-relationships between Spas and other Health and Wellness facilities. *Source*: Smith and Puczkó.

Future trends in Spa development and management

Given that spas and spa hotels and resorts are the main growth sector in all parts of the world, and that spa products are being exported everywhere, it is hardly surprising that the majority of industry research has been directed at spas. A summary of the top trends in spa development and management is offered here, which is based on several different sources. It should be remembered, however, that spas these days are incredibly diverse and tend to incorporate almost all aspects of health and wellness except perhaps surgery and the more esoteric New Age practices.

The spa industry is very strong in North America in terms of number and types of spas available. Because of their significance, there is a high number of spa trend forecasts for and from the North American market. This complex analysis is not typical for Europe or to any other continent, since the different forms of health and wellness facilities tend to be planned, managed and marketed separately. We, therefore, decided that although some of our forecasts are based on the North American trend-watches, we then developed them further.

From the list of main buzzwords Brown (2007) collected it is quite clear that the North American market is very different from other parts of the world. We can see services that are traditional elsewhere, but seem to be coming up in the United States and Canada (e.g. Frigidarium), but we can also see treatments that are almost unknown elsewhere (e.g. 'Metrospiritualiy').

Airport Spas	Frigidarium	Mineral Make up
Anti-aging	Holistic	Nanotechnology
Ayurveda	HRT for Men	Neurobics
Bespoke Spa Treatments	Hyperbaric Chamber	Peptides
Body Facials	Infrared Sauna	Self-Responsibility
Body/Mind/SPIRIT	Kids Spa	Sleep Medicine
Caldarium	Kinesis	Social Hydrotherapy
De-staffed Treatments	Laconium	Spa Butler
Energy Medicine	LOHAS	Spa Culture Tourism
Express Services	Metrospiritual	Tepidarium
TCM	Vibration Therapy	
Unplugged	Wellness	(Brown, 2007)

Health, wellness and new lifestyle trends

In terms of tourism, ISPA (2008) estimates that 63% of United States Spa-goers have visited a spa while travelling away from home. Although women are more likely than men to be spa-goers, spa travelling reduces the gender gap considerably as over 30% of spa travellers are male. However, most trend data seems to indicate that health and wellness is becoming more of a lifestyle than an occasional interest. Guests used to come to a spa once or perhaps twice a year for an hour or so. In the future, they will come more often and spend longer periods of time (Goldsmith, 2008). ISPA (2008) estimates that more than one in 10 spa-goers treat spa-going as part of a larger health and wellness lifestyle, and that more than 2 million spa-goers took part in lifestyle classes in 2005, which includes healthy cooking, achieving balance, and managing stress. Spas are therefore incorporating lifestyle elements, such as fitness, healthy nutrition and stress relieving techniques. This same trend is growing in much of Western Europe or Australia, too. However, other parts of Europe, Central and South-America, Africa or Asia may not have similar patterns, due to tradition, religion or different stages of economic development.

Some people from developed countries are even choosing to live in spas, which are adding residential components or spas are being built into gated communities and condominiums, especially in Florida, New York and Las Vegas. Singer and Monteson (2007) suggest that in the future, spas will be part of up-scale residential and country club communities, and will also be an essential element in mixed-use retail, commercial and condo-hotel developments so that people can enhance their quality of life and find more balance between work and relaxation, well-being, productivity and creativity. SpaFinder (2008) adds that parents will be keener to raise their children in an active, healthy, communal environment (and avoid the growing problems of childhood obesity and diabetes).

The other parts of the world, especially the developed countries, will follow these trends, especially regarding lifestyle changes. In many European countries or in Australia, for example, health consciousness (e.g. diet, exercise) has already peaked and is expected to remain at the same level. This will create a steady demand for health tourism products, however, not to the same extent for medical and wellness services.

Consumer needs and demand

People now expect more from spas and wellness centres than simply being pampered, and the main markets such as 'baby boomers', yuppies or stressed managers are increasingly seeing spa visits as a necessity and an entitlement rather than simply a luxury or vacation treat. 'Savvy Spa-goers are shaping the trends. Spa professionals want to create the best experience possible, so it's a "buyers' market" for consumers who express their wants and needs,' said ISPA President Lynne McNees. 'The spa lifestyle is in fashion, though it's also timeless. As a leading leisure industry, spas have the staying power similar to that of cruise lines, skiing and golf.' (ISPA, 2008).

The Spas Research Fellowship (2008) has shown that customers are likely to become more demanding, as they expect high quality treatments, impeccable hygiene, well-qualified therapists, and value for money. Customers are now much more 'spa wise' and know what their rights are regarding the wellness experience, consequently more litigation and legislation may be an inevitable consequence. Customers also desire experiences that are customized to their personal needs and desires. This includes tailoring products to different ages and genders, for example, as some 30% of North American Spa-goers are men, the demand for products and services designed specifically with men in mind is at an all-time high. Nearly 4 million teenagers have now been to a spa where they learn how to deal with stress, eat nutritiously and care for their skin. 16% of spas now offer teen programs, 34% offer packages and 17% offer for children. Women also want more time to bond with their friends away from family responsibilities and careers, so 'girlfriend' packages are on the increase (e.g. Hen parties and Birthdays). Mother and daughter getaways are also popular, as are mother and baby or family packages. Corporate wellness is also growing, and according to the American Journal of Health Promotions, for every $1 spent on wellness programmes, employers can expect a return of up to $10 through lower medical claims, reduced absenteeism, improved productivity and other factors (ISPA, 2008).

SpaFinder (2008) predicts the search for spa solitude will be trumped by the natural desire for community and a growing awareness that social interaction is an important aspect of health. Spas are already offering more opportunities for socialization, as 8% of United States Spa-goers say they use their time at the spa as an opportunity to socialize. Although many spas enforce silence and calm, the visiting of a spa is likely to become more of a social experience as it was historically (e.g. in Roman times). In Southern European countries it is more common to visit spas in groups and to enjoy the social interaction. The same is true in saunas in countries like Finland and Russia, where major life events were traditionally celebrated. Although many visitors go to spas alone to get away from their everyday routine, there is a growing number of visitors who travel with others, for example, couples for a romantic break; families to enjoy mixed facilities; pre-marriage 'stag and hen' parties enjoying weekend spa breaks; business tourists with colleagues, etc. In holistic centres, one of the major motivations for many of the tourists (the majority of whom travel alone) is to meet like-minded people and enjoy a sense of community. Medical tourism, however, may follow different patterns. It is likely that medical therapeutic tourism more likely has a social element, especially that treatments, therefore the stay can take weeks. Patients travelling for medical surgical reasons may not want an audience (e.g. for a body shaping operation), but in the case of other types of surgery (e.g. dental) it can be a good thing to have moral support from a relative or a friend.

Motivations for visiting spas or wellness centres can vary greatly according to the age, nationality, lifestyle, or gender of a visitor. Although stress relief seems to be the number one reason for going to spas currently, there is also a rise in the number of women having anti-aging cosmetic treatments, even surgery, and healthy nutrition, diet and weight loss are becoming more and more important. Fitness and exercise have always been significant for health and wellness (e.g. a major focus in Greek and

Roman times), but trends vary considerably and are based very much on leisure patterns. For example, the high impact aerobics and circuit training of the 1980s and 1990s has gradually been superceded by activities like yoga or Nordic or Masaai walking. In a few years, the trend may come full circle or favour new activities. Facilities need to be aware of popular leisure trends and achieve a balance somewhere between orthodox medical services and pampering to be competitive, it seems. Although the No. 1 treatment continues to be the Swedish massage, treatments that use two or more therapists are also seen as being on the rise and different massage techniques are becoming better known (e.g. Thai massage, Indian Ayurveda, Hawaiian Lomi Lomi).

Medical tourism has been and remains very much dependent on external financial resources, for example national or private health insurance. Most of therapeutic and surgical treatments are at least co-financed by an external body. This leaves medical tourism very much vulnerable to the economic, social and political changes in every country. While in the United States we can see that corporate employers may consider including medical trips in the health insurance they pay for their employees, in Europe, state health insurance makes attempts to decrease its involvement in financing medical trips.

The major tourist flows of health and wellness tourism, besides domestic and intra-regional tourism (e.g. within Arabia), are likely to follow that of mass tourism:

- From North and West to the East – from Western Europe to Central and Eastern Europe and to South-East and Far-East Asia
- From 'Down Under' to South-East
- From North to Central and South – from North America to Central and South America.

Facilities, services and experiences

Singer and Monteson (2007) predict that spas will pay more attention to creating better facility areas that are more like experiential, self-service treatment areas rather than amenity areas. Spa playgrounds can include aromatherapy steam rooms, environmental saunas, air jet colour therapy tubs, specialty hydro-massage showers, reflexology water walks, relaxation meditation pods, product bars, aqua massage tables, foot massagers, spa 'toy boxes' with a variety of mind-challenging and entertaining puzzles and games, etc. This will appeal to the 'spa virgin' who wants a safe environment, as well as the 'spa veteran' who wants something more than a basic facility area which typically consists of a steam room, sauna and jacuzzi. Spa design will also need to include a variety of accommodations for two or more people as spas become more social. Versatility and flexibility in design and programming will be critical in order to meet the needs and interests of the various markets who visit the spa for everything from privacy to partying and from a 'time-out' to a 'work-out'.

Spas will also need to focus more on hospitality. Spa staff needs to be 'experience makers' and 'memory makers'. This can only happen with customized, personalized service where there are signature WOW moments and features in every area of the spa. Spas do not need to offer a whole spectrum of world-wide spa treatments since this can create stressful decisions for the guests, inadequate training for the staff and too much money tied up in product inventory. It is better to do a few things very well and create your signature touches rather than think that 'more is better'. (Singer & Monteson, 2007).

Spas are also likely to go mainstream in order to attract a wider range of people and not just the wealthy. Treatments and pricing need to be adjusted accordingly, offering simpler, more affordable services. This represents a shift from pampering and luxury to help and healing or leisure and relaxation. If necessary, separate facilities can be created as they were in the past, although this can be considered élitist creating an 'us' and 'them' situation. The idea of a 'hybrid spa' is a resort-based spa that attracts a variety of markets in order to maximize its appeal, profitability and yield management potential. It could appeal to conference guests who would like a la carte treatment, as well as leisure guests who have more time for a half day package or a mini break. It can also be used by the local community for an hour or a full day, perhaps offering them a membership scheme.

Product development and extension

Dosh (2006) refers to consultants' and PricewaterhouseCoopers' opinion that spa treatments have overtaken golf as the most popular supplementary activity during corporate meetings and events, especially in the United States. Resort Spas experienced that as much as half of their current customer base is coming from corporate groups. Based on this trend some forty percent of new luxury and upper-upscale accommodation projects under development include spa facilities according to PricewaterhouseCoopers. The popularity of spas has come at the expense of golf and other activities. It is believed that golf was largely a male sport, whereas spas can be more inclusive. Furthermore organizers of conferences and meetings found that spas were a good way of boosting attendance and motivating staff. It should be noted that although spas may seem to be attractive and new to the MICE market, not everybody likes to be dressed down to swimming costumes in front of their colleagues and bosses! This can result in a relatively high percentage of 'no-show' for corporate events.

In addition to the growth of spas in business and conference hotels, there is also a development of wellness treatments in the transport industry to make travellers more comfortable and recover from their journey more quickly. This service is most likely to be used by business travellers or those who can afford business or first class travel.

Case Study: British Airways Travel Spa (at Heathrow Airport, London)

Elemis travel spas

Flying can be an exciting and exhilarating experience, and to make sure you enjoy your journey with us to the full we do everything we can to ensure your wellbeing and comfort. To help give your skin and body the best possible protection we have teamed up with luxury British Spa and skincare brand Elemis, who will be offering spa therapies and inflight skincare products to rejuvenate your skin, awaken your senses and refresh you on your journey.

Spa therapies

Elemis has designed an exclusive British Airways menu for both men and women. Departing customers (e.g. First passengers) can benefit from treatments designed to aid sleep and relaxation, whilst therapy for new arrivals will leave you feeling re-awakened and energized.

Shiatsu Power Back Massage – select from a choice of three uniquely developed massage sequences combined with 'Elemis Touches' performed by an Elemis Spa Therapist on a luxury massage chair.

Intelligent Massage Chair – select from a choice of three exclusive programmes and with the minimum of fuss you are left in peace.

Intelligent Massage Chair with Elemis Spa-Therapy – select from three exclusive programmes complimented by your choice of one of the following treatments:

- Soothing Scalp
- Flying Feet
- Arm and Hand Hydrator
- Anti-Age facial Reviver
- Tired Eye Reviver

(British Airways, 2008)

The Spas Research Fellowship (2008) describes the expansion of specialized and niche product treatments, for example the development of water-based cures. Although this is something traditional for many cultures and societies, it is relatively new for others (e.g. North America). Spa-goers are also craving more indigenous treatments (Goldsmith, 2008), and prefer the use of natural ingredients. The spa industry, together with pharmaceutical companies and cosmetic brands, will continue to lead innovation in skincare with new technologies and programmes that recognize that beauty is much more than skin deep. Consumers will become more aware of anti-aging foods rich in antioxidants – such as berries, dark green leafy vegetables, salmon, and nuts – as well as a new generation of clinically enhanced skincare products (SpaFinder, 2008)

Spas are also responding to reports from the restaurant industry that the gastro-travel, or in our context, the spa cooking phenomenon has taken off with more people organizing holidays around food. In fact, 19% of United States Spas offer cooking experiences (e.g. lessons and courses), and 51% of

United States Spas offer educational programs and nutritional consultations, 40% offer healthy eating classes, 26% have educational offerings on obesity or weight gain issues and 17% offer exercise programs for children and teens (ISPA, 2008). Detoxing is also a growth development with more people turning to spas and retreats for a range of detox solutions (SpaFinder, 2008).

Fusion treatments are becoming more popular, such as Thai yoga massage (a fusion of yoga stretches and massage), Watsu (water and shiatsu), yogalates (yoga and Pilates) or Aquaveda (hydrotherapy and Ayurveda). Many resorts spas and retreats are also offering 'speciality' weeks in, for example, yoga, sexual health (e.g. tantra), or medical concerns such as easing arthritis or quitting smoking. Healthy sleep also joins exercise, nutrition, and stress management as a main focus of wellness programmes and spas. Hotels and resorts are putting greater emphasis on creating ideal sleep environments using minimal light and sound, offering a 'pillow menu', aromatherapy, and relaxing spa treatments. At destination spas, sleep specialists can help educate, diagnose and treat sleep apnea, insomnia and other disorders (SpaFinder, 2008)

Spas are incorporating technology such as Wi-Fi in relaxation rooms, cyber treatments that combine biofeedback technology with guidance from wellness professionals and light therapy to help those suffering from depression, Seasonal Affective Disorder and insomnia. In addition, new and pioneering therapies are being developed, for example Sound Therapy, Sensory Deprivation (ISPA, 2008).

Delivering services

The Spas Research Fellowship (2008) suggests that new ways of delivering services are likely to be developed in the future. For example, mobile spas have expanded in the United States and are frequently used for parties, office workers, etc. Cruise ship spas (and even hospitals on sea) are becoming more common. Spa treatments could be given whilst people are flying long-haul (e.g. massage or yoga stretches). Spas could provide retirement (holiday) homes for the elderly or day-care services for children. It is even suggested that pet spas could be developed, which is not unusual considering that animal massage and aromatherapy already exists! Spa touches can be used to enhance almost any environment, especially those which are linked to the leisure and tourism industries (e.g. transport, hotels, entertainment venues, shopping centres, etc.). It is also becoming more common for clients to enjoy 'destaffed' centres, for example, Kuyum at Ojai Valley Inn and Spa in California, where same-sex groups of eight can cover themselves in mud in a heated room and experience a guided meditation with a pre-recorded voice (SpaFinder, 2008).

As discussed already, although it is not tourism, many people would like the spa lifestyle to permeate their everyday lives and not just be a holiday treat once a year or less. This might mean visiting or inviting a therapist on a regular basis, learning self-massage techniques, setting up a small yoga studio in the home, installing pools, hot tubs, saunas or jacuzzis.

Case Study: Home Spa

The concept of 'home spa' is very new even to its homeland, that is North America. Home spa means in fact that customers do not have to visit a spa, it comes to their home and 'turns the living room into a luxury hotel'. For example the founders of Green Bliss Eco Spa (2008) believe that everything in life is connected: people, business, and community. The health of each is dependent on the others. Green Bliss is dedicated to providing its customers with an opportunity to renew their spirits and nurture their innate, natural beauty without exposure to the harsh chemicals and invasive procedures practised by other, more traditional spa service providers. They strive to use the most ecologically sound methods to treat and educate their clients while keeping pace with the newest trends emerging in the green and holistic lifestyle movement. Equally important is Green Bliss's dedication to creating and promoting a model for community-based, environmentally responsible business practices. They use products that are Organic and sustainably harvested when possible; from local artisans and craftspeople, from owner-operated, or small business interests and from vendors who engage in fair trade practices.

Customers can enjoy the following home spa services:

- Therapeutic massages
- Skin care and facials
- Hand and foot pampering
- Global body treatment rituals
- Wellness and holistic living packages
- Pregnancy and postnatal treatments and services.

Gurk (2008) describes how in Britain, a company of 200 or more so-called 'Chillers' work for Urban Chill in London and Brighton and service up to 3,000 people a week in pubs and bars. For example, massage is used to ease post-work stress. There is also a nightclub in Dublin called 'Spirit' which 'combines holistic treatments and hands in the air hedonism'. Three dance floors are complemented by three rooms named Body, Mind and Spirit which offer Indian head massage, reiki, deep tissue massage, aura photography and tarot card readings. It is supposed to indicate that people do not need drugs to get high, especially that the 'ecstasy generation' are now in their 30s. Spirit is now the biggest club in Dublin, and the owners have set up a New York version and plan to open seven similar nightspots across the globe, including Cape Town, Sydney, Rio de Janeiro, and Athens.

There appears to be a general expansion of the media alongside that of the health and wellness industry, such as web-based information sites, journals, informative books, CDs for home instruction, chat rooms, and even 'spa friends' on line (90% of North American Spa travellers plan trips using a web site (SRF, 2008). Online retreats and wellness programmes are becoming more and more common. For example, the United Kingdom Kundalini yoga teacher Siri Datta runs regular 40-day online programmes which begin every other New Moon. These online E-Retreats includes: Raw Foods, Kundalini Yoga and Meditation, NLP, and Exercise. Its purpose is 'Spiritual Weight loss of all kinds!' (Anaharta, 2008). The year 2008 is also the Alpro Year of Wellbeing. People are invited to sign up to the website, fill in a detailed online questionnaire about their current state of wellbeing, read articles which are posted by experts, discuss issues in an online forum, and are sent daily hints and tips on how to remain healthy, happy, and balanced.

We can expect that those who log-on to an e-retreat or use a home spa service more easily become health and wellness tourists, than those who do not follow any of these new services.

Examples of Hints and Tips from the Alpro Soya Year of Wellbeing (2008)

Monday 14th January
Notice and compliment positive gestures of others.

Tuesday 15th January
Save water by growing drought-resistant plants such as sedums and lavender, using a watering can rather than a hosepipe and watering early in the morning or in the evening.

Wednesday 16th January
Build up to your 20 minutes of continuous vigorous activity slowly, for example start with a gentle walk doing moderate activity and then after 10 minutes pick up your pace so that you feel challenged for 5 minutes. Slow back down to a moderate level to finish. Repeat this each week, increasing the challenging section by 1–3 minutes each time until you have finally reached 20 minutes.

Thursday 17th January
If you find yourself in a challenging situation, think of a time you were successful in solving a problem before. What did you do? Can you learn something from this example and apply it to your current problem?

Friday 18th January
You don't have to completely cut out fat-containing foods to have a healthy diet, but do keep an eye on portion size. Cheese comes in all shapes, sizes, tastes and textures and is a wonderful food but can be bad for you in excess. If you are a cheese fan, slice it thinly and eat in small amounts with some fruit. Remember a piece of cheddar the size of a matchbox will contain 30–50% of your recommended upper limit for saturated fat intake per day.

Saturday 19th January
Vigorous activity is any movement that raises your heart rate and breathing to a point where you no longer feel you can talk for more than a couple of sentences at a time. Vigorous exercise should however still be 'manageable' at this level, that is you should feel as though you can keep it going for at least 20 continuous minutes.

Sunday 20th January
If you give feedback (positive or negative) to others, refer to the action rather than the person and be sincere. Feedback is more likely to be accepted when it is specific, includes examples, and when those involved can do something concrete about it.

(Alpro Soya Year of Wellbeing, 2008)

Business development

Singer and Monteson (2007) suggest that there will be greater recognition of the business development potential of spas, and that developers will be willing to commit the financial resources for a turn-key spa which includes everything from the building to the training. This means that spa directors will need to be business managers, motivators, and marketers, or they should work together with a team of experts representing all these skills and experiences. It has been seen many times that self-made businesses did not achieve their full potential because of lacking managerial or marketing skills. Only charismatic leaders or gurus can build their business on themselves. Even in their case, the one-man-show often works for a short time only.

There needs to be some realism about how expensive it is to build and operate a spa, especially in terms of the return on investment. The main rule of thumb in spa development is that without more than 50% of demand available locally (with the exception of luxury branded or designer spas) it is not possible to manage a facility successfully. A good awareness of how to sell spas to the tourism market especially business and conference tourists can be a real advantage. There will be increased corporate investment based on added value to an existing enterprise, last seen in the expansion of the worldwide golf industry. In golf developments a signature golf-course, that is a course designed by a leading architect or a famous player, can mean a competitive advantage. It can be expected that spas will copy what we can see in the golf industry and in the case of museum developments (e.g. consider the Guggenheims!). Leading architects will create their own 'signature spas' and visitors will be lured (e.g. Mountain Oasis Spa (Tschuggen Bergoase) designed by Mario Botta, Arosa, Switzerland or Frank Gehry's 'City of Wine' hotel and spa in El Ciego, Spain.

Now corporations are attracted to the added commercial potential of spas, with the potential to enjoy income from more opportunities to charge for services, annexed to existing commercial infrastructures (SRF, 2008). It is estimated that there will be corporate consolidation of more powerful operators giving a distinct marketing barrier for new entrants at the top end. Alongside this the small businesses will continue to expand in numbers providing a distinct personalized local service. This will create greater market segmentation (SRF, 2008). As a means of generating income through private finance, there may be spa timeshare and joint ownership deals to produce venture capital. There may be mega-spa developments in destinations like Las Vegas and Dubai. There will also be more franchising of spa facilities to a specialist operator with the development of stronger branding for the spa itself rather than the products that it uses. Brands that are known for their chic designs are opening spas around the world. Some of the well-known brands include the first Armani-branded spa in Tokyo, Versace Group's spa at its Australian resort, spas at Bulgari's hotels in Milan and Bali, and Prada Beauty's line exclusively at Ritz-Carlton properties.

There are also concerns about the future of the spa industry in its classic form as part of a comprehensive health system. However, there is also talk of a renaissance in which the spa industry becomes a fixed component of the hotel trade. With a decline in state subsidy and interest in medical tourism, spa hotels and cure resorts may no longer be able to attract long-staying medical visitors and therefore have to focus on short-term wellness visitors instead. Although these may be higher spending, the numbers are likely to be much smaller. On the other hand, the spa industry is becoming a component of hotel services on a global scale and this seems to be the largest growth sector. Hotel chains are rapidly adding spa facilities, and 'spa brands' are being franchised. On the one hand traditional spa hotels will face stiff competition from new developments, while on the other they could capitalize on the fact that consumers already consider spa services to be standard offerings and that these consumers have become accustomed to them and are familiar with individual procedures. The traditional facilities are attempting to set themselves apart from the competition and maintain a hallmark of exclusivity in various manners such as employing the appellation of 'medical wellness' certificates, and so on (Visit European Spas, 2008).

Interestingly, Switzerland, one of the countries with the highest prices, recorded a surprisingly positive trend and increase in demand in recent years. Emphasis has been on services and quality. Spas in Great Britain and Ireland are also growing rapidly. They are typically five-star resorts. In addition to a high level of luxury they are accompanied by high levels of professionalism and proven treatment concepts.

However, all health and wellness businesses need to be careful. The market appears to be saturated in some locations and the flow of services and new ideas is slowing, and many trends in tourism are going in a single or opposite direction. For example, there are already concerns in Germany (the largest wellness market) about a saturation of the market. Although 'curiosity' about wellness is on the rise, many services and products are used very seldom, and low-cost providers force further price reductions. The Austrian market also appears to be full. According to estimates from the Institut für Freizeitwirtschaft (The Leisure Time Institute) there has been a reduction in the demand for wellness products by German and local visitors. At the same time Austria has the highest number of per capita providers. In 2004 and 2005 a total of 80 new 'wellness' hotels were opened in Austria; the number of these facilities in the country is now around 750. The trend reached its zenith during this boom but now there are serious concerns amongst hotel owners (Visit European Spas, 2008).

However, the quality of wellness developments were so high in Germany that experts from the German organization Deutscher Wellness Verand have been invited in recent years to serve as advisors for countries developing wellness services and facilities. This organization promotes unified quality standards for wellness products. The group has already helped create standards in neighbouring Poland, Russia, and Slovenia. For example, a Gran Canaria Spa & Wellness project was launched; an initiative which includes 14 facilities and is financed in part by the European Union (EU). A similar association of 16 wellness hotels was also created under the common name of 'body.mind.madeira' on the island of Madeira.

As discussed in Chapter Six, spas and wellness facilities are growing quickly in some regions of the world, for example, Central and Eastern Europe, Asia and the Middle East. For example, Poland and Hungary have built up a large wellness industry over the last few years. Many wellness centres and facilities for health holidays have been created with the use of EU development funds. Competitive pricing is one of the main attractions, therefore many German and other Western European tourists take advantage of this. Traditional spas have largely been modernized by private companies and it is estimated that there will be annual growth of 45–50 providers over the next few years. Slovakia has also been highly praised for professional marketing and favourable prices. Thanks to this, the country recorded an increase in demand in recent years which exceeded that of the Czech Republic. The Slovenian government has also invested significantly in wellness tourism and provided substantial support to the development of infrastructure related to the industry. Hungary is also taking advantage of its position with its 2008 'Year of Waters' campaign:

Case Study: Hungary – The Year of Waters (2008)

Every year the Hungarian National Tourist Office aims to motivate domestic tourism by introducing a yearly campaign. After the Year of Green Tourism in 2007, in 2008 one of the most attractive tourism features of the country, the 'Waters', that is thermal and fresh waters are in focus. During the campaign they emphasize different areas and try to entice tourists with special offers and programmes. Amongst the natural resources of Hungary the healing spring water and thermal water are especially important. On the international scale Hungary is among the top five countries that have the most thermal water (together with Japan, Iceland, Italy, and France). The natural assets based on which the campaign is built are:

- 1,372 thermal water springs
- 385 settlements with either thermal or healing baths
- 221 certified spring water sources and 203 healing water springs
- 13 health resorts of Balf, Bük, Kékestető, Lillafüred, Balatonfüred, Debrecen, Eger, Gyula, Hajdúszoboszló, Harkány, Hévíz, Parád, and Zalakaros
- 56 certified medical hotels
- 66 certified thermal and medical baths (9 of which are in Budapest)
- 5 medical caves
- 5 sources of healing mud
- a mofetta (dry CO_2 bath).

(Hungarian National Tourism Office, 2008)

The growth of the Asian Spa is likely to be between 30% and 60%, annually, for the next 5 years (Asia Spa Festival, 2007). There are efforts to retain local architectural styles as well as indigenous and traditional products. According to SpaArabia Magazine (2007) five trends are shaping the spa experiences in the Arabic world. These are: wellness (procedures that used to be primarily cosmetic now reconfigured as healthful), spa food, authenticity (by evoking regional traditions), masculinity (making spa packages and décor more appealing to men) and elements of fun.

Sustainble health and wellness tourism

Consumers are now factoring in a spa's green commitment when they choose a spa. Both spas and spa consumers are getting serious about terms like 'natural','organic', 'holistic', 'green', 'eco-friendly', and 'sustainable' (SpaFinder, 2008). There are already concerns about issues of sustainability of spas and wellness centres, including the implications of global warming and environmental issues such as water shortage and the recycling of water (SRF, 2008). Many spas are making efforts to become more environmentally conscious, which is also good for business. Spas are positioning themselves with more green products, for example:

- Many skincare companies are getting rid of paraffins and sulphites
- More and more natural ingredients are used in treatments, such as local plants, herbs, and fruits
- Using solar lighting
- Recycling and purifying water flowing into ponds and waterfalls
- Using recycled flooring or furniture
- Using 'waterless' urinals and recycled toilet paper
- Use of non-toxic substances for varnishes and interiors
- Soaps without phosphates, etc.

It is estimated that 76% of United States Spas apply environmentally sustainable practices, and other spas around the world are following suit (Goldsmith, 2008). Holistic retreat and yoga centres are usually environmentally friendly with on-site organic gardens which are sometimes tended by visitors themselves and products made from local ingredients. The main concern, however, has remained the same: how to manage thermal and medical waters in a sustainable way?

There also appears to be a big shift in the sustainability movement in the luxury hospitality world. Such brands as Four Seasons, Hyatt, and Marriott have all made firm environmental commitments, and some Leading Hotels of the World properties donate fifty cents per guest per night to help offset their carbon footprint. The Asian Shangri-la and Banyan Tree hotel chains have opened branches in North America and will also raise the bar in terms of social and environmental responsibility (Goldsmith, 2008). The Little Green Book for Spas is also available from Six Senses providing recommendations on how spas should operate in a more sustainable way.

Case Study: Perfect Earth Tours Spa and Resort

Perfect Earth Tours Spa and Resort in the Yukon territory in Canada describes itself as the world leader when it comes to the combination of Eco Spa luxury and sustainability, offering an uncompromising stand on ecological awareness and first class customer service and appreciation. It is described as

> 'a luxury wilderness resort that also specialises in culinary extravaganzas and soft wilderness adventures. Being aware and compassionate towards our environment does not necessarily mean that one has to forego all the fun and luxurious aspects of life, but times have changed and we no longer can live and take holidays as if there is nothing wrong......we also believe that most of us have worked hard at whatever it is we choose to do with our lives and every now and then would like to reward ourselves with an extreme personal experience that makes all the hard work worthwhile. We would also like to do this without having to possibly feel guilty about the environmental impact our holidays or reward trips have.

Perfect Earth Tours Spa and Resort therefore combines appreciation and protection of the environment within luxury surroundings to show that decadence need not be incompatible with personal and corporate environmental responsibility. This means only products that pass strict personal organic sustainability criteria will be allowed to be used. This includes the following principles:

- Support local organic businesses first.
- Buy organic within western North America if we can't find it locally.
- Use recycled products as much as possible.
- All of our bedding, clothes, furniture are made of some kind of organic material (i.e. hemp, cotton, silk etc.).
- Our vehicles run on Bio-diesel.
- Minimize the use of fossil fuel related items, with the goal of totally eliminating any use of fossil fuels.
- NO PERMANENT structures in the bush. Our entire resort is dismantled at the end of each season.
- NO TRACE resort, which means really no trace!
- Using only alternative energy sources at our resort and as much as possible at home such as solar, wind, geothermal, river and human power.
- 5% of your payment will be donated to a charity of your choice and another 5% of your payment will be donated to a local independent charity in the Yukon.
- If it is not good enough for our children, it's not good enough for us or our clients.

Despite the strict guidelines, the main focus is still on their client's needs and desires.

(Perfect Earth Tours Spa and Resort, 2008)

The Yukon region in Canada where Perfect Earth Tours Spa and Resort is located is building up a large number of health and wellness facilities, especially eco-friendly wilderness retreats with wellness centres. This is based on a comprehensive Feasibility Study for a Yukon Health and Wellness Industry (De la Barre et al., 2005). Other countries and regions (perhaps surprising ones) may lead the way for health and wellness tourism in the future. In theory, anywhere can develop health and wellness tourism, but in practice, only those countries, regions, sites and businesses with creative vision and commercial flair are likely to succeed in the long-term.

Conclusions

In this book we introduced and discussed the history, the most important drivers, resources and challenges of the health and wellness tourism industry. Concluding and synthetizing all arguments we believe that the health and wellness tourism industry will see the following development concepts:

- *Wellpitals* – the blend of hospitals and spas could produce a new phenomenon, a 'wellpital'. A wellpital offers various medical as well as wellness and spa services – without the hospital, clinic or sanatoria, or even a standard hotel feeling and image. This can manifest itself in either the form of an extended spa, modified hospital or even a cruiseship.
- *SpaLiving Environments* – no longer just a North American speciality, more people can enjoy the facilities of spas in their neighbourhood. People can move permanently, or temporarily (e.g. to a summer home) to spa lifestyle communities, which may give boost to time-share developments. Urban dwellers will also have similar services nearby, since more and more spas are developed around urban centres. Holistic and spiritual tourism is never for the masses and the commercialization of these services would just be an oxymoron. However, the application of spiritual and holistic treatments and approaches will become more mainstream, for example applying Feng Shui or Vasati to apartment developments.
- *Eco-Fit Resorts* – these spas or retreats would offer people the chance to relax and improve their physical and mental health through nature-based recreation in eco-friendly surroundings. This may include sports or fitness activities ranging from active adventure (e.g. jungle trekking, sandboarding in the desert) to light movement (e.g. gentle swimming or walking). Special nutritional programmes would also be designed using fresh, organic and local ingredients, and all beauty and pampering treatments would also use traditional and indigenous products.
- *Dreamscapes* – operators will look for new demand segments. In this search, young people and customers of luxury products and brands can

be very appealing for developers. The combination of luxury brands as well as hi-tech equipment, for example music, games or cinema with spas can attract these new segments. A Dreamscape as an experience factory would be a facility which has fantastic, futuristic or breathtaking architecture (signature spa) or location. They have at least one feature which could be described as one of a kind – that is THE largest, tallest, most spectacular, etc. They have the feeling of transporting visitors to another world and completely absorbing them.

- *MySpa* – this is more of a lifestyle trend than tourism related, but it can give some ideas to managers and developers, too. Technological development can provide spas, hospitals, etc. with very sophisticated solutions that give competitive advantage. Real time information about health status during a treatment or retreat can be used to make personalized recommendations. This can then continue after the stay, as an on-line customer care, or can even precede the visit. Guests are collecting more and more experience in health and wellness, and the competition is getting stronger. One of the solutions is to customize supply, that is offer a menu of skills and capacities, and then create something personal to every guest. Certainly, this needs more flexible management and communication, but it will definitely pay back. Gadgets, monitors, personal music players, and game consols will all appear in spas.

- *Hol-Life Retreats* – these are retreat-style wellness centres or spas where people will go for some time away from their stressful lives and workplaces to recover and refocus on themselves and their needs. These do not merely represent an escape from everyday life, however. Instead, people will undertake a number of courses, classes or workshops to learn how to manage and balance their lives better when they return home. This will include all aspects of life for example physical health, social interaction, work-life balance, emotional wellbeing, and spiritual needs.

- *WellWorking* – corporate employers and stressed employees will find the combination of working and well-being more and more necessary. Occupational wellness is no longer new to many western companies and employees (e.g. Google!), but it is expected to be one of the fastest growing forms, most of which is not necessarily tourism, though. As major companies base their human resources management on the so called 'cafeteria' system, when employees can choose from a menu or list of services and benefits they prefer – up to a certain amount a year. Fitness club membership is already among the menu items and we can expect health and wellness oriented trips and treatments to appear soon. In the United States, where health insurance is not compulsory, employers already negotiate to have medical surgical trips covered for the employees.

- *BudgetSpas* – spas almost without exception are expensive places, especially if no external financial support (e.g. for medical treatments) is available. This can and does close out many people from demand, that is those who cannot afford the entrance tickets to pleasure pools, saunaworlds, aquaparks, medical spas, and spa hotels and resorts.

The future localisation of major global concepts							
	Wellpitals	SpaLiving environments	Eco-Fit resorts	Dreamscapes	Myspa	Hol-Life Retreats	Well-working	Budget-Spas
Europe								
Northern			✓	✓	✓		✓	
Western		✓	✓	✓	✓	✓	✓	✓
Central and Eastern	✓						✓	✓
Southern		✓				✓		
America								
North		✓	✓	✓	✓	✓	✓	✓
Central	✓	✓	✓					
South			✓			✓		
Africa			✓			✓		
Asia								
Middle-East	✓	✓		✓			✓	
South-East	✓	✓	✓	✓	✓	✓		✓
Far East				✓			✓	✓
Australia, New Zealand, and South Pacific		✓	✓	✓	✓	✓	✓	✓

Figure 12.6
The Future Localization of Major Global Concepts. *Source*: Smith and Puczkó.

We can expect that following the trend of creating 'budget' versions of services (e.g. flights, hotels or cruises), soon we will see budget spas that provide the basic services for everybody, but then everything else has to be paid for separately, according to what people actually use (Figure 12.6).

Overall, it can be seen that the new trends in health and wellness tourism will be diverse and creative, with both local and global significance. Even those activities which have existed for centuries can be newly discovered elsewhere and packaged differently to new markets. The plethora of innovative developments around the world make health and wellness tourism increasingly competitive for businesses and endlessly exciting for consumers. The final section of this book demonstrates this diversity with a range of international case studies.

PART 3

Operational and management issues

Introduction

This section provides examples of many of the issues raised in Parts One and Two of this book. Although it is not possible to be comprehensive in terms of the coverage of all typologies of wellness tourism sites and destinations, many of the operational and management issues are similar, whatever the location. This includes some of the problems of renovation and regeneration; product innovation and diversification; marketing and promoting destinations; balancing global developments with local features; integrating ancient traditions and new facilities; attracting and mixing market segments; and managing health and wellness tourism businesses.

Renovation and regeneration of historic spas

Many historic spa towns or resorts have suffered from a decline in quality and popularity in recent decades and are facing stiff competition from new purpose-built wellness resorts or hotel spas. Although they can promote their unique heritage, the facilities are sometimes delapidated and in need of renovation, and service levels are often not as developed as they are in some of the newer facilities. This is especially true of many Central and Eastern European destinations, as exemplified in Petroune and Yachina's case study of Russia, which had a flourishing medical tourism sector for many decades, but which suffered from decline in the post-socialist era. A lack of coherent policies and state support has meant the decline of many facilities and services, insufficient modernization, and increasing competition from countries with a better level of quality and innovation.

Sonia Sibila Lebe's case study of Rogaska Slatine describes the oldest spa resort in Slovenia. There has been significant investment in the regeneration of the destination, but competition both within and outside the country has increased at the same time. Rogaska Slatine is also facing a common problem for historic medical spas, which is how to diversify the product to include more general wellness facilities, and to manage the different market segments this will attract. Accommodating medical visitors on the one hand, and wellness visitors on the other, is a challenge which needs to be addressed in terms of the design of facilities and in the promotion of the resort.

Nuno Gustavo's case study of Sao Pedro do Sul Thermal Centre in Portugal suggests that it may be possible to separate facilities for health and wellness tourists, but this is not always easy for spas with fixed structures and limitations on new buildings because of heritage conservation. Although in cities like Bath there has been a successful combination of old and new facilities, in towns like Spa in Belgium, the heritage spa has declined and fallen into disuse in favour of a completely new development. Melanie Smith's case study of Spa suggests that it can be detrimental to the future of an historic spa destination to create modern facilities which could be anywhere, at the expense of heritage facilities which are unique and characteristic of a region or country.

Many onsens in Japan are being redeveloped, and Tamara Rátz describes how some international visitors might be disappointed by the modern facilities that greet them on arrival at an onsen (e.g. concrete rather than traditional buildings, regimented rules and regulations rather than spiritual calm, shopping opportunities, etc.). Whereas Japanese visitors seek relaxation and leisure, visitors may expect a cultural heritage experience. Fortunately, many Japanese onsen are also being redeveloped in an elegant, refined, and traditional way.

Definitional problems arise again and again in the case studies of destinations which were previously medical facilities but are now hoping to attract wellness (i.e. leisure rather than health tourists). Labelling is clearly understood differently around the world, and whereas a CEE visitor would most likely expect a medical facility when visiting a spa, British or Americans would expect something more pampering and luxurious. Central and Eastern European countries are also facing problems of service quality in addition to the more general issues of decline and degeneration of resorts and their facilities. There is a need for improved training of staff and a more holistic and integrated approach to the visitor experience.

Raising the profile of health and wellness destinations

In some destinations, there is a problem with the location of spas and wellness facilities, which are often in relatively remote, inaccessible or unknown parts of the country. Although the destinations may be known by domestic tourists, international visitors may not have awareness of the existence of certain resorts or sites. This is true for example of Eastern Finland, as described by Anja Tuohino and Henna Kangas. The area is well endowed with lakes and natural resources, but it is a challenge to develop an attractive and innovative product based on lake wellness and to raise the profile of the destination as a result. In many countries, the former support of health tourism by the state meant that domestic visitation was guaranteed, and sometimes veterans of wars were even rewarded with regular rehabilitation visits to spas. However, as preventative methods of healthcare are increasingly embraced by governments with a subsequent decline in the support for curative holidays, and veterans are dying out, there is a need to attract new markets. Many of these may come from overseas, especially in countries where the levels of domestic tourism are declining as people prefer to holiday abroad. Research is needed to identify and attract new target markets, providing data for segmentation and cluster analysis. Tuohino and Kangas describe how the e-GOOD cooperation network is using research to identify new segments for Eastern Finland, in particular the Hotel Herttua, as well as helping to develop an innovative lake wellness product.

Veronika Joukes discusses the case of two spas in the relatively under-visited region of Northern Portugal. There has been considerable investment in their redevelopment as the government and investors hope to raise the profile of the region and its resources, and to create local employment. Sometimes it is a risky prospect to invest so significantly in health and wellness destinations where there is no guarantee of success in terms of return on investment through international tourism development. Spas are notoriously expensive to run and extensive marketing and promotion will be required to ensure that these resorts become well known and visited again.

Alon Gelbman discusses the problem of branding wellness tourism in the North of Israel, where promoting wellness is seen as a way of creating an image of exclusivity and prestige. Unfortunately, many of the businesses promoting wellness do not have the resources or facilities to technically call themselves a spa, especially smaller businesses in rural areas. It is notoriously expensive to run spas and to employ qualified staff, therefore the promise created by the image is often not matched by the actual offer.

Product innovation and diversification

As health and wellness tourism becomes more globally competitive there is a definite need to develop new and unique products to attract visitors. Although many hotel developments include spa and wellness facilities, these are arguably incidental for visitors and merely an added attraction. The exception to this is perhaps business and conference tourists, for whom wellness can be an added incentive when offered by their company as part of a trip. Rob Davidson's case study shows that there is a considerable growth in this form of tourism, and that companies are increasingly organizing meetings and conferences within spa hotels. Such hotels can offer the required level of quality and service for business tourists, with the added benefit of relaxation, pampering, and de-stress treatments which can enhance performance and motivation.

Those visitors who want to dedicate the entire holiday to health and wellness may choose their destinations and products more carefully, seeking unique resources, facilities, and treatments. Many locations may not have enough unique natural resources to differentiate them well enough from other destinations. In this case, they need to be creative in their product development. Ilja Castermans describes how one region of the Netherlands has developed a project called *Healing Hills* which focuses on medical tourism, but on recuperation rather than medical intervention. This differs somewhat from other medical tourism destinations which concentrate on the treatment or cure of visitors. In addition, Ilja describes another project called *Wellness in Luxury*, where Valkenburg will be made into a city of wellness and a wellness boulevard will be developed. This is a new and purpose-built development which is likely to include innovation in design, business development, and extensive stakeholder cooperation. The area in itself does not have any resources which would differentiate it from many other areas of Western or Northern Europe, so its future success is likely to lie in the degree of product innovation.

Sonia Ferrari discusses how the Luigiane thermal baths in Calabria, Italy represent an ideal opportunity for extending the tourist season by diversifying the product. Where there has been a traditional focus on therapeutic or curative tourism, there is a need to offer further attractions which are based on a wider concept of wellness. Although health resorts historically tended to offer some leisure and entertainment facilities, these were relatively limited as the focus was more on medical treatments. These days, the healthy visitor may have just as much interest in the local area, including the sea and beach, cultural attractions, food and drink, sports and nature as they would in the wellness facilities. This means that although the thermal baths can provide the necessary infrastructure for a comfortable and relaxing stay, the region can also promote its attractions to a whole range of new markets.

As discussed throughout the book, holistic tourism is also growing and there are numerous product development opportunities in this field, ranging from holistic retreat centres to yoga and meditation holidays. Chantal Laws explores the growth of holistic festivals, focusing in particular on the Big Chill Festival in England, the UK. This kind of event tends to attract a number of younger people who may not be drawn to traditional health and wellness products, as well as older visitors (e.g. in their 30s) who still enjoy music festivals, but who now welcome the chance to relax with holistic treatments and therapies at the same time. Although New Age tourism is viewed by many as being somewhat esoteric, alternative therapies and spiritual activities are once again on the increase, and festival spaces offer the ideal location for the exploration of different, innovative practices.

Roos Gerritsma discusses the growth of yoga tourism in the Netherlands (which is perhaps typical of western Europe). Here, yoga is becoming part of lifestyle enhancement, and people are increasingly discovering the mental and spiritual benefits of yoga as well as the physical ones. Although yoga is still mainly being practised by women, men, children, and people with work-related stress or physical problems are also discovering yoga. Not only are many different forms of yoga offered, but fusion activities are also being developed (e.g. body balance which is based on a combination of yoga, Pilates, and Tai Chi). There is also an intensification in the practice of yoga with all-day or weekend workshops, events, and holidays being developed.

Combining ancient traditions and new developments

Visitors are becoming more attracted by ancient traditions and are prepared to travel long distances to experience indigenous healing and natural products. Although many hotel spas now offer Ayurveda, Thai Massage, or Chinese medicine, some visitors prefer to visit the 'home' of such traditions. Jennifer Laing describes how the Peninsula Hot Springs development in Victoria, Australia is using indigenous Aboriginal products as well as natural resources to attract international visitors. The facilities for tourists are completely new, but the ancient resources and traditions have existed for thousands of years. Visitors are now more and more demanding and may require the high quality facilities of a luxury spa, but with authentic local products and treatments.

This can result in some problems of staff and facilities regulation and visitor protection. For example, Kevin Hannam discusses some of the problems of Ayurvedic tourism in Kerala, India, where many unlicensed practitioners are offering services to visitors who are unable to differentiate a high quality professional Ayurvedic centre from an amateur or unqualified one. Smith and Kelly's (2006) research in Goa also suggested that the regulation of holistic tourism in India is not seen as desirable by practitioners and not always necessary by regional governments. Although Ayurveda may not be the primary motivation for visitors to Kerala, it is a growing attraction and the destination's reputation and image could be damaged by this lack of regulation.

Tamara Rátz describes some of the difficulties of combining the traditional facilities and modern functions of Japanese onsen for both domestic and international visitors. Whereas domestic tourists may be happy with the sometimes stark juxtaposition of ancient traditions and modern developments, international visitors may be disappointed with the lack of cultural heritage experiences. They may consequently wish to visit some of the more 'hidden' and 'authentic' onsen in rural areas, but these can be difficult to access both physically and culturally. It is also the case that many Japanese see these onsen as a place to rediscover and reconnect with their identity, therefore their preservation is essential for the future of cultural continuity.

Sometimes ancient traditions are used as the underlying philosophy for a whole wellness concept, for example a hotel spa development. Jennifer Chan describes the way in which the Chi Spa at the Shangri-la hotel in Sabah, Malaysia, and in other parts of Asia has used Chinese philosophy in its design, treatments, and services. Signature therapies are derived from the Himalayas too, and although this may seem like a hybridization or a displaced offering, it gives a distinctly Asian flavour to the hotel spa, which uses ancient and indigenous traditions from the region.

Roos Gerritsma shows how yoga is increasingly being adapted and blended with other activities to create new forms which are more suitable or attractive for western markets. Yoga holidays are often based on a combination of traditional asanas and meditation with other activities such as nature-based, fitness-oriented, or creative activities. These tend to take place in southern Europe rather than in the traditional 'home' of yoga.

Diversifying health and wellness markets

Many of the case studies address the issues of diversifying markets, a key challenge for all existing and new health and wellness facilities. In a market which has traditionally been dominated by women and older visitors, there is a need to consider other segments, especially as some destinations are already reaching saturation point (e.g. Germany and Austria). Melanie Smith discusses how the new thermal centre in Spa is attracting more younger people and families looking for 'thermoludism' unlike the traditional baths which attracted older medical tourists. As discussed by Sonia Sibila Lebe, historic spas often have problems of mixing medical and wellness visitors, or old and new markets (e.g. older visitors seeking a cure and younger visitors having fun). Nuno Gustavo describes a thermal centre in Portugal which has partly solved this problem by separating the facilities for medical visitors and more general wellness visitors, but this is a major management challenge. Anja Tuohino and Henna Kangas discuss the problem of replacing aging markets, such as veterans, and encouraging new visitors to experience a relatively unknown location.

Rob Davidson describes the growing business and incentive tourism market, who are increasingly using spa and wellness facilities. As discussed earlier in the book, occupational wellness tourism is growing fast, and many companies are offering their employees the chance to enjoy spa and wellness facilities during conferences or meetings, or are even paying for their employees to have treatments or therapies. This can enhance staff motivation, improve productivity, and provide new opportunities for social interaction. It should be remembered that in ancient times, some of the most important business was done in spas!

Those people who welcome a more holistic approach to health will most likely be attracted to some of the newer health and wellness developments, especially spa hotels and destinations offering ancient traditions. The Chi Spa described by Jennifer Chan would attract those people who like a combination of a high quality experience and indigenous practices, who (in this case) are most likely to be incidental wellness tourists or business tourists. Kevin Hannam discusses the growth of Ayurvedic tourism in India, which is increasingly being enjoyed by everyone from package tourists to backpackers. Chantal Laws describes how older visitors are starting to attend holistic festivals and partly reliving the raves of their youth, but with a wellness dimension.

Managing health and wellness businesses

One of the main challenges for many new health and wellness destinations is how to manage their facilities and services. It is becoming more common for hotel chains to manage a string of properties across the world, but to give each one a regional or local flavour. For example, Jennifer Chan describes how the Shangri-la hotel chain makes use of Asian products and treatments to make its spas regionally or locally distinctive. Using international standards and regulation can give businesses the quality and professionalism required by many health and wellness visitors, who are becoming more demanding and discerning. Although this may lead to the same offer being available in multiple locations and thus a reduction in distinctiveness or uniqueness, it is sometimes important to regulate the profession. This is especially important in the case of medical tourism as discussed by Babu George in his case study of Apollo Hospitals in India. There are often fears that medical tourism may be unhygienic or unsafe, especially in developing countries. Kevin Hannam describes some of the problems of Ayurvedic tourism in India, which is generally unregulated. However, more contemporary medical tourism (e.g. surgery) is becoming more professionally organized. The Apollo Hospital Group makes use of the latest equipment, technology and training, and guarantees quality and safety. Although there are concerns that global networks may not care enough for indigenous populations, the advantages for the future image and reputation of the country as an international tourism destination arguably outweigh the disadvantages.

It is often difficult to manage spas and wellness facilities which are starting to develop new products and attract different market segments. Nuno Gustavo discusses the complexity of separating facilities for medical visitors and wellness visitors in a thermal spa in Portugal. This requires not only research on the different needs of visitors, but also the differentiation of spaces, infrastructure and models of management and communication. It is difficult for the kind of spa resort discussed by Sonia Sibila Lebe, which has an attractive heritage environment, but lacks modern facilities. There is often a need to compromise by building a number of new facilities which will lack heritage value, but which meet the standards required by international tourists.

Finally, Alon Gelbman highlights the problems of managing proper wellness facilities and spas, as they tend to be expensive and require considerable investment in qualified staff. As a result, those destinations which claim to be offering wellness or spa tourism, but actually have very basic or limited facilities, are competing with some very sophisticated operations, and as customers become more knowledgeable and demanding, this mislabelling will be less easily tolerated.

Heritage of spa and health tourism in Russia

Inna Petroune and Elena Yachina

Introduction

The large-scale development and popularity of spa resorts was a remarkable feature of the 20th century in Russia. Yet, in the 1990s this sphere was practically ignored by the market reforms. Neither the new Law on Resort Destinations, nor the hectic adjustments introduced were adequate to reconsider the spas' mission and operations in a new systems approach and to reroute health resorts' development into the appropriate health tourism industry. Domestic tourism was in a crisis in the 1990s, and the most notable decay was in the sphere of health resorts, though recreation at spas used to be the most popular purpose and motivation for travel until 1980 in Russia. Unfortunately, a lack of economic indices, social policies, political priorities and conceptual approaches have been a hindrance to health and wellness tourism development in the past. This case study outlines some of these issues further.

A history of spa tourism development in Russia

For the past 280 years Russia has been developing and advancing spa treatment. It was Peter the Great who constructed the first resort in Russia (in 1719 in the suburbs of Petrozavodsk in the Russian NW) and issued a Statement, according to which development of treatment facilities and spas became an item on the state list of priorities. Russian aristocracy supported the idea, and Russian resorts matched and even up-scaled the West European cure destinations in style and fashion. In 1917 there were 36 resorts in Russia, with 60 spas providing treatment with natural water springs, baths, and curative mud. Their total capacity was 3,000 beds. After the revolution the resorts fell under the rule of Narkomzdrav (Committee for Health Care). According to data of 1928, about 242,000 people per year enjoyed treatment at resorts in Russia. In 1940 there were 3,600 spas and rest homes in the Soviet Union with the total capacity for 470,000 guests. The Soviet government took it as a challenge to select and finance the most creative ideas for further development of national resorts.

In 1985 there were 14,000 spas in the Soviet Union, with the capacity of 2.25 million beds. From 1960 they were run by Trade Unions, different ministries, and state-led organizations. Before the 1990s health tourism was a half-social, and half-ideological programme, with highly subsided resort facilities and travel, and the Constitution rights of all citizens to enjoy leisure and recreational opportunities. The core concept of incentive (social) tourism was focused on travel to a health resort (called 'kurort'), where balneological and physiotherapeutical services were provided by a convalescent home or spa (called 'sanatorium') according to advanced methods and under guidance of research institutes and local Councils or local Administrations. The basic operational and occupational standards, administrative regulations and sanitary norms for spas and resorts were generated by the Ministry of Health, as the focus in incentive tourism was on rehabilitation and sound rest of the work force. The indispensable role of spas in Russian health service has always been based on rehabilitation of people who had suffered from a range of specified conditions and illnesses. During the 1990s particular attention was given to hydro-balneotherapy, for which there are well-established recommendations/prescriptions of spa types (climatic, or balneological, or local) and the desired season (depending upon specific manifestations and phases of a disease, the form of a disease, etc.).

The subsidies for travel to spas were provided to employees, workers, farmers, and their families by the state, by Trade Unions and other public organizations, by industrial enterprises and state farms, as a kind of social insurance, an incentive, or an allowance. About 80% of the Trade Unions' vouchers to spas and health resorts used to be distributed for free or at 30–70% discounts, but access to spas was available only for those who obtained doctors' corresponding recommendations. The spas, rest homes, boarding houses, and other types of facilities that provided treatment at resort destinations were funded from the state budget, so that they could pay attractive wages, re-equip, maintain and refurnish their premises, keep and design parks, beaches, sports venues, and use as much electricity, water and heating as they would think they need.

Two types of average package holidays at spas were developed by research institutes, with consideration of the two possible options for a standard holiday duration: either 12 or 24 working days. The two types differed by the methods of treatment provided: (1) a prophylactic course and (2) treatment procedures. Both types of the package holidays included:

- Transportation
- Insurance
- Accommodation (one bed) at a spa – the type and the standard of conveniences were determined by the Trade Union according to the rank of its member or according to availability of resources
- A complete individual diagnostic study, visits to specialist doctors
- Prescription and provision of a number of treatment procedures on site or at another location (all transfers were conveniently arranged)
- Three or four meals a day according to the prescribed diet
- A social programme (cinema, dancing, lectures, competitions, etc.).

As an outcome of privatization policies, the spas obtained different owners, that still neither possessed means nor adequate know-how to keep those huge estates properly. In 1997 the Russian Federation State Committee for Statistics reported that there were 5,327 spas left in Russia with the total all year round capacity of 493,100 beds and with the maximum capacity of 731,000 in high season.

In 1994 the State Committee for Physical Training and Tourism was entrusted by the RF Government with full authority and responsibility to serve as the state executive body maintaining and developing resort business in Russia. Yet, all spas and other resort treatment facilities are still referred to as prophylactic medical establishments regulated by the Health Ministry's statements and circular letters. The Bermuda triangle of problems includes three aspects – authority, providers, and facilitators:

1. The Ministry of Health Care has the authority to encourage health tourism as a scientifically grounded and socially sound service, but it does not have the providers (apart from a small number of specialized spas for children).
2. Whether the spas are economically autonomous, or are under guidance of some major companies, local administrations, ministries – there are numerous regulations imposed by the Ministry of Health, by the State Committee for PH and Tourism, by the owners, and by local administrations. The common trend is to spend seasonal revenues quickly, before taxes are levied. Shortage of funds and fear of commercialization explains why many spas have chosen to change their profiles – and there are less and less players in the field of health tourism.
3. The State Committee for Tourism is responsible for the overall tourism industry, it has a Department for Spas, and its mission is to guide and monitor, to facilitate resorts and spas in their development. But the main tourism facilitator has no adequate financing, while the proposal to the State Duma about introduction of 'holiday vouchers' as a kind of social insurance lacks justification of its suggested legal regulation. Besides, the Russians are only starting to get used to paid services in medicine, so there is generally cautious attitude to the idea.

The average occupancy rate at spas and resort facilities for a number of years ranged around 20–25%, while a 62% occupancy rate constitutes the marginal level at which reconstruction, maintenance, and re-equipment are feasible. By volumes of sales the main distributor of vouchers for spa holidays with treatment was the Federation of Independent Trade Unions. Other major agents included federal and regional welfare foundations, insurance organizations, ministries, and departments of social affairs. They organized and attended fairs of vouchers in Moscow, Sochi, Anapa, and other cities. However, spas prefer direct sales to end users and contracts with trade unions of bigger companies. They do not trust travel agents, who, as it is commonly believed, rip off the customers and ignore doctors' prescriptions of treatment at particular resorts in particular seasons. In Moscow less than 5% of travel agents were traditionally involved in the distribution of spa vouchers.

Weaknesses and strengths of health tourism in Russia

Throughout the 1990s Russian spas' major concerns were:

- Low occupancy rates, seasonality, expensive maintenance of premises
- Extreme competition within the spa sector and across the hospitality industry in their own resort destinations
- Discrepancy between subordination to owners and the regulations generated for years by the RF Ministry of Health, by the RF State Committee for Physical Training and Tourism, by local administrations
- The fixed pricing policies, the diminishing subsidies, the burdens of multiple taxation
- A lack of quality standards in hospitality and catering services for spas, while the health care quality control nearly levels spas with hospitals
- Outdated occupational standards at all levels, all of the existing qualifications, even those of administrative staff, are irrelevant to tourism and hospitality business, too little coordination in education and training
- Negligent role of spas in the destination's strategic management and marketing
- Poor information management and distribution, a very low availability of information technologies, no immediate booking practices
- Inefficient and fragile retail and wholesale methods, based mostly on direct sales.

Apart from the above-mentioned problem areas, there were negative impacts and troubles associated with the overall instability in the Russian economic, social, political, and legal environments. As a result, the capacities of spas, rest homes, boarding houses throughout the country declined, for example, between 1990 and 1993 the total number of beds at resort accommodation facilities decreased by 11% – from 1 million down to 0.89 million. During the same period the number of hotel beds outside the sector dropped by 59% – from 0.26 million down to 0.11 million (Burns, 1998).

However, the 1990s disposed a number of solid strengths and opportunities for spa and health tourism development:

- The centuries old fashion and even family traditions of the Russians for treatment at spas
- Wide public recognition of indispensable efficiency of preventive treatment methods applied at spas
- Accumulated medical expertise, achievements, and developments of national Balneology research centres
- Well-developed infrastructure and superstructure of resorts
- Consideration by the Ministries of positive experience of spa and health tourism abroad
- Association of spas at local and national levels within the sector and across the tourism industry
- Development of new occupational standards based on large-scale interviews in the industry conducted in 1998 within TACIS projects in Russia (TACIS EDRUS 9510 and TACIS BISTRO BIS/95/537/071), their consideration by the State Committee for Physical Training and Tourism, Ministries of Health, General and professional Education, Labour
- Application of the draft occupational standards in the development of spa modules and other health/tourism/resort-relevant modules by secondary, higher and further education and training pilot institutes.

Finally, Russian resort managers have recognized the objective of commercialization of their spas, the need to review the service practices and procedures to encourage and cultivate a hospitality service focus apart from medical and therapeutic objectives. Introduction of yield management principles, knowledge and skills of hospitality operations and product management, upgrading of accounting and sales should be included in a straightforward strategy of market development of spas and resorts, which would underpin their sustainability as health tourism facilities and turn them into a valid sector and a vehicle of the Russian industry of tourism.

Heritage of spas and the development of health tourism

The average age of spa customers is 30–50 years. About 40% of guests are regular clients. The most popular seasons are spring (when chronic health problems are acute) and summer (period of holidays and traditionally preferable season for travel in Russia). Spas offer tremendous discounts in winter, but because of low occupancy many summer conveniences do not pay back, and hence are not available. As Russian spas now have to face competition in the national market with outbound trips, standards of comfort will have to be urgently introduced at spas – to improve design and to upgrade services. This idea of introducing quality standards and quality marks was discussed within the Ministry of Health from March 1999, along with the idea of introducing new educational standards and new spa professions. Congress Tourism is being considered as a reasonable product of spas (at the moment about 80% of all major events in

Russia are brought to Moscow, while resorts will tailor more reasonable prices and environment for the meetings).

From the middle of the 1990s, there were four objectives on the Agenda of resort and spa associations and regions:

- Resorts and spas are to energetically take individual and corporate initiative to define ways of commercializing their business, making it profitable, as there is no return to the old command system of planning, management, and distribution
- Resorts and spas are to vary their products, including the products of adventure tourism, eco-tourism, congress tourism, as seasonality, low incomes and limited leisure time resources result in inadequate occupancy rates
- Associations of resorts and spas are to create reservation procedures and marketing based on Information Technologies, those are to be of two types: providing for information and data bases and providing for trade
- Associations of resorts and spas, together with research centres and education bodies are to create a bank of medical and spa treatment methods, which are most popular, so that this bank could be the foundation of the core product development.

The Health Spa Resort Rogaška Slatina returning to its past glory

Sonja Sibila Lebe

This case study is dedicated to Rogaška Slatina, the oldest spa resort in Slovenia, situated in the south-eastern part of the country, where several hot springs have been discovered and used by locals for centuries. Such sources can be found in several places in Central and Eastern Europe, out of which some proved to be not only warm (thermal) but also healing because of a high concentration of different minerals they were holding. Using some of them, healing spa centres have been erected; great names of other European historic health spa centres are for example, Hévíz (Hungary), Karlovy Vary (Czech Republic), or Baden Baden (Germany).

In the glamour era of European healing spa resorts Rogaška Slatina was known for hosting the European aristocracy, even the K&K emperor family. The cited centres were known for their convalescent and preventive medical treatments and for their exquisite entertainment. Concerts, theatre performances and casinos prevented guests from getting bored. Large parks were an important place for the social life, offering several walking paths but also some hidden corners with benches that allowed undisturbed chatting.

A spa was the best place for a rich widower to find a young wife from a good family or for a rich young widow to find a new, perhaps aristocratic match. Several marriages rooted in a 'cure stay' and in German even a special word has been invented for a gentleman who found the lady of his choice in a spa resort: Kurschatten, meaning 'the spa-shadow.'

The Second World War and the time after it brought severe changes for the Eastern part of Europe: once glamorous spas were converted either into places for the army officers and high rank communist party officials or into remedy places for 'the working class.' Glamour and luxury vanished soon from both of them. As there was no investment into the development of infrastructure, the spas slowly turned into pure medical establishments with a rather poor lodging quality. Even in western European countries spa resorts became more or less an attachment of the medical system, becoming thus less and less attractive for tourists. In several countries the word 'health spa resort' has become synonymous with lower quality hotels with (good) medical services (United Kingdom, Ireland, Scandinavian countries etc.). The clientele has changed completely: today the main segment of visitors in European health spa resorts are convalescents, veterans or retired people who like staying in a well-priced hotel with medical assistance.

The picture fits to the orientation of the guild organization ESPA (Association of Spas and Health Resorts in Europe). Today, its president and her deputy are doctors – and the association is concerned with adopting the code of conduct of medical treatments in European spas – no words about market economy and offering the facilities to tourists.

The description of Eastern Europe fits very well with the situation in Slovene spas after the country became independent in 1991 and experienced a collapse of its heavy industry, followed by a huge unemployment rate. The government looked for solutions in restructuring the economy towards developing the services sector, including tourism. Large investments into tourism infrastructure, especially in the health spas resorts have been made. Their equipment became modern and attractive – and suddenly they were capable of attracting customers from the market who were paying for their stay in spa resorts by themselves (rather than staying there on the expenses of the insurance or veteran company). Over a period of 10 years, all Slovene spas have introduced different kinds of wellness programmes into their offering; this was the main reason why they have all decided to change their names from 'heath spa' into 'thermal wellness resort.'

Rogaška Slatina shares the described development. The place experienced a great history, being known for its healing water sources since Ancient times. The first scientific medical book on Rogaška Slatina and its healing water dates back to the 17th century. In the mid 19th century, the place was the most important holiday resort in the southern part of the Habsburg monarchy and the world's 3rd biggest supplier of mineral water. The next step increasing its popularity was a railway connection in the beginning of the 20th century and the opening of a crystal glass factory, where the work of glassblowers and glasscutters could be admired and where items reaching from simple drinking glass made of transparent glass up to luxury hand-cut items can still be bought. The 21st century brought a stand-still for around 50 years after World War II. Since Slovenia became independent, a great deal has been invested in the renovating and enlarging of the infrastructure.

Today, the core part of the resort is concentrated around a central park and a promenade, surrounded by several beautiful buildings (9 hotels) decorated in the imperial style. Although recently completely renovated and partly enlarged (integration of modern facilities like swimming pools and a congress centre), the architecture has preserved its Habsburg character and brilliance – and this is by no doubt the best decision made and should be recommended to any other resort. Rogaška Slatina is owned by three main parties – which cannot be noticed by visitors. Each group of hotels offers similar spa facilities: saunas, steam baths, jacuzzi, hydromassage, mud wraps, aromatherapy, solarium, large indoor heated pools, fitness suites etc. Covered walkways connect hotels of the same owner with a swimming pool; centres for relaxation as well as a fitness and beauty centre where tourists can try massages and baths. Guests can walk even in wintertime in warmed space from one building into the other either using the corridors under day light or heated subterranean walkways that lead past several small boutiques.

Using huge glass surfaces by renovating and at the time linking together all hotels of one owner has had a double positive outcome: firstly, the orientation became easier for the consumers and secondly, the environment has in a very agreeable way been incorporated into the building. It gives to the resort the flair of openness, almost of a seaside resort, which for sure represents one of the USPs for the resort and the hotel owner; it can be recommended to other hotels or resorts as a perfect architectonic solution.

Some common infrastructural changes could be introduced, like a covered drinking pavilion as common infrastructure has been added recently to make tasting and drinking of the famous magnesium-rich water more agreeable. All hotels are connected with the 'architectural shamespot': an excellent medical centre, which was built in the late 1960s, and does not suit visually the other buildings.

Some 10 years ago the management realized, that their clientele should be strictly divided into the guests coming as convalescents, who want more homelike living, including spending the whole day in their dressing gowns (and who are getting fewer) on the one hand, and on the other hand, guests coming as tourists who want to relax and have a premium leisure time, including full dress for noisy evening events. These two groups do not match at all. In order to make the stay for both groups as agreeable as possible, the spa centre in Rogaška Slatina began to invest in creating the possibility of separating both categories of guests physically from each other into the medical part on the one hand, where the stress is on good accessibility to the medical centre, on quietness and lower prices, and into an even higher concentration and variety of wellness programmes and facilities on the other hand.

The main visitor groups are tourists in 'mature age': 50+, coming today mainly from Italy, Austria, and Russia (about 70%). Only 5 years ago, the most numerous guests were visitors from Austria; the market is developing extremely swiftly and requires a maximal flexibility of the staff (learning additional languages, studying different habits and wishes of unique nationalities; often having to form little 'ghettos' in order to prevent unique groups disturbing each other, etc.). Most of the guests in Rogaška Slatina are asking for slimming cures, relaxing, beauty, sport, and medical programmes. The number of visitors who combine spa visiting with seminars and congresses, or others who just want to enjoy the mineral water and get some pampering (massages of different arts, wining and dining programmes etc.) is steadily increasing.

The strengths of the resort are its tradition, its healing magnesium water and the lovely architecture of the main hotel buildings, as well as the central park and the nearby famous crystal glass factory. The main weakness is still the lack of financing, which goes hand in hand with the split ownership and no interest of several different owners in investing in common infrastructure like building and sharing outdoor swimming pools – it might be described as the main barrier to bringing the place back to its past glory.

A big opportunity for the place is the great cuisine and delicious wines of the region. Within only a 100 km radius, the place has 4 international airports and a great cultural programme and heritage that can be visited. A motorway that will be built by 2012 will bring the place closer for car- and bus tourists. The major threat is seen in new layers of competitors, like Croat coastal hotels that started offering wellness programmes in the low season, as well as swift changes in leisure time patterns of traditional visitor segments.

The conclusion should address two different yet related problems which can easily be solved. In Slovenia all spa resorts, including Rogaška Slatina, are facing a specific problem: which expressions to use when promoting their offering in the global markets? In case they use the word 'wellness hotel' in the United States, it would be understood as a hotel with great sport and recreation possibilities. To use the word for the British and the Irish markets would be a mistake, too as 'wellness' seems to be a relatively underused word there. It would also be a mistake to promote their offer in the United Kingdom as being 'health spa resorts', as the completely renovated Slovene spa hotels with a great array of wellness offer are exceeding by far the level of health spa hotels in the United Kingdom or in Ireland.

In May 2007 Ryanair started its service from London to Maribor Airport, the closest airport to all the spas in Eastern Slovenia (including Rogaška Slatina). Not knowing how to describe their offer in order to attract the desired segment of visitors, the hotels have decided to promote themselves as 'hotels with great value for money in a lovely landscape with plenty of possibilities for active holidays.'

One suggestion is to find a common and everywhere understandable description of what is the meaning of 'spa hotel', 'health spa resort' and 'wellness hotel' – perhaps a home-work for the ESPA organization? We mentioned that the activities of the ESPA leadership are not economic- nor tourism oriented; therefore we suggest to urgently enlarge the ESPA organization (adding a new section?) through the wellness part of the offer and to search for a solution how to designate (label) different kinds of spa centres (classical health spa, wellness spa etc.) in order to mark clearly for the consumers what they can expect from each kind.

Regeneration of an historic spa town: A case study of spa in Belgium

Melanie Smith

The town of Spa is one of the oldest and most famous thermal resorts in the world. It is situated in French-speaking Belgium (Walloon region) on the fringes of the Ardennes. It was already known and appreciated by the Romans, it received famous guests such as Peter the Great, and it became so internationally renowned that in the 16th century the English language started to use the word 'spa' to refer to other thermal resorts. Specific geological conditions helped to create this resort development, namely the mineral and curative qualities of the waters, as well as the peaceful and green surroundings which were considered particularly conducive to health improvement and enhancement. From the mid 16th century onwards, the healing effects of the spring were confirmed (before that it was little more than a village in the woods), and this attracted numerous illustrious visitors. The first private spa institute was founded in 1764 and the first public one in 1820. Spa's heyday came in the 18th century when it was referred to as the 'Café of Europe' (Groote, 2008). 'Les Thermes de Spa' were constructed in 1868, encouraged by King Leopold II. The mineral springs were combined with entertainment, namely the Casino, as well as cafés and organized events. The architecture of the resort became distinctive, with the neo-classical building of the casino, impressive gardens, the Pouhon Pierre-le-Grand (the most important source in Spa) and its beautiful winter garden, the Galerie Léopold II and the Parc de Sept Heures.

After World War I, Spa started to lose its former grandeur as a destination well known to the international élite, and gradually attracted more of a mass market. In 1921 the Spa Monopole Company started to export its mineral water in order to create revenue for the town and promote its image. After World War II, the traditional focus on health tourism was broadened to include more general aspects of leisure. Although there was a growth in the number of spa visitors from 1950 to 1970, this was mainly due to the financial support offered by the social security system. Visitation declined again from 1987 when the social security system no longer funded thermal treatments, thus, the emphasis on leisure rather than medical thermalism started to grow. An agreement between Spa Monopole, Aqualis (Association of local authorities), and the Walloon Region was signed for the building of a new complex in 2001. The project was completed 3 years later on 30th March 2004, and was a successful public-private partnership. The thermal centre's management was entrusted to the French Group Ebrard Thermes, which specializes in the business of spas and health centres (Groote, 2008). The 19th century 'Thermes de Spa' were therefore no longer used.

The new thermal centre focuses on the concept of 'thermoludism' rather than medical or health tourism. Thermoludism is based on a modern, non-medical form of thermalism, which emphasizes relaxation and fun. This means that people go to the spa to rest in and enjoy the warm waters and not specifically to receive a healing experience. Facilities include a large indoor and outdoor swimming pool, jacuzzis, steam baths, saunas, treatment rooms, fitness facilities, and relaxation areas. As a result, less elderly people are visiting the spa and more younger people and families are coming. There are special 6 day programmes for mothers and babies, including a creche for children; programmes for couples; tobacco detoxification, and some traditional treatments, such as peat baths and carbonated copper baths.

Despite these and other attractive offers, competition from new, purpose-built health and wellness centres all over Europe means that travel to this particular thermal centre is not likely if there is a similar facility nearer to home. Although the spa is modern, there are fears that contemporary developments seem to become quickly out-moded in terms of design and facilities, which often have to be renewed every 5–10 years. In addition, there is little to distinguish such new buildings from similar developments elsewhere. There is also insufficient accommodation in the town (there are mainly two and four star hotels but almost no three or five star), limited car parking and poor transport links to other cities. Business and conference tourism would be a welcome addition to the market, but this is difficult without an improved infrastructure.

The tourism institutes in Spa such as the Observatoire Wallon du Tourisme, the Fédération Provinciale or the Maison du Tourisme have recently collected data and built tools to study and analyse their visitors, their expectations and needs. Survey responses for Spa 2006–2007 showed the following:

- The majority of visitors come from close by consisting of 60–65% Belgians, 35–40% are foreign visitors, mainly Dutch, and 2–5% are Germans, Luxemburgers, French, and English. 70% of visitors have been to the region before, often several times.
- The main clientele are couples without children or families with children or senior citizens.
- Seminar tourism is growing as many establishments have special seminar rooms, but there is little or no conference tourism.
- Another target is sports groups because Spa hosts a number of sporting events throughout the year, especially at the motor racing circuit of Spa-Francorchamps.
- 42% of visitors stay in hotels. Spa has 460 hotel rooms with a capacity of 2005 people, and a number of bed and breakfast gites for 85 people, a small number of family homes and campsites (bad weather tends to prohibit camping).
- The average length of stay is only 2–3 days, but day trips are decreasing.
- Tourists mainly come to discover nature, culture and to take part in festivals and sporting events connected to the Francorchamps circuit and the cure centre. It is important to offer a complete range of products relating to the wider area and its attractions.
- The tourist comes mainly to Spa with the proclaimed aim of enjoying well-being. This includes green leisure, spa cure and gastronomy.
- Recent studies show that 15.5% of visitors come for the spa cure centre; 15.5% to relax and take advantage of the peaceful area, and 3% for mountain biking; 20% for cultural visits and events; 25% for guided or signposted walks; 10% for gastronomy; and 12% for other reasons, for example, shopping, local life, family, etc.

Spa is described in a number of different ways in promotional literature, for example:

- Spa 'Pearl of the Ardennes' set in the green heart of Belgium
- Spa 'The Café of Europe' where the rich and famous used to meet

Word-of-mouth is considered the most important promotional tool, as 29% of visitors have been recommended by friends.

The main problems to be overcome in Spa are that wellness tourism is mainly seasonal with peak months in July and August, November and December, and some holidays in February and May. The length of stay of visitors is very short for a health tourism destination. The capacity of the new spa is limited to only 400 people per day and queues can be long on busy days and the facility is then hard to keep clean. Growth of visitors seems to be slowing down as competition from other places in the region increases, for example Aachen, Maastricht and Brussels. Some locals find the spa too expensive. There is also the perception that more exotic locations overseas (e.g. Morocco, Tunisia) are more attractive, with better weather and cheaper prices for the same kind of offer (even though the quality may not be so high). It is generally thought that the quality of other traditional European spa destinations like Baden Baden or Deauville far exceed what Spa can offer.

Renovation of the older part of town with its heritage buildings should be a priority if the town is to retain its uniqueness, character and appeal. Whereas 20 million euro could be found to develop a new spa facility, funds for regeneration of the old town have not been as easily forthcoming. This is partly because other areas in the region of Wallonia are suffering from more extensive post-industrial degeneration, and arguably need more financial support. The application for World Heritage Site status could give extra impetus and support (Spa applied to be on Belgium's Indicative List in January 2008), but this may not be adequate to preserve or re-develop enough of the heritage to make a difference to the future of Spa as an international wellness destination. On the other hand, it is possible to be too nostalgic about the past and too conservative about contemporary developments, which are viewed as risky by some politicians and local people.

The aim of a 2008 symposium in Spa entitled 'The Future of Historic Spa Towns' (Verbecke & Diekmann, 2008) was to identify some possible paths to revitalization for this and other similar historic spa towns. Delegates were somewhat surprised by the decision to construct a new thermal centre in Spa rather than regenerating the historic spa, especially as other spa towns (e.g. Bath in England) have managed to combine new facilities with the historic buildings. This decision seemed to be somewhat at odds with the desire to preserve authenticity, character and uniqueness, which are arguably essential for attracting international tourists or World Heritage Site status. Unfortunately, one of the problems for the town is that there are other towns in this relatively poor region of Belgium which are considered to be higher priority for funding because of their industrial decline. It is also difficult to renovate old, traditional facilities which cannot easily accommodate large numbers of visitors or cannot be adapted because of conservation regulations. It was thought that the new thermal centre was appealing, but could easily have been located anywhere and had no links to the town or local area. Attempts to re-animate the town have been made, but by using sporting events which could also have taken place elsewhere and have no historic or cultural reasons for taking place in Spa.

However, despite the difficulties of revitalizing the town as a health and wellness destination, it still retains a large degree of charm and attractiveness. As stated by Murphy (2008) in his case study of Spa 'It has survived and evolved into a beautiful heritage centre in a scenic region. It now offers a tranquil oasis of health therapy within the frantic post-industrial age of Western Europe'. It just needs to be accepted that health and well-ness are no longer enough to attract international visitors, and that a range of activities within the region need to be included in product development and promotion.

Acknowledgements: Thank you to Myriam Jansen-Verbecke and Anya Diekmann for organizing the 2008 Symposium *The Future of Historic Spa Towns* in Spa, Belgium, during which the material for this case study was collected.

Vidago and Pedras Salgadas spas, the revival of a tourism attraction or a marketing technique for beverages?

Veronique Nelly Paul Marie Joukes

An isolated mountainous region in the North of Portugal

Aquanattur is an exclusive renovation project by private Portuguese investors, with significant financial back-up from the state. They endeavour to link two legendary yet currently out of fashion mineral spas with new insights from the tourism, leisure, recreation, and wellness sectors, while maintaining the traditional medical know-how. This approach has been increasingly supported by the Government over the last 3 years, as demonstrates the law *'Decreto-Lei'* n° 142/2004 of the 11th of June, the National Strategic Plan for Tourism 2006–2015 and the 48 million Euro Aquanattur investment contract negotiated with the Portuguese Investment Agency in 2006.

The spas we focus on are 15 kilometres apart and are located in two small communities, Vidago and Pedras Salgadas, in the Alto Tâmega region, in the Trás-os-Montes ('behind-the-mountains') district, the extreme North of Portugal. It is an interior rural mountainous region that will become accessible by highway, the A24/E801, by the end of 2007. The Vidago and Pedras Salgadas spas are both located approximately 2 hours drive from international airports on both sides of the Portuguese-Spanish border, Porto and Vigo. The region faces all the problems typical for its geographical isolation: low population density, a greying and declining population, decreasing importance of the agricultural employment sector and entrepreneurial initiatives that do not take off. However the region is rich in resources. In the tourism segment alone, it includes (popular) culture, history, handicrafts, a hospitable population, beautiful scenery, and agriculture; it provides an ideal environment for hunting and fishing or outdoor sports and it offers water of all forms (lakes, rivers, river beaches, dams, and mineral springs). All of them are perfect ingredients to diversify the tourist offer and, what is more, all can easily be exploited more intensively.

Two spas with a glorious mythical past, hidden in gorgeous mountains

In 2001 the spas of Vidago (with 658 spa goers) and Pedras Salgadas (251) belonged to the 10 least visited spas of Portugal. However, they have not always played such a low profile role. Around 1870, both of them were already economically exploited. Over the years splendid luxurious hotels with spa and leisure facilities were built and beautifully integrated in vast green parks, following the French model of *'village thermal'*. The Portuguese high society and even the royal family visited these spas regularly between 1875 and 1950. In the 1930s, for example, Pedras Salgadas, received around 2,000 guests per year, while Vidago welcomed some 1,300 visitors per year. Pedras Salgadas saw its visitor numbers decrease from 1948 onwards, while Vidago started suffering severe losses only at the end of the 1980s.

In 1924 the companies Vidago and Pedras Salgadas, together with a smaller and farther northwest spa in Melgaço, were absorbed in the 'Vidago, Melgaço e Pedras Salgadas, sociedade anónima' (VMPS). From the very start, all have been selling their mineral water in two ways: directly to the customer in a spa environment and wholesale after being bottled; the last option being the best economically rewarding undertaking. Moreover, in each locality both activities are being sold under the same name. That way 'Vidago' and 'Pedras Salgadas' not only correspond with a geographical location, but also with the spa situated there and the water that is being bottled there.

The latest spa project formulated for Vidago and Pedras Salgadas merits our attention, as it sparks the imagination. It is of top quality, large scale and was successful in raising massive funds. The local population has high hopes for increased employment opportunities, upgrading of their standard of living and increased wealth for their region. The current national Governors also cherish expectations, as Aquanattur is the fourth project of National Potential Interest approved by them. This means that the proposal meets a certain set of requirements: it creates employment in a disadvantaged region, it uses renewable energy and it breathes life into the local economy. Furthermore the project will be accompanied by a special commission ensuring that all bureaucratic bottlenecks can be passed quickly and that fiscal and financial benefits will be granted once Unicer performs the contract within the fixed time.

Unicer's objective(s) by creating Aquanattur

The Unicer Group was already producing and distributing a range of beverages when it bought VMPS in 2002. This acquisition will diversify the Unicer portfolio with tourism through the renovation of the traditional spa facilities of Vidago and Pedras Salgadas in the Aquanattur project. Broken-down (in Portuguese) Aqua-nat-tur spells out the three pillars of the project – Water, Nature, and Tourism – all of which are important Unicer obligations in terms of sustainability: namely, to preserve natural and hydro-mineral resources available through a concession; respect biodiversity and eco-systems and ensure economic growth through tourism improvement. All this makes Aquanattur more than just another industrial and tourism project. Nevertheless, the main objective of Unicer by creating Aquanattur is to promote their current core products – mineral waters, juices, soft drinks, and beer (Super Bock). They mainly apply a success story from abroad (Vichy in France, Fiuggi in Italy and Spa in Belgium) by letting consumers associate the quality of the spa complex with the beverages carrying the same brand-name. This marketing technique is called 'brand quality association'. This increased quality perception of the beverages should increase sales and support their main objectives of exporting their products widely and dominating the Iberian market.

Unicer remodels Vidago and Pedras Salgadas profoundly

Aquanattur is an all-in-one quality project, coordinated by one of Portugal's most famous architects, Álvaro Siza Vieira. We only outline the different scenarios he conceived for each place. Vidago will be transformed into a 'premium resort' – a secluded hide-away for the happy rich, mostly northern Europeans – while Pedras Salgadas will maintain its link with the local population and its former middle class visitors, by creating a more 'open resort'. The current Palace Hotel in Vidago will be upgraded to a 5-star spa hotel, the nearby golf course will be enlarged to 18 holes and a Golf Academy will be developed. The renowned Contemporary Art and Environment Foundation Serralves have been invited to open an extension in the old style garages. The congress centre, the result of a renovation project of the former baths in 2000, will be maintained and the parks will be environmentally upgraded and certified. The modest casino in

Pedras Salgadas will be transformed into a multifunctional activity centre and the spa therapy zone will be totally renovated. Furthermore, the 3-star hotel 'Avelames' will make way for a brand new 4-star hotel and the ex-garages and bottling installations will house a museum. The park, which includes a public swimming pool, a café, a tearoom, and handicraft ateliers will encourage a close relationship with the people of the Alto Tâmega. Although both spas will be managed independently, they will remain linked by, for example, a 15 kilometre cycling path and several running tracks. All these major works are due for completion by December 2008.

Both region and country will benefit from Aquanattur

Unicer justifies the large public spending in this mega-project in various ways. Firstly they argue that their investment in an interior region will increase that region's business volume thanks to the export of tourism services. This in turn should reduce the differences between the tourist regions of the country, in terms of number of available bedspaces, average occupancy rates, and market share (visitor number) as Aquanattur grows. A second justification is that thanks to the mix of services offered, they will help combat seasonality and create around 110 new jobs (mainly qualified), while maintaining the 220 already existing ones. Furthermore, professional training will be provided for more than just the strict necessary number of new employees, because of the traditionally high personnel turnover in the tourism sector. Unicer also intends to promote the region's exceptional natural, historical, architectural, and gastronomic virtues internationally and to strengthen the image of the region as a high quality and unique tourist destination. They want to push the Douro-region (which includes the Alto Tâmega) to fourth place on the national tourist destination ranking. Unicer also claims that the project will strengthen the tourism marketing efforts of the country as a whole, by promoting emotional values and unique experiences to (potential) customers. While renovating the national spa concept, Unicer will create added value, guarantee higher brand awareness, stimulate cross border tourism promotion and achieve brand rejuvenation. Being the 'first mover' in this region might inspire other economic agents to invest in the region. By attracting more than 38,000 high purchase power tourists per year, Unicer claims the presence of its spas will be a magnet for a considerable number of small and medium private and/or public secondary investments. These, in turn, will further increase the wealth of the region and will stabilize the population numbers and increase its overall development. The local population will also directly benefit as they will be allowed to enjoy some of the new cultural, sportive, social, and tourist infrastructures in Pedras Salgadas.

Will Aquanattur make dreams come true?

We applaud the initiative taken by Unicer and sincerely hope it will meet its objectives. However, we become somewhat reluctant when reading the

Aquanattur promotional website, in which Unicer promises to rejuvenate the long awaited region's tourist attraction power. The first reason to be cautious is because it is a high risk investment. Unicer has no experience in the tourist or spa sector. In several interviews, the former Unicer President admitted that he never would have been able to enter this adventure without the firm support of the State. The current President is renegotiating the contract, in order to get permission to construct the planned buildings over a longer period of time and so, basically, postpone the 2008 deadline. This is necessary as Unicer bought VMPS almost 5 years ago, but has yet to finish the paper work stage.

Henk Verschuur, responsible for the renovation of Bath in Great Britain, experienced that indeed you need a very strong financial back-up if you want to engage in mega spa projects. This appears also to be true in the completely different Portuguese context. Prior to Unicer, Sousa Cintra (1982–1996) and Jerónimo Martins (1996–2002) tried to renovate the spas, albeit on a smaller scale; however, without massive financial support nor a supportive legal environment, they did not succeed and ended up selling VMPS.

The second reason for caution is highlighted in the conclusions of Kathleen Vos's Masters Thesis, analysing the survival strategies applied in four European cultural heritage spa resorts, namely Bath, Spa, Karlovy Vary, and Mariánské Lázne. She concluded that apart from the 'hardware' (recovery of patrimony, construction of new facilities), the 'software', 'orgware', and 'shareware' (what you will do in this environment, how you will promote it, with whom you will collaborate) – concepts developed and defined by the Louvain geography professor MyriamVerbeke – have a vital importance in all recovery processes. Vos argued that the rejuvenation strategies 'renovation, re-imaging, re-organization, and re-relation' are only possible if the software, orgware and shareware are all well exploited. Unfortunately, these concepts have not yet received much attention in the media, nor on the Unicer website.

Finally, we recommend increased public communication to clarify that the first government funding was invested in the modernization and development of the bottling industry of Vidago and Pedras Salgadas and that spa tourism efforts only come next.

Conclusion

The unprecedented governmental financial and strategic support for the rejuvenation of the Vidago and Pedras Salgadas spas gives high hopes that this renovation project will succeed where previous attempts have failed. On top of this Unicer might increase its overall beverage sales significantly once the international market is explored. Even so, we still doubt whether this combined private company interest (increased sales) and state regional development plan will realize entirely the planned sustainable outcome.

We thank Sabine Joukes and Jacques Thijs who helped improving this paper.

The Luigiane thermal baths: A tool for the deseasonalization of the tourist demand in Calabria (Italy)

Sonia Ferrari

The thermal baths: Main features

The Luigiane thermal baths are located in Guardia Piemontese in Calabria, one of the southern regions of Italy, just 1 kilometre away from the Tyrrhenian Sea. The Luigiane thermal baths have ancient origins, witnessed by numerous documents, although the company which currently manages them has been operating since 1936. The baths are the most important thermal centre in the region both for the number of customers and services delivered and for their accommodation capacity. The village of Guardia Piemontese is top ranked in Calabria regarding the entrepreneurial density in the tourism sector (Istituto Tagliacarne).

The specific characteristic of the water of this spa is the high rate of the hydrogen sulphide ratio (173.2 mg/l), making them extremely beneficial. The water also contains a very rare alga, which enriches the mud baths with proteins and vitamins. Thanks to the proximity to the coast and to the various and complex morphology of the land, the Luigiane thermal baths perfectly fit into a local tourist system. This system is built up not only by tourist elements but also by other numerous factors such as the social and economic context, the natural and cultural environment, and by factors of anthropic attraction. Nearby the baths, lies the National Park of Pollino and the Sanctuary of San Francesco of Paola (XII century) is only a few kilometres away. All along the coast, many towers, fortifications and castles of Aragon, Norman, and Bourbon origins can be seen. In addition, Guardia Piemontese claims the unique Occitan community in Calabria which still preserves its own costumes and its ancient language of Provençal origin.

The holiday vocation of this local tourist system is mainly oriented to a *sea*, *sun*, and *sand holiday*. For this reason, the distribution of the tourist flows indicates a strong concentration during the summer months with 79% of arrivals and 91% of Night of Tourism (N.o.T.) concentrated between the months of June and September. This distribution traces the trend of the entire region where the seasonality of the tourist demand is the highest in Italy (VII Report on Tourism in Calabria, Observatory of Tourism in Calabria).

However, the seasonality of the N.o.T. holiday at the Luigiane thermal baths is strongly reduced compared to the rest of the region. Here, in fact, the holiday season begins in the month of May and is extended until the month of November. This is due to the different holiday supply which revolves around thermal tourism. However, the clients of the thermal baths are above all Italians who are also the main presence in the rest of the region. In particular, there is a predominance of Calabrian customers (75%) for thermal treatments, while in the hotels there are numerous tourists coming from other Italian regions.

The Luigiane thermal baths look exactly like a thermal town in terms of quality and typology of accommodation facilities. The place offers five hotels (with a total of about 600 beds), a 'thermal park', a very unique facility including swimming pools, whirlpool baths, mud baths, thermal services, and a fitness centre.

In addition to the two health establishments, the baths are equipped with a physiotherapy centre and a beauty centre. Great attention is dedicated to anti-stress and health therapy. The baths offer a wide range of therapeutic treatments (for respiratory, dermatological, and gynaecological disorders and diseases). The same company offers acceptance and free-time services (hotels, restaurants, thermal park, cinema, etc.).

Survey objectives and method

The present research has two main objectives. On the one hand, it aims at acquiring an understanding of the holiday potential of the tourist destination under survey; on the other, it seeks to investigate the existence of a series of initiatives which aim at diversifying the tourist supply and at increasing the holiday demand.

For the purpose of the present survey, the main opinion leaders and stakeholders were interviewed. In addition, sample of 560 clients of the Luigiane thermal baths were interviewed. The interviews were carried out following a 'one-to-one in person' method and were supported by a questionnaire designed for the purpose. The sample represents 4.5% of the whole universe of the total flow of regional and extra-regional tourists staying in the place from June to September 2006.

Main results of the survey

The results of the research are consistent with the data collected in the thermal sector on a national scale and suggest new patterns of tourist development for the Luigiane thermal baths. The analysis of the demographic variables is perfectly aligned with the results of other national research studies. Table CS5.1 summarizes the main social and demographic features of the sample of interviewees.

The analysis of the flows emphasizes a very high percentage of regional residents visiting the thermal facility essentially for health reasons. Moreover, these customers commonly commute without any overnight stays. Sixty-seven per cent of them come from the same region, whereas 33% come from nearby Italian regions. This leads us to define the phenomenon as a form of 'proximity tourism'.

Table CS5.1 Socio-demographic Data.

		Regional Ref. %	Extra-Regional Ref. %
Sex	M	46	48
	F	54	52
Age	<50	18	15
	50–59	34	38
	59–69	23	30
	>70	25	17
Civil Status	Married	84	91
	Single man	6	4
	Single woman	10	5
Education	primary	89	80
	degree	11	20

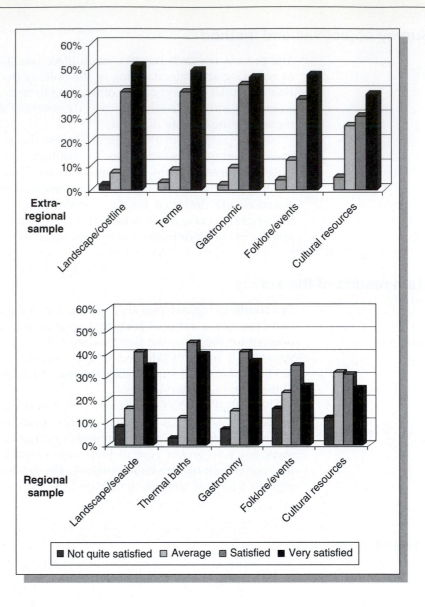

Figure CS5.1
Levels of satisfaction of regional and extra-regional tourists referring to different elements of the tourist offer.

Moreover, 82% of the regional tourists stayed at the baths simply for therapeutic purposes; the hypothesis is confirmed by the channels used to know about and to choose the thermal baths. Thirty per cent of the regional sample informants responded that they knew about the thermal baths through previous experiences and 39% through social and health services. On the other hand, only 26% of extra-regionals had previously stayed at the baths and heard about them from tour operators and travel agencies (16%). Twenty-two per cent of the extra-regional informants knew about the Luigiane baths thanks to 'relatives and friends'. Furthermore, it is interesting to focus on the value of tourism in Calabria in the segment

Table CS5.2 Reasons for Future Travelling.

	Thermal Baths		Nature		Culture		Events		Gastr.		Totals	
	Reg. (%)	Extra (%)	Reg. (%)	Extra (%)	Reg. (%)	Extra (%)	Reg. (%)	Extra (%)	Reg. (%)	Extra (%)	Regional (%)	Extra Reg. (%)
Spring	49	29	26	22	5	18	9	17	11	14	100	100
Summer	12	9	61	41	6	15	17	23	4	12	100	100
Autumn	53	37	12	11	12	12	15	21	8	19	100	100
Winter	31	14	11	16	13	23	27	34	18	13	100	100

of 'return tourism' (tourist flows of Calabrian emigrants who return from abroad to their homeland). Referring further to the extra-regional sample, 29% knew about (and chose) the baths on the basis of 'prior experiences and travels'. This factor indicates a good ability in allowing tourists to acquire a sense of trust. In particular, this may also be attributed to other elements of the local holiday supply as in Figure CS5.1.

The high average age and the family status (Table CS5.1) underline how the Luigiane thermal baths are predominantly chosen for medical cure.

The graph in Figure CS5.1 summarizes the main results found for the regional and extra-regional sample of informants regarding levels of satisfaction of the various elements of the tourist supply. Besides the curative aspects, the numerous elements of the product mix of the Luigiane thermal baths significantly contribute to increase the level of tourists' satisfaction, although a large part of the resources are known by the guests only upon their arrival in the village. These resources, in fact, do not represent 'flagship products'. On the one hand, this is imputable to the perception that tourists/customers have of the thermal sector, seen exclusively as a place where treatment or recovery is received; on the other, it depends on communicative choices directed to therapeutic efficacy and wellness.

In analysing the graphs in Figure CS5.1, it is relevant to point out how both the extra-regional and regional samples of interviewees rate other attractive factors at a high level, although with different values. In the specific case of the extra-regional sample, the findings referring to coast and countryside items (40% satisfied and 41% extremely satisfied) were fairly predictable. Surprisingly, the high values assigned to the remaining items emphasize the high potential of the holiday supply offered by the Luigiane thermal baths. These items include the gastronomy (43%, 46%), the 'events/folklore' (37%, 47%) and the cultural goods (30%, 39%). These data findings are also confirmed by the analysis of the motivations for future stays at the Luigiane thermal baths as in Table CS5.2.

As for the regional sample, the motivations for future returns are essentially therapeutic reasons. The values of motivations like wellness or sea holidays are equally distributed among the other items. Besides, the discovery of the local traditions and manifestations (under the item of events/folklore) or the wine-gastronomy supply shows relevant percentage values.

Conclusions

In conclusion, it seems that with considerable investments exploiting various resources, the Luigiane thermal baths are entering a modern holiday market regarding the field of health. Moreover, it can be claimed that these baths are less focused on the traditional concept of thermal resorts and more on the idea of wellness.

Overall, the survey has underlined that although the shift from a curative centre to a wellness centre is the result of a natural evolution for the Luigiane thermal baths, and more in general for the thermal sector, above all, there are other elements which need to be taken into account. In particular, the surplus value and the differentiation elements of the holiday supply offered by the Luigiane thermal baths are part of an integrated tourist offer which includes other attractive factors. The sources of the local tourist system are, in fact, widely diversified and are able to reach different market targets. Among these, the youth target is firstly addressed. Usually, young people are skeptical about considering thermal resorts as holiday destinations. Elements such as the proximity to the sea and to the natural park of Pollino make the supply more appealing to this target. In addition, besides traditional excursions and natural visits, the Luigiane resort offers the opportunity of practicing a number of sports. The place is also very interesting in terms of religious tourism, thanks to the proximity to the Sanctuary in Paola and to the Sanctuary of the Madonna of Pettoruto in San Sosti. In addition, there is a well-established wine-gastronomy tourism, developed through important communication tools such as the Chilli Pepper Festival in Diamante.

Finally, cultural tourism in a broad sense including cultural and artistic assets, archaeological sites, popular traditions, events and folklore, represents a remarkable surplus value for tourist attraction to the area. In the field of events/folklore, an important element is recorded by the presence of the Occitan Community with its history, language, and costumes.

Summed together, all these elements establish the *uniqueness* of the destination and could, if properly valued, contribute to the rush of a holiday brand based on the *authenticity* of the area.

For all these reasons, the urge to promote the development of the place is strongly advocated. This development should especially be conceived in terms of deseasonalization, by means of an effective communication plan which includes all the aforementioned elements together with the thermal supply. Only in this way, it will be feasible to satisfy the need of well-being, addressing numerous market targets in an original and unique mode.

Hotel Herttua – Spa and rehabilitation centre in Eastern Finland

Anja Tuohino and Henna Kangas

Herttua and Lake Puruvesi region

Hotel Herttua – Spa and rehabilitation centre (www.herttua. fi) is located at Kerimäki on a beautiful, narrow stretch of land on Lake Puruvesi in Eastern Finland, in the province of South Savo(see Figure CS6.1). The municipality has a population of 5,923 (31.12.2005) and covers an area of 875.0 square kilometre of which 281.14 square kilometre is water (www.kerimaki.fi).

Lake Puruvesi is famous for its crystal clear water (transparency over 10 metre) and outstanding fishing possibilities (www. ymparisto.fi). The water is drinkable straight from the lake. The lake provides an excellent fishing environment for both hobby and professional fishermen with its scattered shorelines and numerous islands.

The location of Herttua is multifaceted. First, the surrounding landscape with various landforms and changing types of nature

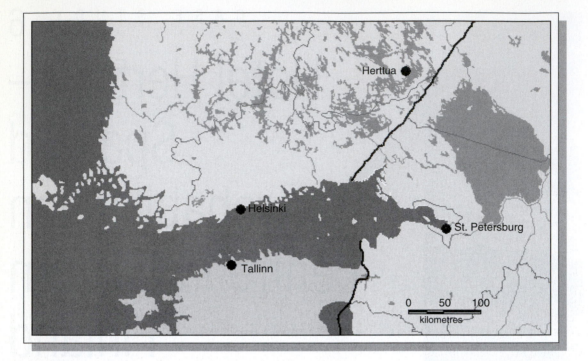

Figure CS6.1
Location of Herttua.

offer an ideal environment for activities. On the other hand, the image of the region is not very strong, even though the geographical location is ideal in the middle of the lakes. The neighbouring city, Savonlinna, is famous for its international opera festival, but the attractiveness of the event is seasonal, during the summer period. In wintertime, the area is just starting to promote its winter activities.

Herttua was established in 1975. Over the past few years, the owners have changed and the present owner, Healthlake Ltd, bought the centre in January 2004. Herttua is one of the biggest employers in Kerimäki; and there are 50 people working in the company.

At present, Herttua is a hotel, a fitness centre as well as a spa and rehabilitation centre. The hotel provides a pleasant site for various purposes, whether it is a peaceful vacation surrounded by nature or a conference or a meeting. There are 85 double rooms, 2 suites, and a luxurious guesthouse built from wooden logs, all of them offer comfortable accommodation in a natural setting. For business purposes there is a log house for 10 persons or a conference room for 200 guests. The restaurant offers local food made of pure raw materials, such as game, berries and fish from Lake Puruvesi.

Herttua is a place which really takes care of the body, soul, and mind. The Lake District around Herttua is an ideal surrounding for various outdoor activities. Marked jogging trails and cross-country skiing tracks, as well as Nordic Walking tracks, follow the diverse hilly countryside. In autumn, forests serve as a resource for mushroom and berry picking. There is also a possibility to recharge by going to the fitness room, Finnish sauna, swimming pool or diving into the crystal clear waves of Lake Puruvesi in addition to trails and tracks. In wintertime, Finland offers exceptional experiences such as snowshoeing or cross-country skiing trips.

For fishermen and fishing ladies Lake Puruvesi can be used in both summer and winter. Rowing boats are freely at disposal for the guests. Herttua offers also indoor activities for exercise in the 17 metres (56 feet) long swimming pool and the keep-fit hall. Massages and beauty treatments are available if reserved beforehand. There is a possibility to play tennis in the indoor hall, too. For golf-fans, there is an 18-hole Kerimaa golf-course available only 9 kilometres away in summer time.

The main segments are rehabilitation customers in the broadest sense. The biggest group of rehabilitation customers are people who want to improve their working ability. This fits Herttua very well because it has targeted rehabilitation programs for people that are working in different professions. This kind of rehabilitation is supported by employers or by public funds (social services). Rehabilitation customers include also veterans but this group is going to decrease in future. There are also different kinds of social holidays supported by public funding. The spa and rehabilitation customers are the main segment in winter time, but in summer time different tourist groups are the main customers, for example opera festival guests and bus groups. These tourists also use the same services as the rehabilitation customers, only their motives to use the services and wellness services are usually different.

Herttua has several unique features close to it. The distance to the Russian boarder is only 60 kilometres by road. This offers new business possibilities since wellness tourism in Russia is increasing rapidly and this offers new possibilities for Herttua in the future.

In addition, many interesting sights are nearby. One of the best-known historical attractions in Finland is Olavinlinna castle in Savonlinna about 25 kilometres from Herttua. Savonlinna Opera Festival is organised in the castle every summer. Herttua also offers transportation to this festival if necessary. The castle is open to the public all year round. The Orthodox Monastery of New Valamo in Heinävesi has developed into a significant centre of Orthodox culture in Finland in recent decades. The monks live the communal spiritual life of a monastery based on the ascetic tradition of the Orthodox Church. The Kerimäki Church, built between 1844 and 1847, is the biggest wooden church in the world (45 metres long, 42 metres wide, and 37 metres high). There are over 3,000 seats. Altogether there can be 5,000 people at a time in the church. In summer time, there was an under water art exhibition in the grounds of Lake Puruvesi. The exhibition can be seen by diving or by rowing on the lake. Finally, a remarkable historical exhibition dealing with Finnish wars 1939–1944 has been built at Herttua hotel. The open-air museum has displays of guns and other heavy equipment used by the Finnish army. Also inside the hotel there is an exhibition concerning the time of wars. Herttua is developing its surroundings and there is already a new plan for the area. For example there is going to be bigger space for an historical open-air museum and the guns and other heavy equipment are going to be situated in places where they were used during the wars.

Challenging future and fundamental pillars of wellness in Herttua

One of the greatest challenges for wellness tourism is an opportunity. Currently the wellness segment of the travel industry in Finland is limited and sketchy. Potential consumers are both unclear as to this segment's breadth and depth, and have rising expectations that may or may not be met.

In Eastern Finland Wellness facilities are diversified and there are various business enterprises offering products under the wellness theme. However, the profile of Eastern Finland's wellness tourism can be described as weak.

At the same time, in terms of resources, Eastern Finland has many lakes, aquatic environments and pure nature. Unfortunately, this rich potential is scarcely utilized. In the case of Herttua, the surrounding lake environment offers an ideal resource for the wellness concept and the development of a Lake Wellness concept.

Today, at the beginning of the 21st century, the needs and images of potential tourists are increasingly important. The ever-increasing competition and new motivations and needs of tourists set a major challenge for tourism (product) development. In the case of Herttua, to enlighten the customer perspective of tourism product development, Herttua is one of the implementers of e-GOOD, a cooperation network of wellbeing services in Eastern Finland, which was created in order to improve their production of services. One of the purposes is to find new innovative solutions for the changing demand among visitors and to find out new potential segments for wellness tourism.

The challenge is how to manage the present variety of products in response to the modern tourists' needs of self-fulfilment, active participation and experiences. And is Herttua together with Lake Puruvesi region a distinguishable destination from the potential visitor's perspective in the context of wellness tourism? Furthermore, how to define what in fact the content of the Wellness concept in Eastern Finland should be?

It can be said that a product development based on nature is not distinctive and unique enough to create a profile. Nature is everywhere, and it does not reflect the differences from or between competitive regions. The question is; would the traveller gain additional value from his/her lake images/experiences, for example, with meanings created through activities and action or through new high-quality innovations, where the local environment and culture would act as catalysts for the creation of the innovations and for product development strategies? Can the new innovative concept of Lake Wellness be an answer? Can a lake be a core product in this innovative concept of Wellness tourism?

Hereafter, in the Herttua case, there is a need for change since the social holidays supported by public funding are decreasing. This means that the company needs to build a new business plan. In future, the aim is to find new business models as well as new products focusing on wellness and well-being. For this, the environment around Herttua is ideal for both mental and physical rest, to give an example.

At the moment, most of the strengths focus on surrounding nature and the facilities the place can offer. The multiply skilled staff fulfil strengths with an excellent hospitality and professionalism. The principal weakness factor is insufficient networking. The company has only a few network partners or subcontractors. The low level of networking is an obstacle to improving conditions.

The possibilities for future development rely on the development of wellness tourism in Eastern Finland. Herttua has an excellent environment for the development of Lake Wellness with a core product of pure Lake Puruvesi. These kinds of products may be profiled in more competitive markets in future, but it all depends on the company's innovation potential and ability to apply the new ideas and process them into new products. In dynamic and changing business environments, new markets, new service systems and new production processes are needed for the new business models. The threats in future include the increasing competitiveness in rehabilitation and wellness tourism sectors.

Lake Wellness concept can be a tool in developing products and services to new and different customer segment. The fundamental pillars of Lake Wellness in Herttua case include:

- spirit and mind; relaxing excursions in the forest and lacustrine environment
- health: Nordic walking around the lake shores or through forests, traditional and preventative treatments
- healthy cuisine; local raw materials and Lake Puruvesi fish
- inner and external beauty; Finnish sauna, peat sauna treatment
- relaxation and comfort; swimming in the pool and in the lake, Finnish sauna experience, baths in hot water barrel
- tailor-made movement; guided tours (see www.loytoristeilyt.fi) in and on the lake, kick sledding or trip skating on the ice of Lake Puruvesi

The possibilities for future development rely on the development of wellness tourism in Eastern Finland. Herttua has an excellent environment for the development of Lake Wellness with a core product of pure Lake Puruvesi. This kind of products may be new profiling products in the more competitive markets in future. All depends on the company's innovation potential and ability to apply the new ideas and process them into new products. In dynamic and changing business environment new markets, new service systems and new production processes are needed for the new business models. The threats in future reflect on the increasing competitiveness in rehabilitation and wellness tourism sectors.

São Pedro do Sul thermal centre: Between health and wellness tourism

Nuno Gustavo

Introduction

The Centre Northern part of Portugal, where the majority of thermal centres are located, presents a high potential for thermal activity as it benefits from climatic and mineralogical characteristics, which are essential to this activity.

One hour from Oporto, right in the centre north of Portugal, we find São Pedro do Sul (SPSUL), basically known for its unique medical water and thermal centre. Its popularity is proven by its demand. In 2004, as in the last years, SPSUL Thermal Centre was the most visited of the 37 Portuguese Thermal Centres. It represented 25.6% of the global Health and Wellness market demand in Portugal (Gustavo, 2006).

Located in the edges of the Vouga river, the historical registers of this thermal centre are lost in time. However, the construction of the thermal set, on the left side of the Vouga river, is attributed to the Romans, which is proved by the existence of important ruins and archaeological remains.

The origins of the Thermal Centre date back to 1884. Currently, and since September 2001, the SPSUL thermal centre provides two thermal buildings the 'D. Afonso Henriques' – BDAH-(Health segment) and 'Rainha D. Amélia' – BRDA-(Wellness segment), which are located contiguously but in independent buildings. Both of them make use of swimming pools and proper equipment for their purposes.

The SPSUL Thermal Centre, a leader of the Health and Wellness market in Portugal, defined a new strategy which is justified, despite other reasons, by the low attractiveness of traditional Portuguese thermal products which goes along with an increasing competition not only between the several European thermal establishments[1] but also between the increasing health and wellness resorts and 'alternative' products offered by non-health and wellness destinations.

Infrastructure and management policy

The customers of the SPSUL Thermal Centre use the following services and facilities: physiotherapy, animation (including visits to the historical and natural patrimony of the region), a thermal museum, a multipurpose room, a library, an auditorium, fluvial beach. Yet, no unit of lodging is integrated into the thermal centre.

All the existing offers of lodging are private and autonomous from the SPSUL Thermal Centre management. They mainly present a low level of service and are pensions, or guesthouses. Yet it is possible to find a few three and four stars hotels.

Currently, the differences between both thermal buildings are only related to the level and cost of the service. The customers of the BRDA make use of a superior level and more expensive service. Thus, they usufruct the following added services/facilities in relation to the BDAH: clothes for the treatments (head caps, bathrobe, and slippers), surrounding music, acclimatization and a higher employee/consumer ratio than BDAH.

In terms of organizational structure there is only one that is common to both thermal buildings, and which is held by the municipal company *Termalistur – Termas de São Pedro Sul*.

It is a functional organizational structure type with three main departments: administrative and financial (Human Resource Services, Provisions and Infrastructure Services, Accounting Services), marketing (Promotion Services), Entertainment (Services and Customer Support Services) and operational (Investigation and Development, Maintenance Infrastructure Services, Thermal and Cleanliness Services, Information System and Computer Services). These three departments are hierarchally dependent on the clinical team and the operational management directors. The *Termalistur* Administration Council is the primary decision-making body in matters of overall strategy and the authorization for investment expenditures. The company has at its service 41 employees of the SPSUL City Council and about 260 contracted workers.

---

[1] Portugal's main competitor destinations are Austria, Italy, Spain, France, Switzerland – study provided by ITP-Instituto de Turismo de Portugal to THR (Asesores en Turismo Hotelería y Recreación), 2006.

The demand

In accordance with the Clinical Report of 2004, the SPSUL Thermal Centre registered a total of 25,237 customers, 5.6% of the customers justified their visit to the SPSUL Thermal Centre with well-being reasons and 94.4% mentioned health reasons (Gustavo, 2006). This trend of the demand verified in the SPSUL Thermal Centre expresses the global behaviour of the demand verified in Portugal. In accordance with ATP,[2] in 2004, 13.1% of the customers of Portuguese thermal centres justified their displacement for well-being reasons and 86.9% for health reasons.

This demand has an anti-symmetrical behaviour, given that the summer months o (June to September) are those where a higher demand is registered (about 50%). In a general way, we verify that the months of greater and lesser demand correspond, respectively, to the months of high and low season, as defined in terms of services prices policy by the SPSUL thermal centre.

A detailed analysis of the average profile of the costumers of SPSUL thermal centre shows the following data (Gustavo, 2006):

- mainly female gender (61.4%)
- an age equal or superior to 65 years (84.5%)
- they essentially come from three districts: Lisbon (23.9%), Aveiro (19.4%) and Coimbra (15.5%)
- in general they are married (72.8%) and have children (78.8%). However this fact is not expressed when customers come to the thermal centre, as only 34.8% is accompanied by his/her family (ascendants and/or descendants)
- only 48% have a paid activity (36% are retired persons)
- the average monthly revenue of a thermal customer family is 1.180 € (but for 48% is no more than 1.000 €)
- the majority of the customers only have the basic education
- the thermal frequency is regular (69% of the customers already have 5 or more years experience)
- during their sojourn in the SPSUL thermal centre (generally once a year for 15 days) the customers modify their daily routines, conjugating the treatments with other activities of leisure
- the thermal frequency is mentioned by 99.3% of the customers, as an important factor with respect to the state of their health for the rest of the remaining year, while 95% of the customers consider the thermal treatment more efficient than medicines, thus the motivation of 94% of the customers derives from pathological reasons. Their decision-making process for the thermal centre was constrained essentially by the opinion of doctors (71%) and friends (26%). The quality of the water of the SPSUL thermal centre is also very relevant when it come to taking a decision (74.7% – very important), as well as the presence of relatives and/or friends (very important for 23.5% and important for 21.1%)
- the accommodation varies from a room or a rented house to hotels (different categories).

---

[2] ATP – Associação das Termas de Portugal.

However, a study carried out in 2004 (Gustavo, 2006) verified the existence of differences in terms of the average profile of the customer of each one of the thermal buildings. Overall, the customer of the BRDA has more spending power, a higher level of education, spends more and consumes more and uses expensive services (e.g. the accommodation). The decision-making process of both clients is also different. When the BRDA's building clients have to choose a thermal centre, they are basically motivated by a medical (scientific) opinion, and not so much by the possible presence of friends. The opposite happens to the BDAH's building clients.

The analysis of the client's profile evidences significant differences between these two profiles, especially in terms of cultural and economic capital. So we are in the presence of two market segments (Gustavo, 2006).

These differences seem limited for two main reasons:

1. in the last decades, in Portugal, the thermal centres had an image which was clearly associated with the prevention and the healing of illnesses, with the SPSUL centre being the leader
2. despite the differences, two SPSUL thermal buildings still have much in common, particularly in terms of physical location, strategy, and management.

SWOT analysis

Strengths	Weaknesses
• Leader of market in Portugal in the health segment	• Image associated clearly with the health segment
• A strategy of differentiation already initiated	• Management by a municipal company
• Located out of a traditional tourism destination, in a region where natural resources are dominant	• They are not located in a traditional tourism destination

Opportunities	Threats
• Growth of the wellness market	• Development of similar and concurrent project in the region; for example SPA hotels and the prequalification of competing thermal centres for the wellness market
• State Systems financing in Portugal, both for the thermal activity, and for the less developed regions	• The main tourism regions in Portugal are also developing infrastructures (projects) for the wellness and health tourism market (mainly wellness tourism)
• Possibility of strategic partnerships with companies of the tourist sector of the region to the level of the management and marketing	

Final recommendations

Thus, by way of a conclusion, we present the following considerations which can be equated in the future, considering the SPSUL or similar cases:

- The definition of a new model of private administration, a more autonomous one, with private participation, aiming at increasing the investment capacity and management and the development of an integrated tourist product (introducing other products such as golf) that allows a balanced tourist demand for the rest of the year.
- Definition of a strategy of joint communication, with the different entrepreneurs of the tourist sector of SPSUL, aiming at the creation of a single and integrated image of the destination.
- An assumed differentiation of the two segments of Health and Wellness Tourism, defining for such spaces, infrastructure, models of autonomous management and communication.
- Valorization of the single qualities of thermal waters as a factor of differentiation, in particular for the health tourism segment, developing the destination branding with marketing and products campaigns (e.g. creation of a branding of bottled water).
- Valorization, development and integration of new infrastructure, new medicinal facilities and new techniques in particular in the context of wellness tourism.
- Development of infrastructure, such as aquatic themed parks, considering that this can be a family vacation destination and not only a single wellness and health vacation destination. This can also be a relevant consideration in terms of a destination's sustainability.

Case 'Healing Hills and Wellness in Luxury'

Ilja Castermans-Godfried

Background

- *Region*: South-Limburg, in the south of the Netherlands. Bigger cities in South-Limburg are Maastricht, Heerlen and Sittard-Geleen. Next to Belgium (Liege) and Germany (Aachen).
- *Start*: January 2005. Province of Limburg wants to become the number two province for tourists in the Netherlands. The province also wants to attract 25% more 'silver' tourists to the region.
- *Horizontal alliances between tourism and health and wellness sector*: People are aging and more people are paying attention to their body and their health. We see that there is a growing demand for care. Combining curative and preventive care with tourism is an example of the horizontal alliances that are effectuated in the south of Limburg.
- *Target groups*: Patients recovering from hip and knee operations and wellness tourists.
- *USP*: Good quality of life, good health care and recovering in beautiful hilly and green surroundings.

SWOT analysis

Opportunity: At this moment about 30% of the Dutch population is 50 years or older. In 20 years this percentage will have augmented to about 40%. A lot of seniors are very affluent and like to travel. It is also a target group that cares about healthy living. In general, this augmenting group of aging people will make the tourism and recreational business the biggest in the world within 25 years.

Strength: South-Limburg offers the tourism product that meets the needs and the wants of senior holiday makers. Especially the 'Heuvelland' (land of hills) is one of the most important areas in the Netherlands for tourism. Many people from within the Netherlands and abroad are attracted to this region. South-Limburg is also of strategic value if you look at it from the point of view of the surrounding Euregional cities Maastricht, Aachen, and Liege, because it offers a lot of possibilities for recreation, overnight stays, and healthy activities.

Threat: Recent years have learned that tourist consumers are less loyal and that competition in the tourism business is increasing.

Weakness: The market share of the 'Heuvelland' has dropped 8% in the last decade. The tourism industry in South-Limburg is characterized by the predominance of small and medium enterprises that do not innovate enough because they are not able to carry the financial consequences on their own. A second problem is that environmental quality (nature and landscape, heritage, culture) is not only affected by urbanization but also by a decrease in agriculture. Traditionally it was agriculture that shaped the rural areas. Environmental quality, however, is one of the pillars of tourism.

Here is where the Province of Limburg comes in. The Province of Limburg is looking for opportunities to attract more tourists to South-Limburg. They want to become the number two province for tourists in the Netherlands. The province also wants to attract 25% more 'silver' tourists to the region. To reach these goals the province has initiated a major project that tries to build horizontal alliances between the tourism industry and other economic sectors in the Heuvelland. Different sectors outside tourism, for example the health care sector, want to invest in the tourism sector and in doing so will help to solve some of the problems mentioned.

This case discusses the horizontal alliances Healing Hills and Wellness in Luxury. With these new product market combinations, alliances between the tourism sector and the health and wellness sector have been created and will lead to tourism product development in the years to come.

Healing Hills

An important current trend in the medical care sector in the Netherlands is that patients are more willing to spend a part of their income on good health care, but at the same time they are far more critical than two decades ago and they want quick and good service for the same amount of money. That is why client friendliness is becoming more and more important also in health care and the medical sector has to learn to treat patients as guests.

Healing Hills is a major project in which the tourism industry and the medical sector cooperate to be better equipped to meet the needs and wants of the patient – guest who is in need of care. Joint care programs are being developed where curative care, in the form of care after an operation, is provided in hotels situated in the 'Heuvelland'. Medical tourism is stimulated in this project, but unlike medical tourism to Turkey and India, patients come to the 'Heuvelland' not for the operation but for necessary after care and recovery.

As a pilot study the Orbis Medical Concern, Oostwegel Châteauhotels and Stichting Zuid-Limburgse Heuvelland Hotels have developed recovery programs for patients who have undergone a knee or hip operation. First, the patient has to go through a pre-operative vitality programme in one of the hotels (5- or 3-stars). Then he undergoes the operation in the hospital. Finally he returns to the hotel for a recovery period of at least 2 days. Next to this programme for the patient, partner, and family programmes have been developed. In the future this project should attract new client groups (medical tourists), for example from the rest of the Netherlands.

Following on from this project other ones can be developed in the short term. Setting up an addiction clinic, organizing lifestyle and rehabilitation health holidays and developing a senior care concept similar to that applied by the Ronald McDonald House are some of the options.

Wellness in Luxury

Wellness is a lifestyle based on healthy life, physical as well as mental. Important elements of wellness are healthy food, relaxation, self-awareness, fitness, and spiritual activities. Nowadays wellness has become a trend due to causes such as the growing need for leisure and relaxation after a demanding week of work, the fact that 40% of the Dutch population is overweight, the aging of the population and the high percentage of sickness absence in comparison to other European countries.

Wellness in Luxury is another major project in which the tourism sector and the health sector cooperate. Within this project five potential product market combinations have been defined and will be developed in the coming years. Two of these product market combinations are 'Mooi Heuvelland' and 'Heuvelland Light'. Within these product market combinations several projects already have been initiated. These projects will be discussed here in short.

Valkenburg, a traditional tourist city in the Heuvelland, wants to become a city of wellness. In the near future a wellness boulevard will be developed. This concept is inspired by the spas in France and Italy. The boulevard will not only be a physical place for wellness in the broadest sense (e.g. retail and wellness therapy), but it also strives to develop a knowledge platform for and by scientists.

The development of this boulevard will take place in three stages. The first stage of this project is already developed. It focuses on preventive care in a tourism setting so that the consumer can change more quickly his/her whole lifestyle. In the short term, two projects will be started.

The first one is a health check arrangement unique in the Netherlands, in which many partners from the tourism industry and the health care sector cooperate. Employers can offer their employees a health check and a health programme at Thermae 2000, a spa and health resort in Valkenburg. It is unique because of the fact that the employee can start immediately with the health programme. This increases the motivation to make a real change in the way of living.

The second wellness project that will be implemented soon is a marl development offered by Thermae 2000, especially (but not solely) for senior guests. A sauna in the form of a marl hut will be built on the premises. The temperature in this sauna will be lower than in normal saunas. Next to this a new cosmetic line with marl and water as the main ingredients will be marketed and special marl workshops for seniors will be given, for example marl carving.

Next to these projects Château St. Gerlach situated in Valkenburg, already has the only specialized Kneipp spa in the Netherlands. Here the guest can choose from different sorts of baths and water massage with added herbs using the basics of Kneipp therapy. Chateau St. Gerlach offers different arrangements.

The second stage of the wellness boulevard will be to add curative care to the offer, and the third stage will be focused on innovative medical treatments and research and development in life sciences. The total project will be completed in about 15–20 years from today.

Good practice and less good practice

Being innovative is the magic word in today's tourism industry. The horizontal alliances that are being created in the 'Heuvelland' region are very innovative. Cooperation outside the boundaries of different sectors and with different partners will probably create a win-win situation in the long term for the consumer and the organizations that participate. However, innovation requires innovators in the consumer market, and from literature we know that this is just a very small part of the total population. Beside that, the small- and medium-sized enterprises in the Heuvelland region are not very innovative, or at least do not have the time nor the money to be innovative. For the wellness projects this might not be a big problem. Almost every accommodation has some wellness aspects in its supply, be it a sauna, a healthy breakfast or a Nordic walking clinic. However, asking patients to recover from an operation far away from their home is another cup of tea. Time will tell if there is really a demand for this offer. One thing is sure: more intense market research is needed and, although a lot of effort has been put into bringing different stakeholders together, the fruits of these efforts cannot yet be seen.

Peninsula Hot Springs: A new spa tourism experience 'Down Under'

Jennifer Laing

Description of chosen site

Peninsula Hot Springs is located on Victoria's Mornington Peninsula and is one of Australia's newest spa operations, open to visitors since June 2005. It offers bathing in natural geothermal pools, as well as private hot mineral baths and a Li'tya Spa Dreaming Centre for beauty and relaxation treatments. Patrons can also use the café, with healthy light meals served based on 'spa cuisine'. Its visitor base is diverse, ranging from young women and couples enjoying weekend packages and 'getaways' in the region and holidaying families with children, to retirees seeking a relaxing and rejuvenating experience. The proximity to the city of Melbourne means that the target market is largely metropolitan or Peninsula dwellers, although its accommodation packages with local businesses may entice more interstate and overseas visitors in the future. Its unique features are its status as the first hot springs to be commercially developed as a spa centre in Victoria and its locale on the picturesque and rugged coast, about 1.5 hour's drive from the elegant and cosmopolitan Melbourne, which makes it well placed to access tourists and day-trippers alike.

Australia, known chiefly for its sun, surf, and sand tourism, now appears to be offering a new tourist experience, centred on the spa and wellness market. This change in focus is being driven in part by government support for developing these health-associated tourism niches, with the State government seeking to position Victoria as 'the destination of choice for visitors seeking a spa and wellness experience', according to *Victoria's Spa and Wellness Tourism Action Plan 2005–2010*, and Tourism Australia recognizing the need to coordinate Australian spa development and supporting the establishment of a spa tourism plan for Australia by the Australasian Spa Association (ASPA).

An example of a new spa tourism operation 'Down Under' is Peninsula Hot Springs, on the Mornington Peninsula, Australia, which opened in June 2005. This facility offers visitors two sources of natural mineral water for bathing – an upper fresh water aquifer and a lower geothermal aquifer. The existence of the latter makes Peninsula Hot Springs the first hot spring spa operation in the State of Victoria and potentially gives it a competitive advantage over more famous and time-honoured facilities in the historic Hepburn Springs/Daylesford spa region, north of Melbourne, which have had to heat their spring water for bathing purposes since their boom days at the turn of last century, when 'taking the cure' was extremely popular for those of European heritage. The idea behind establishing Peninsula Hot Springs, however, came to its founder Charles Davidson, not after visiting the great spas of Europe, but after many visits to Japanese spa towns and resorts during his business travels. He sought to develop a similar venture in his home State in Australia and spent a number of years seeking out a suitable site, before opting for the current one. It appears that there is potential for other hot spring facilities to be developed throughout Victoria, based on geological survey drillings and the success of Peninsula Hot Springs, which may inspire similar ventures in other regions of Victoria and Australia.

The Peninsula Hot Springs complex encompasses indoor and outdoor mineral pools, as well as a Li'tya 'Spa Dreaming Centre' for a variety of beauty and therapeutic services, including massages and facials. The term 'Dreaming' refers to the Australian Aboriginal concept of the 'Dreamtime' and many of the treatments offered at the Springs, have Aboriginal names and incorporate indigenous healing techniques. They have also introduced a new series of massage treatments known as *Makoha*, the Maori word for 'ocean energy' and their New Zealand partner describes them as spreading, 'her people's story through touch in Australia'. *Li'tya* is an Aboriginal word meaning 'of the earth', based on local bush ingredients such as wattleseed and lilly pilly, as combining 'indigenous plant knowhow with the principles of herbalism, aromatherapy, sound, and colour therapy to deliver a wonderfully unique range of sensory treatments with powerful therapeutic effects'. This emphasis on traditional indigenous healing methods and resources mirrors a worldwide trend (Kim & Chung, 2005; McNeil & Ragins, 2005;Smith & Kelly, 2006), with examples including the Indian spa treatments based on the healing system of *Ayurveda*, or 'science of life', Thai spas utilizing Buddhist influences and the Japanese use of *Reiki* meaning 'universal energy' and referring to natural healing therapy. Modern spa patrons appear to seek out places where they can access ancient healing techniques and wellness remedies, albeit in luxurious and ultra hygienic surrounds, and this might be associated with a desire for authenticity and harmony with nature and natural processes (Smith & Kelly, 2006).

Allied services currently offered by Peninsula Hot Springs include a café, which offers light, healthy meals to patrons, based on 'spa cuisine', and a gift shop, which provides the opportunity to purchase products such as scrubs and lotions used by the therapists. Now there are also Peninsula Hot Springs branded spa products that incorporate the natural hot mineral spring water in their ingredients. The Springs' growing popularity, which exceeded initial predictions, has forced the facility to refer visitors to other spa-related tourism ventures in the region during peak periods. This has led the owners to bring forward AU$ 5 million plans for expansion to cope with the surge in demand, particularly at weekends and holiday periods, as well as developing a new facility to cater for young families, in response to feedback from adult visitors who would prefer separate bathing areas to preserve the tranquil nature of the experience. This expansion is also timely given significant investment across the Victorian spa industry, particularly in the Daylesford/Hepburn Springs region, with its AU$ 10 million redevelopment of the Hepburn Springs Bathhouse, due to be completed in 2008.

Development plans for Peninsula Hot Springs in 2009 include constructing the first 21 rooms of 126 room on-site accommodation, which would allow the management to structure their own packages for weekend mini-breaks and longer stays, complementing the offering of nearby resorts which offer a holistic package of spa treatments and health rejuvenation experiences, such as the endota spas at the Peninsula's Peppers Moonah Links resort and Lindenderry Country House and the Woodman Estate Spa Retreat at Moorooduc. At present, lacking on-site lodgings, Peninsula Hot Springs works closely with other tourism operators on the Peninsula, with packages offered such as local accommodation options with vouchers to visit the Springs. This collaboration will continue in the future, given the planned increased capacity of the facility and the owner's ethos that tourism and leisure operations in the area should work together to bring business to the region. The region is also becoming known for its plethora of wineries, as well as golf courses, and these may offer additional partnership opportunities for the Springs, given the obvious links between gourmandizing, recreation, and relaxation, and the fact that some Victorian wineries are now developing their own spa facilities *in situ*, such as Morning Star Estate in Mount Eliza and Immerse in the Yarra Valley.

According to the owners, 'The Hot Springs is a place of quiet relaxation', and this ambience at Peninsula Hot Springs is promoted through the use of design and colour and the inclusion of the existing natural environment into all design. The outdoor pools take advantage of sea breezes and the vast blue of the Australian sky, with native trees and shrubs adding to the unique experience, particularly for international visitors. The architecture of the complex is designed to flow with the natural coastal landscape, with its earth tones. Their next stage of development is aimed at creating 'special places of serenity', including pools with 360° views of the surrounding ocean and bay and sunrises and sunsets. Other new pools will be in a private valley, so that visitors can enjoy peaceful sounds of nature such as frogs croaking and the gentle sound of the surf, and a 'cave-like pool', where silence reigns. Their opening hours, 9.00 a.m. to 9.00 p.m., seven days a week, allow visitors to enjoy the transition and play of light associated with the movement from day and night, additional evidence of the importance placed by the facility on offering a haven from the hustle and bustle of everyday life.

Peninsula Hot Springs has the ability to cater for a variety of different market segments, and its proximity to the elegant urbanity of Melbourne allows it to tap into a diversified and cosmopolitan population, as well as catering to local Peninsula dwellers. For example, they offer Valentine's Day packages for couples, private functions such as pre-wedding weekends for the bride and her attendants and friends, pregnancy treatments for mothers-to-be, and now packages directed at men. Women with busy lives and increasingly stressful jobs might also be successfully targeted with messages about the relaxation benefits of spa going. The family segment is growing, as evidenced by the need for building additional dedicated facilities to cater for their special needs, and another potentially lucrative market segment is the retiree, often living on the Peninsula and looking to preserve physical health as well as rejuvenation through various treatments. Future markets to target might include the interstate and international visitors, who are looking for experiences beyond those traditionally associated with Australia linked with indigenous culture and the Australian landscape and/or natural surrounds. The business traveller is also the focus of marketing efforts. Peninsula Hot Springs has begun to promote memberships, where regulars can take advantage of discounted services, and a corporate club, which they market as the perfect adjunct to a corporate wellness program, linking into the growing awareness of staff health as an employment issue (McNeil & Ragins, 2005) and based around employee visits to the Springs.

It would appear that development of Peninsula Hot Springs has occurred in tandem with a rising demand for wellness services and an ever-increasing appreciation of health and spa experiences and destinations as a potential new growth area for Australian tourism. The next few years will be challenging for its owners, as they strive to balance visitor numbers with a desire to offer an experience which is both calming and rejuvenating, soothing the mind, body, and soul of a diverse target market spanning all community segments. They have announced plans to form an association with growing numbers of spas in the region, both day spas and spa resorts, to provide a strong regional brand which is distinguished from the more established Hepburn Springs/Daylesford area, which *Victoria's Spa and Wellness Tourism Action Plan 2005–2010* argues incorporates, 'some of the best mineral springs and associated spa and wellness tourism infrastructure in Australia'. Emphasizing the local, individual qualities of what is being offered may assist Peninsula Hot Springs to differentiate its product, as well as helping to expand its visitor base to include the international traveller, who may be looking for a distinctively Australian experience, beyond the Rock and the Reef.

Using wellness elements for branding an exclusive image of tourism sites in the north of Israel

Alon Gelbman

This case study of Israel describes and analyses the manner in which wellness elements serve to promote and brand elite images of tourism sites even though the weight of wellness in the tourist product may be relatively small.

Wellness activity is common in many countries around the world. This applies to Israel as well which, in recent years, has undergone extensive and intensive developments in the supply of wellness tourism services and attractions. Wellness tourism services are offered as part of many accommodation packages in Israel, from bed and breakfast units in the rural areas to the most prestigious hotels. These tourism attractions offer an all-encompassing experience with treatment, therapy, and instruction in proper lifestyles intended to cure body and soul, while also offering pampering and relaxation. It would be possible to say that wellness tourism has become an important – and highly sought – component of tourism products in Israel, and in many cases it has become a tourism attraction in its own right.

This study, which was conducted among tourism sites in the north of Israel, a region that attracts most of the country's internal tourism and is characterized by rural areas of green vistas and landscapes, examined the following question: How, if at all, do wellness elements become exclusive image promoters and branders of tourism sites? Methodology included: observations, interviews with tourism operators and content analysis of material intended to position and brand tourism site images on Internet home pages, advertising and reservations sites. The sample for content analysis included 39 tourist destinations in the north of Israel, which present themselves and their tourism product as places of wellness. The tourism sites that were selected include: health villages/hotels, health centres, bed and breakfast and hotel accommodations with health centres and spas. A comparison of the service profiles in the four types of wellness tourism sites that were included in the study are presented in Table CS10.1.

It was found that these tourism sites perceive wellness elements as an important element for branding and positioning themselves as exclusive sites. For the most part, holistic wellness tourism sites offering a broad range of services and activities are considered exclusive and enjoy a prestigious image (see Table CS10.2). However, it appears that tourism sites offering only limited wellness services and activities expend significant marketing efforts to appropriate an image of exclusivity for themselves by emphasizing the wellness services they offer. This trend is especially blatant among small tourism operators of the bed and breakfast accommodations that are so plentiful in the north of Israel. These operators, each with a few accommodation units at the most, offer limited wellness services (mainly massages), but they invest heavily in planning and design to endow their accommodations and facilities with a tranquil, soothing, and pampering ambience. They include elements such as a luxurious whirlpool bath in the bedroom and in the patio overlooking a panoramic view, and try to position and brand themselves in a way that conveys a prestigious image that strongly emphasizes the wellness component of their tourism product (see Table 10.2 and Figure CS10.1). A similar situation can be found among hotels with health or fitness centres. Despite the heavy stress on wellness facilities and activities, these comprise only a limited component of their activity and in many cases are run by outside concessionaires and not by the hotels. The hotels perceive wellness activity as offering high added value for the purposes of positioning and branding their image as luxurious.

The marketing strategies adopted to achieve this positioning and branding include activities such as employing wellness-associated names and extensive use of the term 'spa' (and in many cases distorting the actual meaning of water therapies), emphasizing the calming, tranquil, spiritual, and romantic ambience of an area surrounded by nature and pastoral landscapes, emphasizing natural and rustic foods which fit in well with a healthful atmosphere, and stressing a broad array of therapies and treatments.

Table CS10.1 Typology of Wellness Services in the North of Israel.

Type	Setting	N	Facilities	Activities	Number of Rooms	Price in US $ per Night or per Entrance
A. Wellness villages/ hotels	Mountain and countryside region (north of Israel)	4	• Natural mineral resources • Spa and sauna • Swimming pool • Fitness club	• Various types of massage therapies • Diet program/organic food • Spiritual activities	18–126	$130–$1,700
B. Wellness centers	Developed rural tourism region in the north of Israel	3	• Natural mineral resources • Spa and sauna • Swimming pool • Fitness club	• Various types of massage therapies • Spiritual activities	None	$13–$215
C. Rural/ town guest houses (BB)	Rural settlements in the Galilee and north of Israel	24	• Whirlpool bath mostly. In a few places: spa, sauna or swimming pool	• Various types of massage therapies (mostly outsourced) • Spiritual activities (in some cases only)	1–20	$115–$320
D. Hotels with health/ fitness centers	Tourism cities in the north of Israel	8	• Natural mineral resources • Spa and sauna • Swimming pool • Fitness club	• Various types of massage therapies • Spiritual activities (in some cases only)	17–258	$190–$460

Table CS10.2 Level of Luxurious Wellness Image in Comparison with Facilities, Activities and Holistic Attitude of the Tourism Sites.

Type	Level of Development of Wellness Facilities and Activities	Level of Holistic Orientation	Level of Luxurious Wellness Image
A. Wellness villages/hotels	High/very high	High/very high	Very high
B. Wellness centers	High/very high	Medium/low	High/very high
C. Rural/town guest houses (BB)	Medium/low	Medium/low	High/very high
D. Hotels with health/fitness centers	High/medium/low	Low	High/very high

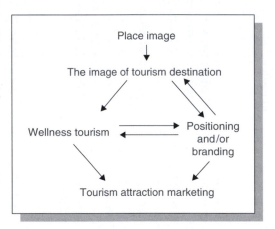

Figure CS10.1
The Model of 'wellness tourism' image of a destination as a tool for tourism marketing.

Most of the sites choose names for themselves with a strong orientation towards wellness elements and, apparently attributing high added value to a name that can attract visitors. For example, many names can be cited that include the word 'spa' such as 'Pastoral Spa', 'Spa in the Forest', 'Hermon Spa'. Apparently the word 'spa' is perceived as a code word with the power to attract tourists. Other names stress a component of nature or geographical location and the unique landscape of their tourism product, as can be seen in names such as 'The Path of Nature', 'The Sea Overlook', or 'The Spa above the Lake', or the 'River Spa', whose names combine both the word 'spa' and their location above a lake or river, evidently assuming that their associations with nature and water might strengthen their image and branding as wellness sites and position them in a unique niche. The excessive use of 'spa', which does not refer to spas in the traditional sense of the word, and the desire of small operators to improve their image and positioning, have created an economic problem. Guest house operators cannot afford to employ a permanent staff of therapists on location. The solution is outsourcing. In the north of Israel companies specialize in offering treatment services for guest houses and small hotels.

One of these companies chose 'Mobile Spa' as its name, reflecting a total dissociation from the original meaning of 'spa' in the sense of water therapy. The service they offer is mainly massages of various types in the bed and breakfast accommodations in the north of Israel, and for many potential clients, the term 'spa' means massage services. In their guest lodgings, tourists can obtain information about treatments and order them either from the hosts or brochures left in the rooms for perusal by the tourists.

The Internet sites of the tourism locations that were investigated use colour pictures, video clips and textual descriptions to underscore their strategy of positioning and branding their facilities as havens of calm, tranquility, and a spiritual and romantic ambience in an environment characterized by nature and pastoral panoramas. These qualities are highly prominent in the advertising material of all these sites. In recent years most tourism reservations in Israel, and especially for guest houses, have been made through Internet reservations sites, and even those who do not reserve by Internet usually visit the home page of the specific sites to learn about them before actually placing their reservations (Flisher et al., 2004). Pictures of the site on the background of a splendid panoramic mountain view, a beach or the banks of a river are very common. In many cases on-site wellness facilities and activities are photographed to create a pastoral, soothing and romantic feeling. In addition, descriptions such as 'rustic, intimate grounds, isolated atop Mount Canaan, pampering hospitality in the European style at an altitude of 900m, overlooking 'an awe-inspiring mountain panorama', or 'a charming spa in an intimate environment offering a breathtaking panorama that touches the soul'. Such descriptions are intended to complement and strengthen the image conveyed through the pictures.

An emphasis on natural and rustic foods that fit in well with a healthful ambience is another prominent element found in the marketing systems of the tourism sites under investigation. Their Internet sites contain pictures of natural food served in rustic utensils made of natural materials, on a background of mountainous Galilee vistas; or two people eating a rustic breakfast on the veranda of the guest house accommodations, sitting in a setting that is soothing and tranquil. These pictures are accompanied by textual descriptions such as the following: 'Inspired by the culinary treasures of the Galilee. You are invited to enjoy pampering brunch and dinner menus of local dishes prepared at home, including fresh herbs, natural freshly prepared fruit juices and special baked goods, using only fresh ingredients with no preservatives'. 'You can order rich Galilee breakfasts prepared from the best produce of the area, as well as pampering spa treatments. In the green garden, around the guest house rooms, you will find not only peace and quiet but also beds for sunbathing and a wooden table on which you can enjoy a meal in a green environment'. Thus, it seems that healthful organic food without preservatives in a green environment, in fields and the heart of nature, can strengthen the wellness image, and thus constitutes an additional component in the exclusive branding of these sites.

A broad range of therapies and treatments are prominent in the pictures. Patients are depicted lying restfully on special treatment beds, enjoying professional quality care from the therapist. In these pictures, extensive thought has been given to the ambience of the room in which the treatment is given, as is described in the text: 'Treatment rooms are insulated against noise, lit with soft, pleasant light, and relaxing background music envelops you'. 'Treatments are given in an atmosphere of candle light, aromatic oils, and calming music'. The textual descriptions accompanying the pictures of the treatments in the sites are varied and highly creative. Texts include messages such as 'We are pleased to invite you to an experience from the fairy tales. Remove yourself from the exhausting routine for a moment so that both your body and soul can be coddled and calmed'; 'We invite you to enjoy a variety of indulging massages, to be rejuvenated through an array of innovative cosmetic treatments, and to experience various relaxation techniques that will balance the flow of energy in your body and teach you how to play an active role in releasing emotional stress and improve the quality of your life'. As can be seen in Table 10.2, there is a great gap between the facilities and treatments offered in holistic wellness sites such as health farms, as opposed to guest house lodgings or hotels with a health centre. The last two invest great effort in enveloping themselves with the image of sites that offer a broad range of high quality treatments, in the hope of improving their branding and positioning as luxurious wellness sites.

From the conclusions of this study, it can be learned that elements of wellness help to foster the image of prestige and luxury in various tourism sites. For hotels and holistic health villages, a luxury image is important because the tourism product they offer is special and expensive. Moreover, behind the image is usually a tourism product that justifies the image. On the other hand, it appears that in many tourism sites, especially bed and breakfast guest houses and hotels with a health or fitness centre, a considerable gap exists between the limited facilities and activities on offer and the image of health and holistics created in their marketing and advertising. Evidently, the reason for this undue emphasis on limited facilities is the high price that can be charged for an elite tourism product, and an image of wellness product is apparently an important contributor to this added value. Wellness tourism has a serious connotation in holistic sites, but distortion of the term, especially by guest houses seeking to upgrade their image, positioning and branding, may harm the entire branch. Symptoms of possible harm are readily evident in the overinvestment by many small tourism guest house operators in facilities that will lead to an excess in supply and a reduction of the prices of wellness services and treatments on offer. Similarly, small tourism operators may find themselves deeply in debt for investments in superfluous – and expensive – facilities. With limited resources and growing competition from many others like themselves, small tourism operators may find the potential for economic feasibility shrouded in doubt. One ramification of the findings of this study is that critical thought should be given to using wellness for image building and marketing tourism products that are not with a higher level of holistic and do not include a large array of facilities and activities that justify the concept of treating body, mind and spirit.

CASE STUDY 11

Ayurvedic health tourism in Kerala, India

Kevin Hannam

Increasing numbers of western tourists are taking the opportunity to engage with both western and non-western forms of healthcare treatment in developing countries with new forms of host–guest relations ensuing. This case study begins by analysing the marketing of the state of Kerala (India) as a centre for non-western healthcare tourism based on the Indian tradition of *ayurveda*. Based on extensive fieldwork in Kerala (2004–2006), it is argued that, for those who seek western medicine, healthcare is the primary motive and tourism is the secondary motive. For those who seek non-western healthcare, tourism is the primary motive and healthcare is the secondary motive. This perhaps highlights the ambivalence of western people towards indigenous forms of health provision as an 'alternative' form of medicine and/or health education.

Marketed as 'God's Own Country' separate from the rest of India, and one of the top fifty must see destinations in the world, Kerala is one of the smallest states in India, but it has the highest density of population. Over 30 million people live in Kerala (some 3% of the Indian population), 85% of them living in small villages, which are continuously distributed throughout the state. Approximately 61% of the population are Hindus, 21% Christians, and 18% Muslims. Kerala has the highest literacy rate in India at 91%, the lowest infant mortality rate in India, the highest life expectancy rate in India, and the highest physical quality of life in India. By India's standards, Kerala is more developed in terms of basic services than other states in India. Indeed the travel writer Bill McKibben went as far to say that: 'statistically Kerala stands out as the Mount Everest of social development; there's truly no place like it' – a quotation that is frequently used in publicity for tourism to Kerala. Beneath the surface, however, other writers have emphasized the 'Hoax of God's Own Country' arguing that – Kerala, India's Model State, is actually hell. They point to Kerala having the highest suicide rate in India, the highest unemployment rate in India and the highest crime rate in India (Wadhwa, 2004). Indeed, Sreekumar and Parayil (2002:529–530) argue that 'Kerala's hard won achievements in social development may be unravelling because of serious economic and financial crises that have afflicted the state in recent times … '

Nevertheless, tourism is of crucial importance to Kerala's development. In 2005, The Chief Minister of Kerala, Mr Chandy emphasized that among other things, 'Tourism drives the State's economy', 'Kerala's economy is largely dependent upon tourism' and that 'Tourism [is] to be the state's new model of development'. According to 2002 statistical data from the State Department of Tourism, Kerala has a 10% share of India's tourism and hosts nearly 6 million tourists each year, including a quarter of a million foreign tourists. The main source countries of western tourists (in ranked order) are the UK, the US, France, Germany, Switzerland, and Italy. Moreover, visitor numbers are increasing year-on-year (by some 5% on average) on the back of successful tourism marketing.

Tourism in Kerala has won worldwide publicity and national and regional awards including:

- One of the 100 great trips for the 21st Century – 'Travel and Leisure Magazine'
- One of the top ten paradises – 'National Geographic Magazine'
- One of the top ten holidays for romance – 'Cosmopolitan Magazine'
- The 'Mecca' of the oldest, holistic health system 'Geo-Saison Magazine'

In its own SWOT analysis the Department of Tourism in Kerala has argued that Kerala's strengths are that it is relatively peaceful, has a well-known brand image, a wide variety of tourism experiences and landscapes, good education, and healthcare systems, relatively good transport and communication infrastructure (compared with the rest of India) and relatively few political problems (again in comparison with the rest of India). Its weaknesses are that it suffers (like most of India) from poor waste management systems, weak quality control mechanisms, militant trade unions (Kerala has had a communist state government for many years) and a high percentage of low yield foreign tourists – backpackers. The opportunities it has identified are in terms of a potential growth in heritage tourism and the development of new markets, while as threats it recognizes environmental pollution, cultural degradation, natural disasters, and continued competition from other states and countries. In terms of the development of specifically health tourism, the Department of Tourism in Kerala has been successful in terms of marketing traditional, holistic 'health' tourism, namely, ayurveda as part of its 'brand equity' and USP's.

Ayurveda has been described by various practitioners as:

- 'A complete and integrated life science'.
- 'The science of life and the art of living'.
- 'A holistic, spiritual and philosophical system of medication that covers all the principels of allopathy, homoeopathy and naturopathy'.

From the Sanskrit, ayurveda is derived from *ayu* (life) and *veda* (knowledge) and is some 2000 years old. Ayurveda views the world as having an intrinsic order and any illness is a departure from that order. According to ayurvedic philosophy we all possess three doshas, humours, or elements, namely: vatha (wind/air), pitha (fire), and kapha (water/earth). Any disease is diagnosed as an imbalance of these in the human body. Treatments, therefore seek to restore the balance of these three elements by either *panchakarma* (internal purification), or diet and massage. Contemporary ayurveda in Kerala is largely focused on forms of massage which is claimed to be particularly beneficial for those suffering chronic ailments such as arthritis and rheumatism. However more austere treatments are available including: induced vomiting, herbal applications through the nose, medicated enema and (under medical supervision) surgical drainage of the blood. Having an ayurvedic massage in Kerala is primarily relaxing and widely available at most hotels but practitioners argue that treatments need to be sustained over 2 weeks or more for any further benefits.

Kerala was the first State in India to sell health tourism abroad by promoting ayurveda. However, it has recently been recognized by the Government of India that 'the oversell of ayurveda has resulted in the mushrooming of unlicensed and ill-equipped healing centres which often have untrained and unqualified personnel. There has also been a growth of shady spas and massage parlours in the garb of ayurvedic treatment' (Basheer, 2003:2). This, the authorities have now realized, could seriously damage Kerala's tourism image.

The study area for our research was, Kovalam, a former fishing village (fishing is still practised and tourists engage with this) just 16 km away from the state capital, Trivandrum. Kovalam is Kerala's most popular beach-side resort and has grown dramatically over the past 30 years with largely unregulated beach side hotel and allied tourist services development as a product of both mass tourism and backpacker tourism from both western countries and Indian day visitors. Kovalam consists of two coves (Lighthouse Beach and Hawah Beach) and the town itself set back from the main beach side developments. Kovalam is described in marketing literature as an evergreen and pleasant climatic beach resort known as the 'Paradise of the South'. A quarter of Kerala's tourists are estimated to visit Kovalam each year. Numerous ayurvedic 'clinics' have been opened in Kovalam alongside and inside the hotel development. Kerala's tourism department has been increasingly concerned with this development and has sought to bring in a licensing scheme so as to regulate this grassroots health tourism industry (Radhakirshnan, 2005). Currently a voluntary certification code of conduct is in practice but not widely accepted (Moosath, 2006).

Although we do not have the space here to develop this our evidence suggests that for some tourists visiting Kerala ayurveda was largely a secondary concern consisting of a few massages: 'Having a massage was enjoyable and made me feel more relaxed but it was very thorough and left me also feeling a bit molested'. (M, 34, Construction Worker, UK). However, for many others, who had previous experience of spa treatments in Germany and Switzerland, the key reason to visit Kerala is for the aesthetic and spiritual nature of ayurveda: 'My ayurvedic treatments have given me spiritual guidance and it made my skin much softer too'. (D, 26, Bank Clerk, Switzerland).

In conclusion, Kerala's indigenous health tourism is developing apace and not without the usual effects of unplanned tourism development. Moreover, although there is no direct link between ayurvedic health tourism and the sex tourism that also exists in Kovalam, sex and 'romance' tourism is widely prevalent. We need to investigate further and question the ethics of the cultural exploitation of indigenous forms of healthcare for aesthetic and possibly sexual gratification in developing countries.

Hot springs in Japanese domestic and international tourism

Tamara Rátz

Introduction

Widespread volcanic activity makes the islands of Japan one of the world's greatest hot spring (onsen) destinations. Bathing in hot springs has been a quintessentially Japanese form of leisure for centuries; the country's oldest hot spring, Dogo Onsen on Shikoku, has a history stretching back over 1500 years. However, the attraction of onsen is about much more than hot water; the essential components of the modern onsen experience are nutrition, sightseeing, exercise, and relaxation in natural surroundings (Seki & Heilman Brooke, 2005). Throughout the centuries, the interpretation and utilization of hot springs in Japan has undergone significant changes. While during the Edo period (1603–1868) travelling to hot springs also represented a spiritual journey, partly a pilgrimage and partly a way to relax one's mind, in the Meiji era (1868–1912) onsen visits became institutionalized events for school and company groups, with an emphasis on learning (Raveri, 2002). In the second part of the 20th century, as the popularity of recreation-oriented tourism increased, many traditional onsen were transformed into large-scale holiday resorts that are among the most visited destinations in the country, offering outdoor and indoor communal bathing facilities, hotel spas, as well as private baths (Chartrungruang & Mitsutake, 2007) in addition to supplementary services such as aromatherapy, foot and hand baths, and a wide range of restaurants and shopping facilities (Mansfield, 2001; Kobayashi, 2004). According to the Japan Spa Association, the country's 16,000 onsen get over 140 million visits every year (population: 127 million) which is an indication of how many people, especially the elderly, return repeatedly (Ellis, 2004).

In recent years, Japanese hot springs have also become a part of the modern medical system, although the number of facilities offering long-term therapy is still rather small, since medical insurance rarely covers onsen stays which tend to be relatively short breaks and are typically regarded as fun trips (Ito, 2003). However, the imminent ageing of the country's population (Aspalter, 2007) is likely to increase the need for enjoyable alternative healthcare solutions offered by hot springs resorts. Onsen therapy is a type of alternative or complementary medicine, not directly curing the cause of the disease, but treating the body as a whole, and assisting in recuperation, rehabilitation, and prevention. In addition to the hot springs, the key elements in Japanese balneotherapy are gases as well as climatic and geographical factors (Ito, 2003). An onsen's chemical makeup is one of the key elements of balneotherapy. According to the 1979 revision of the 1948 Onsen Law, Japan's hot springs are classified into nine categories based on water properties (Ueda, 2006):

- Simple carbon dioxide (carbonated) springs
- Hydrogen carbonate (bicarbonate earth) springs
- Chloride (common salt) springs
- Vitriolic springs
- Ferrous springs
- Sulphur springs
- Acidic springs
- Radioactive springs
- Simple thermal springs with water temperature over 25°C.

As mentioned earlier, gastronomy – with meals generally being included at onsen ryokan – is a key component of the overall onsen experience. International visitors – particularly to the smaller, less mass-oriented hot springs – generally appreciate onsen cuisine which, although unintentionally, represents the key characteristics of the increasingly popular 'slow food' movement. Japanese cuisine has traditionally been based on the principle of consciously enjoying both the flavours and the presentation of the food, and paying particular attention to details such as matching the colour of the plate with the colour of the food, or the type and timing of each course served, relative to the previous course.

Similarly important elements of the onsen experience are the geographical location and the architecture of the destination. Onsen ryokan have always been constructed of natural materials, including timber, paper, bamboo, grass or cloth, in order to form an environment that encourages 'traditional behaviour', that is the personal, relaxing rituals of the Japanese bath (Altman, 2008). While many onsen have been modernized over the last decades – which, in many cases, has led to replacing the atmospheric, wooden Japanese buildings with large concrete structures that are less in harmony with the environment, there are many exceptions where the onsen have been remade in an elegant, traditional Japanese way, with refined artwork, elegant flower arrangements, impeccable and relatively flexible personal service, excellent food served in private rooms and small capacity.

Attitudes and perceptions of domestic and international visitors

Probably the main difference between Japanese and international visitors' perceptions of onsen visits is related to the nature of the experience. While in domestic Japanese tourism hot springs are mostly seen as relaxation-, pleasure- or health-oriented destinations, most Western tourists staying at hot springs are probably more inspired by culture- and heritage-related motivations than by health reasons. Japan has changed significantly in the last 50 years, and the socio-economic and cultural changes are reflected in many aspects of the reality experienced by visitors, including architecture (traditional Japanese thatch-roofed wooden buildings have mostly disappeared) or consumer habits (the ubiquity of shopping facilities is overwhelming). Many international leisure visitors who come to Japan to see a unique culture that is significantly different from their own may feel slightly disappointed by the thoroughly modernized and Westernized country, or even by the seemingly harmonious coexistence of Western lifestyle and the widespread manifestations of traditional cultural heritage. Modern Japan is an overdeveloped country where, to a surprisingly large extent, the tourist milieu (Michalkó & Rátz, 2008), particularly in the metropolitan areas, is composed of concrete high-rise buildings, neon signs, and generally nondescript architecture, so the traditional hot springs are among the few places left in Japan that have retained what Westerners perceive as traditional Japan. Consequently, visiting an onsen is one opportunity for international travellers to get in touch with the so-called 'real Japan' and 'authentic Japanese culture'.

Of course, there are many well-developed onsen towns catering for large numbers of mostly domestic tourists that have already lost their traditional atmosphere, but there are so-called 'hidden' hot springs (Neff, 1995), with just one or a few establishments, catering for a much smaller number and generally more discriminating visitors. However, although these 'hidden' onsen are able to offer a rural, fairly natural, quiet atmosphere, both physical and cultural access may be a challenge for international visitors. While mass-oriented resorts are usually easily accessible by the country's extensive railway network, most small onsen require guests to have their own transportation. Language difficulties pose a similar problem: particularly finding information and establishing contact in any other language than Japanese may be difficult, since on the spot, the helpfulness of the hosts usually overcome language barriers. However, while Japan is generally a tourist-friendly country, the reserved attitude of the Japanese may lead to a deliberate Japanese-only marketing communication policy in more upmarket onsen ryokan, in order to maintain the exclusivity of the place by excluding simply curious Westerners with little or no affiliation to Japanese culture, thus ensuring the satisfaction of their traditional clientele.

The traditional Japanese aesthetics represented by the 'hidden' hot springs draws many foreigners, but also domestic visitors are motivated by the relaxing and nostalgic atmosphere promised by such establishments. In one of the most densely populated countries in the world, where the majority of the population live in crowded urban areas, hot springs breaks may help restore the equilibrium between the social and the personal. In addition, within the contradictory framework of the Japanese tourism industry that aims to internationalize its supply and preserve the vanishing cultural traditions, domestic tourism enjoys an increasing popularity, since travelling to rural areas is perceived by many domestic visitors as a reunion with Japanese identity (Creighton, 1997). Thus, it is also the 'real Japan' that many domestic visitors seek during their holidays, a concept similar to foreign tourists' perceptions in terms of being pre-Western, pre-industrialized and non-urban, but also acknowledged by the Japanese as a place located in the past.

As indicated by information collected by the author through personal observation and conversations with international onsen visitors in Japan during a research trip in spring 2008 (and confirmed by e.g. Tsukada, 2003; Kojima & Kawamura, 2006), foreigners typically perceive an onsen visit as a pleasurable experience because of the warm, soothing water, but also some sort of a cultural challenge since there are strict rules to learn and follow. Since a thorough description of the basics of Japanese bathing etiquette is included in practically any information or promotional material, including guidebooks, websites, and even the onsen changing rooms (all very vigorously emphasizing the correct rules, e.g. not taking soap into the tub, really washing yourself well, taking off jewellery beforehand, bathing without swimsuit, separate pools for men and women, not taking the little towel into the water), it is easy to develop a preconception of an onsen visit as some sort of cultural test as opposed to the relaxing physical experience it actually is. The difference in tone is particularly sharp in comparison with marketing messages of spas outside Japan, which generally focus on the pleasantness of the experience and the variety of services and treatments, not on expected behaviour.

Obviously, many international visitors to Japan are simply not interested in an onsen experience. However, the lack of interest or an unfavourable attitude towards hot springs may also stem from intimidation: the further out of the tourist areas they get, the less likely they will find English speakers and the more likely they will be confused about what is expected of them (Kojima & Kawamura, 2006). Although the bathing rules are not particularly complex, being naked among strangers make many Western tourists uncomfortable, especially as they tend to stand out in a predominantly Japanese crowd. In addition, there are also many behavioural rules and little flexibility in traditional onsen accommodation; for example, it is rather unusual for Japanese onsen ryokan to accept guests travelling alone, which, from an international visitor's point of view, is slightly in contrast with the separate bathing principle, and again, does not make the overall experience easier for foreigners. However, recently there has been some gradual change in terms of rules and flexibility among ryokan owners, partly as a concession to international visitors, but mostly to accommodate a younger, well-travelled Japanese clientele (Altman, 2008).

Note: Based on field research supported by the Japan Foundation Fellowship for Intellectual Exchange within the framework of a three-year research project on health tourism and quality of life (OTKA 67573).

CHI Spa at The Shangri-La's, Sabah, Malaysia: Its philosophy and management concept – 'journey of experiences'

Jennifer Kim Lian Chan

Introduction

In line with the healthy living concept and the increase in awareness for health and fitness in a Malaysian context, spa and wellness has grown and become well accepted as one of the new tourism products and services in Malaysia recently. The Malaysian government has recognized the pioneering spirit of Malaysian spa entrepreneurs, such that spas have made a difference to the spa and wellness industry. The Malaysia Spa and Wellness Awards were held on 4th December 2006 to salute those who had made achievement and for their inspiration in the spa and wellness industry. In many ways, spa and wellness is perceived by the middle and upper income level earners as a form of leisure cum health activity in today's healthy living society.

Over the last 2 years, spa and wellness services have begun to expand rapidly, seemingly as an emerging business sector, and are also recognized as a new form of tourism product for hotel operators in Malaysia. Spa and health centres are commonly found in resort hotels and it is seen as an add-on service to the in-house guests as part of the leisure activities that they can enjoy during their stay. Also, it is a way to generate hotel revenue besides room, food and beverage. The growth of the spa and health services business can be witnessed not only in the resort hotel sector, but it is also evident in the commercial sector such as individual private operated centres located in shopping malls and business commercial buildings in Sabah. Because it is a new form of service business, there has been little attention given by the government in terms of regulations, policies, and standard practices of operating spa and health centres in Malaysia. Although both the hotel and commercial sectors offer almost the same type of spa and massage services, there exists a wide range of price difference between these two sectors. The difference in pricing is mainly due to difference in qualities from its facilities, environment, and professional services as well as product ingredients used.

Despite the fast expansion and popular demand of spa and wellness services/activities by both local and international tourists, there is little understanding of the spa and wellness industry in the Malaysian context. Thus, this case study aims to explore the development and management of spas in the hotel industry in Sabah. Sabah, located on the island of Borneo as part of Malaysia, has been promoted as a nature, culture, and adventure tourist destination with its main target market in European countries. European tourists are attracted by the destination's nature and culture attractions. In addition, luxury resort hotels in Sabah are regarded as important attractors for tourists to spend their holidays in the area. Indeed, these resort hotels are being promoted as one of the place attractions by the local inbound tour operators in their tour packages (Chan & Yeoh, 2001). A study by Chan and Yeoh (2001) confirms that tourists are attracted to visiting Sabah because of the picturesque nature of this beautiful island, its beaches, and internationally renowned beach resorts. The recent trend of spa and health tourism has led to many resort hotel operators in Sabah introducing spa and wellness activities in their hotels, where they have become part of the hotel facilities, providing their in-house guests with a new add-on form of relaxation service. This service is well received by European guests with its reasonable pricing as acknowledged by most hotel operators. The recent tourism development focuses on the concept of healthy living style where spa and wellness are viewed by the hotel operators as one of the potential tourism products and services that can be offered to international tourists during their vacations in Sabah. Yet, there is little understanding of the hotel spa development and management concept. This case study aims to fill in the gap by examining CHI Spa Centre at The Shangri-La's Tanjung Aru Resort and Spa, provided by one of the five star international chain resort hotels located in Kota Kinabalu, Sabah, Malaysia. The case is set to present the unique concept and philosophy of CHI Spa. It attempts to highlight the important issues and challenges faced in developing and managing hotel spas in Malaysia. The objectives of the case are: (a) to describe CHI Spa and its unique physical facilities and service concept; (b) to highlight the good practices and the strengths and weaknesses of CHI Spa; (c) to present some of the operational and managerial issues relating to hotel spas in Sabah, Malaysia.

An overview of CHI – the spa at The Shangri-La

CHI Spa was first introduced at The Shangri-La's Hotel in Bangkok and subsequently to The Shangri-La's Hotel in Penang. The expansion of CHI Spa Centre is stimulated by the demand from the in-house and the market potential of each destination where the hotel is located. Due to the current rapid demand for spa and health services by its in-house guests at The Shangri-La's Tanjung Aru Resort and Spa, Kota Kinabalu, and its market potential in Sabah, The Shangri-La's group decided to expand its CHI Spa to this hotel. CHI Spa was introduced in late 2006 at The Shangri-La's Tanjung Aru Resort and Spa, Sabah, as the third expansion for CHI Spa. CHI Spa Centre is named after the Chinese word in traditional Chinese philosophy meaning 'energy'. Several reasons justify the use of word 'CHI'. First, 'CHI' is the universal life force that governs well-being and personal vitality. It is believed that CHI must flow freely within the body and when blocked, disease and illness will appear. Movement is therefore a key element in releasing these natural blockages. Exercise, stretching, massage, hydrotherapy, and movement of the mind through relaxation and meditation combine to assist the body's natural renewal and form the basis of the CHI, thus forming the SPA philosophy. Indeed, the CHI's signature therapies are based on the Five Elements Theory – Metal, Water, Wood, Fire, and Earth. These must be in balance to harmonize with the positive Yang and negative Yin energy within the body. Second, it was the inspiration from the origin of The Shangri-La legend, high in the mystical Himalayan Mountains, that this magical world brings you the secrets and the unique spa concept fusing ancient healing traditions, philosophies, and rituals from China and the Himalayas.

CHI Spa is currently under construction at a cost of about 8.9 million Malaysian Ringgit. The facilities consist of eight individual villas (three units of villas for double occupancy and five villas for single occupancy), with one common yoga room. Other facilities include steam bath, jacuzzi, and ranges of body therapy services. It is expected to be the official opening for business in September 2007 according to its Spa Manager.

The main underlying concept of CHI Spa is to provide the ultimate in 'privacy, peaceful and high class services' to the hotel guests. Thus, CHI Spa management not only emphasize facilities and services, the landscape, and green environment, but more importantly the journey of experiences created by CHI Spa as mentioned by Ms Rika during an interview session. CHI Spa is built at the edge of the coastal land that offers spectacular views, surrounded by a peaceful green environment and blue sea. This provides a leading advantage in terms of promoting itself as a spa destination within the resort hotel.

The main unique feature of CHI Spa is incorporated into its location, villa concept building features, landscape, and environment/serviscape, which emphasizes 'privacy, spaceless and quality services that make a unique journey of experiences at CHI' rather than just merely a regular therapy and leisure activities that most spa centres offer, said the Manager of CHI Spa. Thus, this concept is a unique selling point for CHI Spa, with an emphasis on 'a journal of experiences that provide privacy and spaceless via the tangible (physical environment and therapy services) and intangible elements (quality of experiences)'. More interesting, CHI Spa concept is fusing ancient healing traditions, philosophies, and rituals from China and the Himalayas. This makes it a unique combination of its ingredients, which make it very different from other spa centres. In addition, its therapy ingredients are 80% from international brands and 20% of local ingredients. Product safety is the main concern for the management and it is ensured that every local ingredient is properly tested and has approval before it is used.

CHI Spa – its short- and long-term objectives

CHI, the Spa at The Shangri-La's is perceived as a 'unique add-on hotel service that provides a journey of body therapy experiences' for its in-house guests and an extension of hotel physical facilities of the resort hotels. The management of The Shangri-La's chain believes that guests would enjoy the feeling of privacy and space in CHI Spa. According to the Manager of CHI Spa, Ms Rika, the short-term objectives of CHI Spa are: (a) to provide guests with a spaceless, private journey of experiences of body therapy in the resort hotel; (b) a better place that offers good facilities and services for the in-house guests than the existing spa and health centre; (c) to provide five star spa services with five star facilities which is in line with its hotel star rating, and (d) to generate hotel revenue. There are three long-term objectives set for CHI Spa which include: (a) to become a leading five star spa centre within the hotel resort that offers a unique journey of experiences; (b) to become an excellent spa location for Sabah and Malaysia, and (c) to become a leader in hotel spas in Malaysia.

In order to realize its short- and long-term objectives, and more importantly to promote CHI Spa as a spa destination within the resort hotel in Sabah, the management of CHI Spa Centre has set its standards high and has developed a set of good practices. Firstly, the uniqueness of the physical facilities of CHI Spa can be evidenced from a good planning and proper concept of spa – physical facilities, imported décor and use of materials, selection of location, and philosophical approach. In this case, CHI, the Spa at The Shangri-La's defines its spa concept in line with Chinese and Himalayan philosophy as well as the use of high quality ingredients that blend with local products. Furthermore, there is a wide range of available herbs that are potentially being used in the body therapy. Secondly, the management of CHI Spa considers that developing its own brand name is important to differentiate itself from other spa centres as well as for customer loyalty. Furthermore, brand is important for spa centres which intend to promote themselves as a spa destination in the future. In order to provide high quality therapy services at CHI Spa, staff training and development are an important element. Currently, certain criteria have been set for the selection of staff /therapies that include previous experiences, personal grooming, and general knowledge of health. In order to overcome the issue of human resources, multiskilling is one of the most important criteria for staff training in CHI Spa. It is perceived that the main critical issues in hotel spa management are the lack of well trained staff and having a proper spa training centre. At the macro level, setting spa industry standards and having government policy in terms of regulating spa and wellness will be quite a challenging task. This is because the spa and wellness industry is new and yet is growing at a rapid speed; so professional human resources are a great shortage.

SWOT analysis

CHI Spa is built within the resort hotel and it is operated under the resort hotel management, thus, its primary market is from its in house guests – European, Japanese, and Korean. There is a potential market segment coming from the walk-in guests from other hotels who are looking for unique spa experiences. Also, guests attending meeting, incentive, convention, and exhibition (MICE) will be an emerging market segment for CHI Spa.

In general, like any kind of business or service, competition will exist for spa and wellness tourism. In the case of CHI Spa, its strength lies in its unique concept, location, use of ingredient, and brand name for its high quality services. Also, it has positioned itself as a quality spa centre that offers a journey of experience. Nevertheless, the major threat for CHI Spa centre is the price competition among other resort hotels and commercial sectors. There will be more and more spa centres and services available for the tourists in Sabah. It may attract some of its in-house guests who do not emphasize so much the quality of services. Since spa and wellness tourism is still regarded as a new tourism product and spas in hotels are only just starting to grow in Sabah, Malaysia; CHI Spa can therefore position itself as a leader in the spa hotel market by focusing on its unique concept and physical environment as well as the experience gained by the guests. CHI Spa can be promoted as a spa destination to differentiate itself from other spa centres. The major weakness of CHI Spa will be the ability to attract in-house guests to use CHI Spa since not all guests are willing to pay high prices for premium services, and they may want to try other places. Some of the challenges faced by CHI Spa management are the availability of professional human resources and an available spa training centre; proper standard guidelines for spa operations set by government and a professional association to accredit the qualifications of staff.

Conclusion

This case presents a unique concept of spa and wellness in terms of its physical facilities and philosophical concept, the use of local ingredients and its potential market. It highlights that CHI Spa is not just a spa centre offering body therapy services; it is the environment, customer privacy, and the total experiences that make it special for the customers and the management. Spa and wellness services offered at spa centres are regarded as professional therapy services for health and well-being, thus a standard of practices must be addressed and become a focal point for the regulatory bodies. Since spa and wellness tourism is very new in Malaysia, yet growing at a rapid speed and seemingly as a new avenue for profit generation, it is important that serious consideration should be paid to the motivational factors for both suppliers and customers as well as having proper guidelines in terms of setting up spa centres which are governed by true spa professionals.

Note: Author would like to express special thanks to Ms. Rika, CHI Spa Manager at The Shangri-La's Tanjung Aru Resort and Spa for her valuable information to this case; a personal in-depth interview was held in April 2007 at The Shangri-La's Tanjung Aru Resort and Spa.

Case study: The Big Chill festival, England, United Kingdom

Chantal Laws

The Big Chill festival is an annual 3-day residential multimedia event that takes place over the first weekend in August, and is currently held in the grounds of Eastnor Castle Deer Park in the Malvern Hills near Hereford, England. The site offers a range of performance, entertainment, camping, and catering facilities, and a Body and Soul area which operates discreetly from the rest of the festival site, whilst being an important and integral part of the festival's ambience.

The performance elements of the festival originate from a monthly Sunday multimedia 'all-dayer' event held at Islington's The Union Chapel in 1994, organized by Katrina Larkin and Pete Lawrence. The event has been described by Lawrence (Potton, 2006) as a festival within a club, and an antidote to the full-on party scene, as the music was played at a level to allow conversation. Perhaps as a natural progression, the event moved outside in 1995 with *The Big Chill Black Mountain Gala* held that summer. This was a relatively small-scale private weekend party in a site favoured by Larkin and Lawrence with around 600–700 guests, yet the elements that have come to typify *The Big Chill* festival experience were already in place, namely: an inspiring location, eclectic and innovative line-up (incorporating live music, DJs, VJs, A/V acts, comedy, dance, and installation), and a relaxed ambience.

Alan James, who played a set at the inaugural party, has described the *Black Mountain Gala* as a 'bucolic frolic' (2002, para. 2, line 3). The choice of setting is seen by James as a fundamental part of the party experience due to its connection with romantic, artistic, and counter-cultural figures which included Oscar Wilde, Pink Floyd, and Eric Gill. The site is also considered to be situated on an important ley line which meant that 'the area was redolent with psychogeographical references' (James, 2002:para. 2, line 18).

The transition from private party to festival proper was hindered by the introduction of the Criminal Justice Act (1995). However, after a number of abortive attempts to organize a similar event in other locations in England, *The Big Chill* found a new home at Dorset's Larmer Tree Gardens and in 1998 the first 'Enchanted Garden' weekender was held. After a stint at Lulworth Castle in 2001, the festival moved to its' current home of Eastnor Castle in 2002. During this time, the number of people attending the events has risen from the hundreds to 35,000 in 2006.

Ostensibly, *The Big Chill* is a music festival and whilst Lawrence is firm that the programming of the music is fundamental to the quality of the event, both he and Larkin believe that the event has a resonance beyond that of a good gig, and they identify the festival as part of 'a lifestyle dedicated to transforming the spirit of our times' (Teimao, 2006). As founders, they seek to provide a highly evolved, all-round experience that is completely unique and gives participants an opportunity to explore the relationship between technology and nature, and the grounding/centring nature of the holistic treatments offered by Body and Soul therapists reflects this. The fostering of a synergistic community that exists beyond the temporal and spatial frames of the festival is also important to the founders, and *The Big Chill* community includes an active online message board. Members of the community are also actively encouraged to feedback and shape the development of *The Big Chill's* activities for the future.

Those who attend the festival have been caricatured as rich hippies (Britten, 2005) due to the relatively luxurious facilities for the festival (particularly compared to the somewhat squalid surroundings of other high profile festivals) and the demographic of the core market segment. *The Big Chill's* loyal audience is predominantly 30 something professionals who experienced the burgeoning of the rave scene in the UK from the late 1980s onwards. For a crowd whose formative clubbing experiences were imbued with a peace, love, unity, and respect ethos, the organizational philosophy that informs *The Big Chill* has a clear resonation and the festival experience can be conceived as the natural maturation of the second 'summer of love' vibe.

Researchers into the development of rave culture such as Partridge (2006) have traced the evolution of the modern music festival to the counter-culture celebrations of the 1960s and 1970s, which had strong and active links with New Age ideologies. Most influential amongst these is the Glastonbury Fayre (now Festival) with which *The Big Chill* is often compared. Glastonbury's Green Fields and *The Big Chill's* Body and Soul area represent a physical manifestation of the desire to engage in alternative experiences in a space apart from everyday life.

Body and Soul at *The Big Chill* is managed and operated by Realease, a company formed by professional holistic therapists who work with a number of music festivals to provide healing areas. At Eastnor, the space is designed around the elements with a central shrine for grounding and channelling, and there is a clear entrance to the space to produce a sense of apartness from the more frenetic energies created in the main festival arenas. The Body and Soul area has been expanded following research with the festival community in 2003, and for 2007 a team of 160 therapists will be working at the festival, to offer treatments in both communal and individual areas. Additionally, Body and Soul provides workshops and classes, as well as dedicated rooms for pregnant women and new mothers, spa and beauty treatment areas, and a tea room offering organic, fairly traded food and drink. The atmosphere is further enhanced through provision of a gathering space and small acoustic stage, to provide a transition back to the throng of the main festival (Realease, 2007).

Engaging in holistic health practices is a clear medium by which festival participants can achieve a transformative state of being, and for some this may be the main reason to attend. However, for many participants it is the experience of dancing en masse to rave-derived music that offers an opportunity for transcendence from the everyday to the sublime. In this respect, the location and setting is key and, as Duffy (2000) states, the music festival may offer a ritual or sacral experience of marking one's place in a landscape that can lead to greater self-awareness and reflection.

In this regard *The Big Chill* can be conceived as an holistic/wellness tourism product at a number of levels, as the festival opens up a unique experiential space in which 'the body, mind, and spirit are integrated by the individual to live more fully within the human and natural community' (Myers et al., 2005 cited in Smith & Kelly, 2006:1). This may be achieved through the direct experience of healing practice in the Body and Soul area, or within the sublime festival setting, yet it also informs the ethos of the organization which promotes a kind of transcendent spirituality that it can be argued is a core element of the existential wellness tourism experience. The extent to which individual festival-goers would consciously identify this as their aim in attending the festival requires further investigation; however, the collective contribution to the fostering of a Big Chill community outside of the event strongly indicates the kind of deliberate engagement that Smith and Kelly (2006) promote as a qualifier for the contemporary wellness tourism experience.

The Big Chill promotes a type of responsible hedonism (Brinton, 2005) that would appear to be a hybrid of the truly New Age celebrations and the overtly commercial offerings of the V Festival and Carling Weekender. It is the boutique scale of the festival that allows this synthesis to occur with little tension to date, and *The Big Chill* has become an iconic event that now in turn influences other UK festivals both firmly established, such as Glastonbury, and emerging, such as Bestival on the Isle of Wight and the Wychwood Festival in Cheltenham.

However, this very burgeoning of the UK festival market may pose a threat to *The Big Chill*, as demand for attendance rises. The organization has already attracted criticisms of elitism, and the dramatic increase in audience capacity from 2002–2006 demonstrates that commercialization of the festival is perhaps inevitable. As *The Big Chill* grows, both as a festival in the UK and as an event phenomenon at international destinations such as Goa, the Greek Islands, New Zealand, and Japan, perhaps questions as to whether the Big Chill community will be able to maintain its spiritual ethos without concession should be raised.

The successes of the organization and management of *The Big Chill* to date are situated in the careful management of the development of the festival and the diversification of *The Big Chill* brand. The integrity of the festival and the loyalty of its audience remain largely uncompromised, however the festival is at a tipping point where brand diversification may lead to dilution, and where iconic status may attract more aggressive sponsor involvement. As *The Big Chill* continues to grow and the demand for the Body and Soul area increases, the synergistic relationship between health and hedonism which the festival embodies is in the balance.

The growing Yoga community in the Netherlands: How Yoga is becoming a lifestyle product including tourism activities

Roos Gerritsma

Yoga is hot in the Netherlands. We can see an increase in the Yoga offer in a broader sense: from Yoga lessons at Yoga schools to a blend of Yoga and other techniques in fitness centres, from Yoga at home, thanks to DVDs and the Internet, to the arrival of a new Yoga lifestyle magazine. Yoga isn't only a body and mind technique you can experience during class anymore, or wisdom you can read about. Nowadays it has become a continuous lifestyle including 1-day Yoga workshops or weekends in the Netherlands and many travel opportunities for those who would like to experience Yoga during a vacation abroad. Through different media we can discover a variety of Yoga travel package deals and reviews from Dutch Yoga tourists.

Yoga appears in all forms

Although probably tens of thousands people are doing Yoga in the Netherlands, it is impossible to find exact data about the number of practitioners. There is no national list of Yoga schools and there are many fitness centres offering a form of Yoga, or a blend of Yoga and other techniques attended by only part of their members. The fact is that the number of certified Yoga teachers rose from about 450 ten years ago to at least 750 today[1] (Dutch Society for Yoga Teachers, 2008), but the profession of Yoga teacher isn't regulated (yet). It can be very expensive to rent or buy your own Yoga school (or Studio or Institute), and it isn't always simple to share the place for other activities than Yoga. Seventy percent of the certified Yoga teachers in the Netherlands are between 40 and 60 years old. Characteristic for the Netherlands is the mix of several types of Yoga. They are not always as easy to recognize as a specific one like Iyengar Yoga. Over the past years Bikram (a 90 min sequence of 29 asanas in a heated classroom of 38–40°C), and Power Yoga (a dynamic form of Yoga based upon Ashtanga Yoga) which tend to be more physical and less focused on meditation have become popular forms. According to the president of the Dutch Society of Yoga Teachers, Mrs Mascini, most people start with a more dynamic Yoga and end up with the more meditative styles. She also sees a growing group of young people attending the classes, especially women in their 30s, struggling with the combination of motherhood, having a responsible job and other obligations that give them a feeling of being burned out. Most of the time people start to practise Yoga due to physical complaints. In general we can say that Yoga in Yoga-only schools or fitness centres is being practised more in the big cities than in smaller towns. On average we see about 80% women and 20% men, where the more dynamic forms of Yoga attract a higher percentage of men. But not only adults are practising Yoga. There are dozens of places for childrens' Yoga and several organizations that offer Yoga at work, to reduce stress and improve the health of employees. Also individual Yoga is possible for those who can afford it. Some Dutch wellness resorts are also providing (aqua) Yoga sessions for their visitors.

During research conducted amongst 101 Yoga and Pilates students, 75% joined the classes for relaxation reasons, 42% to get more energy, 24% for a better respiration, and 9% to meditate (Body, Mind and Balance, 2008). The respondents consider Yoga/Pilates mainly as a way of taking care of their body (marked 68 times) and less for their mind (marked 43 times).

---

[1]Dutch Society for Yoga Teachers (Vereniging voor Yogaleerkrachten Nederland) – 31 March 2008, told by the President, Mrs. Mascini.

In fitness centres Yoga is often taught more in a blend with other body and mind techniques. The world wide fitness group Les Mills has 808 locations in the Netherlands (Les Mills, 2008). They don't offer Yoga, but 'Body Balance' which is a combination of Yoga, Tai Chi, and Pilates. The classes can only be given by instructors who get a les Mills license. There are now 1,450 registered body balance instructors. Only large fitness schools can afford such a license. In the Netherlands and Flanders, there are now 549 clubs offering body balance. In general, they all offer classes five times a week. On average 20 people attend a class. This means that more than 50,000 people are joining such a body balance class every week (van de Broek, 2008).

(New)media and advertisements

Like in other countries, there is an increase in lifestyle magazines that focus on a healthy body, mind, and spirit in the Netherlands. The largest one, Happinez has a circulation of 230,000, including 60,000 subscribers. In October 2008, it will celebrate its 5th anniversary. Happinez has even become the largest monthly women's magazine of the Netherlands (Dutch Institute for Media Auditing, 2008). Another example is the lifestyle magazine Yoga. What started as a successful special edition on Yoga with the Psychology magazine, resulted in a brand new magazine, named Yoga – health, spirituality, and lifestyle, in January 2007 with a circulation of 60,000 (which is a lot for such a niche market). It appears four times a year and works together with Yoga TV which is an online 'relaxation' website. Every month they put a new lesson online which people can follow wherever and whenever they want. Others can add their own Yoga lesson as well, like You Tube for Yoga aficionados. All together there is a huge variety of online Yoga lessons to be found. On the Internet there are several virtual Yoga communities through sites like Hyves, My Space, and Potential Buddha. Members discuss new asanas (movements), where to find Yoga eco mats or clothes, what Yoga events with DJs and VJs will take place and describe their Yoga travel experiences. All previously named media publish advertisements for all sorts of Yoga products and services.

Yoga at a Spanish beach

For those who consider Yoga more as a lifestyle and not as a Wednesday-evening activity only, there are lots of things to do, see, read, or experience. A growing market in this seems to be 1 day Yoga workshops or weekends in the Netherlands itself or Yoga travel abroad. The offer in the Netherlands is mainly focused on either a specific technique during a short workshop (head and neck, how to practise at home, block instructions for Yoga teachers) or a mix of Yoga and other activities such as meditating or singing during a weekend. In contrast to the travels abroad, promises of extraordinary nature and exclusive locations aren't often used to promote these Yoga activities.

Specialized Dutch wellness tour operators and individual Yoga teachers are organizing Yoga trips to countries like Spain, Greece, Indonesia, Portugal, and Italy. Some call it 'spiritual travels', others prefer to brand Yoga travels as: 'Relaxing and Recharging'. An average programme contains not only several hours of Yoga exercises per day – often at sunrise – but also time for creativity (dance, singing, and painting), therapy like group sessions or other activities like walking. Almost all organizers provide either mainly or strictly vegetarian food and fruit/vitamin juices. The programme usually takes 5–7 days and costs around 650 to 1,100 Euros excluding the travel costs. For the summer of 2008, the Dutch Yoga tourists can choose from at least 35 different possibilities (Sibley, 2008). Values like authenticity of place, nature, purity, a safe atmosphere for learning and good weather conditions are frequently used in the marketing of Yoga travels. The accommodations tend to be pretty luxurious and are often situated in idyllic environments, next to the beach, in beautiful nature or picturesque villages. Exemplary is wellness tour operator La Contessa (2008), which promotes its Yoga travel as follows: 'Power Yoga at the Garda Lake – yoga holiday in Italy for 655 Euros. Do you desire a special yoga vacation that focuses on relaxing, inspiration, and pure enjoyment? (…) Yoga with a view of the impressive mountain landscape with the sun on your skin – that's combining the pleasant with the pleasant'. They also mention tourist attractions in the neighbourhood like a visit to Venice or the overwhelming silence on the estate where the participants will stay. They all guarantee well-trained Yoga teachers who speak Dutch and sometimes English. In order to get to know one's teacher already, they show pictures and a CV of the teacher(s) in the (online) brochure. Most of the programmes are open to any level of Yoga experience, some are meant as a refresher course for Yoga teachers.

Dutch Yoga tourists share their experiences or gained insights of those Yoga trips in different virtual communities. They often write their reviews on the website of the Yoga travel organizer as well. Although we should always be aware of the subjectivity, these reviews are almost exclusively very positive. A quote that seems to cover the opinion of many is one from Ankie: 'What a great week. The Atalanta Centre felt as a warm bath of love and attention. I feel as if I'm back on track and in touch with my inner force'.[2] Judging from the photos and reviews of many websites, most Yoga holidays are booked by women. Sometimes the participants can book also for their partners who may not want to join in with the Yoga programme, but can enjoy the accommodation, food, and surroundings.

This growing Yoga community and the group of Dutch Yoga tourists offer several research opportunities for the future. Interesting themes could be for example: constructing profiles of Yoga students and of those who go on a Yoga trip; What marketing strategies will be developed to sell

---

[2] www.Atlanta.nl

the growing awareness of the experienced benefits from Yoga (travel)?; What roles do health insurance and commercial companies play in this market? And finally, Yoga is being practised world wide and encompasses many (virtual) communities and includes an enormous Yoga travel market which brings up the question how the Dutch Yoga community has been positioned in that.

Note: The Body, Mind and Balance (2008) research amongst 101 Yoga and Pilates practitioners was carried out by the following students of Inholland University, Minor Sports, Wellness and Lifestyles: Sheridin Ho-a-Hing, Rachida Prada, Jindra Proost, and Fanny Tang.

Medical tourism in India: A case study of Apollo Hospitals

Babu P. George

Introduction

Medical tourism is a silent revolution that has been sweeping across the healthcare landscape of India for almost a decade. According to the Confederation of Indian Industries (CII, 2007), India is unique as it offers holistic medicinal services. With yoga, meditation, ayurveda, allopathy, and other systems of medicines, India offers a unique basket of services to an individual that is difficult to match by other countries. Also, clinical outcomes in India are at par with the world's best centres, besides having internationally qualified and experienced specialists. With the international media constantly telecasting scenes of white people getting knees replaced, hips resurfaced, and dental works done in India by the West-trained doctors at throw-away prices, often in the ambience of a five star resort; the demand from the nationals of Western Europe and the USA for medial treatment in India is on the increase.

The domestic medical industry in India is trying all out to grab its pie from the evolving global health bazaar. Statistics suggest that the medical tourism industry in India is worth $333 million. According to the Government of India, India's $17-billion-a-year healthcare industry could grow 13% in each of the next 6 years, boosted by medical tourism, which industry watchers say is growing at 30% annually. It is forecasted that medical tourism will fetch India $2.3 billion by 2012 (Incredible India, 2006). If nothing goes wrong, it will become a major driver of the Indian economy along with information technology, biotechnology, and technology-enabled consumer services. Probably realizing the potential, major corporate groups in the healthcare business have made significant investments in setting up modern hospitals in major cities. Many have also designed special packages for patients, including airport pickups, visa assistance, and boarding and lodging (The Economist, 2004).

In the recent past, the healthcare sector in India has witnessed an enormous growth in infrastructure in the private and voluntary sector. The private sector which was very modest in the early stages has now become a flourishing industry equipped with the most modern state-of-the-art technology at its disposal. It is estimated that 75–80% of healthcare services and investments in India are now provided by the private sector. An added plus had been that India has one of the largest pharmaceutical industries in the world. It is self sufficient in drug production and exports drugs to more than 180 countries. Unlike many of its competitors in medical tourism, India also has the domestic technological sophistication and infrastructure to maintain its market niche, and Indian pharmaceuticals meet the stringent requirements of the US Food and Drug Administration.

The Apollo Group

The Apollo Hospitals Group, the largest healthcare group in Asia, is today recognized as the architect of healthcare in India. With over 7,000 beds in 38 hospitals, a string of nursing and hospital management colleges, and dual lifelines of pharmacies and diagnostic clinics providing a safety net across Asia, Apollo may be rechristened metaphorically as a healthcare powerhouse. Its history of accomplishments, with its unique ability of resource management and able deployment of technology and knowledge to the service of mankind, justifies its recognition in India and abroad. Apollo has got one of the largest and the most sophisticated sleep laboratories in the World. It has pioneered orthopaedic procedures like Total Hip and Knee Replacements, the Illizarov procedure, and the Birmingham Hip Resurfacing technique. Its stated vision is to bring healthcare of international standards within the reach of every individual. According to Apollo, it is committed to the achievement and maintenance of excellence in education, research, and healthcare for the benefit of humanity.

Apollo's business began to grow in the 1990s, with the deregulation of the Indian economy, which drastically cut the bureaucratic barriers to expansion and made it easier to import the most modern medical equipment. The first patients were Indian expatriates who returned home for treatment; major investment houses followed with money and then patients from Europe, the Middle East, and Canada began to arrive. Services provided by the International Patient Service Centres of Apollo Group, located within India and Abroad, include: local travel arrangements, airport transfers, coordination of doctor's appointment, accommodation for relatives and attendants, locker facilities, provision of cuisine options, provision of interpreters, arrangements with leading resort chains for post-operative recuperation, among others.

Apollo: a SWOT analysis

The major strengths of Apollo are listed below

Apollo is one of the earliest entrants into the medical tourism business in India and has got the associated first mover advantages. Almost 70% of the Apollo doctors have been trained, have studied or worked in institutions and hospitals in the West. Apollo has recorded exceptionally good clinical outcomes and post-treatment success rates. Apollo conducts itself in a conscientious manner in all transactions and deals with people professionally and transparently, while maintaining privacy and confidentiality deserved by its customers. Over the years, Apollo has successfully engineered trust, integrity, and confidentiality to its unique advantage. Wherever admissible, Apollo tries to integrate the diverse ancient healing traditions with the latest in modern medicine and this holistic approach as brought it a great deal of acclaim. With over 7,000 beds in 38 hospitals, Apollo has hospitals spread across the length and breadth of the country. Treatment can be arranged in a particular unit which is geographically closer to a particular destination type which the patient or the ones accompanying may want to see. Apollo offers unrivalled price–value advantage, too.

Apollo's investment in the best and latest technology in the world is well appreciated. Apollo Telemedicine Networking Foundation (ATNF), established in 1999, is the pioneer in launching the first rural telemedicine centre in the country. The telemedicine initiative can in fact be employed to boost its medical tourism business. At this stage, Apollo should try to integrate its medical tourism activities with the telemedicine initiatives since the telemedicine offers a very good alternative for preliminary and post-treatment consultations. It will give a big positive push to its patient relationship management too. The Virtual Patient Visit scheme at Apollo offers the friends and relatives of patients the opportunity to gather frequently updated information about treatment progress, the consultant's opinion about the patient, patient's remarks, and a multimedia rich medium to convey the messages to and from both sides. If the Virtual Patient Visit scheme and the telemedicine initiative could somehow be integrated, the friends and relatives of the patient could better understand the stage and the result of treatments being undergone.

However, it suffers from the following weaknesses

Apollo's patient relationship management programme is almost flawless. However, one significant weakness afflicting Apollo is its relative lack of understanding of the accompanying persons also as customers to deal with. While the Virtual Patient Visit scheme permits remotely located persons to get to know about the patient's recovery status, managing the experience of those physically accompanying and those who visit from the host country in between are almost neglected. Apollo should either establish a travel-cum-hospitality desk to provide hospitality and excursion facilities for these groups or get into a suitable partnership scheme with an external service provider for the same. Competitors have already identified this as an area of opportunity and have begun to come forward with packaged offers for the accompanying persons as well.

To successfully run the medical tourism business, it is high time Apollo realizes that it requires employees with domain expertise in tourism in addition to the traditional medical support staff. However, this is a weak spot with Apollo and people with qualifications in the areas of tourism and hospitality have to be recruited and assigned important roles in medical tourist relations management.

If it wants to make a further positive difference, the opportunities for Apollo are

Apollo has got the pioneering status in attracting medical tourists to India and has developed over time unassailable brand equity. Now, it is faced with a great opportunity, both to enrich and to expand the medical tourism business. Apollo should establish off-campus centres equipped with tele-medicine facilities, especially in countries like the USA and Canada from where it receives the majority of patient inflows. These off-campus centres would be the preliminary points of contact between the patients and the hospital. These contact centres, in addition to giving elementary care and clinical information, can help to process the travel documentation, including arranging visas for the patients and the ones accompanying them. For example, hospitals like Cromwell in the UK have representatives in India and Pakistan, while hospitals in Singapore are also setting up offices such as in Indonesia and the Middle East. These agents help to establish and maintain relationships such as with local hospitals, doctors, embassies, sponsor corporations, or insurers. Apollo can get into deals with middlemen agencies like Global Health Tours (GHT) who help people to decide and manage their treatments abroad.

E-marketing of medical tourism services provides an opportunity for Apollo to reach the customer directly, bypassing the middlemen. This will help the firm to provide services at a lower price, on-time, and in a highly customized manner. E-marketing clubbed with the marketing initiatives through the patient contact centres to be established in the important medical tourist originating countries can do a successful brick and mortar marketing job for the Apollo. The staff at the various contact centres should ideally have sufficient training in the cultural norms and expectations of the medical tourists of the respective countries to tailor-make the service offerings. Since medical service is a credence service, long-term relationship building and maintaining the same will be the key to sustained business. No firm that wants to continue in this business should look towards one-time transaction-specific approaches. Firms should tap on referrals, positive word of mouth, etc., since these carry more credential that an impersonal advertisement.

Apollo has thus far concentrated upon curative medical care for the medical tourists. While specialization has its own advantages, there is a lucrative market out there for the preventive cure as well. Research has revealed that especially those who accompany a curative patient would like to undergo preventive treatment during their stay in India. Significantly enough, preventive medical treatments given in the alternative tradition like ayurveda and homoeopathy are the ones utmost in demand. If Apollo cannot cater to this demand, it should further examine the potential of outsourcing the same to another provider under a licensing agreement. Yet, it seems fairly feasible for Apollo to manage itself the demand for allopathic preventive medical treatment.

Another lucrative opportunity waiting to be exploited by Apollo is to get into the area of medical insurance. Critics of medical tourism warn that travelling patients put themselves at risk. Should complications arise, patients might not be covered by insurance or be able to seek adequate compensation via malpractice lawsuits. This decision, again, depends on whether it wants to get into an altogether different business. It may be noted that a sister concern of Apollo, Apollo Health Street already is in the business of remotely executing the non-core health information management activities of foreign healthcare groups such as medical transcription, coding, revenue cycle management, and claims processing.

Yet Apollo faces the following threats

One of the major threats for Apollo, like any other large-scale private initiative in India, comes from citizen's groups: a widely held perception is that it does not care for the disadvantaged sections of the society. Many critics cite that medical tourism by the corporate hospitals like Apollo has unleashed a range of unhealthy and unethical practices. Apollo rebuffs the criticism raised by various groups that it has neglected India's millions of poor. The official website says that it has set aside free beds for those who can't afford care, has set up a trust fund and is pioneering remote, satellite-linked telemedicine across India. Even from a purely rational economic point of view, it is in the interest of Apollo to cater to the needs of the bottom of the pyramid, since the economies of scale derivable from the same can make it a cost leader as well.

Of course, Apollo face stiff competition from hospital groups like the Escorts, Wockhardt, Fortis, Manipal, Christian Medical College, Tatas, Birlas, Aravind, Leelavati, and so on. Some of these competitors have specialized in certain sub-domains like eye care, dental care, knee care, heart care, etc., and hence offer superior treatment for these diseases. The benefits of comprehensive care offered by Apollo are somehow to be blended with the advantages of specialization to successfully overcome the threat factor.

The threat from the public sector hospitals that strive to fill the deficit caused by reduced governmental funding is also significant. For example, public sector hospitals like All India Institute of Medical Sciences (AIIMS) have been receiving patients from over 16 countries including European nations and there is a steady increase in the number of patients, mainly for complex surgical procedures. The AIIMS has also initiated a dedicated International Healthcare Service team, which will take care of the patient right from arrival till their departure coordinating all aspects of medical treatment.

Conclusion

Apollo's capabilities have received international acclaim resulting in the replication of its Indian models at international locations. Apollo group is also in talks with private healthcare groups and government authorities in Nigeria, South Africa, Tanzania, Mauritius, Yemen, Muscat, Bahrain, Vietnam, Malaysia, Thailand and other neighbouring countries to establish its presence in world class clinical efficiencies. The question now is from here to where?

Since competitive advantages for the different components of the medical tourism system lie with different players, forming inter-organizational networks with a common marketing front might turn out to be a great idea for Apollo. This coordinated move will synergize the operations and minimize the scope of service failures. For example, with the objective of promoting and establishing Kerala, one of the most sought after tourist destinations in India, as a medical tourism destination, Kerala Tourism Development Corporation (KTDC), Amrita Institute of Medical Sciences and Intersight Tours have already signed an MOU. The consortium plans to promote Kerala as a medical tourism destination, where medical treatment will be provided at AIMS, holiday options will be provided by KTDC, and the logistics of travel will be provided by Intersight. Cooperation often is a more sustainable strategy than a confrontational approach.

What is called International Patient Care is already a seamless process, with the guests buying inclusive arrangements that feature air travel, local transportation, translation services, air-conditioned five star accommodation, together with their personalized choice of global cuisine. To attract foreign patients, healthcare providers may consider leveraging on both business and clinical considerations. Also, well coordinated efforts among the travel, the hospitality, and the healthcare trade are imperative for the sustainable growth of this business. A sincere commitment to these coordinated moves allows each stakeholder to focus on its own competencies and may even alleviate the level of competition – allowing for better long run revenues throughout the entire sector.

The use of spas by meetings participants: The case of the United States

Rob Davidson

Meetings and spas

Meetings and spas have been closely associated ever since ancient times, when men would regularly assemble in Roman and Greek baths to discuss affairs of state and other issues.

In recent times, there has been a worldwide renewal of interest in holding meetings in venues offering spa facilities. Spa treatments are now widely used to attract, reward and relax meeting attendees. Organizers of corporate meetings in particular – events held by companies for their staff – are increasingly choosing venues with spa facilities as the places in which their meetings are held. The reasons for the resurgence of interest in using spas as the setting for meetings of work colleagues are various:

- A meeting held in a spa facility or a hotel offering spa treatments is usually an extremely memorable event for the participants.

The reasoning is that if participants remember the venue, they are more likely to be able to recall the information they learned during the meeting. This is particularly the case for meetings held for the purpose of training staff.

- When participants are relaxed and refreshed as a result of using the spa facilities, they become more focused and ready to learn at the meeting.
- When attendance at the meeting is optional and/or financed by the participants themselves, organizers often understand that they can increase their attendance by adding spa elements to their programmes, as activities for participants.
- The growing focus on health, wellness and longevity means that members of the increasingly stressed, over-worked population are often attracted to the potential benefits offered by spa facilities as an adjunct to the business events they attend.
- Spa facilities can be a source of much-needed relief for meetings participants who have been sitting down all day.
- A spa experience can be a rewarding networking event, allowing participants to relax together in an atmosphere conducive to social interaction.

In the United States, the trend of holding meetings in venues with spa facilities has been widely supported by the companies who finance such events. They increasingly recognize that a better-balanced, well-rested employee with the strong sense of wellbeing that time spent in a spa can provide will perform better at work. That, together with the ability easily to incorporate a team-building component into spa-based meeting, represents the most significant benefit for employers' investment in these events.

Treatments used by meetings participants

There is no one standardized way for meetings planners to incorporate spa components into the events they organize. The strategic objectives of the meeting generally determine how and when a spa option is added. The types of spa treatments offered to participants varies depending on whether the organizers of the event want them to be indulged, invigorated or inspired.

However, it is generally accepted that most medical treatments do not combine well with meetings, and so these are rarely part of the packages offered to participants. In order to satisfy the preferences of groups attending meetings, a spa must offer a wide selection of treatments, as well as opportunities for the participants to learn something of value to their wellbeing and/or appearance. Workshops on topics such as skin care, stress reduction, diaphragmatic breathing, healthy cooking, dressing for success, and relaxation techniques tend to be popular.

From the point of view of the facility owner, it is increasingly clear that spas equal business. Benchmark Hospitality, an independent hospitality management company, put spas at the top of its 2006 'Top Ten Hospitality Trends for the Year' list. According to Benchmark, spas were the 'hottest trend going in hotels'. Hannelore R. Leavy, founder and executive director of the Day Spa Association and the International Medical Spa Association – both based in Union City, New Jersey, has insisted that a quality spa is an essential facility for any property that hopes to attract large groups. She maintains that spas in the United States have become profit centres for the meetings venues in which they are located:

'If you wish to compete, a spa is as necessary as a swimming pool was in the 1960s, or a fitness centre in the 1980s. And it can't just be a miniature spa. Up to the mid-1990s, resorts didn't care whether the spa made money or not; now it's a very important income source for the owner/developer. The spas are there to fill the rooms and the meeting planner will choose the resort that has the spa and can accommodate the delegates.'

Lynne Walker McNees, president of the International SPA Association (ISPA), has stated that members of her association are making a special effort to accommodate corporate groups: 'Spa activities are a great way to entertain a group, while also helping them bond and have fun. Spa suites can accommodate several people at the same time for relaxing treatments. Spa treatments are also being increasingly integrated with the actual meetings attended by the participants. The president of the ISPA, for example, reported seeing growing numbers of instances whereby therapists offer chair massages in the actual meeting room, to relieve participants' stress. Spa therapists and masseurs can also join attendees during breaks in the meetings and offer 5-minute treatments such as hand or neck massages before the meeting resumes'.

Networking in spas

For many planners, the provision of time for networking between meetings participants, outside the actual meetings sessions, is a key element of the events they organize. Increasingly, they have realized that spa time and networking do not have to be mutually exclusive, and that a spa experience can also be a rewarding networking event. In a relaxed, informal setting of a spa, sharing and relationship-building between participants often follow effortlessly. A group spa event can therefore include the usual treatments but can also incorporate more qualities of a networking event. One example of this use of spas is the case of the annual retreat organized by Tastefully Simple, a Minnesota-based company specializing in convenient, easy-to-prepare gourmet foods, for its top consultants. According to the planner of these retreats, the most popular event of these conferences is Spa Night: 'We did this for the first time last year and realized that the relaxation truly inspired our consultants. They loved sitting around with their colleagues and having some time for themselves. Spa Night is a great way to thank them, and they deserve this'. In 2006, the Tastefully Simply spa night took place at the Barton Creek Resort & Spa in Texas. The company had exclusive use of the spa facility for the evening, which featured customized spa treatments, and the participants gathering in the spa's relaxation room for cocktails and hors d'oeuvres between treatments.

Whether a spa component is optional and individual or incorporated into a group networking event, a post-meeting activity for participants or a source of relief and relaxation during breaks, it is clear that the long association between spa facilities and meetings is experiencing a great resurgence in the United States and worldwide.

(Dobrian, 2005; Chiarello, 2006)

Bibliography

Ables, S. L. (ed.) (2000) *Spirituality in Social Work Practices: Narratives of Professional Helping*. Denver: Love.

Accor Thalassa (2008) http://www.accorthalassa.com/gb/sejour/bienfaits-eau.shtml (accessed 2nd April 2008).

Adams, T. B. (2003) 'The Power of Perceptions: Measuring Wellness in a Globally Acceptable, Philosophically Consistent Way', *Wellness Management*, www.hedir.org (accessed 20th September 2005).

Aho, S. (2007) 'Spa Rehabilitation of War Veterans: A Finnish Speciality of War Compensation', ATLAS Spa and Wellness Special Interest Group Meeting, Budapest, 25th–28th June 2007.

Alexander, J. (2001) *The Holistic Therapy File*. London: Carlton Books Ltd.

Alpine Wellness (2008) www.alpinewellness.com/en (accessed 10th March 2008).

Alpro Soya Year of Wellbeing (2008) http://ayearofwellbeing.com (accessed 20th March 2008).

Altman, D. (2008) 'A Relaxing Tradition Dips a Toe in the 21st Century', *The New York Times*, 20 January 2008, http://travel.nytimes.com/ (accessed 4th April 2008).

American College of Sports Medicine (2007) http://www.acsm.org/AM/Template.cfm?Section=Home_Page&template=/CM/ContentDisplay.cfm&ContentID=6183 (accessed 4th December 2007).

American Holistic Health Association (AHHA) (2007) http://www.heall.com/body/altmed/definitions/holistic.html (accessed 3rd Oct 2007).

American Spa Magazine (2008) http://www.americanspamag.com/americanspa/article/articleDetail.jsp?id=30389 (accessed 12th March 2008).

American Therapeutic Recreation Association (2007) http://www.atra-tr.org/about.htm (accessed 3rd October 2007).

Ananda Answers (2008) hppt://www.anandaanswers.com (accessed 15th March 2008).

Ananda Retreats (2008) http://www.ananda.it (accessed 4th April 2008)

Anaharta (2008) 'Mini Size Me and Live Vibe Tribe Retreat', http://www.anaharta.com/1LVTWorkshopsAndRetreats.php (accessed 10th Janary 2008).

Apollo Hospitals (2007) www.apollohospitals.com (accessed on 10th March 2007).

Arasha Resort (2008) http://www.arasharesort.com/arasha.htm#what (accessed 4th April 2008).

Arias, J. (2001) *Paolo Coelho: Confessions of a Pilgrim*. London: Harper Collins.

Asia Spa Festival (2007) http://www.asiaspafestival.com (accessed 24th November 2007).

Aspalter, C. (2007) 'The asian cure for health care', *Far Eastern Economic Review*, 170(9), pp. 56–59.

Assenov, I. & Suthin, K. (2007) 'Medical Travel: Factors Impeding the Growth of the Industry', ATLAS Spa and Wellness Special Interest Group Meeting, Budapest, 25th–28th June 2007.

Atlanta (2008) http://www.Atlanta.nl (accessed 31st March 2008).

Australian Spa Association (2006) http://www.australasianspaassociation.com/the_spa_world/documents/ASPASpaIndustryDefinitions300104.doc (accessed 24th November 2007).

Azara, I., Hughes, S., Hunter, G. & Stockdale, I. (2007) 'Profiling Day Spa Visitors and Motivations to experience Wellness 'at home', ATLAS Spa and Wellness Special Interest Group Meeting, Budapest, 25th–28th June 2007.

Bachvarov, M. & Liszewski, S. (2004) *Spas in Central-Eastern Europe: Between Decline and Revitalisation*. Greifswald: University of Greifswald Press.

Bacon, W. (1998) 'Economic systems and their impact on tourist resort development: The case of the Spa in Europe', *Tourism Economics*, 4(1), pp. 21–32.

Bad Blumau (2008) http://www.blumau.com (accessed 26th November 2007).

Balch, O. (2006) 'Buenos Aires or Bust', *Guardian Unlimited*, Tuesday 24th October, http://www.guardian.co.uk/argentina/story/0,,1930436,00.html (accessed 24th November 2007)

Bali Romeo (2008) http://www.baliromeo.com (accessed 5th April 2008).

Barr, D. (2005) 'Spa: A splash of gay glamour. Homo away from home', *The Times*, 30th Novermber.

Basheer, K. (2003) 'Centre's policy a shot in the arm for State', *The Hindu*, 30th November.

Bauman, Z. (2001) *Community: Seeking Safety in an Insecure World*. Cambridge: Polity.

Bauman, Z. (2003) *Liquid Love*. Cambridge: Polity.

BBC News Online (2000) 'Models Link to Teenage Anorexia', 30th May http://news.bbc.co.uk/1/hi/health/769290.stm (accessed 24th October 2007).

BBC News Online (2006) 'Half of nation do no exercise', 8th December http://news.bbc.co.uk/2/hi/health/6220358.stm (accessed 26th October 2007).

Beard, M. (1901) *The Quotable Traveler (1994)*. Philadelphia: Running Press.

Beautiful Break (2008) www.beautifulbreak.com (accessed 14th March 2008).

Beck, L. & Cable, T. (1998) *Interpretation for the 21th century. Fifteen guiding principles for interpreting nature and culture*. Champaign, IL: Sagamore Publishing.

Beckerson, J. & Walton, J. K. (2005) 'Selling air: Marketing the intangible at British resorts', in Walton, J. K. (ed.) *Histories of Tourism: Representation, Identity and Conflict*. Clevedon: Channel View Publications, pp. 55–68.

Bergsma, M. (1997) 'Report on the State of Russian Tourism market. Inbound, outbound and domestic tourism', *TACIS EDRUS* 95 (10), April, p. 36.

Best Health Austria (2008) http://www.best-health-austria.com/ (accessed 30th March 2008).

BMWA (2002) Health Tourism and Overseas Treatment in England: Analysis of Trends and Systems, www.bmwa.gv.at (accessed 7th February 2008).

BMWA (2002) 'Bestandsaufhahme der Entwicklungspotenziale im Gesundheitsturismus', Modul 1.Wien: BMWA.

Body, Mind and Balance (2008) Research amongst 101 Yoga and Pilates practitioners carried out by students of Inholland University, Minor Sports, Wellness and Lifestyles.

Bond, M. (2003) 'The Pursuit of Happiness', *New Scientist*, 179, pp. 40–43.

Britten, F. (2005) 'Happy campers', *Sunday Times*, July 17th, p. 18.

British Airways (2008) http://www.britishairways.com/travel/healthwb/public/en_gb#elemis (accessed 15th March 2008).

British Spa Association (2008) 'BISA Spa Accreditation' http://www.spaassociation.org.uk/4.html (accessed 4th April 2008).

Brown, A. (2007) Spa Trends 2007, http://spas.about.com/od/stressmanagement/a/trends2007.htm (accessed 17th March 2008).

Brown, M. (1998) *The Spiritual Tourist*. London: Bloomsbury.

Burns, P. (1998) 'Tourism in Russia: Background and structure', *Tourism Management*, 19(6), pp. 555–565.

Bywater, M. (1990) 'Spas and health resorts in the EC', *EIU Travel & Tourism Analyst*, 6, pp. 52–67.

Canadian Therapeutic Recreation Association (2007) http://www.canadian-tr.org (accessed 24th November 2007).

Canadian Tourism Association (2005) Business Strategy for Spa Health and Wellness Tourism http://dsp-psd.pwgsc.gc.ca/Collection/C86-199-2004E.pdf (accessed 24th November 2007).

Carrasco, D. (1996) *Those Who Go on a Sacred Journey: The Shapes and Diversity of Pilgrimages*. London: SCM Press Ltd.

CBC News (2007) 'More than 30% of Canadians say they are workaholics', Tuesday May 15th, http://www.cbc.ca/canada/story/2007/05/15/workaholics-study.html (accessed 12th November 2007).

Chaline, E. (2002) *Zen and the Art of Travel*. London: MQ Publications Ltd.

Chambers, T. (2006) 'Essence of a Resort and Day Spa', 30thDecember, http://resortdayspa.com (accessed 7th February 2008).

Chan, J. (2007) 'Broad definition and meaning of Health and Wellness Tourism in Sabah , Malaysia', Discussion Paper for ATLAS Spa and Wellness Special Interest Group.

Chan, J. K. L. & Yeoh, E. L. (2001) *A Mongraph–Marketing and Positioning Sabah as Tourist Destination*. Kota Kinabalu: Special Publication Universiti Malaysia Sabah Third Convocation (September 2001). ISBN 983-2188-78-4.

Chandler, A. (2007) Body, Mind, Spirit Expo http://www.bodysoulspiritexpo.com/enewsplus/enews.php3?nid=74 (accessed 3rd October 2007).

Chartrungruang, B. & Mitsutake, M. (2007) *A Study on the Promotion of Tourism between Japan and Thailand: Travel Images of Japan and its Hot springs Sites in the Viewpoints of Thai Tourists*. Paper presented at the CAUTHE 2007 Conference, Sydney, Australia.

Chiarello, A. (2006) 'Royal Treatment', *The Meeting Professional Magazine*, 26(6), www.mpiweb.org (accessed 25th March 2008).

Chopra, D. (1993) *Ageless Body, Timeless Mind: The Quantum Alternative to Growing Old*. New York: Crown Publishing.

CII (2007) 'The official website of Confederation of Indian Industry', www.ciionline.org (accessed on 31st March, 2007).

Cleaver, M. & Muller, T. (2002) 'The socially aware baby boomer: Gaining a lifestyle-based understanding of the new wave of ecotourists', *Journal of Sustainable Tourism*, 10(3), pp. 173–190.

Cohen, E. (1996) 'A Phenomenology of tourist experiences', in Apostopoulos, Y., Leivadi, S. & Yiannakis, A. (eds) *The Sociology of Tourism: Theoretical and Empirical Investigations*. London: Routledge, pp. 90–111.

Cohen, E. (1972) 'Towards a sociology of international tourism', *Social Research*, 39(1), pp. 64–82.

Competitive Team (2004) 'Medical Tourism. Cluster Study, Ministry of Planning and International Cooperation', http://www.competitiveness.gov.jo/files/Medical%20Toursim_presented.pdf (accessed 2nd April 2008).

Connell, J. (2006) 'Medical tourism. The newest of niches', *Journal of Tourism Recreation Research*, 31(1), pp. 99–102.

Connor, S. (2003) 'Can Buddhists Transcend Mental Reservations?' 22nd May, http://www.biopsychiatry.com/happiness/buddhist.html (accessed 26th November 2006).

Cortijo Romero (2006) www.cortijo-romero.co.uk (accessed 10th November 2006).

Crebbin-Bailey, J., Harcup, J. & Harrington, J. (2005) *The Spa Book*. London: Thomson.

Creighton, M. (1997) 'Consuming rural Japan: The marketing of tradition and nostalgia in the Japanese travel industry', *Ethnology*, 36(3), pp. 239–254.

Crossette, B. (1998) *The Great Hill Stations of Asia*. New York: Westview Press.

Cruz, J. F. A. D. (2002) 'Engarrafamento de águas minerais naturais e de nascente e termalismo em 2001', *Boletim de Minas*, 39(2), pp. 87–107.

Crystal Wood Stables (2008) http://www.crystalwoodstables.com/aboutthe rapeuticriding.htm (accessed 20th March 2008).

CTG Heathcare (2008) http://www.ctghealthcare.co.uk/?title=health_spa__turkish_bath&menuid=21279 (accessed 24th March 2008).

D'Angelo, J. (2005) *Spa Business Strategies: A Plan for Success*. New York: Delmar.

Daintree Lodge (2007) http://www.daintree-ecolodge.com.au (accessed 20th November 2007).

Damask Rose Tours (2008) http://www.damaskrosetours.com/yoga-retreats/yoga-at-rishikesh.html (accessed 7th February 2008).

Dann, G. & Cohen, E. (1996) 'Sociology and tourism', in Apostopoulos, Y., Leivadi, S. & Yiannakis, A. (eds) *The Sociology of Tourism: Theoretical and Empirical Investigations*. London: Routledge, pp. 301–314.

Dann, G. (1977) 'Anomie, eco-enhancement and tourism', *Annals of Tourism Research*, 4, pp. 184–194.

Davie, G. (1994) *Religion in Britain since 1945: Believing without Belonging*. Oxford: Blackwell.

De Botton, A. (2002) *The Art of Travel*. London: Penguin.

De Groote, P. (2008) 'Spa, the mother spa resort of Europe', in Jansen Verbecke, M. & Diekmann, A. (eds) *The Future of Historic Spa Towns: Spa Symposium Workbook*. Belgium: Castermans, pp. 25–34.

De la Barre, K., De la Barre, S. & Taggart, M. (2005) 'Feasibility Study for a Yukon Health and Wellness Industry', May, http://www.tirc.gov.yk.ca/files/2005HealthandWellnessPartI.pdf (accessed 3rd April 2008).

De Palma, B. (2007) 'What Will I find in Silence? Only What I take with Me', http://www.firehorse.com.au/philos/vipassana/welcome.html (accessed 21st November 2007).

Destination Spa Group (2005): Survey on Destination Spa-goers & Vacationers (A Study by M. H. Tabacchi, Cornell University), http://www.destinationspa-group.com/cornell.htm.

Destineering (2007) http://www.destineering.com/life-coaching-retreats.php (accessed 12th November 2007).

Deutscher Wellness Verband (2008) 'Medical Wellness', http://www.wellness verband.de/medical/index.php (accessed 27th March 2008).

Devereux, C. & Carnegie, E. (2006) 'Pilgrimage: Journeying beyond self', *Journal of Tourism Recreation Research*, 31(1), pp. 47–56.

Dickman, S. (1997) *Arts Marketing: The Pocket Guide*. Sydney: Centre for Professional Development and Australia Council.

Diener, E. & Seligman, M. E. P. (2004) 'Beyond money: Toward an economy of well-being', *Psychological Science in the Public Interest*, 5(1), pp. 1–31.

Diener, E. (2005) 'Guidelines for National Indicators of Subjective Well-Being and Ill-Being', http://www.psych.uiuc.edu/~ediener/Guidelines%20for%20National%20Indicators.pdf (accessed 4th December 2007).

Dobrian, J. (2005) 'Meetings mean massages', *The Meeting Professional Magazine*, May, 25(5), www.mpiweb.org (accessed 25th March 2008).

Dosh, C. (2006): 'Hotels Meeting Spa Demand with New Facilities', Business Travel News, November 6, http://www.btnmag.com/businesstravelnews/headlines/frontpage_display.jsp?vnu_content_id=1003352725 (accessed 25th January 2008).

Duffy, M. (2000) 'Lines of drift: Festival participation and performing a sense of place', *Popular Music*, 19(1), pp. 51–64.

Dunn, H. (1959) 'High-level wellness for man and society', *American Journal of Public Health*, 49(6), pp. 786–792.

Dutch Institute for Media Auditing (2008) http://www.hoi-online.nl (accessed 31st March 2008).

Dutch Society for Yoga Teachers (Vereniging voor Yogaleerkrachten Nederland) (2008) Statement by the President, Mrs. Mascini, 31st March 2008.

Dysli, E. (2008) 'Wellness, Selfness, Mindness', http://www.wellnessplus.ch/uploads/media/Wellness-Selfness-Mindness_01.pdf (accessed 15th February 2008).

Eakin, J. S. (2005) *Salons and Spas: The Architecture of Beauty*. Beverley, MA: Rockport Publishers Inc.

Eco, U. (1986) *Travels in Hyper-Reality*. London: Picador.

Ecospas (2008) http://www.ecospas.com (accessed 27th March 2008).

Edensor, T. (2001) 'Performing Tourism, staging tourism: (Re)producing tourist space and practice', *Tourist Studies*, 1(1), pp. 59–81.

Eliade, M. (1971) *The Myth of Eternal Return*. Princeton: Princeton University Press.

Elias, M. (2002) 'What makes people happy? Psychologists now know', *USA Today*, December 9th, 2002.

Elkins, D. N., Hedstrom, L. J., Hughes, L. L., Leaf, J. A. & Saunders, C. (1988) 'Toward a humanistic-phenomenological spirituality', *Journal of Humanistic Psychology*, 28(4), pp. 5–18.

Ellis, J. (2004) 'Onsen Obsession', *Far Eastern Economic Review*, 167(35), pp. 58–59.

ESPA (2006) European Spa Association, http://espa-ehv.com (accessed 21st January 2008).

ESPA (2007) European Spa Association, http://espa-ehv.com (accessed 30th March 2008).

Euromonitor International (2008) *Travel and Tourism in Japan*. Euromonitor International.

Europe Spa (2008) http://www.europespa.euwww.europespa.eu. (accessed 19th March 2008).

European Tourism Institute (2008) http://www.eti.dewww.eti.de. (accessed 3rd March 2008).

Fiji Times (2007) http://www.fijitimes.com (accessed 9th May 2007).

Findhorn (2007) http://findhorn.org (accessed 24th November 2007).

Flisher, A., Angel, Y. & Chechik, A. (2004) *Rural Hospitality in Israel 2004*. Rehovot: The Hebrew University (Hebrew).

Florida, R. (2002) *The Rise of the Creative Class*. New York: Basic Books.

Foley, J. (2003) *Great Spa Escapes: The Definitive Guide to the Best Spas in the World, and What They Have to Offer*. London: Dakini Books Ltd.

Forgen, C. (2005) 'What is Your Health Personality', Medicinenet.com, http://www.medicinenet.com/script/main/art.asp?articlekey=47048 (accessed 29th November 2008).

Fosarelli, P. (2002) 'Fearfully wonderfully made: The interconnectedness of body-mind-spirit', *Journal of Religion and Health*, 41(3), pp. 207–229.

Foss, P. (2008) Spas for men, Why visit a spa and how to make the best of it? MyNippon, http://www.mynippon.com/men/spas.htm, latest visited 28 March, 2008.

Fralix, P. (2007) 'The personality divide: Getting better results with different types of people', *MEDICALSPAS*, July/August, pp. 20–22.

Fruchthendler, S. & Colbert, J. (2001) *Big Bang Marketing for Spas*. Crofton, MD: Tuff Turtle Pub Inc.

Future Foundation (2007) http://www.futurefoundation.org (accessed 10th January 2008).

Gallup, G. & Lindsay, D. M. (1999) *Surveying the Religious Landscape: Trends in U.S. Beliefs*. Harrisburg: Morehouse Publishing.

Garcia-Altes, M. (2005) 'The development of health tourism services', *Annals of Tourism Research*, 33(1), pp. 262–266.

Germany Tourism (2008) http://germany-tourism.de (accessed 15th March 2008)

GfK Lifestyle Research (2005) 'Euro-Socio-Styles', http://www.gfk.hr/omnibus/consumers.htm (accessed 5th April 2008).

GlobalChoice Healthcare, 2008) www.globalchoicehealthcare.com (accessed 17th February 2008).

Glouberman, D. (2002) *The Joy of Burnout*. London: Hodder and Stoughton.

Glouberman, D. (2004) 'Skyros Soul', http://www.skyros.com/skyros_soul.html (accessed 20th February 2004).

Golden Door Spa (2008) http://www.goldendoor.com (accessed 2nd April 2008).

Goldsmith, M. (2008) 'Spa Trends 2008: The Evolved Spa', http://www.healinglifestyles.com/index.php?page=jan2008-insight-spatrends20082 (accessed 12th February 2008).

Goodrich, J. N. & Goodrich, G. E. (1987) 'Health-care tourism – an explanatory study', *Tourism Management*, September, pp. 217–222.

Götz, A. (2008) 'Inkább vízimajmok voltunk', Index, http://index.hu/tudomany/tortenelem/vizimaj6108 (accessed 2nd April 2008).

Graburn, N. H. (2002) 'The ethnographic tourist', in Dann, G. M. S. (ed.) *The Tourist as a Metaphor of the Social World*. Wallingford: CABI, pp. 19–40.

Grainger, L. (2007) 'Sun, Sea and….Psychotherapy', Telegraph online, 8th July http://www.telegraph.co.uk/fashion/main.jhtml?view=DETAILS&grid=&xml=/fashion/2007/07/08/sttherapy08.xml (accessed 2nd October 2007).

Gray, J. (2002) *Men Are from Mars, Women Are from Venus: How to Get What You Want in Your Relationships*. London: HarperCollins.

Green, B. & Aldred, L. (2002) 'Money is just spiritual energy: Incorporating the new age', *Journal of Popular Culture*, 35(4), p. 61.

Green Bliss Ecospa (2008) http://greenbliss.com (accessed 2nd April 2008).

Green, M. (2008) 'Seaspa, Worldwide Spareview', March/April, http://www.spareviewmag.com/24/seaspa.html (accessed 20th March 2008).

Guardian Unlimited (2005) 'Fat to fit: How Finland Did it', January 15th, http://www.guardian.co.uk/befit/story/0,15652,1385645,00.html (accessed 17th November 2007).

Gupta, R. (2007) 'Qatar, Saudi Arabia, Oman and Dubai', *Spa Scope, SpaArabia*, March/April, pp. 7–11.

Gurk, S. (2008) 'Mine's a Pint and a Pummel', Times online, http://www.timesonline.co.uk/tol/life_and_style/health/features/article687318.ece (accessed 16th February 2008).

Gustavo, Nuno (2006) *Social Representations of the São Pedro Thermal Centre-Goers*. M.A. thesis, University of Coimbra (Faculty of Sport Sciences and Physical Education).

Haikko Spa (2008) http://www.mjgunivers.fi/haikko.htm (accessed 28th March 2008)

Hall, C. M. (1992) 'Adventure, sport and health tourism', in Weiler, B. & Hall, C. M. (eds) *Special Interest Tourism*. London: Belhaven Press, pp. 141–158.

Hallab, Z. (2006) 'Catering to the healthy-living vacationer', *Journal of Vacation Marketing*, 12(1), pp. 71–91.

Hamilton, C., Eckersley, R. & Denniss, R. (2008) *The Wellbeing Manifesto*. Australia: The Australia Institute.

Hardy, J. (2002) 'Yoga Holidays', http://www.travelintelligence.net/wsd/articles/ (accessed 20th February 2004).

Haridwar Tour Packages (2008) http://www.zoomtra.com/Holiday-Packages/ Haridwar.aspx/6990 (accessed 25th February 2008).

Harrison, E. (2006) 'Divine Trash: The Psychology of Celebrity Obsession', Cosmos, February, http://www.cosmosmagazine.com/node/414) (accessed 3rd October 2007).

Hartman Group (2007) *Wellness Lifestyle Insights 2007: Emerging Trends to Shape the Future Marketplace*. Bellevue, WA: Hartman Group.

Heelas, P. (1996) *The New Age movement: The celebration of the self and the sacralization of modernity*. Oxford: Blackwell.

Heelas, P. & Woodhead, L. (2005) *The Spiritual Revolution*. Oxford: Blackwell.

Heller, D. (2005) 'Selfness statt Wellness', http://www.spa-concept.de/Cover-3.3597.0.html (accessed 15th February, 2008).

Henderson, J. C. (2004) 'Healthcare in Southeast Asia', *Tourism Review International*, 7, pp. 111–122.

Herttua (2005) 'Herttua – Etusivu', http://www.herttua.fi (accessed 8th February 2007).

Hiranyikara (2008) www.hiranyikara.com (accessed 23rd March 2008).

HNTO (2002) *The Marketing Concept of Health Tourism*. Budapest: HNTO.

Hole in the Wall Camps (2008) www.holeinthewallcamps.org (accessed 10th March 2008).

Holistic Healing (2008) 'Native American Indian Healing Traditions', http://healing. about.com/od/tools/a/nativetools.htm (accessed 27th March 2008).

Holloway, J. C. (2004) *Marketing for Tourism*. Harlow: Prentice Hall.

Horváth, E. (1998). A nemzetközi aktív turizmus multiplikátor hatásainak becslése input-output model alkalmazásával', PhD dissertation, Budapest University of Economic Sciences, Budapest.

House of Lords Report (2000) 'Complementary and Alternative Medicine (CAM)', http://www.parliament.the-stationery-office.co.uk/pa/ld199900/ldselect/ ldsctech/123/12301.htm (accessed 21st September 2005).

House of Male (2008) http://www.houseofmale.com (accessed 5th April 2008).

Humphreys, C. (2007) 'Escaping the Rat Race', ABC News.com, 30th June http:// www.geocities.com/RainForest/6783/DalyNewsSimplicity980630#top.html (accessed 24th October 2007).

Hungarian National Tourism Office (2008) http://www.hungary.com (accessed 4th April 2008).

Incredible India (2006) *Medical Tourism Brochure*. Ministry of Tourism, Government of India, August, 2006.

Indiatravelite (2007) http://www.indiatravelite.com/feature/oshocom1.htm (accessed 2nd November 2007).

Inskeep, E. (1991) *Tourism Planning: An Integrated and Sustainable Development Approach*. New York: Van Nostrand Reinhold.

Intelligent Spas (2006) 'Female Versus Male Spa Consumers: Survey of Behaviours', Expectations, Preferences and Predications, http://www.intelligentspas.com (accessed 20th March 2008).

Intelligent Spas (2007) http://www.tourism.australia.com/Marketing.asp?lang=EN&sub=0437&al=2576 (accessed 24th November 2007).

ISPA (2003) *The International SPA Association's 2003 Spa-goer Study: Japan*. Lexington: ISPA.

ISPA (2004) *Consumer Trends Report: Variations and Trends on the Consumer Spa Experience*. Lexington: ISPA.

ISPA (2006a) *The International SPA Association's 2006 Spa-goer Study: U.S. and Canadian Consumer Attitudes and Spa Use*. Lexington: ISPA.

ISPA (2006a) *ISPA 2006 Spa-goer Study. U.S. and Candian Consumer Attitudes and Spa Use*. Lexington: ISPA.

ISPA (2006b) *Consumer Report: Spa-goer and Non-Spa-goer Perspectives*. Lexington: ISPA.

ISPA (2007) '2007 ISPA Global Consumer Report', http://www.experienceispa.com/ISPA/Media Room/Press Releases/ISPAs 13th Annual Media Event.htm (accessed 5th November 2007).

ISPA (2008) 'Key Spa Industry Trends', http://www.experienceispa.com/ISPA/Media+Room/2008+Trend+Release.htm (accessed 12th February 2008).

ITER CADSUS (2005) http://www.iter-cadses.it/en/mainl.htm (accessed 28th March 2008).

Iter Spa Itineraries (2005) 'Interreg III B Cadses', http://www.iter-cadses.it/en/index.html (accessed 10th November 2008).

Ito, M. (2003) 'Getting Into Hot Water for Health', *The Japan Times*, 25 May 2003, http://search.japantimes.co.jp (accessed 3rd April 2008).

IUOTO (1973) *Health Tourism*. Geneva: United Nations.

Iyengar, B. K. S. (1989) *Light on Yoga*. London: Unwin Hyman.

James, A. (2002) 'The Big Chill Black Mountain Gala', http://www.bigchill.net/media/1995firstfestival.doc (accessed 28th December 2006).

Jansen-Verbecke, M. & Diekmann, A. (2008) *The Future of Historic Spa Towns: Spa Symposium Workbook*. Belgium: Castermans.

Jansen-Verbecke, M. (2000) 'Cultuurtoerisme en stedelijke revitalisatie', *Leuvense Geografisch Papers*, 11, pp. 7–24.

Jennings, E. T. (2007) *Curing the Colonizers: Hydrotherapy, Climatology, and French Colonial Spas*. Durham, NC: Duke University Press.

Jordan, P. (ed.) (1999) *Atlas of Eastern and Southeastern Europe – International Tourism Attractions 1998*. Vienna: Österreichisches Ost-und Südeuropa Institut.

Jordan Times (2008) 'Jordan international conference seeks to promote medical tourism', 25th January 2008.

Just the Flight (2006) 'Spiritual Tourism in Malaysia', (http://www.justtheflight.co.uk/news/15165150-malaysia-promotes-spiritual-tourism.html, February (accessed 20th November 2007).

Kangas, H. & Tuohino, A. (2007) 'Lake Wellness – a new concept in lake tourism development in Eastern Finland' (unpublished paper, forthcoming).

Kaspar, C. (1992) *Turisztikai menedzsment*. Budapest: KIT.

Kelly, C. & Smith, M. K. (2008) 'Holistic tourism: Integrating body, mind and spirit', in Jafari, J., Bushell, R. & Sheldon, P. (eds) *Wellness and Tourism: Mind, Body, Spirit*, Place. Innovation and Tourism Book Series (forthcoming).

Kerimäen kunta (2005) 'Kerimäen kunta – etusivu', http://www.kerimaki.fi (accessed 8th February 2007).

Kim, M. & Chung, A. Y. (2005) 'Consuming Orientalism: Images of Asian/American women in multicultural advertising', *Qualitative Sociology*, 28(1), pp. 67–91.

Kinsey, M. (2005) 'Eating Disorders on the Rise', 3rd January, http://media.www.dailyfreepress.com/media/storage/paper87/news/2005/03/01/Science/Eating.Disorders.On.The.Rise-880957.shtml (accessed 24th October 2007).

Kirsch, M. (2003) 'All Tomorrow's Parties', http://www.ideasfactory.com/performance/features/perf_feature18.htm (accessed 2nd January 2007).

Kobayashi, M. (2004) 'Onsen in Tokyo. Value-added relaxation for urbanites', *Japan Spotlight, Economy, Culture & History*, 39(5), pp. 8–13.

Kögler, A. (2007). 'Wellness and Quality', ATLAS Spa and Wellness Special Interest Group Meeting, Budapest, 25th–28th June 2007.

Kojima, J. & Kawamura, K. (2006) 'The delights of Japanese hot springs. 19 relaxing onsen retreats', *Kateigaho International Edition, Japan's Arts and Culture Magazine*, 10, pp. 135–151.

Kotler, P., Bowen, J. T. & Makens, J. C. (2005) *Marketing for Hospitality and Tourism*. Pearson International.

Kovács, B., Horkay, N. & Michalkó, G. (2006) 'A turizmussal összefüggő életminőség-index kidolgozásának alapjai', *Turizmus Bulletin*, X(2), pp. 19–26.

Kowalski, R. (2001) *The Only Way Out is In*. Charlbury: JC Publishing.

KPMG Consulting (2002) *The Marketing Concept of Health Tourism in Hungary*. Budapest: Hungarian National Tourism Office.

Kuoni (2008) www.kuoni.co.uk/spa (accessed 8th March 2008).

La Contessa (2008) http://www.lacontessa.eu (accessed 1st March 2008).

Larrinaga, C. (2005) 'A century of tourism in Northern Spain: The development of high-quality provision between 1815 and 1914', in Walton, J. K. (ed.) *Histories of Tourism: Representation, Identity and Conflict*. Clevedon: Channel View Publications, pp. 88–103.

Lea, J. (2006) 'Experiencing festival bodies: Connecting massage and wellness', *Journal of Tourism Recreation Research*, 31(1), pp. 57–66.

Leading Spas of Canada (2006) *2005 Canadian Spa Goers Survey*. Canada: MedSci, Sooke.

Lee, G. (2004) *Spa Style Europe*. London: Thames & Hudson.

Lehto, X., Brown, S., Chen, Y. & Morrison, A. M. (2006) 'Yoga tourism as a niche within the wellness sector', *Journal of Tourism Recreation Research*, 31(1), pp. 25–36.

Les Mills (2008) http://www.lesmills.com (accessed 2nd April 2008).

Lomine, L. (2005) 'Tourism in Augustan society (44BC – AD69)', in Walton, J. K. (ed.) *Histories of Tourism: Representation, Identity and Conflict*. Clevedon: Channel View Publications, pp. 71–87.

Loverseed, H. (1998) 'Health and spa tourism in North America', *Travel & Tourism Analyst*(1), pp. 46–61.

MacKenzie, J. M. (2005) 'Empires of travel: British guide books and cultural imperialism in the 19th and 20th centuries', in Walton, J. K. (ed.) *Histories of Tourism: Representation, Identity and Conflict*. Clevedon: Channel View Publications, pp. 19–38.

Magyar, R. (2008) 'Hosszú az út a lélektől a lélekig', *Turizmus Trend*, 3, pp. 24–25.

Mandelbaum, R. & G. Lerner (2008) 'Hotel Operators Massage More Profits from their Spa Operations', Hotel Online, 8 February, http://www.hotel-online.com/News/PR2008_1st/Feb08_SpaProfits.html (accessed 12th January 2008).

Mansfield, S. (2001) 'Lips of fire. Beppu spa offers old-style sightseeing rituals that are reason enough to visit', *Japan Spotlight, Economy, Culture & History*, 37(1), pp. 25–29.

Marks & Spencers (2005) 'Spending Habits of Bridget Jones Generation', 5th September, http://www6.marksandspencer.com/pressreleases/Press35.pdf (accessed 4th January 2008).

Mathieson, A. & Wall, G. (1982) *Tourism. Economic, Physical and Social Impacts*. Harlow: Longman.

Mayr Centre (2008) www.viva-mayr.at/en (accessed 10th March 2008).

McCabe, S. (2002) 'The tourist experience and everyday life', in Dann, G. M. S. (ed.) *The Tourist as a Metaphor of the Social World*. Wallingford: CABI, pp. 61–76.

McNeil, K. R. & Ragins, E. J. (2005) 'Staying in the spa marketing game: Trends, challenges, strategies and techniques', *Journal of Vacation Marketing*, 11(1), pp. 31–39.

Medindia (2008) 'Nepal: Alternative Medicine News', Thursday, September 28th, 2006, http://www.medindia.net/news/view_news_main.asp?x=14637 (accessed 24th March 2008).

MedRetreat (2008) www.medretreat.com (accessed 17th March 2008).

Meeberg, G. A. (1993) 'Quality of life: A concept analysis', *Journal of Advanced Nursing*, 18(1), p. 32.

Middleton, V. T. C. & Clarke, J. (1998) *Marketing in Travel and Tourism*. Oxford: Butterworth-Heinemann.

Michalkó, G. & Rátz, T. (2008) 'The role of the tourist milieu in the social construction of the tourist experience', *JOHAR: Journal of Hospitality Application & Research*, 3(1), pp. 22–32.

Miller, C. (1994) 'People want to believe in something', *Marketing News*, 28(25), pp. 1–3, 1c.

Mintel (2006) 'Health and Wellness Holidays', http://www.mintel.com/press_release.php?id=271145 (accessed 28th November 2007).

Misserli, H. R. (2004) 'Health and wellness tourism', *Travel and Tourism Analyst*, 2004/3.

Moldova Tourism (2008) http://www.turism.md/eng/section/262/ (accessed 15th February 2008).

Montes, C. (2006) *Spas and Wellness Hotels*. New York: teNeues Publishing.

Monteson, P. A. & Singer, J. (2004) 'Marketing a resort-based spa', *Journal of Vacation Marketing*, 10(3), pp. 282–287.

Moore (1852) in *The Quotable Traveler (1994)*, Philadelphia: Running Press.

Moosath, A. (2006) 'Brand ayurveda', *Business Line*, 10th March.

Müller, H. & Kaufmann, E. L. (2000) 'Wellness tourism: Market analysis of a special health tourism segment and implications for the hotel industry', *Journal of Vacation Marketing*, 7(1), pp. 5–17.

Müller, H. (2001) 'Wellness tourism: Market analysis of a special health tourism segment and implications for the hotel industry', *Journal of Vacation Marketing*, pp. 5–17, 2001/1.

Mullholland, C. (2005) 'Depression and Suicide in Men', http://www.netdoctor.co.uk (accessed on 20th September 2005).

Mundt, I. (1994) 'Ecotourism or ego-tourism?', *Race and Class*, 46, pp. 50–52.

Murphy, P. (2008) *The Business of Resort Management*. Oxford: Butterworth-Heinemann.

Müller, H. & Kaufmann, E. L. (2001) 'Market analysis of a special health tourism segment and implications of the hotel industry', *Journal of Vacation Marketing*, 7(1), pp. 5–17.

Myers, J. E., Sweeney, T. J. and Witmer, M. (2000) 'A holistic model of wellness', http://www.mindgarden.com/products/wells.htm (accessed 20th September 2005).

Nahrstedt, W. (2008) 'From medical wellness to cultural wellness: New challenges for leisure studies and tourism policies, Keynote Speech', *The Future of Historic Spa Towns Symposium, Spa, Belgium*, 13th–14th March, p. 2008.

Napier, E. (2002) *A Place to Spa*. London: Conran Octopus Ltd.

National Center for Alternative and Complementary Medicine (2007) http://nccam.nih.gov (accessed 8th Oct 2007).

The National Tourism Development Authority of Ireland (2007) 'Health and Wellness Positioning Strategy for Key Markets', http://www.failteireland.ie (accessed 21st February 2008).

National Wellness Institute (2007) http://www.nationalwellness.org (accessed 29th November 2007).

Native American Healing Traditions (2007) http://healing.about.com/od/tools/a/nativetools.htm (accessed 24th November 2007).

Neff, R. (1995) *Japan's Hidden Hot Springs*. Boston: Charles E. Tuttle Publishing Co.

Neves, F. M. G. D. R. (2002) *O turismo termal no Norte de Portugal. Vidago e Pedras Salgadas: o desenvolvimento de duas estâncias termais*. Coimbra: Universidade de Coimbra, Unedited Tese de mestrado.

New Economics Foundation (NEF) (2004) http://www.wellbeingmanifesto.net/uk_manifesto.pdf (accessed 4th December 2007).

New Zealand Tourism (2007) (http://www.nzmaoritourism.com/Home/Hells_Gate___Wai_Ora_Spa_IDL=4_IDT=1375_ID=8268_.html (accessed 20th November 2007).

NMI (2006) 'Health and Wellness Trends Database', http://www.nmisolutions.com/hwtd_segment.html#eatdrink (accessed 2nd November 2007).

Nordic Well (2007) http://www.nordicwell.com/nordicwell/apps/nordicwell.jsp?pid=380 (accessed 20th November 2007).

OneSeven (2008) http://www.oneseven.com.sg (accessed 3rd April 2008).

ÖTM (2007) *A turizmus-specifikus életminőség index kidolgozása*. Budapest: ÖTM, unpublished research paper.

Parádai, A. (2007) 'A wellness uj hullámai (New trends in wellness)', *Mozgás*, October, pp. 20–21.

Parasuraman, A., Zeithaml, V. A. & Berry, L. L. (1985) 'A conceptual model of service quality and its implications for further research', *Journal of Marketing*, 49(4), pp. 41–50.

Partridge, C. (2006) 'The spiritual and the revolutionary: Alternative spirituality, British free festivals, and the emergence of Rave culture', *Culture and Religion*, 7(1), pp. 41–60.

Pascarella, S. (2008) 'Enjoy Rugged Relaxation at Adventure Spas', http://www.usatoday.com/travel/deals/inside/2005-10-12-column_x.htm (accessed 24th March 2008).

Pearce, D. G. (1989) *Tourist Development*, 2nd edition. Harlow: Longman.

Pechlaner, H. & Fischer, E. (2006) 'Alpine wellness: A resource-based view', *Journal of Tourism Recreation Research*, 31(1), pp. 67–77.

Perfect Earth Tours (2008) http://www.perfectearthtours.com (accessed 20th March 2008).

Pernecky, T. & Johnston, C. (2006) 'Voyage through numinous space: Applying the specialization concept to new age tourism', *Journal of Tourism Recreation Research*, 31(1), pp. 37–46.

Pesek, T. J., Helton, L. R. & Nair, M. (2006) 'Healing across cultures: Learning from traditions', *EcoHealth*, 3, pp. 114–118.

Pilzer, P. Z. (2008) *The Wellness Revolution: How to Make a Fortune in the Next Trillion Dollar Industry*, 2nd edition. London: John Wiley & Sons.

Plog, S. C. (1974) 'Why destinations rise and fall in popularity', *Cornell Hotel and Restaurant Administration Quarterly*, 14(4).

Post, P. (1996) *The Modern Pilgrim: A Christian Ritual Between Tradition and Postmodernity*. London: SCM Press Ltd.

Potton, E. (2006) 'A cool welcome', *The Times*, May 27th, p. 6.

Premium Spa Resorts (2008) www.premiumsparesorts.com/en/resorts/specials/Men-only-spa-angebote/ (accessed 3rd April 2008).

PROGESTUR (2006) 'Entrevista ao Dr. Manuel Marques, Director de Turismo da UNICER', Newsletter Progestur, Mar/Abr 2006, http://www.progestur.net/n102/nl_02.html (accessed 13th August 2006).

Puczkó, L. & Bacharov, M. (2006) 'Spa, bath, thermae: What's behind the labels?', *Journal of Tourism Recreation Research*, 31(1), pp. 83–91.

Puczkó, L. (2006) 'Interpretation in cultural tourism', in Smith, M. K. & Robinson, M. (eds) *Cultural Tourism in a Changing World: Politics, Participation and (Re)presentation*. Clevedon: Channel View, pp. 227–243.

Radhakrishnan, S. (2005) 'Bill to check unhealthy practices in ayurveda treatment', *The Hindu*, 10th August.

Rátz, T. & Puczkó, L. (2002) *The Impacts of Tourism. An Introduction*. Hameenlinna: Hame Polytechnic.

Raveri, M. (2002) 'Introduction', in Hendry, J. & Raveri, M. (eds) *Japan at Play: The Ludic and the Logic of Power*. London: Routledge, pp. 1–21.

Ravilious, K. (2005) 'The recipe for success: Get happy and you will get ahead in life', *The Guardian*, Monday 19th December.

Raw Food Planet (2007) http://www.rawfoodplanet.com/Links/Vacationsretreats-links.html (accessed 28th November 2007).

Ray Morgan Research Centre (1997) http://www.roymorgan.com.au (accessed 12th June 2006).

Realease (2007) 'Body and Soul', http://www.bigchill.net/story/2021/bodyandsoul.html, (accessed 5th April 2007).

Registro de la Oficina de Acogida de Peregrinos (2004) Oficina de Sociología del Arzobispado de Santiago de Compostela. Santiago de Compostela.

Religious Tolerance (2006) http://www.religioustolerance.org/newage.htm (accessed 15th October 2007).

Retreats Online (2006) www.retreatsonline.com (accessed 15th November 2006).

Reuters (2006) 'Luxury Rehab Eases Troubles with a Rubdown', December 15th, http://www.msnbc.msn.com/id/16227377 (accessed 8th October 2007).

Rew, K. (2007) 'My yoga holiday from hell', Sunday 11th March, http://travel.guardian.co.uk/article/2007/mar/11/restandrelaxation.canaryislands.escape (accessed 27th January 2008).

Richards, G. (2006) *TRAM Global Medical Tourism Report*. Tilburg: ATLAS.

Rogner (2008) http://www.rogner.com (accessed 4th February 2008).

Rojek, C. (1993) *Ways of Escape: Modern Transformations in Leisure and Travel*. London: Macmillan Press Ltd.

Royal Spas (2008) www.royal-spas.net (accessed 2nd April 2008).

Ryan, C. (ed.) (1997) *The Tourist Experience: A New Introduction*. London: Cassell.

Sacred Sites (2008) 'Kumbha Mela', http://www.sacredsites.com/asia/india/kumbha_mela.html (accessed 27th March 2008).

San Antonio College (2005) 'Wellness', http://www.accd.edu/sac/wellness/wellpage.htm. (accessed 21st September 2005).

Saracci, R. (1997) 'The World Health Organisation Needs to Reconsider its Definition of Health', http://bmj.bmjjournals.com (accessed 20th September 2005).

Saratoga State Park (2008) 'Park History', http://www.saratogaspastatepark.org/history.html (accessed 27th March 2008).

Schneiders, S. (1989) 'Spirituality in the Academy', *TS*, pp. 676–697.

Scottish Executive Committee (2006) http://www.scotland.gov.uk/Publications/2006/01/13110743/0 (accessed 24th October 2007).

Seaton, A. V. & Bennett, M. M. (1996) *The Marketing of Tourism Products: Concepts, Issues and Cases*. London: International Thomson Business Press.

Seaton, A. V. (2002) 'Tourism as metempsychosis and metensomatosis: The personae of eternal recurrence', in Dann, G. M. S. (ed.) *The Tourist as a Metaphor of the Social World*. Wallingford: CABI, pp. 135–168.

Seki, A. & Heilman Brooke, E. (2005) *The Japanese Spa: A Guide to Japan's Finest Ryokan and Onsen*. Boston: Tuttle Publishing.

Shah, H. & Marks, N. (2004) *A Well-Being Manifesto for a Flourishing Society*. London: New Economics Foundation.

Sharpley, R. (1994) *Tourism, Tourists and Society*. Huntingdon: ELM Publications.

Sharpley, R. (ed.) (2002) *The Tourism Business: An Introduction*. Sunderland: Business Education Publishers Ltd.

Sibley, S. (2008) Yoga Travel Research Carried Out At Inholland University, Minor Sports, Wellness and Lifestyles, The Netherland.

Singer, J. L. & P.A. Monteson (2007) 'Spas – How to Stay On-trend and Make Money', Hotel Online, http://www.hotel-online.com/News/PR2007_1st/Feb07_SpasOnTrend.html (accessed 15th January 2008).

Six Senses (2008) http://www.sixsenses.com (accessed 30th March 2008).

Skyros (2008) http://skyros.co.uk (accessed 14th March 2008).

SLH (2005) 'Small Luxury Hotels of the World', http://www.slhpress.com/template.phtml?frompage=feature&cid=21&sid=50&aid=700 (accessed 21st February 2008).

Slovak Government (2005) http://pdc.ceu.hu/archive/00002751/01/Tourism Strategy.pdf (accessed 4th March 2008).

SLH (2005) Spa Book, Small Luxury Hotels of the World, http://www.slhpress.com/template.phtml?frompage=feature&cid=21&sid=50&aid=700 (accessed 28th March 2008).

Smith, M. K. & Kelly, C. (2006) 'Holistic tourism: Journeys of the Self?', *Journal of Tourism Recreation Research*, 31(1), pp. 15–24.

Smith, M. K. (2003) 'Holistic holidays: tourism and the reconciliation of body, mind, spirit', *Journal of Tourism Recreation Research*, 28(1), pp. 103–108.

Sonwai Spa at The Hyatt Regency, Scottsdale, USA (2008) www.insider-scottsdale.com/scottsdalemensspas.htm (accessed 2nd March 2008).

Sonnentherme (2008) http://www.sonnentherme.com (accessed 4th March 2008)

South African Tourist Board (2008) http://www1.southafrica.net/Cultures/en-US/consumer.southafrica.net/Things+to+Do/Attractions/EntertainmentLeisure/African+Spas.htm?SEARCH=%2fcultures%2fen-US%2fconsumer.southafrica.net%2fsearchresults.aspx%3fKeyword%3dspa (accessed 14th February 2008).

South Pacific Tourism Organisation (SPTO) (2007) 'Weekly Newsletter', http://www.spto.org (accessed 12th December 2008).

SPAA (2005) 'The Spa Association 2005 Consumer Study', www.thespaassociation.com (accessed 12th January 2008).

Spa Audit (2008) http://spaaudit.com (accessed 15th March 2008).

Spa Finder Magazine (2005) 'Live at a Spa', www.spafinder.com (accessed 2nd February 2008).

Spafinder Magazine (2007) www.spafinder.com (accessed 11th March 2008).

Spagasm (2008) www.spagasm.com (accessed 4th March 2008).

Spa Index (2008) www.spaindex.com (accessed 5th March 2008).

Spa of Colonial Williamsburg (2008) http://www.colonialwilliamsburg.com/visit/recreation/spaServices (accessed 24th March 2008).

SpaFinder (2007) http://www.spafinder.com/spalifestyle/spa101/history.jsp (accessed 12th February 2008).

SpaFinder (2008) 'Spa Etiquette', http://www.spafinder.com/spalifestyle/spa101/etiquette.jsp (accessed 20th March 2008).

Spas of America (2008) www.spasofamerica.com (accessed 5th March 2008).

Spas Research Fellowship (2008) http://www.thespasdirectory.com/discover_the_spa_research_fell.asp?i=10 (accessed 14th February 2008).

Spa Uno (2008) www.spauno.com (accessed 4th April 2008).

Spirit Rock Meditation Centre (2007) http://www.spiritrock.org/display.asp?catid=3&pageid=13 (accessed 21st November 2007).

Sreekumar, T. & Parayil, G. (2002) 'Contentions and contradictions of tourism as development option: The case of Kerala, India', *Third World Quarterly*, 23(3), pp. 529–548.

Stanford Encyclopedia of Philosophy (2007) http://plato.stanford.edu/entries/well-being (accessed 24th October 2007).

Steiner, C. & Reisinger, Y. (2006) 'Ringing the fourfold: A philosophical framework for thinking about wellness tourism', *Journal of Tourism Recreation Research*, 31(1), pp. 5–14.

Sturebadet (2008) http://www.sturebadet.se/ (accessed 13th March 2008).

Sukko Spa (2008) www.sukkospa.com (accessed 4th April 2008).

Swarbrooke, J. & Horner, S. (1999) *Consumer Behaviour in Tourism*. Oxford: Butterworth Heinemann.

Sylge, C. (2007) *Body & Soul Escapes*. Bath: Footprint Handbooks Ltd.

Tai Chi Finder (2007) http://www.taichifinder.co.uk/article_info.php?articles_id=3 (accessed 8th November 2007).

Talaso Pontiente (2007) http://www.talasoponiente.com/interior.asp?MP = 11&MS=30&MT=0&TR=C&IDR=40 (accessed 8th November 2007).

A Taste of Health (2008) http://atasteofhealth.org (accessed 15th February 2008).

Teimao, R. (2004) 'What The Big Chill Is All About', http://www.bigchill.net/story/841/whatthebigchillisallabout.html (accessed 28th December 2006).

The Economist (2004) *Medical Tourism to India*, October 7th.

The National Tourism Development Authority of Ireland (2007) *Health and Wellness Positioning Strategy for Key Markets*. Bord Failte Ireland.

The Sanctuary (2007) http://www.sanctuarybb.com/overview/director.htm (accessed 2nd November 2007).

Thompson, M. (2007) 'Feng Shui', http://michaelthompson.org/fengshui (accessed 2nd January 2008).

Tierra Atacama Hotel and Spa (2008) http://www.tierraatacama.com/hotel/detalle_eng.asp?id=4 (accessed 24th March 2008).

Tilden, F. (1977) *Interpreting Our Heritage*, 3rd edition. Chapel Hill: The University of North Carolina Press.

Tourism Australia (2007) 'Wellbeing Factsheet', http://www.tourism.australia.com/content/Research/Factsheets/Wellbeing_Experiences.pdf (accessed 24th November 2007).

Tourism Victoria (2005) *Victoria's Spa and Wellness Tourism Action Plan 2005–1010*.

TRAM (2006) *Global Medical Tourism Report*. Tilburg: ATLAS.

Djerba-les-Bains (2008) http://www.tunisietourisme.com.tn/guide-e/activites/activite_reduite.htm (accessed 25th March 2008).

Trem Y Mor (2007) http://www.tremymor.co.uk/5.html (accessed 28th November 2007).

Tsukada, K. (2003). 'Hot-Spring Aficionados Visit a Top-Notch Ryokan', Katei-gaho International Edition, Japan's Arts and Culture Magazine', http://www.jnto.go.jp/eng/indepth/featuredarticles/kie/ryokan/index.html (accessed 31st March 2008).

Turtle Cove (2008) http://www.turtlecove.com/index.html (accessed 4th April 2008).

Tyrell, B. & Mai, R. (2001) *Leisure 2010 – Experience Tomorrow*. Henley: Jones Lang La Salle.

Ueda, M. (2006) 'What taking the waters means today', *Kateigaho International Edition, Japan's Arts and Culture Magazine*, 10, p. 149.

UK Life Coaching (2007) http://www.uklifecoaching.org (accessed 8th Oct 2007).

UNICEF (2007) 'Innocenti Research Center', http://www.unicef-irc.org (accessed 3rd December 2007).

UNICER (2006a) 'Aquanattur. Parques de Vidago & Pedras Salgadas. Um reencontro com o futuro', Unicer, http://www.aquanattur.com (accessed 13th August 2006).

UNICER (2006b) Report and Accounts 2005. Unicer-Bebidas de Portugal, SGPS, SA, Unicer, http://www.unicer.pt (accessed 13th August 2006).

UNICER (2006c) Sustainability Report 2005. Unicer-Bebidas de Portugal, SGPS, SA, Unicer, http://www.unicer.pt (accessed 13th August 2006).

Urry, J. (1990) *The Tourist Gaze: Leisure and Travel in Contemporary Societies*. London: Sage.

Valtion ympäristöhallinto (2007) 'Valtion ympäristöhallinto', www.ymparisto.fi (accessed 8th February 2007).

Van de Broek, J. (2008) Data from the Marketing Department of Les Mills, the Netherlands, 31st March.

Van der Meulen, D. & O'Brien, K. (2006) *Spa Style Arabia*. London: Thames & Hudson.

Van der Post, L. (1994) *The Quotable Traveler*. Philadelphia: Running Press.

Verschuur, H. (2005) 'Novas termas de Bath', *II Congreso Internacional de Turismo Termal*, Ourense.

Vichy Thermes (2008) www.vichy-thermes.tm.fr (accessed 27th March 2008).

Victoria Safaris (2008) http://www.victoriasafaris.com/africa/healthtourism.htm (accessed 31st January 2008).

Vipassana Meditation (2007) http://www.dhamma.org/en/code.shtml (accessed 9th November 2007).

Virtual Byron (2008) http://www.virtualbyron.com/visitors/history.php (accessed 24th March 2008).

Visit European Spas (2008a) 'What is the future of "wellness tourism"?' (http://www.visiteuropeanspas.com/article/wellnesstourism (accessed 19th February 2008).

Visit European Spas (2008b) 'Thalassotherapy', (http://www.visiteuropeanspas.com/article/wellnesstourism (accessed 27th February 2008).

Vos, K. (2006) Traditionele thermale kuuroorden als dragers van cultureel erfgoed en toerisme, Leuven, KU Leuven: Unpublished MA thesis.

Wadhwa, S. (2004) 'The hoax of God's own country', *Outlook*, 12th July.

Walsh, K. (1992) *The Representation of the Past: Museums and Heritage in the Post-modern World*. London: Routledge.

Walton, J. K. (2005) *Histories of Tourism: Representation, Identity and Conflict*. Clevedon: Channel View Publications.

Wang, N. (1999) 'Rethinking authenticity in tourism experience', *Annals of Tourism Research*, 26(2), pp. 349–370.c

Way to Poland (2008) http://www.waytopoland.com/x.php/1,362/Health-Resort-at-the-Salt-Mine-of-Bochnia.htm (accessed 27th March 2008).

Weil, A. (1995) *Spontaneous Healing: How to Discover and Enhance your Body's Natural Ability to Heal Itself*. New York: Knopf.

Wellbeing Cluster (2008) http://www.wellbeingcluster.at/ecoplus/cluster/wbc (accessed 27th February 2008).

Wellbeing Escapes (2007) http://www.wellbeingescapes.co.uk/welcome.php (accessed 3rd October 2007).

Wellbeing Factsheet (2007) http://www.tourism.australia.com/content/Research/Factsheets/Wellbeing_Experiences.pdf (accessed 24th November 2007).

Wellness Hotels Deutschland (2008) http://www.w-h-d.de/de/wellness_hotels_deutschland_gepruefte_qualitaet (accessed 26th March 2008).

Wellness of Scandinavia (2001) http://www.wellnessofscandinavia.com (accessed 25th November 2008).

Wells, D. (2007) 'The Male Only Spa Phenomenon. Global grooming hotspots for the guys', (http://www.gaywired.com/article.cfm?section=90&id=16619) 09/26/2007.

Whitman, C. & Fadra, M. (2007) '15 Keys to Improving Med Spa Efficiences', *MEDICALSPAS*, July/August, pp. 14–18.

White, G. (2003) *Hot Bath: The story of the spa*. Bath: Nutbourne Publishing Ltd.

Whittall, J. (2003) '2003 Guide to Men's Spa Service', MenEssentials, February, www.menessentials.com (accessed 5th March 2008).

Wildfitness (2008) http://www.wildfitness.com/page/eco_wildfitness.htm (accessed 27th March 2008).

Williams, S. (2003) *The Reluctant Spa Director and the Mission Dream*. Haverford, PA: Infinity Publishing.

Witepski, L. (2005) 'Botox in the Bush', British Airways High Life Magazine, http://www.surgeon-and-safari.co.za/news/british-airways-hl.html (accessed 12th November 2007).

Wolsko, C., Lardon, C., Hopkins, S. & Ruppert, E. (2006) 'Conceptions of wellness among the Yup'ik of the Yukon-Kuskokwim delta: The vitality of social and natural connection', *Ethnicity and Health*, 11(4), pp. 345–363.

Wong, C. (2007) 'Alternative Medicine: Detox Diet', http://altmedicine.about.com/cs/dietarytherapy/a/DetoxBasics.htm (accessed 24th October 2007).

Woods Smith, D. (1994) 'Theory of Sprituality', http://www.housesofhealing.com/source/Spirarticle94.pdf (accessed 14th February 2008).

World Health Organisation (1948) http://www.who.int/about/en (accessed 20th October 2007).

World Health Organisation (1984) *Health Promotion: A Discussion Document*. Copenhagen: WHO.

World Tourism Organization (1997) *Tourism Highlights 1996*. Madrid: WTO.

World Values Survey (2003) in Bond, M. (2003) 'The Pursuit of Happiness', New Scientist, 179, pp. 40–43.

Wright State University (2003) 'Wellness Wheel', http://www.wright.edu/admin/wellness/wellnesswheel.htm (accessed 21st September 2005).

Yoga Holidays (2008) http://www.yogaholidays.net/magazine/Rishikesh.htm (accessed 7th February 2008).

Yoga Magazine (2007) 'Find your ideal type', Issue 56, September 2007, pp. 66–71.

Yoga Travel (2007) http://www.yogatravel.co.uk/morocco.htm (accessed 20th November 2007).

Yoga TV (2008) http://yogatv.nl (accessed 31st March 2008)

Zara Spa Dead Sea (2008) http://www.zaraspa.com/main.asp (accessed 24th March 2008).

Index

5/09